Palgrave Studies in Religion, Politics, and Policy

Series Editor
Mark J. Rozell, Schar School of Policy and Government, George Mason University, Arlington, VA, USA

This series originated under the co-editorship of the late Ted Jelen and Mark J. Rozell. A generation ago, many social scientists regarded religion as an anachronism, whose social, economic, and political importance would inevitably wane and disappear in the face of the inexorable forces of modernity. Of course, nothing of the sort has occurred; indeed, the public role of religion is resurgent in US domestic politics, in other nations, and in the international arena. Today, religion is widely acknowledged to be a key variable in candidate nominations, platforms, and elections; it is recognized as a major influence on domestic and foreign policies. National religious movements as diverse as the Christian Right in the United States and the Taliban in Afghanistan are important factors in the internal politics of particular nations. Moreover, such transnational religious actors as Al-Qaida, Falun Gong, and the Vatican have had important effects on the politics and policies of nations around the world.

Palgrave Studies in Religion, Politics, and Policy serves a growing niche in the discipline of political science. This subfield has proliferated rapidly during the past two decades, and has generated an enormous amount of scholarly studies and journalistic coverage. Five years ago, the journal Politics and Religion was created; in addition, works relating to religion and politics have been the subject of many articles in more general academic journals. The number of books and monographs on religion and politics has increased tremendously. In the past, many social scientists dismissed religion as a key variable in politics and government.

This series casts a broad net over the subfield, providing opportunities for scholars at all levels to publish their works with Palgrave. The series publishes monographs in all subfields of political science, including American Politics, Public Policy, Public Law, Comparative Politics, International Relations, and Political Theory.

The principal focus of the series is the public role of religion. "Religion" is construed broadly to include public opinion, religious institutions, and the legal frameworks under which religious politics are practiced. The "dependent variable" in which we are interested is politics, defined broadly to include analyses of the public sources and consequences of religious belief and behavior. These would include matters of public policy, as well as variations in the practice of political life. We welcome a diverse range of methodological perspectives, provided that the approaches taken are intellectually rigorous.

The series does not deal with works of theology, in that arguments about the validity or utility of religious beliefs are not a part of the series focus. Similarly, the authors of works about the private or personal consequences of religious belief and behavior, such as personal happiness, mental health, or family dysfunction, should seek other outlets for their writings. Although historical perspectives can often illuminate our understanding of modern political phenomena, our focus in the Religion, Politics, and Policy series is on the relationship between the sacred and the political in contemporary societies.

Mark R. Royce

Ecclesiology, Idealism, and World Polity

The Concordats of the Apostolic See

Mark R. Royce
Political Science
Northern Virginia Community College
West Springfield, VA, USA

ISSN 2731-6769　　　　　ISSN 2731-6777　(electronic)
Palgrave Studies in Religion, Politics, and Policy
ISBN 978-3-031-57032-2　　　ISBN 978-3-031-57033-9　(eBook)
https://doi.org/10.1007/978-3-031-57033-9

© The Editor(s) (if applicable) and The Author(s), under exclusive license to Springer Nature Switzerland AG 2024

This work is subject to copyright. All rights are solely and exclusively licensed by the Publisher, whether the whole or part of the material is concerned, specifically the rights of translation, reprinting, reuse of illustrations, recitation, broadcasting, reproduction on microfilms or in any other physical way, and transmission or information storage and retrieval, electronic adaptation, computer software, or by similar or dissimilar methodology now known or hereafter developed.
The use of general descriptive names, registered names, trademarks, service marks, etc. in this publication does not imply, even in the absence of a specific statement, that such names are exempt from the relevant protective laws and regulations and therefore free for general use.
The publisher, the authors and the editors are safe to assume that the advice and information in this book are believed to be true and accurate at the date of publication. Neither the publisher nor the authors or the editors give a warranty, expressed or implied, with respect to the material contained herein or for any errors or omissions that may have been made. The publisher remains neutral with regard to jurisdictional claims in published maps and institutional affiliations.

Cover illustration: Contributor: Perseomedusa/Alamy Stock Photo

This Palgrave Macmillan imprint is published by the registered company Springer Nature Switzerland AG
The registered company address is: Gewerbestrasse 11, 6330 Cham, Switzerland

If disposing of this product, please recycle the paper.

To the Affectionate Memory of the Rev. Dr. Chester F. Russell

Contents

1	**A Peculiar Treaty Form**	1
	The Imputation of Concordatorial Authoritarianism	2
	An Original Analysis	4
2	**At the Intersection of Canon, Comparative, and International Law**	7
	A Peculiarity of Canon Law	8
	A Rarity in Comparative Law	13
	A Development Within International Law	19
3	**Research Presentation**	37
	Ad Fontes	37
	The Concordats of the Apostolic See	39
	Case Cluster I: Concordatorial Fascism, 1906–1953	63
	The Theory of Concordatorial Fascism	63
	The Concordats with the Dictators	65
	Mit Brennender Sorge	68
	Case Cluster II: The German Reich, *1925–2019*	71
	The German Sonderweg	71
	Diplomatic Ecclesiology	71
	The Dilemma of Worms	74
	Case Cluster III: Latin American Counter-Revolution, 1887–1994	76
	Spanish Catholic Neo-Conservatism	76

	Concordatorial Counter-Revolution	78
	The Theology of Liberation	80
	Case Cluster IV: European Secularism, 1801–2020	80
	Positivist Theory	80
	The Concordats with Secular Europe	82
	The Qualification of Positivist Theory	86
	Case Cluster V: The Second Vatican Reformation, 1968–2016	86
	Christian Democratic Norms	86
	The Concordats of the Council	88
	Profession of International Order	91
	Case Cluster VI: The Benediction of the Third World, 1993–2015	92
	Soul Force	92
	Concordatorial Agape	93
	Pontifical Humanitarianism	95
	An English Realist Synthesis	96
4	**Concordatorial Fascism, 1906–53**	119
	(Im)pious Contracting Parties	119
	Ecclesiological Treaty Norms	128
	Weeping and Gnashing of Teeth: The "Pius Wars"	131
5	**The German *Reich*, 1925–2019**	149
	Politik and Recht	149
	The Concordats of Worms	157
	The Question of International Validity	163
6	**Latin American Counter-Revolution, 1887–1994**	171
	Neocolonialism	172
	Concordatorial Counter-Revolution	180
	A Theology of Liberation	184
7	**European Secularism, 1801–2020**	195
	Pure Theory of Law	196
	Positivist Concordats	205
	"Identitarian" Reaction	209

8	The Second Vatican Reformation, 1968–2019	221
	Pontifical Idealism	221
	The Conciliar Concordats	233
	The Standardization of Catholic Norms	238
9	The Benediction of the Third World, 1993–2016	249
	Pontifical Constructivism	250
	Constructivist Concordats	259
	Interfaith Idealism	265
10	A Distinguished Treaty Form	271
Appendix: The Secret Concordat with China		273
Index		285

List of Figures

Fig. 3.1 The relationship between canon law and treaty norms   62
Fig. 8.1 The International theory of Paul VI   224

List of Tables

Table 3.1	Concordatorial terms	60
Table 3.2	"Most Favored Nations"	61
Table 4.1	Concordatorial fascism	121
Table 5.1	The German *Reich*	151
Table 6.1	Latin American counter-revolution	173
Table 7.1	European secularism	200
Table 8.1	The second vatican reformation	229
Table 9.1	The benediction of the Third World	253

CHAPTER 1

A Peculiar Treaty Form

One of the most peculiar treaties of the twentieth century was initialed on the eighth, and signed on the twentieth of July, 1933 amid the imperial opulence of the infant Vatican City-state, the contracting parties attired in the immaculate clerical or formal dress of the interwar period. Representing Pope Pius XI was Cardinal Secretary of State Eugenio Pacelli, representing German President Hindenburg and German Chancellor Hitler was Vice-Chancellor Franz von Papen; and also in attendance, unofficially, was Pacelli confidante and erstwhile German Centre Party leader Msgr. Ludwig Kaas.[1] The specific terms of the resulting "Solemn Convention" (SOLLEMNIS CONVENTIO) between the Holy See and the German *Reich* (*AAS* 25 [1933], 389–416) shall be examined in due course. Nor is there any strictly analytical need to recall the conspiracies, crimes against peace, war crimes, and crimes against humanity soon to be unleashed by the Nationalist Socialist regime upon millions of betrayed and slaughtered innocents. The point of departure of ecclesiological, ideational, and international interest is rather that this agreement, along with a small assortment of others like it contracted with authoritarian rulers, is largely responsible for the dissemination within liberal democratic discourse of the generally authoritarian connotations of the word CONCORDAT, which under canon, comparative, and international law denotes the treaties of the Apostolic See in Rome.

© The Author(s), under exclusive license to Springer Nature Switzerland AG 2024
M. R. Royce, *Ecclesiology, Idealism, and World Polity*, Palgrave Studies in Religion, Politics, and Policy, https://doi.org/10.1007/978-3-031-57033-9_1

The Imputation of Concordatorial Authoritarianism

The institutional Roman Catholic Church has contended with generations of Protestant, Enlightened, and Liberal-idealist opponents and with *laïque*, Leninist, and Maoist enemies; but as its primary diplomatic instrument, by which the Church seeks to extend and solidify its presence and prerogative in a given country, the concordat has long been the subject of peculiar misperception.[2] Such misunderstanding, fairly or unfairly, results primarily from salient historiography of the Second World War, which has long presented a category of disturbing questions concerning the rôle of the Catholic Church in Axis and occupied Europe, the record of Eugenio Pacelli as Cardinal Secretary of State (1930–1939) and as Pope Pius XII (1939–1958), and the ecclesiological, comparative, and international implications of the Lateran Pacts of 1929 and the *Reich* Concordat of 1933. The frequent scholarly tendency to view the institutional Church as variously confined, captured, compromised, or coöpted by fascism and Nazism departs in large measure from Guenter Lewy's *The Catholic Church and Nazi Germany* (1964), wherein he states, "In a mood of naïve trust and wishful thinking about Hitler's promises of religious peace, and anxious to protect the Church's organizations, schools, and newspapers, the German bishops supported the signing of the [*Reich*] Concordat" (325). He boldly continues soon thereafter, "When 6,000,000 human beings were murdered for being 'non-Aryan'…the Pope in Rome, the spiritual head and supreme moral teacher of the Roman Catholic Church, remained silent" (341).

A large body of historical research has therefore taken shape to attempt to explain the supposed inability of the Church to prevent the authoritarian reaction, total war, and genocide in Europe from 1929 to 1945[3]; in which several central tendencies emerge. With respect to doctrine, the Catholic or universal church did not at all ascribe to the neopagan amalgamation of Dark Age tribalism with imperialist Social Darwinism characteristic of the Nazi racial ideology,[4] but nevertheless appears to have had serious concerns that a perceived lack of cooperation with the "realist" fascist leaderships might result in the ascent of the marginalized pagan elements exceedingly hostile to the Church, a tendency that included men such as "super-fascist" Julius Evola of Italy,[5] or the prime mover of pagan revival within the Nazi movement Alfred Rosenberg.[6] The Church was also deeply antithetical to the axiomatic apostasy of the Marxist-Leninist worldview, with its uncompromising denials of the existence and providence of God and frightful assertion that an industrial proletariat—however inherently deserving of overdue economic justice—could achieve earthly paradise through the violent revolutionary overthrow of the international bourgeoisie.[7] Interwar Catholic nations, according to such authors, thus gravitated toward centralized, concordatorial connections with fascist rulers as the most expedient apparent means of navigating the uncertainty of the increasingly totalitarian times, although the vitality of lay Catholic action is concomitantly held to have suffered as a result.[8] Rhodes concludes in *The Vatican in the Age of the Dictators, 1922–1945* (1973), "The care of souls, liberty to celebrate Mass and administer Sacraments, above all to impart religious education to the young...is what the Church aspires to...If it believes that this apostolic activity can be furthered by a concordat, it will conclude one" (354).

The publication of John Cornwell's incendiary *Hitler's Pope: The Secret History of Pius XII* (1999) would further rivet critical attention upon the particular priest who, as the fourth chapter will demonstrate, functioned as pontiff or pontifical legate for 9 out of the 11 concordats concluded between 1929 and 1953, inclusive, rendering him the single individual most directly responsible for the respective treaties between the Catholic Church and fascist governments. The ongoing scholarly debate—which can not unworthily arouse strong feelings and emotions—between the accusers, critics, sympathizers, and defenders of Pacelli whatever their respective motives has been described as the "Pius Wars,"[9] will be properly addressed in the fourth chapter, and shall perhaps continue with the opening of the Vatican archives from 1939 to 1958.[10]

Finally, the larger historiography surveyed above connecting via concordat the Vatican with the Dictators forms the overall posture for the most comprehensive English-language study of the treaties of the Holy See: Frank J. Coppa's edited *Controversial Concordats: The Vatican's Relations with Napoleon, Mussolini and Hitler* (1999). Coppa and his contributors establish that although the Holy See bore no affection and little admiration for those delinquent and apostate supermen, nevertheless tremendous institutional incentives were present in each case to induce the Holy See, through international treaty, to attempt to minimize the damage they yet might inflict upon the Catholic faith. In "Napoleon, the Concordat of 1801, and Its Consequences," (33–80)

William Roberts explains that the treaty with Bonaparte had lasting international implications, in that it "would later serve as a model for treaties defining church-state relations all over Europe and comprise a type of charter to which both secular rulers and Popes would often appeal" (78); and he cites the subsequent Bavarian (1817), Prussian (1821), Swiss (1845), and Spanish (1851) concordats as partial continuations of the initial Napoleonic example. In "Mussolini and the Concordat of 1929" (81–119), Coppa contends that the Lateran Pacts ultimately did place the institutional Church beyond totalitarian fascist control, although they simultaneously much emboldened the regime. In "The *Reich* Concordat of 1933" (120–81), Joseph Biesinger laments, "Whether or not intended by the Vatican, the Concordat did provide some respectability and prestige to the Nazi state. Through the Concordat Hitler created his one-party state by eliminating the Center Party and destroying the hated power of political Catholicism" (142). The at least marginal utility of the concordat in the consolidation of the Napoleonic and to a greater degree the Axis Powers has therefore resulted in such authoritarian associations.

An Original Analysis

This study acknowledges the force, but questions the totality and finality of the above representations. Notwithstanding their manifold sins and wickedness, fascism and Nazism came and went upon the stage of Europe; whereas the Holy See existed for centuries before, and has endured for decades after those authoritarian movements. Secondary school students are sometimes introduced to the Concordat of Worms of 1122; and any instrument of such antiquity, it stands to reason, has likely enjoyed a wide-ranging career. An original analysis of the concordats of the Holy See should therefore seek to comprehend not merely the distressing examples with select European tyrants, however salient, but the history and applications of the treaty form in its entirety, by posing the following research question: *What are the norms of concordats as a whole, and what are the implications for international relations?*

Notes

1. Owen Chadwick describes his role in inducing the German Centre to vote in favor, "one of the most controversial acts of German

history." *Britain and the Vatican During the Second World War* (Cambridge: Cambridge University Press, 1986), 86.
2. Anonymous maintain a "Concordat Watch" website for the purpose of preserving comparative church and state separation.
3. Rita Almeida de Carvalho, "Interwar Dictatorships, the Catholic Church and Concordats: the Portuguese New State in Comparative Perspective," *Contemporary European History* 25, no. 1 (2016): 37–55; Frank J. Coppa, "Between Morality and Diplomacy: The Vatican's 'Silence' During the Holocaust," *Journal of Church and State* 50 (2008): 541–68; Matthew Feldman and Marius Turda, "'Clerical Fascism' in Interwar Europe: An Introduction," *Totalitarian Movements and Political Religions* 8, no. 2 (2007): 205–212; Oded Heilbronner, "Catholic Resistance during the Third Reich?", *Contemporary European History* 7, no. 3 (1998): 409–14; Jay John Hughes, "The Pope's 'Pact with Hitler': Betrayal or Self-Defense?", *Journal of Church and State* 17 (1975): 63–80; Peter C. Kent, *The Pope and the Duce: The International Impact of the Lateran Agreements* (New York: St. Martin's Press, 1981); Oliver Logan, "The Pontificate of Pius XI: The Impact of New Material from the Vatican Archives," *European History Quarterly* 42, no. 4 (2012): 664–72; Albert C. O'Brien, "Benito Mussolini, Catholic Youth, and the Origins of the Lateran Treaties," *Journal of Church and State* 23 (1981): 117–29; John F. Pollard, "The Papacy in Two World Wars: Benedict XV and Pius XII Compared," *Totalitarian Movements and Political Religions* 2, no. 3 (2001): 83–96; Richard Steigmann-Gall, *The Holy Reich: Nazi Conceptions of Christianity, 1919–1945* (Cambridge: Cambridge University Press, 1999).
4. See Frank J. Coppa, "Pope Pius XI's 'Encyclical' *Humani Generis Unitas* Against Racism and Anti-Semitism and the 'Silence' of Pope Pius XII," *Journal of Church and State* 40 (1998): 775–95.
5. Richard Drake, "Julius Evola, Radical Fascism and the Lateran Accords," *The Catholic Historical Review* 74, no. 3 (1988): 403–19.
6. Author of *The Myth of the Twentieth Century: An Evaluation of the Spiritual-Intellectual Confrontations of our Age* (Ostara Publications, [*Mythus des XX. Jahrhunderts*, 1930] 2016).
7. See especially Lauren N. Faulkner, "Against Bolshevism: Georg Werthmann and the Role of Ideology in the Catholic Military

Chaplaincy, 1939–1945," *Contemporary European History* 19, no. 1 (2010): 1–16.
8. Jorge Dagnino, "The Intellectuals of Italian Catholic Action and the Sacralisation of Politics in 1930s Europe," *Contemporary European History* 21, no. 2 (2012): 215–33.
9. This controversy is summarized in Joseph Bottum and David G. Dalin (eds.), *The Pius War: Responses to the Critics of Pius XII* (Lanham, MD: Lexington Brooks, 2004); David Cymet, *History vs. Apologetics: The Holocaust, the Third Reich, and the Catholic Church* (Lanham, MD: Lexington Books, 2010); and José M. Sánchez, *Pius XII and the Holocaust: Understanding the Controversy* (Washington, D.C.: The Catholic University of America Press, 2002).
10. *L'Osservatore Romano*, 4 March 2019.

CHAPTER 2

At the Intersection of Canon, Comparative, and International Law

"I, bishop Calixtus, servant of the servants of God, do grant to thee beloved son, Henry-by the grace of God august emperor of the Romans-that the elections of the bishops and abbots of the German kingdom, who belong to the kingdom, shall take place in thy presence." "In the name of the holy and indivisible Trinity, I, Henry, by the grace of God august emperor of the Romans, for the love of God and of the holy Roman church and of our master pope Calixtus, and for the healing of my soul, do remit to God, and to the holy apostles of God, Peter and Paul, and to the holy catholic church, all investiture through ring and staff."[1] In this initial Concordat of Worms of 1122, the ceremonial rhetoric and plaintive emotion of the respective speakers may appear difficult to fully disentangle from the substance of their bilateral agreement, whereby the German state should continue to endow bishops with civil, but no longer with ecclesiastical authority. But this celebrated medieval rapprochement between pontiff and emperor would serve to initiate the practice of the negotiation of treaties between the Holy See and civil commonwealths, called concordats.

A concordat is "a treaty of international law by which the Holy See, on one hand, and a sovereign state, on the other, regulates the collection of questions concerning the institutions and activities of the Catholic Church in a given territory."[2] The research findings of the following chapter shall

© The Author(s), under exclusive license to Springer Nature Switzerland AG 2024
M. R. Royce, *Ecclesiology, Idealism, and World Polity*, Palgrave Studies in Religion, Politics, and Policy, https://doi.org/10.1007/978-3-031-57033-9_2

demonstrate the usefulness and accuracy of this definition. But in this place, discussion shall consist of the identification and explanation of the three main branches of *law* which generally occupy mutually exclusive teaching and research communities, but at the intersection of which the concordats of the Apostolic See emerge: the canon law of the Roman Catholic Church, the comparative law of the sovereign nation-states, and the incipient international law of the emerging cosmo-polis.

A Peculiarity of Canon Law

The roots of the canon law of the Roman Catholic Church lie in the life and doctrine of the Biblical Apostles. The special naming of Peter (Mat. 16:18–19) is interpreted as the intended exaltation of him as their Prince, whom the Roman pontiff, amid the Cardinals, is said to succeed.[3] The first church council (Acts 15) established the precedent of ecumenical decision-making, the probable baptism of infants (Acts 16:13–15, 30–33) would serve as the basis for the administration of that blessed sacrament, and the Pauline description of an appropriate supper of the Lord (I Cor. 11:20–34)—including pertinent words of Christ not actually recorded in the Gospels—inaugurated the world-historical transformation of Eucharistic theology. But with the eventual conversion of the Roman Empire to Christianity, New Testament theory and practice became institutionalized throughout the Western world, as the law of the Roman state was by degrees transformed into the law of the Roman church. Neoclassicist Hannah Arendt remarks in *Between Past and Future* (1954), "Thanks to the fact that the foundation of the city of Rome was repeated in the foundation of the Catholic Church…the Roman trinity of religion, authority, and tradition could be taken over by the Christian era" (126).

During the first centuries of Christianity in the West, it was typical to appeal to the amorphous "sacred canons" of the early church as the collective source of law and authority.[4] What is known as the "old law" prevailed until the textual intervention of Gratian (1140–1150), the "new law" prevailed until the Council of Trent (1545–1563), and the "newest law" is post-Trent. In 1582, Gregory XIII ordered the general distribution of a Corpus Iuris Canonici; and canon law remained in this state of relative disorder until the decisive code of 1917 (*AAS* 9 [1917-II]).

In 1904, Pope Pius X appointed Archbishop of Caesarea Cardinal Pietro Gasparri to chair a select committee tasked with a total revision and codification of the canon law of the Roman Catholic Church.

The selection matters in part because he also served as Secretary of the Sacred Congregation for extraordinary affairs, and he would function as contracting plenipotentiary for seven concordats concluded between 1922 and 1929, inclusive. His Eminence energetically set about his monumental task and after institutional delays connected with the outbreak of the Great War, a new Code of Canon Law was prepared for entry into force on the Day of Pentecost (19 May), 1918.

Its 2414 canons comprehend the entire ecclesiology of the Catholic faith, and mention shall be made throughout of the numerous points of intersection between the contents of canon law and the contents of concordats. But, strikingly, the concordatorial question is addressed in no less than the third canon, which reads, "The canons of this Code in no way abrogate from or in any way abrogate treaties entered into by the Apostolic See with various Nations; those treaties, therefore, maintain their present force, notwithstanding any contrary prescriptions of this Code."[5] This canon appears to make the vital point that *when in conflict*, the provisions of a concordat override the provisions of canon law. A handful of other canons, meanwhile, touch upon concordats or relate to pontifical diplomacy more generally. Organizationally, the research and development of concordats are assigned by the Cardinal Secretary of State to a Congregation for extraordinary ecclesiastical affairs (CONGREGATIONEM PRO NEGOTIIS ECCLESIASTICIS EXTRAORDINARIIS, CIC/1917, c. 255), one of several divisions of the Office of the Secretary of State (CIC/1917, c. 263). Meanwhile, the code insists upon the inalienable right of the Apostolic See to formally engage in international relations. "It is the right of the Roman Pontiff," it reads, "independent of civil power, to send into any part of the world Legates, with or without ecclesiastical jurisdiction."[6] Characteristic protocols concerning the rights and duties of such legates are thereafter furnished (CIC/1917, c. 266–70).

Conceived by Pope John XXIII in much the same reformist spirit responsible for the Second Vatican Council, the new Code of Canon Law of 1983 (*AAS* 75 [1983-II]) was promulgated by Pope John Paul II on 25 January and entered into force on the First Sunday of Advent (27 November). It states of itself, "The Code must be regarded as the essential instrument for the preservation of right order, both in individual and social life and in the Church's zeal;"[7] and its canons concerned with concordats are very similar to those of the code of 1917. Once again, the third canon states, "The Canons of this Code do not abrogate, nor do they derogate from, agreements entered into by the Apostolic See with nations or other civil entities. For this reason, these agreements continue in force as hitherto, notwithstanding any contrary provisions of this Code."[8] The phrase, "or other civil entities" (ALIISVE SOCI-ETATIBUS POLITICIS) shall become important when the frequency with which the German *Länder* contract their own concordats is identified and discussed. At a more general level, two other canons from the 1983 code appear significant. First, "The Roman Pontiff has an inherent and independent right to appoint Legates and to send them to particular Churches in various countries or regions, or at the same time to States and to public Authorities."[9] Such a pontifical legate, second, "who at the same time acts as envoy to the State according to international law, has in addition the special role: 1° of promoting and fostering relationships between the Apostolic See and the Authorities of the State; 2° of dealing with questions concerning relations between Church and State, especially, of drawing up concordats and other similar agreements, and giving effect to them."[10] Therefore whereas the 1917 code had tasked curial officials in Rome with the composition of concordats, the 1983 version appears to diffuse and decentralize this responsibility to accredited pontifical representatives.

With the eruption in 1789 of the revolution in France, the sacred canons of the Catholic Church were put to their greatest historical test, as Europe's oldest nation-state with the deepest connections to the institutional Church was suddenly converted into the international fountainhead of anti-clerical belief and practice. The decisive attempt at reconciliation was the Latin-language concordat of 15 July 1801 between the Apostolic See and the Gallic Republic, with its First Consul (Napoleon) appointed as executor. In an apparent demonstration that a concordat remains in force notwithstanding revolutionary transformation within the contracting party, this treaty was preserved throughout the imperial proclamation of 1804, the Restoration of 1814, the Second Republic of 1848, the Second Empire of 1852, and the Third Republic of 1870; and it was not abolished, as the following chapter will demonstrate, until the passage of the law of separation of 1905. The enormous importance of the concordat with Napoleon, however, generated in the French language the first significant body of scholarship on the topic, in which primarily historical discussions involving canon law, international law, republicanism, and church and state in France, among other subjects, were intermittently pursued through the 1930s.[11] The magisterial history of Count

Boulay de la Meurthe provides in six volumes a minute account of the development of the 1801 concordat,[12] while Baudrillart writes from a clerical perspective, emphasizing concordats as papal concessions and the grievous harm of the unilateral French denunciation.[13] Much of this literature is concerned with the specifics of the French case, and many of the contentious points involved have been transformed by the Lateran Pacts and by postwar ecclesiological developments. But the as it were capstone entry of the Napoleonic school, Henri Wagnon's *Concordats et Droit International: Fondement, Élaboration, Valeur et Cessation du Droit Concordataire* (1935), remains of enduring significance.

The most important study of concordats prior to the Second World War, its author Monsieur Wagnon held a doctorate in canon law but defended the validity of concordats within international law, arguing against *laïque* attempts to deny to the Holy See legitimacy as a transnational actor. He defines his subject as, "a convention concluded between the civil and ecclesiastical power…a bilateral treaty, born of the common accord of the two parties, establishing a rule of law that they are duty bound to maintain and to faithfully observe."[14] One of the main contemporary objections that Wagnon sought to rebut was the largely personal nature of the early versions like that of Worms above, in which a pontiff and a monarch simply exchange public letters. His parsimonious reply is that *almost all* ancient treaties assumed this form, and therefore those of the Holy See ought not to be singled out for such criticism. Medieval kings, he furthermore argues, did in their pride and jealousy abrogate treaties of every sort with everyone, and there is therefore little to no historical or legal basis for conceptualizing concordats any differently from bilateral conventions between two civil powers. He therefore concludes, "The Catholic Church, personified by its organ, the Holy See, is a normal person of the international community, that is to say…of the international juridical life. And the treaty, the concordat, is precisely one of the most important acts of this juridical life."[15] Wagnon also empirically applies his theory to his native land, furnishing a decisive analysis of the continued applicability of the Napoleonic concordat to four European regions at the periphery of French hegemonic power: it does not apply in Belgium or in Luxembourg because of the total independence acquired by the respective Belgian and Luxembourger churches nor to the Netherlands because it never had any effect there at any time. It does remain in force, however, in the picturesque lands of Alsace-Lorraine, because they are part of France and because the French government was seen to respect its continuation there even after the passage of the 1905 law of separation.[16]

As a result of this revolutionary struggle between church and state in France involving, though not limited to the agreement with Bonaparte the greatest works of contemporary concordatorial scholarship as a whole appear in French. A chronological survey is contained in Jean Julg's *L'Église et les États: Histoire des concordats* (1990). Julg provides a very useful narrative history of concordats, beginning with those of Worms (1122), of Vienna (1448), and with François I (1516), and then continuing into more recent periods. Resisting theoretical synthesis, he emphasizes historical context, critical junctures, and the particularities of each case. The laurel of the subject matter, however, currently belongs to Msgr. Dr. Roland Minnerath, Archbishop of Dijon (2004–2022) and the greatest contemporary scholar of concordats. His *L'Église et les États Concordataires* (1846–1981): *La souveraineté spirituelle* (1983) furnishes similar historical material to Julg, but with greater emphasis on change and continuity in church doctrine. His primary argument is that, whether in a correlative or causal capacity, the newfound doctrines of religious liberty expressed in the concordats of the 1960s and 1970s correspond to the changing ecclesiological norms manifest in the outcomes of the Second Vatican Council, and in the revolutions in human rights and self-determination shaping international relations. He writes, "In the preceding doctrine, the unity of perspective was centered in God, the creator of temporal societies and founder of the Church. Now, the transcendent principle is the dignity of the human person as fundamental source of individual and communal rights."[17] Said another way, the recent concordatorial *oeuvre* acknowledges and accepts a liberal international order in which equality of all creeds and persons before the law is a major principle. "The doctrine of post-conciliar concordats," he continues, "ratifies here the constitutional principle of the equality of citizens before the law and the administration of justice."[18] Minnerath's second book on concordats, *L'Eglise catholique face aux États. Deux siècles de pratique concordataire, 1801–2010* (2012) reiterates many of the findings of his previous work, especially the correspondence between the Christian democratic philosophy of the Vatican II documents and recent concordats and the explicit concordatorial affirmation of the importance of equality before the law and representative institutions. Yet his more recent textual analysis demonstrates greater interest in establishing the Catholic Church and the Holy See as an independent, willing, and dynamic partner in the normative reconstitution of international politics, rather than as simply a passive, belated, and reluctant late convert. He writes in a thesis passage, "In a perfect continuity of two centuries of concordatorial practice, the Catholic Church does not solely claim its right of religious liberty, but presents it to the states as a subject that treats with them on terms of equality in order to define the concrete implications and modalities of this right."[19] This research shall seek to extend the pioneering efforts of particularly Julg and Minnerath but shall do so for somewhat different reasons, in a different language, and with different results.

A Rarity in Comparative Law

Concordats equally belong to comparative law, being treaties acknowledged by the legal systems of respective independent nation-states. They operate by the principle of PACTA SUNT SERVANDA,[20] in which acknowledged plenipotentiaries convene on equal footing and draw up a treaty that engages the powers of their respective governments; and there is no clear recorded instance of the head of state or contracting plenipotentiary to a concordat ever subjecting the pontifical legate to any sort of serious indignity. The peaceful exchange of ambassadors, on the contrary, has always and everywhere been scrupulously observed, as is revealed in the treaty texts themselves. "An Apostolic Nuncio shall reside in Poland and an Ambassador of the Republic shall reside in the Holy See."[21] "There shall continue to be an Ambassador of the Dominican Republic to the Holy See and an Apostolic Nuncio in Trujillo City" (*AAS* 46 [1954], 434 {II.2}).[22]

The PACTA SUNT SERVANDA principle involves three important elements with respect to concordats. First, of all the official instruments present in the annual *Acts of the Apostolic See*, only concordats remotely resemble an international treaty, and yet they do so strongly and consistently. The super-majority appears in side-by-side, equally authentic Italian and vernacular texts, with the contents usually divided into articles and sections. The names, titles, and signatures of the contracting plenipotentiaries are always provided, and in some cases, rank and/or precedence are entered into the treaty articles themselves. "In relation to Art. 14 § 1 of the Fundamental Agreement, signed by the Holy See and the State of Israel, the 'Special Representatives' shall have, respectively, the personal rank of Apostolic Nuncio and Ambassador" (*AAS* 86 [1994],

726 {Additional Protocol 1}). The ratification principle, second, should also be adduced, with a representative explanation taken from a Maltese concordat: "The present Agreement shall come into force when the Parties exchange an official communication that the full implementation of all its provisions through the appropriate legal instruments according to their respective legal systems has taken place" (*AAS* 89 [1997], 688 {11}). Given that, on the part of the constitutional monarchic Apostolic See, signature has heretofore always proven equivalent to ratification, a concordat *enters into force* once the contracting party has by whatever means necessary approved the treaty through its own legal system and formally informed the Apostolic See of the successful completion of this action. Finally, concordats almost always include toward the end language to the effect that should any disagreement or dispute arise as to the requirements of the treaty terms, it will be settled by mutual consultation. "If there should arise any divergence of interpretation or application of a disposition of the present concordat, the Holy See and the German *Reich* shall proceed in one mind toward an amicable solution."[23] "Bosnia and Herzegovina and the Holy See will resolve, by common accord, through diplomatic means, any doubts or difficulties which might arise in the interpretation and application of the provisions of the present Agreement" (*AAS* 99 [2007], 945 {18.1}).[24]

The aforesaid elements, furthermore, appear to fully conform to the terms of the Vienna Convention on the Law of Treaties between States and International Organizations or between International Organizations (1986), the most important instrument regulating such matters. "The present Convention," it opens, "applies to…treaties between one or more States and one or more international organizations" (1.a). The Apostolic See is indisputably an international organization. It continues, "'Treaty' means an international agreement governed by international law and concluded in written form…between one or more States and one or more international organizations" (2.1.a.i). A concordat is indisputably a written agreement. The characteristic processes of concordatorial ratification, furthermore, also appear to satisfy the Vienna convention. "The consent of a State to be bound by a treaty," it holds, "may be expressed by signature, exchange of instruments constituting a treaty, ratification, acceptance, approval or accession, or by any other means if so agreed" (11.1). Contracting states all over the world, as shall be repeatedly demonstrated, have relied upon all of the above to signal their consent to be bound by a concordat. Finally, the convention, like concordats, states that treaties may be amended by the mutual agreement of the contracting parties (39.1).

In addition to treaty form, treaty content should also be considered. Concordats primarily concern the establishment or adjustment of the numerous points of institutional intersection between the Catholic Church and the civil power of the contracting party, with such church and state issues decisive in every scholarly account of the conclusion of a particular concordat.[25] The Lateran Pacts of 1929, to adduce the strongest example, declare Roman Catholicism the Italian state religion (*AAS* 21 [1929], 210 {1}), but the revised concordat with the Italian Republic in 1984 explicitly disestablishes (*AAS* 77 [1985], 532 {additional protocol 1}). Such bilateral agreement on much of the relationship between church and state via treaty can be divided into an assortment of recurring questions.

The first, the most important, and the most comprehensive series involve recognition of the juridical personality of the Catholic Church and the Apostolic See as formulated in canon law (CIC/1917, c. 100, 218–19, 1518, 1556, 1569; CIC/1983, 113–15, 1273, 1404, 1417), in that any subsequent arrangements are predicated on this formal acknowledgment.[26] Most concordats at or near their beginning furnish language acknowledging the independence, autonomy, and apostolic mission of the Church, and the intention of the contracting civil power to respect them. "The Catholic religion shall be freely and publicly exercised in Latvia."[27] "The Portuguese Republic recognizes the juridical personality of the Catholic Church…and the Catholic Church is guaranteed the free exercise of its authority."[28] Such passages represent the base-line affirmation. Such general introductory remarks can however on occasion be rather more expansive, as in the case of the concordat with, of all possible signatories, the Palestine Liberation Organization: "The PLO recognizes the freedom of the Catholic Church to exercise her rights to carry out, through the necessary means, her functions and traditions, such as those that are spiritual, religious, moral, charitable, educational and cultural" (*AAS* 92 [2000], 855 {5}).

One particular dimension is insistence upon respect for *ordinary power* (CIC/1917, c. 197, 2214; CIC/1983, c. 1311), which under canon law "is joined to a certain office by the law itself."[29] An ordinary is an executive official of an ecclesiastical formation, and the Church through its concordats is keen to ensure that the decisions of local ordinaries shall not be peremptorily overridden by organs of the state. A concordat with

Croatia thus affirms, "The competent ecclesiastical authority can erect, modify, abolish, or recognize the juridical ecclesiastical person, according to the norms of canon law."[30] Ordinary power can include the imposition of ecclesiastical taxation—a consolidated regime in much of Germany[31]— as well as the inviolability of confession. Non-negotiable under canon law (CIC/1917, c. 889; CIC/1983, c. 889), and an impervious norm since the Middle Ages, information divulged to a priest in his capacity as confessor cannot be disclosed to a third party under any circumstances; and recent concordats have emphasized the sacrosanct character of the confessional seal (*AAS* 92 [2000], 798 {8.1}; 93 [2001], 139 {8.1}; 95 [2003], 104 {7}; 99 [2007], 941 {8.2}; 106 [2014], 199 {8§3}).

The corporate and institutional life of the Church is also promoted through its concordats. The import of the sacred canons (CIC/1917, c. 1247§1; CIC/1983, c. 1246) concerning Sabbath rest sometimes enters into the respective treaty texts, as do the preservation of feast and other holidays. "The [Spanish] State recognizes all Sundays as festival days. By common agreement shall be determined other religious festivities to be recognized."[32] The preservation of ecclesiastical property is also a frequent treaty term, which even Chancellor Hitler agreed to safeguard (*AAS* 25 [1933], 399 {17}) in accordance with canon law (CIC/1917, c. 531, 1495; CIC/1983, c. 634, 1255). A concordat with Colombia for example "guarantees to the Church the right to possess and to administer its own cemeteries."[33] Less frequently, the state is engaged in the actual building up of the physical premises of the Church. "The government of Bolivia shall aid in the construction of churches."[34] Mention is often made however of cultural cooperation between the Catholic Church and the contracting civil commonwealth, involving mutual efforts at historical preservation. Treaty passages taken from concordats with two of the Baltic countries are illustrative in this regard. "The cultural and historical patrimony of the Catholic Church is an important part of the national heritage, therefore the Catholic Church and the Republic of Lithuania shall continue to co-operate to preserve this heritage" (*AAS* 92 [2000], 788 {13.1}). "The cultural and artistic heritage of the Catholic Church is to be considered as an important part of the national heritage of the Republic of Latvia" (*AAS* 95 [2003], 108, {22.1}). There is also an occasional reference to the preservation of Church access to print and broadcast media. "The Catholic Church shall have access to public mass media, Catholic radio and television programmes shall be broadcast [in Lithuania]" (*AAS* 92 [2000], 787 {12.1}).

Concluding this discussion of concordatorial recognition of the juridical personality of the Catholic Church, there are two recurring treaty terms concerning the armed forces. First, in conformity with canon law (CIC/1917, c. 121, 141; CIC/1983, c. 289), officiating priests or sometimes all religious are excluded from military service, during peacetime or sometimes at all times. "The Spanish state recognizes that clerics and religious, be they professors or initiates...are exempt from all military service."[35] Second, concordats routinely guarantee ministerial access to the troops, usually through some form of independent institutionalization to oversee the spiritual wellbeing of those in uniform. "The Holy See shall constitute in Bolivia a Military Vicarage in order to attend to the spiritual care of the members of the Armed Forces."[36] "The Military Ordinary shall be named by the Holy See prior to the notification of Sir President of the Republic of Boliva."[37]

Episcopacy also furnishes an assortment of related concerns. The Catholic Church in any given nation is governed by its bishops, and therefore the contents of concordats often address what institutional relationships are to exist between the civil power and the episcopal sees of these elevated priests. Most arresting perhaps to a liberal sensibility is the occasional loyalty oath extracted from the bishops prior to or upon the taking possession of their dioceses. "I swear and promise before God and upon his holy Gospels obedience and fidelity to his Highness the Prince of Montenegro."[38] "I promise and I engage myself to preserve respect and fidelity to the Haitian Constitution in view of the pursuit of the common good of the country and of the defense of the interests of the nation."[39] The first case chapter exploring the concordats with the fascist dictators will explore, among other subjects, the terrible implications of this episcopal oath. For now, the loyalty oath is sometimes accompanied by the commitment to offer special prayers for the regime. For example, "on Sundays and on the day of celebration of national independence, the officiating priests shall recite a liturgical prayer for the prosperity of the Republic of Lithuania and its President."[40] Provision is also typically made for the preservation of episcopal correspondence vis-à-vis the Holy See and the dioceses, as in this 1929 concordat with the Kingdom of Romania: "Direct communication of Bishops, Clergy, and people with the Holy See and vice-versa, in spiritual matters and ecclesiastical affairs, shall be absolutely free."[41] In conformity with canon law (CIC/1917, c. 329; CIC/1983, c. 375, 377), modern concordats also, like their ancient predecessors, insist upon the right of the Apostolic See to nominate bishops. "The nomination of the Archbishops and Bishops [of Argentina] is the competence of the Holy See."[42] "The right of naming the Archbishop [of Monaco] is the exclusive competence of the Holy See."[43]

The institutionalization of Catholic education in both schools and universities also serves as a major theme of concordats.[44] Under canon law, Catholic parents are instructed, if possible, to enroll their children in Catholic schools (CIC/1917, c. 1374; CIC/1983, c. 798); and most of the comparative treaty texts assertively make provision for this vital component of the Church's teaching *magisterium*. "The [Bavarian] State guarantees the institution and function of a teaching ecclesiastical high school."[45] "The Church holds full liberty [in Peru] to establish educational centers at every level, in conformity with national legislation."[46] "The Italian Republic, recognizing the value of the religious culture and taking into account its part of the historic patrimony of the Italian people, shall continue to assure, within the framework of the schools, the teaching of the Catholic religion in the public schools."[47] Naturally, subsidiary terms are contained within this overall objective. One is episcopal, ordinary, or other ecclesiastical control over both syllabi and instructors (CIC/1917, c. 1365, 1381; CIC/1983, c. 250, 252, 256, 803, 805–06, 810). "For the teaching of religion [in Spain], nothing can be adopted but textbooks approved by the ecclesiastical authority."[48] "Teachers of the Catholic religion [in Lithuania] must have the written authorization (*missio canonica*) of the local Bishop" (*AAS* 92 [2000], 784 {3.2}). Another is, amid separate Catholic and public schools, full equality of opportunity between them. "The Land [of the Rhineland-Palatinate] assures the students of the Higher Scientific Educational Ecclesiastical School an internship equivalent to that of the Higher Scientific Educational Land School."[49] Catholic universities, meanwhile, also occupy an important place within canon law (CIC/1917, c. 587, 1349, 1354, 1379; CIC/1983, c. 234, 237, 659), and concordats frequently create or otherwise empower them. "In its time the Land shall erect a Catholic theological faculty at the University of Göttingen."[50] "A chair of Catholic theology is erected at the University of the Saarland."[51]

The final series of recurring provisions concern holy matrimony, a sacrament and very important dimension of the life of the Roman faith. Characteristically, concordats require in conformity with canon law (CIC/1917, c. 1014; CIC/1983, c. 1060) that canonical marriage be equated with civil marriage, enjoying all the rights and privileges pertaining thereto. "The Austrian Republic recognizes the civil effect of marriage contracted in conformity with canon law."[52] Less frequently, ecclesiastical tribunals that under canon law (CIC/1917, c. 1960; CIC/1983, c. 1671) rule upon dissolution and other failures of marriage are recognized by the contracting commonwealth. "The judgments of nullity and the decrees of ratification of nullity of marriage given by the ecclesiastical tribunals are recognized as producing civil effects [in Malta]" (*AAS* 89 [1997], 687 {7}).

In summation, the negotiation, signature, and ratification of the treaties of the Apostolic See in every important respect resemble those between two or more civil powers. The primary concerns of all concordats lie at the intersection of civil and ecclesiastical power, with recognition of the juridical personality of the Church, the efficacious institution of episcopacy, the furtherance of Catholic education, and the protection of covenant marriage the central recurring themes. Through respective treaty ratification processes—whatever they may be—the contents of concordats become comparative law.

A Development Within International Law

Concordats also occupy a conceptually distinct position within international law, of which there has always been some apprehension since the Peace of Westphalia, but which was profoundly enhanced under American leadership after the Second World War. Among its major instruments are the Geneva Conventions (1906–1907, 1949) setting down the laws of war among nation-states, and the example of the International Military Tribunal for Germany (1945–1946) for those select individuals who willfully refuse to comply. The Charter of the United Nations and Statute of the International Court of Justice (1945) and the Universal Declaration of Human Rights (1948) more generally apply the concepts of state sovereignty, personal autonomy, and rule of law, while the Allies reëstablished the structure of a liberal global economy through an International Monetary Fund and International Bank for Reconstruction and Development (1944), as well as shortly thereafter through a General Agreement on Tariffs and Trade (1948). The Helsinki Final Act greatly intensifying complex interdependence was added in 1975. What the inquisitive student of these world-historical alterations tends to soon recognize, however, is the prevailing secular-humanism of much of their especially

American historiography. Usually described as either *neoliberalism* or, if somewhat more to the Left, *liberal-idealism*, the general framework inclines toward the substitution of enlightened pursuit of self-interest for humble submission to God as the foundation for the increasingly cooperative norms of international politics.[53] Philosopher John Rawls for example triumphantly declares in *The Law of Peoples* (1999), "Compare democratic societies with the nation-states of the earlier modern period in Europe. England, France, Spain, Hapsburg Austria, Sweden, and others fought dynastic wars for territory, true religion, for power and glory, and a place in the sun…[but] since constitutional democratic societies are safe from each other, peace reigns among them" (8). Similar in Kantian ethos although more circumspect and scholarly is the following thesis passage from Alexander Wendt's landmark *Social Theory of International Politics* (1999):

> Lockean assumptions have dominated Westphalian politics for the past three centuries. Hobbesiansim has occasionally reared its head, but each time has been beaten back down by status quo states…however…a new international political culture has emerged in the West within which non-violence and team play are the norm, in which case there might not be any such return to the past. I will call this culture "Kantian" (297).

Professor Wendt's Hobbes-to-Locke-to-Kant international evolution certainly furnishes an exceedingly useful and suggestive heuristic, but it unintentionally fails to acknowledge the life and doctrine of the carpenter of Nazareth which each of those authors professed,[54] and probably incurs the risk of oversimplifying international history.[55]

A more balanced historical perspective takes into account the great importance of the Catholic Church in shaping centuries of international order, with its sacrament of Holy Communion (1 Cor. 11:20–34) lovingly joining all willing people long before the development of any human rights political theology. Theoretical contribution begins with Augustine's *City of God* ([*De Civitate Dei*, 426] 1957), in which Church and Empire can without loss pursue their separate destinies, while the *Summa Theologica* ([1265–1274] 1920) of Thomas Aquinas synthesizes Christian theology and Aristotelian philosophy to redefine the high Middle Ages. Dante's *Monarchy* ([*De Monarchia*, 1313] 1996) and Sir Thomas More's *Utopia* ([1516] 1992) both became vital texts for the shaping of modern political theory, while authors such as Robert Bellarmine,

Francisco Suárez, and Francisco de Vitoria helped conceptualize the emerging Spanish and Portuguese empires as normative extensions of the Counter-Reformation. At the level of practice, the Catholic Church ruled medieval Europe alongside its Kings and Queens, patronizing the Frankish empire of Charlemagne, approving of the Holy Roman Empire of Germany, resisting what remained of Byzantine imperialism, initiating the Crusades, directly ruling the Papal States, and almost single-handedly preserving literacy and learning; and its ecumenical councils including those at Nicaea (325), Constance (1414–1418), and Trent (1545–1563) decisively shaped the lived experience of the inhabitants of Western Christendom. To further pursue such argumentation, however, would prove tedious. Whatever the reader's philosophical persuasion, the general significance of the Catholic Church as an international actor is a historical fact, but what richly deserves emphasis is the profound degree to which the conclusion of the Lateran Pacts of 1929 would reinvigorate learned debate as to the intentions and capabilities of the Holy See within the international order.

As shall be described in detail in Chapter 4, those series of conventions between the Holy See and the fascist government of Italy created the city of the Vatican as a sovereign state within international politics, at once resolving the vexatious "Roman question" and enabling the Roman pontiff to attain to the same rank as civil heads of state. The Lateran Pacts were generally well-received at the time,[56] and generally understood to have created an independent albeit miniscule state within the international system.[57] They also inaugurated generations of scholarly literature concerned with the Holy See as a transnational actor.

One series of issues can be classified as concerned with the *institutional capability* of the Holy See to act internationally. Relatively few scholars have defended the position that the Holy See and/or the Vatican City-state can be denied such participation strictly on the grounds of asserted inability to fully conform to the Montevideo Convention (1933)[58]; rather most studies of the subject since the Second World War concur in assigning a robust if *sui generis* presence to the Holy See within international law.[59] The Holy See demonstrates its sovereignty by sending ambassadors—called *nuncios*—to other countries, and by in turn receiving their plenipotentiaries in Rome. The Holy See regularly concludes concordats. The Holy See is also a Permanent Observer to the United Nations organization, maintaining a mission in New York; and recent research has emphasized how the *catholicity* of the Roman pontiff appears to place him in a unique position to understand and address the increasing legal, political, economic, and ecological challenges of world polity.[60] The Holy See must not however be confused with the Vatican City-state,[61] which issues its own passports and can shelter money within its bank or persons within its walls beyond the reach of Italian, European, or even international law. In an increasingly multi-polar, and for the sake of argument ideal-driven international system, the Holy See and Holy Father appear in the eyes of many *poised* to make historic contributions. Diez remarks, "We have witnessed a solidarization of international society that has had a transformative impact on diplomatic practices and created a window of opportunity for actors such as the Pope to increase their influence both on the society of states and on a transnational, 'world' society of individuals."[62]

The *normative intent* of the Holy See on the international plane has also received sustained critical attention. Whereas learned opinion in majority-Protestant Britain and America until the Second World War generally held Roman Catholicism inimical to individual freedom, this concern is no longer nearly so strong or widespread, given that the results of the Second Vatican Council and the subsequent conduct of the Holy See have demonstrated sincere and seemingly irrevocable commitment to the rights of man and of the citizen.[63] Catholic countries, usually aided by their bishops and the Holy See, furthermore dominated the cascade of democratic transitions that accompanied the decline and fall of the Soviet Empire,[64] with Samuel Huntington clarifying that the "third wave" between 1974 and 1990 "was overwhelmingly a Catholic wave."[65] The strong advocacy of the Holy See for human rights at a global level has also been observed and welcomed,[66] even if secular commentators remain reluctant to accept the Christian claim to have originated the concept, while the recent papacy is credited with renewed and intensified inter-faith dialogue.[67]

The skill, splendor, and steadfastness of the diplomacy of particular popes have also resulted in fertile scholarly exploration.[68] Pius XII (1939–1958) may have equivocated with respect to Nazism, but he was resolutely anti-Communist, crucial to the Christian Democratic victory at the Italian polls in 1948 that cemented the new republic to the Western democratic sphere.[69] John Paul II (1978–2005) is often interpreted as a global citizen and high priest of the democratic world,[70] with Formicola describing him as a "catalyst for a new world order" to include "social justice and political change in the world."[71] The first Polish pontiff, in particular furnished significant theological, institutional, and diplomatic resistance to European Communism, probably hastening its collapse.[72] The great intellect of Benedict XVI (2005–2013) and its application to international policy received acknowledgement,[73] while a refreshing Third World perspective is identified with Francis (2013-),[74] including even his avoidance of costly regalia in favor of more humble attire. "The radicalism of Franciscan metaphysics," comments Thomas, "is relevant to international relations."[75]

Recent English-language research specifically concerned with concordats, finally, generally observes the democratic-idealist ecclesiological transformations surveyed above. Damián Němec's *Concordat Agreements between the Holy See and the Post-Communist Countries, 1990–2010* (2012) exhaustively codes the comparative treaty texts to demonstrate the democratic nature of most of their contents, while Petkoff (2007) does much the same concerning religious rights internationally.[76] Especially decisive is Ferrari (2004), who argues that the democratizing spirit of Vatican II has been fully reflected in subsequent concordats with European countries, to some degree with those with Latin American countries, but not at all with respect to Morocco or Tunisia.[77]

To thus summarize the conceptual background provided in this chapter, concordats appear at the intersection of the canon law of the Roman Catholic Church, the comparative law of the nation-states, and the international law of the state system. The sacred canons, first, outline their institutional space. Comparative law, second, observes their bilateral negotiation and subjects of mutual concern. International law, finally, acknowledges them as an institutional expression of the independent action of the Apostolic See on the international plane. The next and most crucial task of the inquiry is to empirically identify, rigorously describe, and conceptually account for the full extent of concordats.

Notes

1. Ernest F. Henderson, *Select Historical Documents of the Middle Ages* (London: George Bell and Sons, 1910), 408–09.
2. Roland Minnerath, "Concordat," *Encyclopædia Universalis* (Paris: [1990] 2000), www.universalis.fr/encyclopedie/concordat. *Un traité de droit international par lequel le Saint-Siège, d'une part, et un état souverain, d'autre part, règlent l'ensemble des questions concernant les institutions et les activités de l'église catholique sur un*

territoire donné. The following chapter shall provide further clarification and justification of the terms and concepts to be employed in the research.
3. The same also, following the Lord's Ascension, *stood up in the midst of the disciples* and urged them to initiate the proclamation of his Gospel (Acts 1:15).
4. See the decisive "Preface" by Cardinal Pietro Gasparri in Edward N. Peters (curator), *The 1917 or Pio-Benedictine Code of Canon Law* (San Franciso: Ignatius Press, 2001).
5. Codicis canones initas ab Apostolica Sede cum variis Nationibus conventiones nullatenus abrogant aut iis aliquid obrogant; eae idcirco perinde ac in praesens vigere pergent, contrariis huius Codicis praescriptis minime obstantibus.
6. Romano Pontifici ius est, a civili potestate independens, in quamlibet mundi partem Legatos cum vel sine ecclesiastica iurisdictione mittendi (CIC/1917, c. 265).
7. Codex, utpote quod est primarium documentum legiferum Ecclesiae, innixum in hereditate iuridica et legifera Revelationis atque Traditionis, necessarium instrumentum censendum est, quo debitus servetur ordo tum in vita individuali atque sociali, tum in ipsa Ecclesiae navitate (*AAS* 75 [1983-II], xi).
8. Codicis canones initas ab Apostolica Sede cum nationibus aliisve societatibus politicis conventiones non abrogant neque iis derogant; eaedem idcirco perinde ac in praesens vigere pergent, contrariis huius Codicis praescriptis minime obstantibus.
9. Romano Pontifici ius est nativum et independens Legatos suos nominandi ac mittendi sive ad Ecclesias particulares in variis nationibus vel regionibus, sive simul ad Civitates et ad publicas Auctoritates (CIC/1983, c. 362).
10. § 1. Legais Romani Pontificis officium committu ipsius Romani Pontificis stabili modo gerendi personam apud Ecclesias particulares aut etiam apud Civitates et publicas Auctoritates, ad quas missi sunt. § 2. Personam gerunt Apostolicae Sedis ii quoque, qui in pontificiam Missionem ut Delegati aut Observatores deputantur

apud Consilia internationalia aut apud Conferentias et Conventus (CIC/1983, c. 365 § 1).

11. Among the most important of these historical accounts of the concordat with Napoleon and of how it transformed the balance of civil and ecclesiastical power in France are André Latreille, *Napoléon et le Saint-Siège (1801–1808). L'ambassade du cardinal Fesch à Rome* (Paris: Alean, 1935); François Désiré Mathieu, *Le Concordat de 1801: Ses Origines, Son Histoire; D'Après des Documents Inédits* (Paris: Perrin, 1904); Augustin Theiner, *Histoire des deux Concordats de la république Française et de la république cisalpine* (Paris: Bar-le-Duc, 1869); and Henri Welschinger, *Le Pape et l'Empereur, 1804–1815* (Paris: Plon, Nourrit et Cie, 1905).
12. *Documents sur la Négociation du Concordat et sur les autres rapports de la France avec le Saint-Siège in 1801* (Paris: Ernest Leroux, 1891–1905).
13. Alfred Baudrillart, *Quatre cent ans de Concordat* (Paris: Poussielgue, 1905).
14. *Le concordat est une convention conclue entre le pouvoir ecclésiastique et le pouvoir civil…un traité bilatéral, né de l'accord des volontés des deux parties, établissant une règle de droit qu'elles sont tenues en justice de maintenir et d'observer fidèlement*, 23.
15. *L'Église catholique, personnifiée par son organe, le Saint-Siège, est une personne normale de la communauté internationale, c'est-à-dire… de la vie juridique internationale. Or le traité, le concordat, est précisément un des actes le plus importants de cette vie juridique*, 77.
16. A suggestive semantic point emerges from this French literature. In Anglo-American law and political philosophy, the *right* of an individual to A or B is strongly, sometimes diametrically juxtaposed against the force of *law* in respect Y or Z. But in French, these two key concepts are comprehended within the same word, *droit*.
17. *Dans la doctrine précédente, l'unité de la perspective était place en Dieu, créateur des sociétés temporelles et fondateur de l'Eglise. Maintenant, le principe transcendant est la dignité de la personne humaine, source fondatrice de droits individuels et communautaires*, 122.
18. *La doctrine des concordats post-conciliaires ratifie ici encore la principe constitutionnel de l'égalité des citoyens devant la loi et l'administration de la justice*, 203.

19. *Dans une continuité parfait sur deux siècles de pratique concordataire, l'Église catholique ne revendique pas seulement son droit à la liberté religieuse, mais se pose face aux États comme un sujet qui traite à égalité avec eux pour preciser les implications concrètes et les modalités d'application de ce droit*, 354.
20. "Treaties must be observed," the general norm undergirding all contractual international law.
21. *Un Nonce Apostolique résidera en Pologne et un Ambassadeur de la République résidera auprès du Saint-Siège* (*AAS* 17 [1925], 274 {III}).
22. *Continuarán acreditados un Embajador de la República Dominicana cerca de la Santa Sede y un Nuncio Apostólico en Ciudad Trujillo.*
23. Se in avvenire sorgesse qualche divergenza sull'interpretazione o sull'applicazione di une disposizione del presente Concordato, la Santa Sede ed il Reich Germanico procederanno di comune intelligenza ad una amichevole soluzione / Sollte sich in Zukunft wegen der Auslegung oder Anwendung einer Bestimmung dieses Konkordates irgendeine Meinungsverschiedenheit ergeben, so werden der Heilige Stuhl und das Deutsche Reich im gemeinsamen Einvernehmen eine freundschaftliche Lösong herbeiführen (AAS 25 [1933], 408 {33}).
24. To date there is only one clear example of such terms in operation, when Lithuania and the Apostolic See corrected by mutual agreement a detected textual error (*AAS* 113 [15 Sep. 2021], 88–94). Chapter 7 will furthermore explore a different application of the procedure with respect to Austria.
25. Among the most decisive comparative or case-studies are Carlos Salinas Araneda, "The Efforts to Sign a Concordat Treaty between Chile and the Holy See in 1928," *The Catholic Historical Review* 101, no. 1 (2015): 100–21; P.W. Browne, "The Pactum Callixtinum: An Innovation in Papal Diplomacy," *The Catholic Historical Review* 8, no. 2 (1922): 180–90; William J. Callahan, "Church and State in Spain, 1976–1991," *Journal of Church and State* 34, no. 3 (1992): 503–19; Maria Elisabetta de Franciscis, *Italy and the Vatican: The 1984 Concordat between Church and State* (New York: Peter Lang, 1989); Mauro Giovanneli, "The 1984 Covenant between the Republic of Italy and the Vatican: A Retrospective Analysis after Fifteen Years," *Journal of Church and*

State 42, no. 3 (2000): 529–38; Herbert J. Miller, "Conservative and Liberal Concordats in Nineteenth-Century Guatemala: Who Won?", *Journal of Church and State* 33, no. 1 (1991): 115–30; Stephen T. Rusak, "The Canadian 'Concordat' of 1897," *The Catholic Historical Review* 77, no. 2 (1991): 209–34; John B. Toews, "Pope Eugenius IV and the Concordat of Vienna (1448): An Interpretation," *Church History* 34, no. 2 (1965): 178–94; and Charles R. Wells, "Napoleon's Concordat with Pope Pius VII, 1801," Annual Report of the American Historical Association for the year 1895 (Washington, D.C.: Government Printing Office, 1896): 467–85.

26. Thus during the Cold War, no concordat was ever negotiated with a Communist state. The Apostolic See was however partially able to do so afterward. See Damián Němec, *Concordat Agreements between the Holy See and the Post-Communist Countries, 1990–2010* (Leuven: Peeters, 2012).

27. *La religion-catholique sera librement et publiquement exercée en Lettonie* (*AAS* 14 [1922], 577 {I}).

28. La Repubblica Portoghese riconosce la personalità giuridica della Chiesa Cattolica…È garantito alla Chiesa Cattolica il libero esercizio della sua autorità / A República Portuguesa reconhece a personalidade juridical da Igreja Católica…É garantido à Igreja Católica o livre exercicio da sua autoridade (*AAS* 32 [1940], 219 {I–II}).

29. Potestas regiminis ordinaria ea est, quae ipso iure alicui officio adnectitur (CIC/1983, c. 131).

30. L'autorità ecclesiastica competente può erigere, modificare, abolire o riconoscere le persone giuridiche ecclesiastiche, secondo le norme del Diritto Canonico / *Nadlezna crkvena vlast moze osnivati, mijenjati, dokidati ili priznavati crkvene pravne osobe, prema odredbama kanonskoga prava* (*AAS* 89 [1997], 278 {2.3}).

31. For example, La Chiesa Cattolica nel Baden ha diritto di riscuotere imposte sulla base dei registry civili / Die katholische Kirche in Baden hat das Recht, aufgrund der bürgerlichen Steuerlisten nach… der landesrechtlichen Bestimmungen Kirchensteuern (AAS 25 [1933], 181 {4}).

32. La Stato riconosce come giorni festivi tutte le domeniche. Di comune intesa si stabilirà quali alter festività religiose sono riconosciute come giorni festivi / El Estado reconoce como días

festivos todos los domingos. De común acuerdo se determinará qué otras festividades religiosas son reconocidas como días festivos (*AAS* 72 [1980], 32 {III}).

33. Lo Stato garantisce alla Chiesa il diritto di possedere e amministrare propri cimiteri / *El Estado garantiza a la Iglesia el derecho de poseer y administrar sus propios cementerios* (*AAS* 67 [1975], 431 {XXVII}).

34. *El Gobierno de Bolivia ayudará a la construcción de iglesias* (*AAS* 50 [1958], 75 {XIV.1}).

35. *El Estado español reconoce que los clérigos y religiosos, ya sean profesos, ya novicios…están exentos de todo servicio militar* (*AAS* 43 [1951], 84 {XII}).

36. *La Santa Sede constituye en Bolivia un Vicariato Castrense para atender al cuidado espiritual de los miembros de las Fuerzas Armadas* (*AAS* 43 [1951], 84 {XII}).

37. *El Ordinario Militar sera nombrado por la Santa Sede previa notificación al señor Presidente de la República de Bolivia* (*AAS* 81 [1989], 529 {III}).

38. Io giuro e prometto dinnanzi a Dio e sopra i Santi Evangeli obbedienza e fedeltà a Sua Altezza il Principe del Montenegro / Iuro ac promitto coram Deo et sanctis Evangeliis, celsissimo Amani Principi obedientiam fidelitatemque me pfaestiturum (ASS 19 [1886–87], 220 {IV}).

39. *Je promets et je m'engage à garder respect et fidélité à la Constitution d'Haïti en vue de la poursuite du bien commun du Pays et de la défense des intérêts de la Nation* (*AAS* 76 [1984], 954 {5}).

40. *Les dimanches et le jour de la fête nationale de l'indépendance, les prêtres officiants réciteront une prière liturgique pour la prospérité de la République de Lithuanie et de son Président* (*AAS* 19 [1927], 427 {VIII}).

41. *La communication directe des Evêques, du Clergé et du peuple avec le Saint-Siège, et viceversa, en matière spirituelle et en affaires ecclésiastiques, sera absolument libre* (*AAS* 21 [1929], 443 {IV}).

42. *El nombramiento de los Arzobispos y Obispos es de competencia de la Santa Sede* (*AAS* 59 [1967], 128 {III}).

43. *Le droit de nommer l'Archevêque est de la compétence exclusive du Siège Apostolique* (*AAS* 73 [1981], 652 {II}).

44. See John J. Doyle, Education in Recent Constitutions and Concordats. Ph.D. dissertation, Catholic University of America (Washington, D.C.: 1933). Perhaps the strongest example of such institutionalization is the creation via concordat of the Maltese "Religious Counsellor," a powerful commissar entrusted with the Catholic education of Maltese students (*AAS* 90 [1998], 35–39 {1–8}).
45. Lo Stato garantisce l'istituzione ed il funzionamento di una Alta Scuola pedagogica ecclesiastica / Der Staat gewährleistat einer kirchlichen Pädagogischen Hochschule (*AAS* 61 [1969], 165 {5§4}).
46. *La Iglesia tiene plena libertad para establecer centros educacionales de todo nivel, de conformidad con la legislación nacional* (*AAS* 72 [1980], 811 {XIX}).
47. La Repubblica italiana, riconoscendo il valore della cultura religiosa e tenendo conto che i principi del cattolicesimo fanno parte del patrimonio storico del popolo italiano, continuerà ad assicurare, nel quadro delle finalità della scuola, l'insegnamento della religione cattolica nelle scuole pubbliche (*AAS* 77 [1985], 528 {9.2}).
48. *Para la enseñanza de la Religión, no podrán sera adoptados más libros de texto que los aprobados por la Autoridad eclesiástica* (*AAS* 45 [1953], 646 {XXVII.8}).
49. Il Land assicura agli student dell'Alta Scuola scientifico-educativa ecclesiastica possibilità di tirocinio pari a quelle degli studenti dell'Alta Scuola scientifico-educativa del Land / Das Land wird die schulpraktische Ausbildung der Studenten der kirchlichen Erziehungswissenschaftlichen Hochschule in gleicher Wise sicherstellen wie diejenige der Studenten der Erziehungswissenschaftlichen Hochschule des Landes (*AAS* 62 [1970], 162 {final protocol}).
50. A suo tempo il Land erigerà una Facoltà teologica cattolica nell'Università de Göttingen / Das Land wird zu gegebener Zeit eine katholisch-theologische Fakultät an der Universität in Göttingen errichten (*AAS* 57 [1965], 838 {4(1)}).
51. Nell'Università del Saarland viene eretta una Cattedra di Teologia cattolica / An der Universität des Saar lands wird ein Lehrstuhl für katholische Theologie errichtet (*AAS* 60 [1968], 780 {§1}).
52. La Repubblica Austriaca riconosce gli effetti civili ai matrimoni contratti in conformità del diritto canonico / Die Republik Oesterreich erkennt den gemäss dem kanonischen Recht geschlossenen

Ehen die bürgerlichen Rechtswirkungen zu (*AAS* 26 [1934], 258 {VII§1}).
53. Prominent examples central to the graduate instruction of international relations and law include Michael E. Brown, Sean M. Lynn-Jones, and Steven E. Miller (eds.), *Debating the Democratic Peace* (Cambridge, MA: MIT Press, 1996); Michael W. Doyle, "Liberalism and World Politics," *American Political Science Review* 80, no. 4 (1986): 1151–69; G. John Ikenberry, *Liberal Leviathan: The Origins, Crisis, and Transformation of the American Order* (Princeton: Princeton University Press, 2011); Robert O. Keohane, *After Hegemony: Cooperation and Discord in the World Political Economy* (Princeton: Princeton University Press, 1984); Robert O. Keohane and Joseph S. Nye, Jr., *Power and Interdependence: World Politics in Transition* (Boston: Little, Brown, 1977); Andrew Moravcsik, "Taking Preferences Seriously: A Liberal Theory of International Politics," *International Organization* 51, no. 4 (1997): 513–53; Douglass North, *Institutions, Institutional Change, and Economic Performance* (Cambridge: Cambridge University Press, 1990); John M. Owen IV, *Liberal Peace, Liberal War: American Politics and International Security* (Ithaca, NY: Cornell University Press, 1997); Kenneth A. Oye (ed.), *Cooperation under Anarchy* (Princeton: Princeton University Press, 1986); Bruce Russett, *Grasping the Democratic Peace: Principles for a Post-Cold War World* (Princeton: Princeton University Press, 1993); and Anne-Marie Slaughter, *A New World Order* (Princeton: Princeton University Press, 2005).
54. HOBBES, *Leviathan* (Cambridge: Cambridge University Press, [1651] 1991): "The (*Unum Necessarium*) Onely Article of Faith, which the Scripture maketh simply Necessary to Salvation, is this, that JESUS IS THE CHRIST" (407). LOCKE, *The Reasonableness of Christianity* (Stanford: Stanford University Press, [1695] 1958): "God, out of the infiniteness of his mercy...promised a deliverer, whom in his good time he sent; and then declared to all mankind, that whoever would believe him to be the Saviour promised, and take him now raised from the dead, and constituted the Lord and Judge of all men, to be their King and Ruler, should be saved" (75). KANT, *Religion within the Boundary of Pure Reason* (Edinburgh: Thomas Clark, [*Die Religion innerhalb der Grenzen der bloßen Vernunft*, 1793] 1885), "But upon the principles of MORAL

RELIGION (which, amid all the public ones that have hitherto appeared, THE CHRISTIAN RELIGION alone is)" (62).

55. Most problematic perhaps would be the apparent characterization of both the United States and much more so the Soviet Union during World War II as "status quo states," as neither was defending much entrenched international position, and both professed a revolutionary ideology at home. Wendt's more recent *Quantum Mind and Social Science: Unifying Physical and Social Ontology* (Cambridge: Cambridge University Press, 2015), meanwhile, is considered unmoored from the more limited task of the refinement of international theory; and consequently the formidable burden of its contents is not assumed.

56. Philip Bernadini, "The Lateran Concordat with Italy," *The Catholic Historical Review* 16, no. 1 (1930): 19–27; André Géraud, "The Lateran Treaties: A Step in Vatican Policy," *Foreign Affairs* 7, no. 4 (1929): 571–84. And even by those who bore no affection for the regime: Elisa A. Carrillo, "Alcide de Gasperi and the Lateran Pacts," *The Catholic Historical Review* 49, no. 4 (1964): 532–39.

57. Marcel Brazzola, *La Cité du Vatican est-elle un État?* (Paris: Recueil Sirey, 1932); Charles G. Fenwick, "The New City of the Vatican," *The American Journal of International Law* 23, no. 2 (1929): 371–74; Gordon Ireland, "The State of the City of the Vatican," *The American Journal of International Law* 27, no. 2 (1933): 271–89. A further interesting data point is that the inter-war Latvian (1922) and Romanian (1927) concordats were formally registered—by their respective governments—with the League of Nations in Geneva.

58. For the minority view, see Yasmin Abdullah, "The Holy See at United Nations Conferences: State or Church?", *Columbia Law Review* 96, no. 7 (1996): 1835–75; and John R. Morss, "The International Legal Status of the Vatican/Holy See Complex," *European Journal of International Law* 26, no. 4 (2015): 927–46. The argument runs that the Montevideo Convention requires a permanent population, a defined territory, government, and relations with other states and independence for conferral of statehood under international law; but that the Apostolic See, populated by rotating avowed celibates, clearly fails the first criterion.

59. Gaetano Arangio-Ruiz, "On the Nature of the International Personality of the Holy See," *Revue Belge De Droit International*

(1996): 354–69; Robert John Araujo, "The International Personality and Sovereignty of the Holy See," *Catholic University Law Review* 50, no. 2 (2001): 292–360; Matthew N. Bathon, "The Atypical International Status of the Holy See," *Vanderbilt Journal of Transnational Law* 34 (2001): 608–15; Hyginus Eugene Cardinale, *The Holy See and International Order* (Toronto: Macmillan, 1976); Horace F. Cumbo, "The Holy See and International Law," *International Law Quarterly* 2, no. 4 (1948–1949): 603–20; Robert A. Graham, *Vatican Diplomacy: A Study of Church and State on the International Plane* (Princeton: Princeton University Press, 1959); Geoffrey R. Watson, "Progress for Pilgrims? An Analysis of the Holy See-Israel Fundamental Agreement," in Marshall J. Breger (ed.), *The Vatican-Israel Accords: Political, Legal, and Theological Contexts* (Notre Dame: University of Notre Dame Press, 2004): 203–34.

60. Alan Chong and Jodok Troy, "A Universal Sacred Mission and the Universal Secular Organization: The Holy See and the United Nations," *Politics, Religion, & Ideology* 12, no. 3 (2011): 335–54; Edward J. Gratsch, *The Holy See and the United Nations, 1945–1995* (New York: Vantage Press, 1997); Roman A. Melnyk, *Vatican Diplomacy at the United Nations: A History of Catholic Global Engagement* (Lewiston: The Edwin Mellen Press, 2009); Jodok Troy, "Two 'Popes' to Speak for the World: The Pope and the United Nations Secretary General in World Politics," *The Review of Faith & International Affairs* 15, no. 4 (2017): 67–78; Ivan Vallier, "The Roman Catholic Church: A Transnational Actor," *International Organization* 25, no. 3 (1971): 479–502. One might also add to the above that the Holy See was considered a "participating State" to the Conference on Security and Co-operation in Europe Final Act (Helskini, 1975) that formulated the global *détente* policy.

61. Noel Dias, "Roman Catholic Church & International Law," *Sri Lanka Journal of International Law* 13, no. 107 (2001): 107–134; Cedric Ryngaert, "The Legal Status of the Holy See," *Goettingen Journal of International Law* 3, no. 3 (2011): 829–59; Stephen E. Young and Alison Shea, "Separating State from Church: A Research Guide to the Law of the Vatican City State," *Law Library Journal* 99, no. 3 (2007): 589–610.

62. "Diplomacy, Papacy, and the Transformation of International Society," *The Review of Faith & International Affairs* 15, no. 4 (2017): 32.
63. Edward Bell, "Catholicism and Democracy: A Reconsideration," *Journal of Religion & Society* 10 (2008): 1–22; José Casanova, "Civil Society and Religion: Retrospective Reflections on Catholicism and Prospective Reflections on Islam," *Social Research* 68, no. 4 (2001): 1041–80.
64. John Anderson, "Catholicism and Democratic Consolidation in Spain and Poland," *West European Politics* 26, no. 1 (2003): 137–56; Daniel Philpott, "The Catholic Wave," *Journal of Democracy* 15, no. 2 (2004): 32–46.
65. *The Third Wave: Democratization in the Late Twentieth Century* (Norman, OK: University of Oklahoma Press, 1991), 76.
66. Timothy A. Byrnes, "Sovereignty, Supranationalism, and Soft Power: The Holy See in International Relations," *The Review of Faith & International Affairs* 15, no. 4 (2017): 6–20; Allen D. Hertzke, "Roman Catholicism and the Faith-Based Movement for Global Human Rights," *The Review of Faith & International Affairs* 3, no. 3 (2005–06): 19–24.
67. Melanie Barbato, "Diplomatic Language in the Deepavali Messages of the Pontifical Council for Interreligious Dialogue," *The Review of Faith & International Affairs* 15, no. 4 (2017): 93–104.
68. David Alvarez, "The Professionalization of the Papal Diplomatic Service, 1909–1967," *The Catholic Historical Review* 75, no. 2 (1989): 233–48; Mariano P. Barbato, Robert J. Joustra, and Dennis R. Hoover (eds.), *Modern Papal Diplomacy and Social Teaching in World Affairs* (London and New York: Routledge, 2019); Peter C. Kent and John Pollard (eds.), *Papal Diplomacy in the Modern Age* (Westport, CT: Praeger, 1994); Janne Haaland Matlary, "The Just Peace: The Public and Classical Diplomacy of the Holy See," *Cambridge Review of International Affairs* 14, no. 2 (2001): 80–94; Anthony Rhodes, *The Vatican in the Age of the Cold War* (Wilby, Norwhich: Michael Russell, 1992); René Schlott, "Papal Requiems as Political Events since the End of the Papal State," *European Review of History: Revue europeenne d'histoire* 15, no. 6 (2008): 603–14.

69. Peter C. Kent, *The Lonely Cold War of Pope Pius XII: The Roman Catholic Church and the Division of Europe, 1943–1950* (Montreal: McGill-Queen's University Press, 2002).
70. Robert J. Araujo, "John Paul II—A Man of God and a Servant of Man: The Pope at the United Nations," *Ave Maria Law Review* 5, no. 2 (2007): 367–98; Drew Christiansen, "Catholic Peacemaking, 1991–2005: The Legacy of Pope John Paul II," *The Review of Faith & International Affairs* 4, no. 2 (2006): 21–28; Chester Gillis (ed.), *The Political Papacy: John Paul II, Benedict XVI, and their Influence* (London and New York: Routledge, 2006); Bernard J. O'Connor, *Papal Diplomacy: John Paul II and the Culture of Peace* (South Bend, IN: St. Augustine's Press, 2005).
71. *Pope John Paul II, Prophetic Politician* (Washington, D.C.: Georgetown University Press, 2002), 8.
72. Andrew M. Essig and Jennifer L. Moore, "U.S.-Holy See Diplomacy: The Establishment of Formal Relations, 1984," *The Catholic Historical Review* 95, no. 4 (2009): 741–64; Maryjane Osa, "Creating Solidarity: The Religious Foundations of the Polish Social Movement," *East European Politics and Societies* 11, no. 2 (1997): 339–65; Michael Sutton, "John Paul II's Idea of Europe," *Religion, State, and Society* 25 (1997): 17–30; George Weigel, *The Final Revolution: The Resistance Church and the Collapse of Communism* (Oxford: Oxford University Press, 1992).
73. Jurgen Habermas and Joseph Ratzinger, *The Dialectics of Secularization: On Reason and Faith* (San Francisco: Ignatius Press, 2006); Bernard J. O'Connor, "A Diplomacy of Candor: Pope Benedict XVI on the Global Stage," *The Review of Faith & International Affairs* 4, no. 2 (2006): 41–43.
74. Pasquale Ferrara, "The Concept of the Periphery in Pope Francis' Discourse: A Religious Alternative to Globalization?", *Religions* 6, no. 1 (2015): 42–57; Roland Flamini, "Peter and Caesar: Is Pope Francis Shifting the Vatican's Worldview?", *World Affairs* (2014): 35–33; Austen Ivereigh, *The Great Reformer: Francis and the Making of a Radical Pope* (New York: Atlantic Books, 2015).
75. "A Trajectory Toward the Periphery: Francis of Assisi, Louis Massignon, Pope Francis, and Muslim-Christian Relations," *The Review of Faith & International Affairs* 16, no. 1 (2018): 24.

76. Peter Petkoff, "Legal Perspectives and Religious Perspectives of Religious Rights under International Law in the Vatican Concordats, 1963–2004," *Law and Justice: The Christian Law Review* 158, no. 30 (2007): 30–53.
77. Silvio Ferrari, "The Fundamental Agreement between the Holy See and Israel and the Conventions between States and the Church since the Vatican II Council," in Marshall J. Breger (ed.), *The Vatican-Israel Accords: Political, Legal, and Theological Contexts* (Notre Dame: University of Notre Dame Press, 2004): 96–116.

CHAPTER 3

Research Presentation

"It is astonishing to what an extent the historian has been Protestant, progressive, and whig, and the very role model of the nineteenth-century gentleman," (3) opens Professor Sir Herbert Butterfield in his provocative "Whig Interpretation of History" (1965 [1931]). He continues, "The historian tends in the first place to adopt the whig or Protestant view of the subject, and very quickly busies himself with dividing the world into the friends and enemies of progress" (5). The tip of Butterfield's polemical spear is that the ubiquitous *Whig* historiography sheds much pertinent detail in order to construct and support a linear progression concluding with our Enlightened, Protestant-bourgeois selves, with Catholics and Tories routinely dismissed as obstacles that had to be overcome. Assuming Butterfield is correct, then it should come as no surprise that much remains to be explored concerning the international relations of the neither Protestant, progressive nor whig Apostolic See.

Ad Fontes

This research presentation chapter, the methodological heart of the work, shall attempt to provide an answer to the overall research question by establishing the treaty norms of concordats and then by arriving at suitable theoretical contextualization. These tasks begin with proper collection of the necessary data, in this case, the treaties of the Apostolic See. Discussion therefore turns to the only primary source of this information.[1]

From 1865 to 1908, inclusive, the Catholic Church published ACTA SANCTAE SEDIS, or *Acts of the Holy See* (*ASS*), and since 1909 has published ACTA APOSTOLICAE SEDIS, or *Acts of the Apostolic See* (*AAS*). Uninterrupted throughout both intervals, the series is the annual gazette of the Holy or Apostolic See, publishing all official papal instrumentation. Roughly seven hundred pages per volume, the *Acts of the Holy See* totals 30,021 pages and at least one concordat is present in 7 out of its 41 volumes, while the *Acts of the Apostolic See*, through the year 2021, totals 105,369 pages and at least one concordat is present in 69 out of 114 volumes. The base language is Latin, although, as has already been demonstrated, numerous others are utilized, especially in concordats. Under canon law (CIC/1917, c. 9; CIC/1983, c. 8), the contents of the *AAS* enter into force three months after publication, but per the findings of the second chapter, concordats lie outside canon law and adhere to their own procedures. Nevertheless, the above official gazettes constitute the only open-source for the necessary data, and have been examined for any and all apparent treaties between the Holy or Apostolic See and a civil commonwealth. They are furthermore public domain, and therefore outside the Secret Vatican Archives, which have not been at all consulted. The source material having been identified, a few further points of clarification are in order prior to reporting the results.

First, no "independent" or "outside" attempt at verification has been made, primarily for reasons of methodological consistency. The primary other route to the accumulation of the data—the League of Nations Treaty Series (1920–1946) and the United Nations Treaty Series (1945-)—have not been consulted because they comprehend a narrower longitudinal interval, because they are secondary sources, and because, as merely a Permanent Observer to the United Nations, it is not abundantly clear that the Apostolic See is bound by the terms of the UN Charter (102.1) to register its treaties with the Secretariat. Neither is there any consideration for concordats that might be secret, nor accommodation of the prospect of perfidy. The institutional Latin Church, as heir to the empire of Rome, as confessor to the Kings and Queens of Europe, and as guardian of the thoughts of the hearts of millions certainly keeps many secrets; but that it should fabricate treaties in an obscure publication attentively read almost exclusively by specialists is not regarded as a serious possibility.[2]

Second, two terminological adjustments are necessary at this juncture. First, English-language scholarship generally speaks of the *Holy See*. This expression, although universal among scholars and still frequently employed by organs of the Church itself, is revealed to be incorrect. In 1909, the bishopric in the city of Rome renamed itself the *Apostolic See*, and by this term, it ought to be known. Next, it is of the utmost importance to distinguish the Apostolic See from the micro-state in and around Rome over which its resident bishop rules as Prince, and consequently, the term *Vatican City-state*, where applicable, shall be utilized, being in the author's opinion the most parsimonious and effective translation of the Italian, *Stato della Città del Vaticano*.

Finally, several interpretive points are useful. The author has developed a citation system through which to communicate the concordatorial material. For example, "Bosnia and Herzegovina and the Holy See will resolve..." (*AAS* 99 [2007], 945 {18.1}). The parenthetical citation means, "*Acts of the Apostolic See*, volume 99, of the year 2007, page 945, treaty portion article 18, Sect. 1." Second, all date ranges henceforth provided are inclusive, unless otherwise indicated. Third, in accordance with the primary intended location of the inquiry within the advanced study of international relations the Catholic Church's preferred *she/her* pronouns will generally be avoided, unless where their use is deemed to enhance clarity and delivery. With the aforementioned points in order, the research findings may now be presented.

The Concordats of the Apostolic See

Table of Concordats

I. Concordats of the Holy See
Henry V (1122)
Constance (1418)
François I (1516)
Victor Amadeus of Sardinia (1727)
Marie of Portugal (1778)
Joseph II of Austria (1784)
Victor Amadeus III of Sardinia (1795)
Charles Emmanuel IV of Sardinia (1797)
Gallic Republic (1801)

(continued)

(continued)

Table of Concordats

Cisapline Republic (1803)
Tuscany (1815)
Maximilian of Bavaria (1817)
Ferdinand I (1818)
William I of the Netherlands (1827)
Lucerne, Berne, Soleure, Zoug (1828)
Ferdinand II of Naples (1834)
Charles-Albert of Sardinia (1841)
Nicholas I of Russia (1847)
Leopold II of Tuscany (1851)
Isabel II of Spain (1852)
Republic of Costa Rica (1852)
Republic of Guatemala (1852)
Franz-Joseph I of Austria (1855)
Peter V of Portugal (1857)
William I of Württemberg (1857)
Frederick of Baden (1859)
Isabel II of Spain (1859)
Republic of Haiti (1860)
Honduras (1861)
Nicaragua (1861)
San Salvador (1862)
Venezuela (1862)
Ecuador (1862–1881)
[Commencement of *Acts of the Holy See* (1865)]

Pontiff	**CONTRACTING PARTY**	Head of State or Government
(Pontifical Legate, Title)	*(Contracting Location, Date, Language(s))*	*(Contracting Plenipotentiary, Title)*
Pius VII	**FRENCH GOVERNMENT** (15 July 1801 [invoked 1906], Latin)	Napoleon Bonaparte
Leo XIII	**KING OF PORTUGAL** (Rome, 23 June 1886, Portuguese/Latin)	Luís I (GB da Silva Ferrâ de Carvalho Martens, Ambassador Extraordinaire)
(Ludovico Iacobini, Cardinal Secretary of State)		
Leo XIII	**KINGDOM OF MONTENEGRO** (Rome, 18 Aug. 1886, Italian/Latin)	Nikola I
(Ludovico Iacobini, Cardinal Secretary of State)		(Giovanni Sundêcic, Secretary Particulaire)

(continued)

(continued)

Pontiff (Pontifical Legate, Title)	CONTRACTING PARTY (Contracting Location, Date, Language(s))	Head of State or Government (Contracting Plenipotentiary, Title)
Leo XIII (Rampolla del Tindaro, Cardinal Secretary of State)	REPUBLIC OF COLOMBIA (Rome, 31 Dec. 1887, Latin)	Raphael Nuñes (Ioachim Ferdinandum Vélez, Legate Extraordinaire)
Pius X (Aristide Rinaldini, Nuncio)	SPANISH GOVERNMENT (Madrid, 19 June 1904, French)	Alfonso XIII (Faustino-Rodríguez Sampedro, Minister)
Pius X (Vico, Nuncio)	KINGDOM OF CONGO (Brussels, 26 May 1906, French)	Leopold II (Cuvelier)
Pius X (Merry del Val.)	RUSSIA (Rome, 22 July 1907, French)	Nicholas II (S. Sazonow)
Pius X (Aristide Rinaldini, Nuncio)	SPAIN (Madrid, 12 July 1904, Italian)	Alfonso XIII (Faustino-Rodríguez Sampedro, Minister)

[Commencement of *Acts of the Apostolic See* (1909)]
II. Concordats of the Apostolic See

Pius XI (Pietro Gasparri, Cardinal Secretary of State)	GOVERNMENT OF LATVIA (The Vatican, 30 May 1922, French)	Jānis Čakiste (Zigfiids A. Meierovics, Foreign Minister)
Pius XI (Eugenio Pacelli, Nuncio)	STATE OF BAVARIA (Munich, 24 Jan. 1925, German/Italian)	Heinbich Held (Eugen von Knilling, Franz Matt, And Wilhelm Krausneck, Ministers)
Pius XI (Pietro Gasparri, Cardinal Secretary of State)	REPUBLIC OF POLAND (Warsaw, 2 June 1925, French)	Stanisław Wojciechowski (Amb. Ladislas Skrzynski andMP Stanislas Grabski)
Pius XI (Luigi Maglione, Nuncio)	FRENCH REPUBLIC (Paris, 4 Dec. 1926, French)	Gaston Doumergue (Aristide Briand)
Pius XI (Pietro Gasparri, Cardinal Secretary of State)	KINGDOM OF ROMANIA (The Vatican, 10 May 1927, French)	Ferdinand I (V. Goldis, Minister for Religion and the Arts)
Pius XI (Pietro Gasparri, Cardinal Secretary of State)	GOVERNMENT OF LITHUANIA (The Vatican, 27 Sep. 1927, French)	Antanas Smetona (Augustinas Voldemaras, Foreign Minister)

(continued)

(continued)

Pontiff (Pontifical Legate, Title)	CONTRACTING PARTY (Contracting Location, Date, Language(s))	Head of State or Government (Contracting Plenipotentiary, Title)
Pius XI	**GOVERNMENT OF CZECHOSLOVAKIA** (1928?, French)	Tomáš Garrigue Masaryk
Pius XI (Pietro Gasparri, Cardinal Secretary of State)	**PORTUGUESE GOVERNMENT** (The Vatican, 3 May 1928, Italian/Portuguese)	Óscar Carmona (Augusto de Castro Sampaio Corte-Real, Ambassador Extraordinaire)
Pius XI (Pietro Gasparri, Cardinal Secretary of State)	**ITALY** (Rome, 11 Feb. 1929 [treaty portion], Italian)	Victor Emanuel (Benito Mussolini, Prime Minister)
Pius XI (Pietro Gasparri, Cardinal Secretary of State)	**PORTUGAL** (Rome, 11 April 1929, Italian/Portuguese)	Óscar Carmona (Augusto de Castro Sampaio Corte-Real, Ambassador Extraordinaire)
Pius XI (Eugenio Pacelli, Nuncio)	**PRUSSIAN FREE STATES** (Berlin, 14 June 1929, Italian/German)	Paul von Hindenburg (President Otto Braun, Ministers Carl Heinrich Becker, And Hermann Höpker-Aschoff)
Pius XI (Eugenio Pacelli, Cardinal Secretary of State)	**ROMANIAN GOVERNMENT** (Vatican City-state, 30 May 1932, French)	Charles II (Yaleritj Pop, Justice Minister)
Pius XI (Eugenio Pacelli, Cardinal Secretary of State)	**BADEN FREE STATE** (Konstanz, 12 Oct. 1932, Italian/German)	Paul von Hindenburg (President Josef Schmitt, Ministers Eugen Baumgartner, And Wilhelm Mattes)
Pius XI (Eugenio Pacelli, Cardinal Secretary of State)	**REPUBLIC OF AUSTRIA** (Vatican City-state, 5 June 1933, Italian/German)	Wilhelm Miklas (President Engelbert Dollfuß And Minister Kurt Schnuschnigg)
Pius XI (Eugenio Pacelli, Cardinal Secretary of State)	**GERMAN *REICH*** (Vatican City-state, 20 July 1933, Italian/German)	Paul von Hindenburg and Adolf Hitler (Franz von Papen, Vice Chancellor)
Pius XII	**PORTUGUESE REPUBLIC**	António Salazar

(continued)

(continued)

Pontiff (Pontifical Legate, Title)	CONTRACTING PARTY (Contracting Location, Date, Language(s))	Head of State or Government (Contracting Plenipotentiary, Title)
(Luigi Maglione, Cardinal Secretary of State)	(Vatican City-state, 7 May 1940, Italian/Portuguese)	(Ministers Eduardo Augusto Marques and Mario de Figueiredo, and Amb. Vasco Francisco Caetano de Quevedo)
Pius XII (Domenico Tardini, Sec. of the S. Congregation for Extraordinary Ecclesiastical Affairs)	**PORTUGUESE REPUBLIC** (Vatican City-state, 18 July 1950, Italian/Portuguese)	António Salazar (Pedro Tovar de Lemos, Ambassador Extraordinaire)
Pius XII (Domenico Tardini, Sec. of the S. Congregation for Extraordinary Ecclesiastical Affairs)	**SPANISH STATE** (Vatican City-state, 5 Aug. 1950, Spanish)	Francisco Franco (Joaquín Ruiz-Gimenez, Ambassador)
Pius XII (Domenico Tardini, Sec. of the S. Congregation for Extraordinary Ecclesiastical Affairs)	**SPAIN** (Vatican City-state, 27 Aug. 1953, Italian/Spanish)	Francisco Franco (Minister Alberto Martin Artajo and Amb. Fernando Maria Castiella y Maiz)
Pius XII (Domenico Tardini, Sec. of the S. Congregation for Extraordinary Ecclesiastical Affairs)	**THE DOMINICAN REPUBLIC** (Vatican City-state, 16 June 1954, Italian/Spanish)	Pedro Santana (Rafael Leonidas Trujillo Molina, Generalissimo)
Pius XII (Luigi Muench, Nuncio)	**LAND OF NORTH RHINE-WESTPHALIA** (Bad Godesberg, 19 Dec. 1956, Italian/German)	Konrad Adenauer (Minister-President Fritz Steinhopf and Minister Paul Luchtenberg)
Pius XII (Umberto Mozzoni, Nuncio)	**REPUBLIC OF BOLIVIA** (La Paz, 1 Feb. 1958, Italian/Spanish)	Hernán Siles Zuazo (Manuel Barrau Peláez, Minister of Foreign Relations and Religion)
John XXIII (Giovanni Dellepiane, Nuncio)	**REPUBLIC OF AUSTRIA** (Vienna, 23 June 1960, Italian/German)	Julius Raab (Ministers Bruno Kreisky and Heinrich Drimmel)

(continued)

(continued)

Pontiff (Pontifical Legate, Title)	CONTRACTING PARTY (Contracting Location, Date, Language(s))	Head of State or Government (Contracting Plenipotentiary, Title)
John XXIII (Domenico Tardini, Cardinal Secretary of State)	REPUBLIC OF BOLIVIA (Vatican City-state, 15 March 1961, Spanish)	Hernán Siles Zuazo (Fernando Diez de Medina, Ambassador Extraordinaire)
John XXIII (Carlo Martini, Nuncio)	GOVERNMENT OF PARAGUAY (Asunción, 20 Dec. 1961, Spanish)	Alfredo Stroessner (Raúl Apena Pastor, Minister of Foreign Relations)
John XXIII (Opilio Rossi, Nuncio)	REPUBLIC OF AUSTRIA (Vienna, 9 July 1962, Italian/German)	Alfons Gorbach (Ministers Bruno Kreisky and Heinrich Drimmel)
Paul VI (Luigi Dadaglio, Nuncio)	REPUBLIC OF VENEZUELA (Caracas, 6 March 1964, Italian/Spanish)	Rómulo Betancourt (Marcos Falcón Briceño, Minister of Foreign Relations)
Paul VI (Amleto Giovanni Cicognani, Cardinal Secretary of State)	TUNISIAN REPUBLIC (Vatican City-state, 27 June 1964, French)	Habib Bourguiba (Mongi Slim, Secretary of State for Foreign Affairs)
Paul VI (Opilio Rossi, Nuncio)	REPUBLIC OF AUSTRIA (Vienna, 7 July 1964, Italian/German)	Josef Klaus (Ministers Bruno Kreisky and Theodor Piffl-Percevic)
Paul VI (Corrado Bafile, Nuncio)	LOWER SAXON LAND (Hannover, 26 Feb. 1965, Italian/German)	Ludwig Erhard (Georg Diederichs, Minister-President)
Paul VI (Corrado Bafile, Nuncio)	BAVARIAN FREE STATE (Munich, 2 Sep. 1966, Italian/German)	Ludwig Erhard (Ludwig Huber, Minister for Teaching and Culture)
Paul VI (Umberto Mozzoni, Nuncio)	ARGENTINE REPUBLIC (Buenos Aires, 28 Jan. 1968, Italian/Spanish)	Juan Carlos Onganía (Nicanor Costa Méndez, Minister of Foreign Relations and Religion)
Paul VI (Bruno Torpigliani)	GOVERNMENT OF EL SALVADOR (San Salvador, 11 March 1968, Spanish)	Fidel Sánchez Hernández (Alfredo Martínez Moreno)
Paul VI (Corrado Bafile, Nuncio)	SAARLAND (Bad Godesberg, 9 April 1968, Italian/German)	Kurt Georg Kiesinger (Werner Scherer, Minister for Religion, Teaching, and Culture)

(continued)

(continued)

Pontiff (Pontifical Legate, Title)	CONTRACTING PARTY (Contracting Location, Date, Language(s))	Head of State or Government (Contracting Plenipotentiary, Title)
Paul VI (Ambrogio Marchioni, Archbishop Nuncio)	**SWISS FEDERAL COUNCIL** (Berne, 14 July 1968, French)	Swiss Federal Council (Pierre Micheli, Ambassador)
Paul VI (Opilio Rossi, Nuncio)	**REPUBLIC OF AUSTRIA** (Vienna, 7 Oct. 1968, Italian/German)	Josef Klaus (Ministers Kurt Waldheim and Theodor Piffl-Percevic)
Paul VI (Corrado Bafile, Nuncio)	**BAVARIAN FREE STATE** (Munich, 7 Oct. 1968, Italian/German)	Kurt Georg Kiesinger (Minister-President Alfons Goppel, Ministers Ludwig Huber and Konrad Pöhner)
Paul VI (Corrado Baule, Nuncio)	**RHINELAND-PALATINATE** (Mainz, 29 April 1969, Italian/German)	Kurt Georg Kiesinger (Peter Altmeier, Minister-President)
Paul VI (Opilio Rossi, Nuncio)	**REPUBLIC OF AUSTRIA** (Vienna, 29 Sep. 1969, Italan/German)	Josef Klaus (Ministers Wilfried Platzer and Alois Mock)
Paul VI (Corrado Bafile, Nuncio)	**SAARLAND** (Bonn, 12 Nov. 1969, Italian/German)	Willy Brandt (Alois Becker, Minister-President)
Paul VI (Corrado Bafile, Nuncio)	**BAVARIAN FREE STATE** (Bonn-Bad Godesberg, 17 Sep. 1970, Italian/German)	Willy Brandt (Ludwig Huber, Minister for Teaching and Worship)
Paul VI (Opilio Rossi, Archbishop Nuncio)	**REPUBLIC OF AUSTRIA** (Vienna, 8 March 1971, Italian/German)	Bruno Kreisky (Ministers Rudolf Kirchschläger and Leopold Gratz)
Paul VI (Corrado Baule, Archbishop Nuncio)	**RHINELAND-PALATINATE** (Mainz, 15 May 1973, Italian/German)	Willy Brandt (Helmut Kohl, Minister-President)
Paul VI (Corrado Bafile, Archbishop Nuncio)	**LOWER SAXON LAND** (Hannover, 21 May 1973, Italian/German)	Willy Brandt (Alfred Kubel, Minister-President)
Paul VI (Corrado Bafile, Archbishop Nuncio)	**BAVARIAN FREE STATE** (Munich, 4 Sep. 1974, Italian/German)	Helmut Schmidt (Minister-President Alfons Goppel, Ministers Hans Maier and Ludwig Huber)
Paul VI (Giovanni Villot)	**PORTUGUESE REPUBLIC** (Vatican City-state, 15 Feb. 1975, Italian/Portuguese)	António Salazar (Francisco Salgado Zbnha)
Paul VI	**SAARLAND**	Helmut Schmidt

(continued)

(continued)

Pontiff (Pontifical Legate, Title)	CONTRACTING PARTY (Contracting Location, Date, Language(s))	Head of State or Government (Contracting Plenipotentiary, Title)
(Corrado Bafile, Archbishop Nuncio)	(Bonn-Bad Godesberg, 21 Feb. 1975, Italian/German)	(Franz Josef Röder, Minister-President)
Paul VI (Angelo Palmas, Archbishop Nuncio)	REPUBLIC OF COLOMBIA (Bogotá, 2 July 1975, Italian/Spanish)	Misael Pastrana Borrbro (Alfredo Vásquez Carrizosa, Minister of Foreign Relations)
Paul VI (Opilio Rossi, Archbishop Nuncio)	REPUBLIC OF AUSTRIA (Vienna, 9 Jan. 1976, Italian/German)	Bruno Kreisky (Ministers Erich Bielka and Fred Sinowatz)
Paul VI (Giovanni Villot)	SPANISH STATE (Vatican City-state, 28 July 1976, Italian/Spanish)	Adolfo Suárez (Marcelino Oreja Aguirre)
Paul VI (Ambrogio Marchioni, Archbishop Nuncio)	SWISS FEDERAL COUNCIL (Berne, 2 May 1978, French)	Swiss Federal Council (Amb. Emanuel Diez and Counsellor Alfred Wyser)
Paul VI (Guido Del Mestri, Archbishop Nuncio)	BAVARIAN FREE STATE (Munich, 7 July 1978, Italian/German)	Helmut Schmidt (Alfons Goppel, Minister-President)
Paul VI (Luigi Accogli, Nuncio)	REPUBLIC OF ECUADOR (Quito, 3 Aug. 1978, Spanish)	Alfredo Poveda Burbano (José Ayala Lasso, Minister of Foreign Relations)
John Paul II (Giovanni Villot)	SPANISH STATE (Vatican City-state, 3 Jan. 1979, Italian/Spanish)	Adolfo Suárez (Marcelino Oreja Aguirre)
John Paul II (Mario Tagliaferri, Nuncio)	REPUBLIC OF PERU (Lima, 19 July 1980, Spanish)	Francisco Morales Bermúdez Cerrutti (Arturo García, Minister of Foreign Relations)
John Paul II (Mario Cagna, Archbishop Nuncio)	REPUBLIC OF AUSTRIA (Vienna, 24 July 1981, Italian/German)	Bruno Kreisky (Willibald Pahr and Fred Sinowatz, Federal Ministers)
John Paul II (Achille Silvestrini, Archbishop)	PRINCIPALITY OF MONACO (Vatican City-state, 25 July 1981, French)	Rainier III (César Charles Solamito, Ambassador Extraordinaire)
John Paul II (Agostino Casaroli, Cardinal)	ITALIAN REPUBLIC (Vatican City-state, 18 Feb. 1984, Italian)	Bettino Craxi
John Paul II	LAND OF NORTH RHINE-WESTPHALIA	Helmut Kohl

(continued)

(continued)

Pontiff (Pontifical Legate, Title)	CONTRACTING PARTY (Contracting Location, Date, Language(s))	Head of State or Government (Contracting Plenipotentiary, Title)
(Guido Del Mestri, Archbishop Nuncio) John Paul II (Achille Silvestrini, Archbishop)	(Düsseldorf, 26 March 1984, Italian/German) **REPUBLIC OF HAITI** (Port-au-Prince, 8 Aug. 1984, French)	(Johannes Rau, Minister-President) Jean-Claude Duvalier (Jean-Robert Estimé, Minister of Foreign Affairs and Religion)
John Paul II (Joseph Uhaé)	**SAARLAND** (Saarbrücken, 12 Feb. 1985, Italian/German)	Helmut Kohl (Werner Zeyer)
John Paul II (Santos Abril y Castellò, Nuncio)	**REPUBLIC OF BOLIVIA** (La Paz, 1 Dec. 1986, Spanish)	Víctor Paz Estenssoro (Guillermo Bedregal Gutiérrez, Minister of Foreign Relations and Religion)
John Paul II (Joseph Uhaé, Archbishop Nuncio)	**BAVARIAN FREE STATE** (Munich, 8 June 1988, Italian/German)	Helmut Kohl (Franz Josef Strauβ, Minister-President)
John Paul II (Joseph Uhaé, Archbishop Nuncio)	**LOWER SAXON LAND** (Hannover, 8 May 1989, Italian/German)	Helmut Kohl (Herrn Ernst Albrecht, Minister-President)
John Paul II (Donato Squiccairini, Archbishop Nuncio)	**REPUBLIC OF AUSTRIA** (Vienna, 10 Oct. 1989, Italian/German)	Franz Vranitzky (Alois Mock and Hilde Hawlicek, Federal Ministers)
John Paul II (Carlo Furno)	**FEDERATIVE REPUBLIC OF BRAZIL** (Brasilia, 23 Oct. 1989, Portuguese)	José Sarney (Paulo Tarso Flecha de Lima)
John Paul II (Joseph Mercieca, President of the Episcopal Conference)	**REPUBLIC OF MALTA** (Valletta, 16 Nov. 1989, Italian/English)	Ċensu Tabone (Ugo Mifsud Bonnici, Minister of Education)
John Paul II (Pier Luigi Celata)	**REPUBLIC OF MALTA** (2) (Valletta, 28 Nov. 1991, Italian/English)	Edward Fenech Adami (Ugo Mifsud Bonnici)
John Paul II (Pier Luigi Celata, Archbishop Nuncio)	**REPUBLIC OF SAN MARINO** (San Marino, 2 April 1992, Italian)	Germano De Biagi and Ernesto Benedettini (Gabriele Gatti, Secretary of State for Foreign Affairs)
John Paul II	**IVORY COAST**	Félix Houphouët-Boigny

(continued)

(continued)

Pontiff (Pontifical Legate, Title)	CONTRACTING PARTY (Contracting Location, Date, Language(s))	Head of State or Government (Contracting Plenipotentiary, Title)
(Janusz Bolonek, Archbishop Nuncio)	(Abidjan, 20 May 1992, French)	(Amara Essy, Minister of Foreign Affairs)
John Paul II (Pier Luigi Celata, Archbishop Nuncio)	REPUBLIC OF MALTA (Valleta, 3 Feb. 1993, Italian/English)	Eddie Fenech Adami
John Paul II (Józef Kowalczyk, Archbishop Nuncio)	REPUBLIC OF POLAND (Warsaw, 28 July 1993, Italian/Polish)	Hanna Suchocka (Krzysztof Skubiszewski, Minister of Foreign Relations)
John Paul II (Lajos Kada, Nuncio)	LOWER SAXON LAND (Hannover, 29 Oct. 1993, German/Italian)	Helmut Kohl (Gerhard Schröder)
John Paul II (Claudio M. Celli)	STATE OF ISRAEL (Jerusalem, 13 Dec. 1993, English/Hebrew)	Yitzhak Rabin (Yossi Beilin)
John Paul II (Angelo Acerbi)	REPUBLIC OF HUNGARY (Budapest, 10 Jan. 1994, Italian/Hungarian)	Péter Boross (Für Lajos)
John Paul II (Lajos Kada, Nuncio)	LANDS OF SAXONY-ANHALT, BRANDENBURG AND THE SAXON FREE STATE (Magdeburg, 13 April 1994, German/Italian)	Helmut Kohl (Minister-Presidents Christoph Bergner, Frank E. Portz, and Steffen Heittmann)
John Paul II (Lajos Kada, Nuncio)	LAND OF BRANDENBURG AND THE SAXON FREE STATE (Görlitz, 4 May 1994, German/Italian)	Helmut Kohl (Minister-Presidents Manfred Stolpe and Hans Joachim Meyer)
John Paul II (Lajos Kada, Nuncio)	THURINGIAN FREE STATE (Erfurt, 14 June 1994, German/Italian)	Helmut Kohl (Bernhard Vogel, Minister-President)
John Paul II (Lajos Kada, Nuncio)	FREE AND HANSEATIC STATE OF HAMBURG, LAND OF MECKLENBURG-WEST POMERANIA, AND LAND OF SCHLESWIG–HOLSTEIN	Helmut Kohl (Senate President Henning Voscherau, Minister-Presidents Steffie Schnoor and Marianne Tidick)

(continued)

(continued)

Pontiff (Pontifical Legate, Title)	CONTRACTING PARTY (Contracting Location, Date, Language(s))	Head of State or Government (Contracting Plenipotentiary, Title)
	(Hamburg, 22 Sep. 1994, German/Italian)	
John Paul II (Oriano Quilici, Nuncio)	REPUBLIC OF VENEZUELA (Caracas, 24 Nov. 1994, Spanish)	Rafael Caldera (Miguel Angel Burrelli Rivas, Minister of Foreign Relations)
John Paul II (Angelo Sodano, Cardinal)	REPUBLIC OF ITALY (Vatican City-state, 3 Dec. 1994, Italian)	Silvio Berlusconi (Emanuele Scammaca del Murgo)
John Paul II (Mario Tagliaferri, Nuncio)	KINGDOM OF SPAIN (Madrid, 21 Dec. 1994, Spanish/Italian)	Felipe González (Luis Solana, Minister of Foreign Affairs)
John Paul II (Pier Luigi Celata)	REPUBLIC OF MALTA (Valletta, 6 Jan. 1995, Italian/English)	Eddie Fenech Adami (Guido de Marco)
John Paul II (Donato Squiccairini)	REPUBLIC OF AUSTRIA (Vienna, 21 Dec. 1995, Italian/German)	Franz Vranitzky (Wolfgang Schüssel and Elisabeth Gehrer)
John Paul II (Giovanni Lajolo, Archbishop Nuncio)	SAXON FREE STATE (Dresden, 2 July 1996, German/Italian)	Helmut Kohl (Kurt Biedenkopf, Minister-President)
John Paul II (Giulio Einaudi)	REPUBLIC OF CROATIA (3) (Zagreb, 19 Dec. 1996, Italian/Croatian)	Zlatko Mateša (Jure Radie)
John Paul II (Giovanni Lajolo, Archbishop Nuncio)	THURINGIAN FREE STATE (Erfurt, 11 June 1997, German/Italian)	Helmut Kohl (Bernhard Vogel, Minister-President)
John Paul II (Angelo Sodano, Carinal)	REPUBLIC OF HUNGARY (Vatican City-state, 20 June 1997, Italian/Hungarian)	Árpád Göncz (Horn Gyula)
John Paul II	LAND OF MECKLENBURG-WEST POMERANIA	Helmut Kohl
(Giovanni Lajolo, Archbishop Nuncio)	(Schwerin, 15 Sep. 1997, Italian/German)	(Berndt Seite, Minister-President)
John Paul II (Andrea C.L. di Montezemolo)	STATE OF ISREAL (Jerusalem, 10 Nov. 1997 [10 Heshvan 5758], English/Hebrew)	Benjamin Netanyahu (David Levy)
John Paul II	LAND OF SAXONY-ANHALT	Helmut Kohl

(continued)

(continued)

Pontiff (Pontifical Legate, Title)	CONTRACTING PARTY (Contracting Location, Date, Language(s))	Head of State or Government (Contracting Plenipotentiary, Title)
(Giovanni Lajolo, Archbishop Nuncio)	(Magdeburg, 15 Jan. 1998, German/Italian)	(Reinhard Höppner, Minister-President)
John Paul II (Angelo Sodano, Cardinal)	REPUBLIC OF HUNGARY (Vatican City-state, 3 April 1998, Italian/Hungarian)	Horn Gyula
John Paul II	REPUBLIC OF KAZAKHSTAN	Nursultan Nazarbayev
(Angelo Sodano, Cardinal)	(Vatican City-state, 24 Sep. 1998, English/Kazakh/Russian)	(Kasymzhomart K. Tokaev)
John Paul II (Giulio Einaudi)	REPUBLIC OF CROATIA (Zagreb, 9 Oct. 1998, Italian/Croatian)	Zlatko Mateša (Jure Radió)
John Paul II (Angelo Sodano, Cardinal)	REPUBLIC OF ESTONIA (Tallinn, 23 Dec. 1998, English)	Mart Laar
John Paul II	PALESTINE LIBERATION ORGANIZATION	Yasir Arafat
(Celestino Migliore)	(Vatican City-state, 15 Feb. 2000, English)	(Emile Jarjoui)
John Paul II	REPUBLIC OF LITHUANIA (3)	Andrius Kubilius
(Erwin Josef Ender)	(Vilnius, 5 May 2000, English/Lithuanian)	(Algirdas Saudargas)
John Paul II	ORGANIZATION OF AFRICAN UNITY	Salim Ahmed Salim
(Silvano Tomasi, Archbishop Nuncio)	(Adis Ababa, 19 Oct. 2000, French/English)	(Secretary General)
John Paul II	REPUBLIC OF LATVIA	Einars Repše
(Erwin Josef Ender)	(8 Nov. 2000, English/Latvian)	(Ingrīda Labucka)
John Paul II	SLOVAK REPUBLIC	Mikulàs Dzurinda
(Angelo Sodano, Cardinal Secretary of State)	(Vatican City-state, 24 Nov. 2000, Italian/Slovak)	(Prime Minister)
John Paul II	GABONESE REPUBLIC	Jean-François Ntoutoume Emane
(Jean-Louis Tauran, Cardinal Secretary of State)	(Vatican City-state, 26 July 2001, French)	(André Mba Obame, Minister for National Education)
John Paul II	SAARLAND	Gerhard Schröder

(continued)

(continued)

Pontiff (Pontifical Legate, Title)	CONTRACTING PARTY (Contracting Location, Date, Language(s))	Head of State or Government (Contracting Plenipotentiary, Title)
(Giovanni Lajolo, Archbishop Nuncio)	(Saarbrücken, 19 Sep. 2001, German/Italian)	(Peter Müller, Minister-President)
John Paul II (Jean-Louis Tauran, Cardinal Secretary of State)	**REPUBLIC OF SLOVENIA** (Ljubljani, 14 Dec 2001, Italian/Slovene)	Janez Drnovšek (Dimitrij Rupel, Minister for Foreign Affairs)
John Paul II (Giovanni Bulaitis)	**REPUBLIC OF ALBANIA** (Tiranë, 23 March 2002, English/Albanian)	Pandeli Majko
John Paul II (Henryk J. Nowacki)	**SLOVAK REPUBLIC** (Bratislava, 21 Aug. 2002, Italian/Slovak)	Mikuláš Dzurinda (Josef Stank)
John Paul II (Giovanni Lajolo, Archbishop Nuncio)	**THURGINIAN FREE STATE** (Erfurt, 19 Nov. 2002, German/Italian)	Gerhard Schröder (Bernhard Vogel, Minister-President)
John Paul II (Jean-Louis Tauran)	**ITALIAN REPUBLIC** (Vatican City-state, 15 Oct. 2003, Italian)	Silvio Berlusconi (Lamberto Dini)
John Paul II (Giovanni Lajolo, Archbishop Nuncio)	**LAND OF BRANDENBURG** (Potsdam, 12 Nov. 2003, German/Italian)	Gerhard Schröder (Matthias Platzeck, Minister-President)
John Paul II	**FREE AND HANSEATIC STATE OF BREMEN**	Gerhard Schröder
(Giovanni Lajolo, Archbishop Nucnio)	(Bremen, 21 Nov. 2003, German/Italian)	(Henning Scherf, Senate President)
John Paul II (Henryk Józef Nowacki, Apostolic Nuncio)	**SLOVAK REPUBLIC** (Bratislava, 13 May 2004, Italian/Slovak)	Rudolf Schuster
John Paul II (Angelo Sodano, Cardinal Secretary of State)	**PORTUGUESE REPUBLIC** (18 May 2004, Italian/Portuguese)	José Manuel Durão Barroso
Benedict XVI	**FREE AND HANSEATIC STATE OF HAMBURG**	Angela Merkel
(Erwin Josef Ender, Archbishop Nuncio)	(Hamburg, 29 Nov. 2005, German/Italian)	(Ole von Beust, President)
Benedict XVI	**BOSNIA AND HERZEGOVINA**	Ahmet Hadžipašić
(Alessandro D'Errico)	(Sarajevo, 19 April 2006, English)	(Ivo Miro Jović)

(continued)

(continued)

Pontiff (Pontifical Legate, Title)	CONTRACTING PARTY (Contracting Location, Date, Language(s))	Head of State or Government (Contracting Plenipotentiary, Title)
Benedict XVI (Erwin Josef Ender, Archbishop Nuncio)	**BAVARIAN FREE STATE** (München, 19 Jan. 2007, German/Italian)	Angela Merkel (Edmund Stoiber, Minister-President)
Benedict XVI (Fernando Filoni)	**REPUBLIC OF THE PHILIPPINES** (Manila, 17 April 2007, English/Italian)	Gloria Macapagal Arroyo (Alberto G. Romulo)
Benedict XVI (Giovanni Bulaitis, Apostolic Nuncio)	**REPUBLIC OF ALBANIA** (Tirane, 3 Dec. 2007, Italian/Albanian)	Bamir Topi (Zoti Ridvan Bode, Minister of Finance)
Benedict XVI (Tarciso Bertone, Cardinal Secretary of State)	**PRINCIPALITY OF ANDORRA** (Vatican City-state, 17 March 2008, Italian/Catalan)	Albert Pintat
Benedict XVI (Dominique Mamberti, Cardinal Secretary of State)	**FEDERATIVE REPUBLIC OF BRAZIL** (Vatican City-state, 13 Nov. 2008, Portuguese/Italian)	Luiz Inácio Lula da Silva (Celso Amorim, Minister for Foreign Affairs)
Benedict XVI (Dominique Mamberti, Cardinal Secretary of State)	**FRENCH REPUBLIC** (Paris, 18 Dec. 2008, French)	Nicolas Sarkozy (Bernhard Kouchner, Minister for Foreign and European Affairs)
Benedict XVI (Jean-Claude Périsset, Archbishop Nuncio)	**LAND OF SCHLESWIG–HOLSTEIN** (Kiel, 12 Jan. 2009, German/Italian)	Angela Merkel (Peter Harry Carstensen, Minister-President)
Benedict XVI (Edmund Farhat, Apostolic Nuncio)	**REPUBLIC OF AUSTRIA** (Vienna, 5 March 2009, Italian/German)	Werner Faymann (Michael Spindelegger)
Benedict XVI (Jean-Claude Périsset, Apostolic Nuncio)	**LOWER SAXON LAND** (Hannover, 6 April 2010, German/Italian)	Angela Merkel (Christian Wulff, Minister-President)
Benedict XVI (Alessandro D'Errico, Archbishop Nuncio)	**BOSNIA AND HERZEGOVINA** (Sarajevo, 8 April 2010, Bosnian/Croatian/Serbian/Italian)	Mustafa Mujezinović (Selmo Cikotić, Minister of Defense)
Benedict XVI	**FREE AND HANSEATIC STATE OF HAMBURG**	Angela Merkel

(continued)

(continued)

Pontiff (Pontifical Legate, Title)	CONTRACTING PARTY (Contracting Location, Date, Language(s))	Head of State or Government (Contracting Plenipotentiary, Title)
(Jean-Claude Périsset, Archbishop Nuncio)	(Hamburg, 18 May 2010, German/Italian)	(Herlind Gundelach, Senator for Science and Research)
Benedict XVI (Claudio Gugerotti)	REPUBLIC OF AZERBAIJAN (Baku, 29 April 2011, English/Azerbaijani)	Ilham Aliyev (Hidayet Orucov)
Benedict XVI (Tarciso Bertone, Cardinal Secretary of State)	MONTENEGRO (Vatican City-state, 24 June 2011, Italian/Montenegrin)	Filip Vujanović (Igor Lukšić)
Benedict XVI (Zenon Grocholewski, Cardinal)	MINISTRY OF EDUCATION OF THE REPUBLIC OF CHINA (Taipaei, 2 Dec. 2011, English)	Ma Ying-jeou (Ching-Ji Wu)
Benedict XVI (Antonio Arcari, Nuncio)	REPUBLIC OF MOZAMBIQUE (Maputo, 7 Dec. 2011, Italian/Portuguese)	Armando Guebuza (Oldemiro Júlio Marques Baloi, Minister of Foreign Affairs)
Benedict XVI (Jean-Claude Périsset, Archbishop Nuncio)	LOWER SAXON LAND (Hannover, 8 May 2012, German/Italian)	Angela Merkel (David McAllister, Minister-President)
Benedict XVI (Luigi Bonazzi, Nuncio)	REPUBLIC OF LITHUANIA (Vilnius, 8 June 2012, English/Lithuanian)	Dalia Grybauskaitė (Audronius Ažubalis, Minister of Foreign Affairs)
Francis (Dominique Mamberti, Cardinal Secretary of State)	REPUBLIC OF CAPE VERDE (2) (Praia, 10 June 2013, Italian/Portuguese)	José Maria Neves (Jorge Alberto da Silva Borges, Minister of Foreign Affairs)
Francis (Franco Coppola, Archbishop Nuncio)	REPUBLIC OF BURUNDI (Bujumbura, 5 July 2013, French)	Pierre Nkurunziza (Laurent Kavakure, Minister of Exterior Relations and International Cooperation)
Francis (Piero Pioppo, Apostolic Nuncio)	REPUBLIC OF EQUATORIAL GUINEA (Mongomo, 25 Oct. 2013, Italian/Spanish)	Teodoro Obiang Nguema Mbasogo (Agapito Mba Mokuy)
Francis	REPUBLIC OF CHAD	Idriss Déby

(continued)

(continued)

Pontiff (Pontifical Legate, Title)	CONTRACTING PARTY (Contracting Location, Date, Language(s))	Head of State or Government (Contracting Plenipotentiary, Title)
(Jude Thaddeus Okolo)	(N'Djaména, 6 Nov. 2013, French)	(Moussa Faki Mahamat)
Francis	**REPUBLIC OF THE CAMEROON**	Paul Biya
(Piero Pioppo, Archbishop Nuncio)	(Yaounde, 13 Jan 2014, French/English/Italian)	(Pierre Moukoko Mbonjo, Minister of External Relations)
Francis	**REPUBLIC OF MALTA**	Joseph Muscat
(Aldo Cavalli, Apostolic Nuncio)	(Valletta, 27 Jan. 2014, Italian/English)	(George W. Vella, Minister for Foreign Affairs)
Francis	**HUNGARY**	Viktor Orbám
(Alberto Bottari de Castello)	(Budapest, 10 Feb. 2014, Italian/Hungarian)	(Semjén Zsolt)
Francis	**REPUBLIC OF SAN MARINO**	Valeria Ciavatta and Luca Beccari
(Apostolic Nunciature)	(Rome, 24 June 2014, Italian)	(Secretary of State for Foreign Affairs)
Francis	**REPUBLIC OF SERBIA**	Aleksandar Vučić
(Dominique Mamberti, Cardinal Secretary of State)	(Belgrade, 27 June 2014, Italian/Serbian)	(I. Dačić)
Francis	**UNITED STATES OF AMERICA**	Barack Obama
(Paul R. Gallagher, Secretary for Relations with States)	(Vatican City-state, 10 June 2015, English)	(Kenneth Hackett, US Ambassador to the Holy See)
Francis	**STATE OF PALESTINE**	Mahmoud Abbas
(Paul R. Gallagher, Secretary for Relations with States)	(Vatican City-state, 26 June 2015, English)	(Riad Al-Malki, Minister of Foreign Affairs)
Francis	**LAND OF MECKLENBURG-WEST POMERANIA** (Schwerin, 27 July 2015, German)	Angela Merkel
Francis	**MINISTRY OF FOREIGN AFFAIRS**	Sabah IV
(Paul R. Gallagher, Secretary for Relations with States)	**OF THE STATE OF KUWAIT** (Vatican City-state, 10 Sep. 2015, English/Arabic)	(Sabah Khaled Al-Hamad Al-Sabah, First Dep. Prime Minister and Minister of Foreign Affairs)

(continued)

(continued)

Pontiff (Pontifical Legate, Title)	CONTRACTING PARTY (Contracting Location, Date, Language(s))	Head of State or Government (Contracting Plenipotentiary, Title)
Francis (Paul R. Gallagher, Archbishop Secretary for RelationsWith the State)	DEMOCRATIC REPUBLIC OF CONGO (Vatican City-state, 20 May 2016, French)	Joseph Kabila (Raymond Tshibanda, Minister for Foreign Affairs and Interational Cooperation)
Francis (Franco Coppola, Archbishop Nuncio)	CENTRAL AFRICAN REPUBLIC (Bangui, 6 Sep. 2016, French)	Faustin-Archange Touadéra (Charles Armel Doubane, Minister of Foreign Affairs and African Integration)
Francis (Paul R. Gallagher, Secretary for Relations with States)	GOVERNMENT OF THE UNITED ARAB EMIRATES (Vatican City-state, 15 Sep. 2016, English/Arabic)	Khalifa bin Zayed Al Nahyan (Abdullah bin Zayed Al-Nahyan)
Francis (Paul R. Gallagher, Secretary for Relations with States)	GOVERNMENT OF THE ITALIAN REPUBLIC (Vatican City-state, 15 Oct. 2016, Italian)	Giuseppe Conte (Pier Carlo Padoan, Minister of Economics and Finance)
Francis (Brian Udaigwe, Apostolic Nuncio)	REPUBLIC OF BENIN (Cotonou, 21 Oct. 2016, French)	Patrice Talon (Aurélien A. Agbénonci, Minister for Foreign Affairs and Cooperation)
Francis (Pietro Parolin, Cardinal Secretary of State)	REPUBLIC OF CONGO (Brazzaville, 3 Feb. 2017, Italian/French)	Denis Sassou Nguesso (Clément Mouamba, Prime Minister)
Francis (Giuseppe Versaldi, Cardinal)	REPUBLIC OF ITALY (Rome, 13 Feb. 2018, Italian)	Giuseppe Conte (Marco Bussetti)
Francis (Emil Paul Tscherrig, Apostolic Nuncio)	REPUBLIC OF SAN MARINO (San Marino, 28 June 2018, Italian)	Stefano Palmieri and Matteo Ciacci (Nicola Renzi, Secretary of State for Foreign Affairs)
Francis (Nikola Eterović, Apostolic Nuncio)	LAND OF MECKLENBURG-WEST POMERANIA (Berlin, 4 June 2019, German)	Angela Merkel (Katy Hoffmeister, Justice Minister)

(continued)

(continued)

Pontiff (Pontifical Legate, Title)	CONTRACTING PARTY (Contracting Location, Date, Language(s))	Head of State or Government (Contracting Plenipotentiary, Title)
Francis (Paul R. Gallagher, Secretary for Relations with States)	**BURKINA FASO** (Vatican City-state, 12 July 2019, French)	Roch Marc Christian Kaboré (M. Alpha Barry, Minister of Foreign Affairs and Cooperation)
Francis (Paul R. Gallagher, Secretary for Relations with States)	**REPUBLIC OF ANGOLA** (Vatican City-state, 13 Sep. 2019, Italian/Portuguese)	João Manuel Gonçalves Lourenço (Manuel Domingos Augusto, Minister for Exterior Relations)
Francis (Pedro López Quintana, Apostolic Nuncio)	**REPUBLIC OF AUSTRIA** (Vienna, 12 Oct. 2020, German)	Sebastian Kurz (Susanne Raab)

The above table of concordats furnishes the only complete and annotated list of all of the international treaties of the Apostolic See. Two main sections partition the concordats of the Holy and Apostolic Sees, respectively, with the former divided into those before and after the commencement of *Acts of the Holy See*. Analysis begins with the full-text availability initiated in 1865 and runs through all available volumes. Down the center column run the contracting parties, and below them the contracting locations, dates, and languages other than Latin, with the languages given in order of appearance. On the left-hand side, one finds the respective pontiffs and pontifical legates along with their titles, while on the right-hand side appear the heads of state or government and contracting plenipotentiaries, along with their titles. The author's translations, where applicable, are more literal, and textual fidelity is preserved amid both the presence and absence of information. For ease of reference, an alphabetized and abridged version of the results is also provided below.

Table of Concordats

Alphabetized and abridged

Contracting Party	Year(s)
Albania	2002, 2007
Andorra	2008
Angola	2019
Argentina	1968
Austria	1933, 1960, 1962, 1964, 1968, 1969, 1971, 1976, 1981, 1989, 1995, 2009, 2020
Azerbaijan	2011
Baden	1932
Bavaria	1925, 1966, 1968, 1970, 1974, 1978, 1988, 2007
Benin	2016
Bolivia	1958, 1961, 1986
Bosnia & Herzegovina	2006, 2010
Brandenburg	2003
Brandenburg and Saxon Free State	1994
Brazil	1989, 2008
Bremen	2003
Burkina Faso	2019
Burundi	2013
Cameroon	2014
Cape Verde	2013 (2)
Central African Republic	2016
Chad	2013
Charles-Albert (Sardinia)	1841
Charles Emmanuel IV (Sardinia)	1797
Cisalpine Republic	1803
Colombia	1887, 1975
Congo	1906
Dem. Rep. of	2016
Rep. of	2017
Constance	1418
Costa Rica	1852
Croatia	1996 (3), 1998
Czechoslovakia	1928
Domenican Republic	1954
Ecuador	1862, 1978
El Salvador	1968
Equatorial Guinea	2013
Estonia	1998
Ferdinand I (1818)	1818
Ferdinand II (Naples)	1834

(continued)

(continued)

Table of Concordats

France	1801, 1926, 2008
François I	1516
Franz-Joseph I (Austria)	1855
Frederick (Baden)	1859
Gabon	2001
Gallic Republic	1801
German *Reich*	1933
Guatemala	1852
Haiti	1860, 1984
Hamburg	2005, 2010
Hamburg, Mecklenburg-West Pomerania, and Schlewig-Holstein	1994
Henry V	1122
Honduras	1861
Hungary	1994, 1997, 1998, 2014
Isabel II (Spain)	1852, 1859
Israel	1993, 1997
Italy	1929, 1984, 1994, 2003, 2016, 2018
Ivory Coast	1992
Joseph II (Austria)	1784
Kazakhstan	1998
Kuwait	2015
Latvia	1922, 2000
Leopold II (Tuscany)	1851
Lithuania	1927, 2000 (3), 2012
Lower Saxon Land	1965, 1973, 1989, 1993, 2010, 2012
Malta	1989, 1991 (2), 1993, 1995, 2014
Marie (Portugal)	1778
Maximilian (Bavaria)	1817
Mecklenburg-West Pomerania	1997, 2015, 2019
Min. of Education, Rep. of China	2011
Monaco	1981
Montenegro	1886, 2011
Mozambique	2011
Nicaragua	1861
Nicholas I (Russia)	1847
North Rhein-Westphalia	1956, 1984
Organization of African Unity	2000
Palestine Liberation Organization	2000
Palestine, State of	2015
Paraguay	1961

(continued)

(continued)

Table of Concordats

Peru	1980
Peter V (Portugal)	1857
Philippines	2007
Poland	1925, 1993
Portugal	1886, 1928, 1929, 1940, 1950, 1975, 2004
Prussia	1929
Rhineland-Palatinate	1969, 1973
Romania	1927, 1932
Russia	1907
Saarland	1968, 1969, 1975, 1985, 2001
San Marino	1992, 2014, 2018
San Salvador	1862
Saxony-Anhalt	1998
Saxony-Anhalt, Brandenburg, and Saxon Free State	1994
Saxon Free State	1996
Schleswig–Holstein	2009
Serbia	2014
Slovak Republic	2000, 2002, 2004
Slovenia	2001
Spain	1904 (2), 1950, 1953, 1976, 1979, 1994
Swiss Federal Council	1968, 1978
Thuringia	1994, 1997, 2002
Tunisia	1964
Tuscany	1813
United Arab Emirates	2016
U.S.A	2015
Venezuela	1862, 1964, 1994
Victor Amadeus (Sardinia)	1727
Victor Amadeus III (Sardinia)	1795
William I (Netherlands)	1827
William I (Württemberg)	1857

The results are provided exclusively in English, but to furnish some awareness of the dense linguistic context, frequency Table 3.1 provides the concordatorial terms utilized in the respective treaty texts together with quantification of their occurrences. The term that appears with by far the greatest frequency (141 instances) is CONVENTIO, Latin for "agreement" or "compact."[3] Next in order of primary appearance (40 instances) is the German *Vertrag*, "treaty."[4] The other terms may be examined

Table 3.1
Concordatorial terms

Term*	Frequency
Conventio	141
[Sollemnis Conventio]	[14]
[Convenzione]	[10]
[Convenio]	[3]
[Convention]	[2]
[Solenne Convenione]	[1]
Vertrag	40
[Zusatzvertrag]	[7]
Agreement	15
Accord	5
[Accordo]	[63]
[Acuerdo]	[8]
[Ugovor]	[6]
[Acordo]	[5]
[Megállapodás]	[3]
[Accord-Cadre]	[6]
[Acord]	[1]
[Zmluva]	[1]
Concordat	3
[Concordato]	[12]
[Konkordat]	[5]
[Concordata]	[2]
Protocoll	3
Conventum	2
Marrëveshje	2
Memorandum of Understanding	2
Pactio	3
Modus Vivendi	1
Pacta	1
Trattato	1

*raw frequency from title and/or subtitle
°Latin alphabet only.

as interest dictates, but to reply to the most obvious question as to why such treaties are usually referred to as "concordats" when the term itself emerges as surprisingly rare requires recollection of the historical importance of French concordatorial scholarship explored in the previous chapter. Via path-dependent logic, Napoleon titled his 1801 treaty with the Holy See a "concordato," (*ASS* 37 [1904–1905] 76), French canonists began consistently employing the term to refer to such arrangements, it entered into canon law as such and finally became during the twentieth century the recognized designation for the treaties of the Apostolic See.

Table 3.2, meanwhile, appropriates an expression from the General Agreement on Tariffs and Trade to furnish the most frequent contracting parties over the given longitudinal interval. This simple presentation of the data is certainly useful and throughout the further development of the study there shall be occasional reason to return to it. But a much more analytically rigorous, theoretically provocative, and contextually vivid approach is required. The prevailing methodological tendency within political science is to furnish, from a potentially much larger list of observations, a representative sample of "cases" that together demonstrate instructive variation across an outcome. Given the longitudinal unfolding of the total list of concordatorial observations, the large number of those observations, and the importance of identifying major trends and transformations within those observations, the results shall be grouped into six overarching "case clusters" that together furnish the gamut of variation on the unifying thesis described below (Fig. 3.1).

There is an overall relationship between the dominance or inferiority of Roman Catholic canon law within the contracting party and ecclesiological or ideational norms expressed through its concordat. Where canon law is long-standing, uninterrupted, monopolist, or otherwise DOMINANT, the treaty norms are characteristically more ECCLESIOLOGICAL, of or pertaining to the Church as an institution. Where canon law is new, intermittent, minimal, or otherwise INFERIOR, the treaty norms are characteristically more IDEATIONAL, of or pertaining to the Church as an adherent to values. This relationship may be problematized in

Table 3.2 "Most Favored Nations"

Contracting party	Frequency
Republic of Austria	13
Bavarian Free State	8
Spanish Government	7
Lower Saxon Land	6
Republic of Malta	6
Italy	6
Portugal	6
Government of Lithuania	5
Saarland	5
Republic of Croatia	4

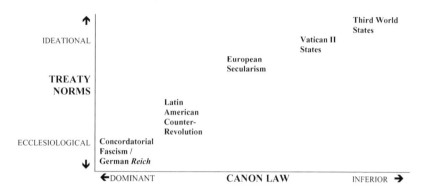

Fig. 3.1 The relationship between canon law and treaty norms

two different although not contradictory ways depending upon one's preferred epistemology. It is *causal* insofar as the entry into force of the Pio-Benedictine Code of Canon Law discussed in the preceding chapter predated the agreement of most concordats, but it is also *dialectic* in that canon law and treaty norms are constantly in constructive and reconstructive dialogue with one another. With regard to the research method, concordats are treaties, treaties are law, and law is self-referential; whereby the necessary evidence of the dominance or inferiority of canon law and the ecclesiological or ideational character of treaty norms is sufficiently contained within the texts of the concordats themselves, although relevant scholarly literature shall of course be furnished throughout each case cluster discussion to facilitate demonstration of its respective outcome. The eminent jurist Hans Kelsen—to be properly introduced in case section four—is abundantly clear on this point, affirming in the *General Theory of Law and State* (1945), "Law regulates its own creation inasmuch as one legal norm determines the way in which another norm is created, and also, to some extent, the contents of that norm" (124). The following six case cluster discussions—each consisting of the background, outcome, and aftermath of the group of respective treaties—shall be satisfactorily problematized through the respective texts themselves, and shall together demonstrate the full range of variation across the norms of the concordats of the Apostolic See.

Case Cluster I: Concordatorial Fascism, 1906–1953[5]

The Theory of Concordatorial Fascism[6]

Conceptualization of the authoritarian political force known as *fascism* has long proven challenging,[7] with the word itself enjoying a perhaps insufficiently discreet resurgence during the Trump administration.[8] Most strongly associated with the European reaction of the 1930s, with the Axis total war of the 1940s, and with the Latin American counter-revolution of the 1950s–1980s, fascism, like any political tendency, was not an undivided monolith, but rather broadly comprehended individuals as different as Philippe Pétain and Heinrich Himmler, and institutions as different as the German *Abwehr* and the Croatian *Ustaše*. What overall framework shall suffice? The most influential and enduring description to emerge from interwar fascist Europe itself is the vivid characterization of fascism as *political religion* capable of appealing to the masses with much of the spiritual force of traditional religious belief. German-American Eric Voegelin, its originator, writes in his 1938 treatise of that title, "The 'Führer'…is the point where the spirit of the people breaks into historical reality; the inner-worldly god speaks to the Führer in the same way the transcendent God speaks to Abraham, and the Führer transforms god's words into commands for his immediate followers and for the people."[9] The most influential and representative theorist of fascism is usually said to be Giovanni Gentile, whose *Origins and Doctrine of Fascism* (*Origini e dottrina del fascismo*, 1929) locates the movement primarily within the legacy of Mazzini and the example of the *Risorgimento*, while its inaugural practitioner was indisputably Benito Mussolini, who in "The Political and Social Doctrine of Fascism" (1933) explains the following: "The foundation of Fascism is the conception of the State, its character, its duty, and its aim. Fascism conceives of the State as an absolute, in comparison with which all individuals or groups are relative, only to be conceived of in their relation to the State."[10]

Conceptual provision of what shall be described as a specifically *concordatorial* fascism, however, belongs to Msgr. Dr. Ludwig Kaas (1881–1952), professor of canon law and theology, Weimar parliamentarian, and final head of the interwar German Centre Party who in 1933 induced it to support the Enabling Act and, as a close confidant of Cardinal Secretary of State Pacelli, helped negotiate the *Reich* concordat.[11] Amid the approaching triumph of reactionary authoritarianism within constitutively Roman Catholic Italy, Germany, Spain, and

Portugal, this eminent priest published "The Concordat Type of Fascist Italy" (1933),[12] wherein he acclaims the Lateran Pacts as a historic ecclesiological achievement. The most important critical reflection on the subject of concordats by an actual treaty negotiator, it furnishes the thesis of this tendency.

Overall, Kaas appears *agnostic* with respect to the authoritarian character of fascist Italy, uninterested in its advantages or enormities. His authorial intent is rather to vindicate the Lateran Pacts as "a unique phase of the latest concordatorial history" (*einzigartige Phase der neusten Konkordatsgeschichte dar*, 489), satisfactorily resolving the Roman question and significantly clarifying the relationship between the Apostolic See and the Italian state. Favorably reviewing the treaty terms outlined below, he personally furnishes no criticism; and furthermore asserts that the nearly unanimous approval of the Italian Senate—only Benedetto Croce[13] dissented—demonstrates the absence of any reasonable grounds for objection. Within the unequivocal endorsement of the treaties and the bilateral diplomacy that created them, several observations predominate. Kaas, first, is correct that the Lateran Pacts unlike any concordat before or since constitutionally establish Roman Catholicism as the state religion, thereby furnishing the strongest ecclesiological guarantee supplied by any contracting party to any concordat. Second, the elevation to treaty status of Catholic education, in his mind, is agreeable, while further emphasis is placed on the withdrawal of the state from ecclesiastical appointments and consequent expansion of the reach of canon law. Concerning the socio-political position of Catholic Action—soon to result in bilateral conflict considered below—Kaas appears, once again, in favor of the treaty terms, arguing that its "confinement to the purely religious sphere and the prohibition of any activity that extends into partisan politics is to an extent also without doubt in the putative church interest" (510).[14] The overall verdict, therefore, is that the Lateran Pacts demonstrate successful concordatorial engagement with fascism, success being defined as ecclesiological preservation or even enhancement. "It is hoped," he concludes, "that the concordatorial encounter between the Vatican and the 'totalitarian state' will not recede into history as an anecdotal incident but remain as a viable, enduring work" (522).[15]

The Concordats with the Dictators

The theory of concordatorial fascism expounded by Kaas dominates the period 1929–1950, during which a concordat was negotiated with every independent[16] fascist state in Europe; but the two primary distinctive instruments of the cases within this cluster emerged before and endured after that specific interval. The first is an oath of episcopal loyalty[17] whereby bishops within the contracting party must swear obedience to its regime prior to taking possession of their dioceses, and the oath sometimes also enjoins the bishop-designate to encourage his subordinate priests to similar obedience. In addition to the Lateran Pacts and the *Reich* concordat discussed below, the concordats with the French Government (1801), the Kingdom of Montenegro (1886), the Government of Latvia (1922), the Republic of Poland (1925), the Government of Lithuania (1927), the Kingdom of Romania (1927), the Government of Czechoslovakia (1928?), the Swiss Federal Council (1978), and the Republic of Haiti (1984) all contain a version of this oath, which has no basis in canon law. The first example is found in the concordat with the French Government of 1801, which reads:

> I swear and promise before God and upon his Holy Gospels, obedience and fidelity to the government established by the constitution of the French Republic. I furthermore promise to engage in no communication, to partake of no council, to belong to no league, whether at home or abroad, which menaces the public peace; and if I am informed of anything prejudicial to the state, within my diocese or elsewhere, to make it known to the government .(*ASS* 37 [1904–1905], 77 {VI})[18]

Although Bonaparte in his insatiable lust for power may have originated this template, of much greater importance is the extent to which the Apostolic See became accustomed and amenable to such terms, agreeing to an oath of episcopal loyalty in ten subsequent concordats, the last with Haiti under Jean-Claude "Baby Doc" Duvalier.

The second major instrument of concordatorial fascism—once again, absent from canon law—is the promise by the Church within the contracting party to offer common prayers for the peace and prosperity of the regime. The 1801 concordat with Bonaparte's government again furnishes the original example, stating, "After the divine office, the following prayer shall be recited in all the churches of France: 'DOMINE, SALVAM FAC REMPUBLICAM; DOMINE, SALVOS FAC CONSULES' [LORD, save the Republic; LORD, save the Consuls]" (*AAS* 37 [1904–1905] 77 {VIII}). The concordats with Montenegro (1886), Poland (1925), Lithuania (1927), Romania (1927), Italy (1929), and Germany (1933) will all repeat some version of this resolution; and it bears emphasizing how important is the practice and content of common prayer to the lived experience of the Catholic faithful, with the *Catechism of the Catholic Church* (1995) stating, "Vocal prayer is an essential element of the Christian life. To his disciples, drawn by their Master's silent prayer, Jesus teaches a vocal prayer, the Our Father" (2701).

But it is the Lateran Pacts of 1929 and the *Reich* concordat of 1933 that furnish the most compelling examples of the overall tendency based on the above instruments. Beginning with the first, the Lateran Pacts consisting of a treaty (*trattato*) with four appendices and a concordat (*concordato*) is the longest as well as the most complex of any concordat (*AAS* 21 [1929], 209–97), furnishing the ultimate example of ecclesiological treaty norms prevailing amid Roman linkage to authoritarian political power. Within the treaty portion (209–21), Article 1 constitutionally establishes Roman Catholicism as the Italian state religion (1), and Article 2 provides recognition of the international sovereignty of the Apostolic See "as an inherent attribute of its nature" (*come attributo inerente alla sua natura*, {2}). Any "attack and provocation" (*l'attentato e la provocazione*) against the pontiff shall be punished as that against the king ({8}), while cardinals are elevated to the status of "princes of the blood" (*Principi del sangue*, {21}), conferring a kind of royal inviolability.

In addition to these robust guarantees, the Roman pontiff is endowed with civil authority according to three gradations. First, a "Vatican City-state" (*stato della città del Vaticano*) is created north and west of St. Peter's Square, with the Italian authorities tasked with maintaining order up to its steps ({3}), and with Italy more generally agreeing to guarantee water, communications, postal, and telephone services ({6}). Aircraft may not fly over this sacerdotal micro-state ({7}), which furthermore declares itself neutral and non-aligned in world affairs ({24}). Within the Vatican walls, the pontiff is legally supreme, being endowed with "sovereignty and exclusive jurisdiction" (*la sovranità e la giurisdizione esclusiva*, {4}). Second, the pope is granted "extra-territorial privilege" (*privilegio di extraterritorialità*, {Appendix I}) over eight main properties considered essential to the ecclesiology of the Catholic faith, and which are thereby rendered exempt from taxation or expropriation: the papal basilicas of Saint John Lateran, Saint Paul Outside the Walls, and Santa Maria

Maggiore, the Castel Gandolfo, and the Dataría, Cancelleria, *Proganda Fide*, and Sant'Uffizio palaces ({13–15}), with the palaces furthermore acquiring "immunity" (*immunità*) if or when the Holy Father should be physically present ({15}). Finally, papal administration is acknowledged over the Gregorian University, the Biblical, oriental, and archaeological institutes, the Russian and Lombard colleges, the palaces of Sant'Apollinare, and the priest's house of San Giovanni e Paolo ({16}), with Italy agreeing to pay 750,000,000 lire in compensation for the loss of the papal states ({appendix IV, 1}).

The concordat (275–94) meanwhile endows churches with protection from police searches ({9}) and immunity from demolition ({10}). Catholic holidays are constitutionally established ({11}), marriage upheld as a sacrament ({34}), and instruction in the Catholic faith declared the "fundamental and crowning" (*fondamento e coronamento*) achievement of public education ({36}). The concordat of the Lateran Pacts also includes a strong oath of episcopal loyalty, which on account of the grave importance of the exact wording is recorded in full:

> Before God and upon the Holy Gospels, I swear and promise, as becomes a Bishop, loyalty to the Italian state. I swear and promise to respect and to engage my clergy to respect the King and Government established according to the constitutional law of the State. I swear and promise to neither participate in any agreement nor to assist in any council that could threaten the Italian state or the public order and to prohibit similar participation among my clergy. Solicitous of the interest of the Italian state, I will seek to avoid any damage that might threaten it. (*AAS* 21 [1929], 283 {20})[19]

The terms of the oath revised and expanded those of the 1801 concordat recorded above, and helped make captive the Italian Catholic clergy to the Italian fascist regime.

The shorter but equally significant concordat with the German *Reich* of 1933 (*AAS* 25 [1933], 389–416), meanwhile, consists of both guarantees to and impositions upon the Church. The Catholic Church in Germany receives through the treaty the right to the public exercise of the religion ({1}), as well as the preservation in force of the concordats with Bavaria (1925), Prussia (1929), and Baden (1932) ({2}). Churches are protected from demolition ({17}), as in Italy, and the continuity of Catholic education is assured ({21–25}).[20] Its pressures and constraints, conversely, include the provision that priests active in Germany must be German citizens ({1.a}), as well as the promise that the Apostolic See will soon hand down guidelines for the disestablishment of clerical influence within German politics ({32}). A special "prayer for the prosperity of the *Reich* and the German people" ({30}) is agreed,[21] while the infant National Socialist regime extracts obedience from the German bishops according to the following ominous terms:

> Before God and upon the Holy Gospels, I swear and promise, as becomes a Bishop, fidelity to the German *Reich* and to the State. I swear and promise to respect and to engage my clergy to respect the Government established according to the constitutional laws of the State. Solicitous as I ought to be of the wellbeing and interest of the German State, I shall seek to avoid, in the exercise of the sacred ministry entrusted to me, any danger which might threaten it. (*AAS* 25 [1933], 389 {16})[22]

The subsequent work of the International Military Tribunal for Germany would begin to establish how profound were the implications of the loyalty oaths Hitler took care to extract from the members of the German armed forces; yet the influence of the oath of his *spiritual* personnel, established through the concordat, ought to also be properly appreciated.

Mit Brennender Sorge

The primary ecclesiological outcome of the concordats with authoritarian and Axis Europe were two encyclicals of Pius XI concerned with the abuses of the governments of Mussolini and Hitler, respectively.[23] The first was *Non abbiamo bisogno* (29 June 1931), an encyclical on Catholic Action in Italy (*AAS* 23 [1931], 285–312) written in protest of the dissolution (30 May 1931) of its youth organizations and in exposition of the resulting temporary suspension of diplomatic relations.[24] Although not shared by Mussolini himself, anti-clericalism formed a surprisingly strong and pervasive tendency within the fascist coalition, championed by Grand Council member and Party Secretary (1925–1926) Roberto Farinacci and by the trenchant ideologue Julius Evola whom he protected.[25] The most prolific author of the occult-authoritarian tradition, Evola throughout his indicatively titled *Revolt Against the Modern World* (*Rivolta contro il mondo moderno*, 1934), the most representative of his many books, furnishes much by no means implausible anthropology amid its turgid and tergiversatory acclamation of the violent glory of ancient civilizations, but its categorical denial of any Christian salvific, much less Petrine primal theology would have been recognized under contemporary canon law (CIC/1917, c. 1325§2) as *apostasy*, of or pertaining to the total rejection of the Christian faith. *Non abbiamo bisogno* identifies and opposes such theory and practice, beginning with an expression of the "astonishment and grief at seeing Catholic Action societies persecuted and assailed here, in the very center of the Apostolic Hierarchy" (287).[26] The document continues with a further protest of the rising tide of anti-clerical intimidation and violence, the reiteration of previous assurances made to the Catholic Action networks, and forceful but diplomatic statements as to the continued good faith of endangered ecclesiastical associations before engaging in an almost total confrontation with the doctrine of fascism. "A real pagan worship of the State," argues the encyclical, "is 'Statolatry' no less in contrast with the natural rights of the family than it is in contradistinction with the supernatural rights of the Church" (302).[27] Furthermore, the previous chapter of this study demonstrated the profound concordatorial emphasis on the preservation of Catholic education as central to the ecclesiological survival of the Church; and the encyclical also intervenes on that question specifically. "A conception of the State," it argues, "which makes the rising generations belong to it entirely, without any exception, from the tenderest years up to adult life, cannot be reconciled by a Catholic either with Catholic doctrine or with the natural rights of the family" (305).[28] The venerable Pius therefore confronted, although it would eventually require the Allied armies to destroy the authoritarian state of fascist Italy.

The same also delivered, with visibly increasing desperation, *Mit Brennender Sorge* (14 March 1937) to all Church leaders within Germany (*AAS* 29 [1937], 168–88). The racism and anti-Semitism, if not necessarily the genocidal intent of the Nazi regime was clearly apparent from the outset. "One blood belongs in one *Reich*,"[29] Hitler had declared on the second page of *Mein Kampf* (1936); and among the 25 points of the Nazi program of 1920 were the prohibition of Jewish citizenship on racial grounds (4), emigration of all foreigners who had moved in since 1914 (8), and Germanization of the newspapers (23).[30] The *paganism* of the Third *Reich*, however, took somewhat longer to come into focus, being heavily reliant upon the public argumentation and bureaucratic maneuvering of a man regarded even by many Nazis as a perverse extremist: *Reichsminister* Dr. Alfred Rosenberg.[31] His *Myth of the Twentieth Century* ([*Der Mythus des zwanzigsten Jahrunderts*, 1930] 2016), the most influential thesis of Nazism after *Mein Kampf*, unfolds a Nordic occult *Weltanschauung* in which "blood represents that MYSTERIUM which has overcome and replaced the other sacraments" (61). Arguing forcefully against both international Judaism and Roman Catholicism, he asserts, "Rome cannot tolerate any organization which is conscious of its people and honor...therefore it must promote dissension and sow war and racial decomposition" (111). Devoting an entire chapter (III.V) to the churches and educational policies, Rosenberg places on record his general approval of the Lateran Pacts, but at the same rejects ecclesiastical education, the monstrous assertion that Our Lord was a Jew, and the entire Old Testament, vaguely prophesying instead a "coming German folkish church...[which] must cultivate the values of honor, pride, inward freedom, aristocracy of soul, and faith in the indestructibility of the soul of man" (372).[32] The 1937 encyclical attempts to vigorously respond. Asserting the good faith and sincere intentions of the Apostolic See in agreeing to the concordat, the pontiff declares, "the other contracting party emasculated the terms of the treaty, distorted their meaning, and eventually considered its more or less official violation as normal policy" (170).[33] Proceeding with respective defenses of Catholic education, the Old Testament, papal primacy, and Sabbath rest, as well as issuing a preëmptive interdict against any Rosenbergian *Reich* church, Pius identifies a newfound "provocative neo-paganism" (*provocante neopaganesimo*, 172) operative within a larger "myth of blood and race" (*mito del sangue e della razza*, 174) incommensurate with the fundamentals of the Catholic faith. In words that appear to portend the forthcoming crucifixion of Europe, the ailing pontiff writes, "Whoever exalts race, or the people, or the State, or a particular form of State...to an idolatrous level, distorts and perverts an order of the world planned and created by God" (171).[34] The Supreme Pontiff Pius XI therefore repeatedly bewailed the inability of his concordats to satisfactorily adjust the reactionary, racist, and militarist posture of their contracting parties.

Case Cluster II: The German Reich, 1925–2019[35]

The German Sonderweg

The central research question of modern German studies is why totalitarianism triumphed in Germany but not in the outwardly comparable Western democracies of France, Britain, and the United States. The surviving German people who supported or who acquiesced to Hitler's tyranny doubtless remained forever haunted by this grievous introspection; but much postwar academic debate postured a comparative "special path" (*Sonderweg*) toward modernity horrifically climaxing in the Nazi disaster. In its most robust version, Hans-Ulrich Wehler in *The German Empire, 1871–1918* (1985) departs *in toto* from the Hegelian ultra-conservative disposition of traditional German historicism in favor of a social scientific emphasis on the influence of historical, especially economic structure. Memorably describing the Hohenzollern monarchy as an "autocratic, semi-absolutist sham constitutionalism" (55) in the style of Bonaparte, and introducing concepts such as "social imperialism" (173), Wehler contends that eventual German collapse resulted primarily from relentless processes of economic transformation in irremediable collision with the intransigent monarchist conservatism of the throne, the aristocracy, and the state. "Otto von Bismarck," he writes, "was to fight vehemently and with staggering success on behalf of the groups that lent him support, groups representing the old Prussia and its ruling elites against the forces of social and political progress. But the consequences were to prove completely disastrous in the long run for the majority of Germany's population" (23). Intervening decades have necessarily produced conceptual qualification and adjustment[36]; but conceding to the theory some explanatory value, the numerous concordats with the German states, as a whole, furnish the case cluster that appears to provide the most smooth and linear institutional continuity to medieval antiquity, pursuing many of the same lines of argument introduced in the initial Concordat of Worms of 1122.

Diplomatic Ecclesiology

In German constitutional thought, the *Länder* are usually understood as furnishing the territorial divisions of the larger *Staat*, all of which is somehow enfolded within the transcendent and immutable greater *Reich*. From 1925 to 2019, an arresting 42 concordats were concluded with various German states, including at least one with all of the current *Länder* except Berlin and Hesse. During the Weimar period, the concordats with Bavaria (1925), with the Prussian Free States (1929), and with the Baden Free State (1932) established a process by which a primary ecclesiological objective of the Catholic Church would be pursued through bilateral diplomacy: the preservation, and where possible the enhancement of the Church's teaching *magisterium*. As explained in the preceding chapter, the insistence upon the ecclesiological right of the Catholic Church to properly educate its adherents in faith and morals is one of the primary objects of canon law, and it is also the primary concern of this cluster of German concordats.

The numerous concordats with the German *Länder* identically adhere in both form and content to the first three within the cluster noted above, and together insist upon three general rights of the Church in collective defense of its *magisterium*. First, there is agreed the right of the Church to exist and to carry out its apostolic mission. "The Bavarian State guarantees the free and public exercise of the Catholic religion."[37] "The Prussian State shall give legal protection to the freedom of profession and exercise of the Catholic religion."[38] This fundamental ecclesiological liberty, as has been seen, consistently assumes several institutional forms, beginning with the preservation of Sabbath rest. "The legal protection of Sundays, state-sponsored church holidays and church holidays is guaranteed [in Bremen]."[39] It continues with the burial of the dead. "The church cemeteries [in Saxony-Anhalt] enjoy the same protection as the municipal cemeteries. The parishes have the right to create new cemeteries."[40] Church architecture, furthermore, is very frequently preserved by treaty agreements. "The Church and the Land [of Mecklenburg-West Pomerania] share responsibility for the protection and preservation of ecclesiastical monuments."[41] There is also consistent though not ubiquitous reference to ecclesiastical privilege in public broadcasting, whereby local authorities must in various ways avoid giving needless offence to the Church and ensure that Catholic perspectives are seen and heard. "The [Lower Saxon] Land will ensure that broadcasting...does not harm the religious sentiments of the Catholic population. The Catholic Church should be given adequate airtime and allowed to represent its interests appropriately in the questions of the program."[42]

The right of the Church to educate is also strongly and comprehensively emphasized throughout the treaty cluster, with reference to both elementary and high schools. "The [Saxon] Free State guarantees the provision of regular Catholic instruction as a regular subject in public schools. The subject of the religious instruction is the teaching of Catholic doctrine in faith and morals."[43] "The right of the Catholic Church in Bavaria to have an appropriate influence in the education of the students of their creed is guaranteed without prejudice to the right of the parents to rear their children."[44] Enforcement of this right is frequently secured through concordatorial agreement on clerical inspection of schools, whereby ecclesiastical authorities may assess the form and content of classroom instruction. At the university level, meanwhile, a library of provisions grants to the Church both positive approval of curricula and syllabi as well as veto or interposition on faculty tasked with instruction of Catholic theology. "[In Thuringia] guidelines, curricula, and textbooks for Catholic religious instructions are to be laid down in agreement with the Catholic Church."[45] "Professors and university lecturers in Catholic theology and religious education [in Saxony] are only hired or appointed when the competent state ministry has ascertained from the competent diocesan bishop that no reservations are present with respect to life and doctrine."[46]

The ecclesiological right of the Church to govern, third, is also consistently secured through concordatorial diplomacy with German contracting parties. Key elements include the imposition of ecclesiastical taxes on the basis of the available civil lists, the separation of powers with respect to the appointment of bishops, and as needed the creation of new dioceses, with three concordats[47] following the reunification of Germany devoted specifically to that purpose. The government of religious orders is also, though less frequently addressed in the treaty texts. "Orders and religious congregations [in Bavaria] can be founded freely in accordance with the canonical provisions."[48]

With regard to the overall argument pursued throughout the respective treaty clusters, it suffices to say that the ecclesiological norms of the concordats with the German states are expressed almost exclusively through the prism, and on the basis of canon law. The comparative constitutional law of the Federal Republic of Germany (1949-) is very seldom, and international law is not at all mentioned apart from the anecdotal assurance of Saxony-Anhalt that it has taken into account the requirements of existing international broadcasting treaties (*AAS* 90 [1998], 494 {final protocol 11.1}). The connection is developed through sustained references to canon law throughout, but rendered seemingly impervious once the decisive role of SAPIENTIA CHRISTIANA (1979) is considered.

The respective final protocols of the concordats with North Rhine-Westphalia (*AAS* 77 [1985], 303 {I.iv.1}), the Saarland (*AAS* 78 [1986], 228 {1.2}), Saxony (*AAS* 89 [1997], 634 {v}), Saxony-Anhalt (*AAS* 90 [1998], 492 {5.1(2)}), Thuringia (*AAS* 95 [2003], 244 {2(2)}), and Lower Saxony (*AAS* 87 [1995], 569 {3}) explicitly establish the Apostolic Constitution of SAPIENTIA CHRISTIANA of the Supreme Pontiff Pope John Paul II on Ecclesiastical Universities and Faculties of 15 April 1979 (*AAS* 71 [1979], 469–528) as the basis for the relationship between the civil and ecclesiastical power. Citing the Second Vatican Council as well as unidentified new pedagogical trends, the document proceeds toward the following profound adjustment: "Only Universities and Faculties canonically erected or approved by the Holy See and ordered according to the norms of this present Constitution have the right to confer academic degrees which have canonical value." (6).[49] This pontifical assumption of control over canonical education is to rely especially upon the position of the Chancellor, who shall serve as the connection between the Apostolic See and the Catholic university or faculty (12), and who is endowed with ordinary power (13.1). Faculty are furthermore rendered suitable by their life and doctrine, Baccalaureate, Licentiate, and Doctoral degrees are identified and discussed, and respective faculties of Sacred Theology, Canon Law, and Philosophy are established. The main text of the constitution concludes, "Each University or Faculty must, before 1 January 1981, present its proper Statutes, revised according to this Constitution, to the Sacred Congregation for Catholic Education. If this is not done, its power to give academic degrees is, by this very act, suspended" (89).[50] The ecclesiological treaty norms of the German concordats thus result from both historic and pervasive presence of canon law within those same contracting parties.

The Dilemma of Worms

The most important conceptual challenge resulting from the concordats with the component parts of the greater German *Reich* is an intensification of the problem of "succession of states," long a major point of contention within international jurisprudence. In his *Principles of International Law* ([1952] 2012), Kelsen explains, "When the territory of one state becomes, totally or partially, part of the territory of another state or of several other states…the question arises whether and to what extent, according to general international law, the obligations and rights of the predecessor devolve on the successor. This is the problem of so-called succession of states" (295–96). The subsequent Vienna Convention on Succession of States in respect of Treaties (1978) generally answers Kelsen's query in the *negative*: as a rule, new states do not inherit the treaty obligations of whatever previous stationary bandit formerly held a monopoly on violence over that portion of the Earth's surface.[51] But the problem nevertheless remains salient in this context because the concordats with the German states characteristically speak of those with Prussia (1929) and with the German *Reich* (1933) treated in the previous section as still in effect. "The Concordat between the Holy See and the German *Reich* of 20 July 1933 and the Treaty of the Prussian Free States with the Holy See of 14 June 1929…remain unaffected [in Schleswig–Holstein]."[52] "The valid Concordat between the Holy See and the German *Reich* of 20 July 1933, insofar as it binds the State of Brandenburg, and in appreciation of the treaty of the Prussian Free States with the Holy See of 14 June 1929, conclude the following contract."[53]

With regard first to Prussia, few if any states within international history appear more irrevocably crucified, dead, and buried. An administrative behemoth comprising the bulk of the northern half of Germany—including East Prussia on the opposite side of the Free City of Danzig[54]—the contracting Prussian Free States of 1929 were central to the internal administration of both Weimar and Nazi Germany. But the invincible Red Army devoured most Prussian territory as Hitler committed suicide and the Soviet Union installed Communist governments that lasted for the duration of the Cold War. Citing its tradition of "militarism and reaction,"[55] Allied Control Council Law No. 46 (25 February 1947) had furthermore abolished Prussia, it is not numbered among the contemporary *Länder,* and Königsberg has been renamed Kaliningrad and is now controlled by a violently irredentist Russia. It is therefore difficult to understand, on the basis of customary international law, how its concordat could be regarded as remaining in effect.

The *Reich* Concordat, for its part, remains of the utmost importance for the subject matter as a whole not merely on account of its Hitlerian associations, but also because it furnishes the sole existing example of the judicial review of a concordat at a comparative or international level.[56] In September 1954, Lower Saxony passed a comparatively *laïque* school law that closed Catholic schools, enhanced the burden of exception on

Catholic parents, canceled the right of clerical inspection, and dismantled teacher training guarantees. In response, the Federation petitioned the Constitutional Court, arguing that its exclusive competence in foreign relations had been violated. Lower Saxony responded, with Hesse and Bremen joining in *amicus*.

In addition to clarifying federal roles and responsibilities within the young German republic, the Constitutional Court reached two overall conclusions regarding the *Reich* concordat. First, it had been lawfully negotiated, agreed, ratified, and entered into force. The Enabling Act of 23 March 1933 clearly invested Chancellor Hitler and President Hindenburg with the authority to enter treaties into force without parliamentary approval, several other treaties had been concluded during the same interval on the same grounds with proper notice provided in the *Reich* Law Gazette, and the concordat itself neither specified a time limit nor provided its own means of denunciation. The court also held—as the treaty title does clearly state—that the contracting party was not the criminal and vanquished Nazi state, but rather the insuperable German *Reich*, over and above temporal principality and power. The occupying Allies never repealed the concordat nor would they have had the authority to do so, and the Basic Law (123.2)[57] is conclusive that *Reich* treaties remain binding on the Federal Republic. "The *Reich* Concordat," ruled the German Constitutional Court, "did not lose effectiveness through the collapse of the National Socialist dictatorship. The contracting party was the German *Reich*...Therefore, the argument that the concordat only remained in force for the duration of the Nazi system is unconvincing" (I.4.a).[58] This ruling in favor of the continued validity of the concordat with the German *Reich* establishes an important precedent.

Case Cluster III: Latin American Counter-Revolution, 1887–1994[59]

Spanish Catholic Neo-Conservatism

In his landmark *Church and State in Latin America: A History of Politico-Ecclesiastical Relations* ([1934] 1966), J. Lloyd Mecham describes how the authoritarian Church of the Iberian Counter-Reformation attempted to reassert ecclesiological control in the face of the "abolition of tithes, suppression of religious orders, confiscation of ecclesiastical property, and like measures...of vengeance wreaked upon the clergy by their political opponents" (416) of the Latin American revolutions. Notable manifestations of Catholic counter-revolutionary doctrine included the theory of the "perfect society" (*sociedad perfecta*) cited in the concordat with the Dominican Republic (*AAS* 46 [1954], 435 {III.1}), the vehemently illiberal *Syllabus of Errors* (1864) of Pius IX,[60] or the declaration of papal infallibility (*ASS* 6 [1870–1871], 45–47 {IV}) of the First Vatican Council (1869–1870). The most forceful and accomplished exposition of specifically Spanish Catholic neo-conservatism, however, remains the 1851 essay on Catholicism, liberalism, and socialism of Juan Cortés.

Professor, parliamentarian, diplomat, and royal counselor, El Sr. Marqués de Valdegamas Don Juan Donoso Cortés (1809–1853)[61] delivered the primary response of Catholic conservatism to the revolutions of the nineteenth century, at once succeeding the Counter-Reformation of St. Ignatius and laying the ideological foundations for General Franco's modern phallangist regime. Six works define his *oeuvre*.[62] The Lessons in Political Right (*Lecciones de Derecho politico*) delivered at the Madrid Athenaeum in 1836 open a succession of contributions to political theory that continue with "The Absolute Monarchy in Spain" (*La Monarquía absoluta en España*, 1838), the decisive parliamentary intervention of 4 January 1849 styled the "Discourse on Dictatorship," and the respective discourses on the situations in Europe and in Spain. Most of the ideas developed within those previous works are however combined and strengthened in the sustained *Essay on Catholicism, Liberalism, and Socialism* (*Ensayo sobre Catholicismo, el Liberalismo, y el Socialismo*) of 1851,[63] the greatest theoretical statement of Spanish Catholic counter-revolution.

Cortés derives an informed opposition to both liberal and socialist ideas on the basis of a proper understanding of the full implications of Biblical doctrine, especially with respect to the inevitability of human sin but the imperturbability of the love and power of Christ. Largely ignoring the legacy of the religious wars and other abuses characteristically cited by the opponents of the Church, Cortés opens with effusive praise for Catholicism as having "placed in order and in concert all human things" (*ha puesto en orden y en concierto todas las cosas humanas*, 51), given that it "is love, since God is love" (*es amor, porque Dios es amor*, 62). The Catholic Apostolic Church occupies the central position within his formulation. Eternal, infallible, above all principality and power, "The Church represents the natural man without sin, as from the hands of God, full of original justice and sanctifying grace."[64] Her much debated doctrinal intolerance, more specifically, "has saved the world from chaos" (*ha salvado el mundo del caos*, 43), and her long resisted pontiff "is king" (*es rey*, 46) by both divine and human right. Man must recognize, accept, and grow to love his subordinate position within a cosmic order ruled by a perfect God, administered by spiritual angels, and populated by imperfect fellow men, in which evil (*mal*) is equivalent to disorder (*desorden*), based on the recognition that "submission to the divine will is the highest good."[65]

Liberal and (pre-Marxist) socialist doctrine, however, willfully ignore or pervert the lordship of Jesus Christ, with ruinous consequences for the individual and the society. Liberalism, a "region without a name" (*región sin nombre*, 192) between socialism and Catholicism, confines its recognition of evil strictly to political and legal institutions that the enlightened might effectively adjust; while socialism, though commendable to some degree in its idealism, seriously errs in its central contention that sinful man can by his own effort transform society. Socialist solidarity, upon closer examination, offers nothing not already contained within the mystical body of Christ; wherefore Cortés pronounces it "a semi-Catholicism, and nothing more" (*un semi-catolicismo, y nada más*, 281). War and revolution have of course occurred throughout history, but the modern *ideas* behind these disorders, argues Cortés, in various ways distort the true message of the Gospel, increasing their popular appeal but also intensifying their historic danger.

Concordatorial Counter-Revolution

The treaty norms of the concordats with Latin America primarily reflect the ecclesiology of the Spanish counter-revolution theoretically explored above. The most comprehensive are those with the Dominican Republic (*AAS* 46 [1954], 433–57), with the Republic of Venezuela (*AAS* 56 [1963], 925–32), and with the Republic of Colombia (*AAS* 67 [1975], 421–34), although the latter employs somewhat different wording. "The Catholic, Apostolic, Roman religion shall continue as that of the Dominican Nation and shall enjoy the rights and privileges which correspond to Divine and Canon Law" ({I}).[66] "The Venezuelan State shall continue to assure and guarantee the free and plain exercise of the spiritual power of the Catholic Church" ({I}).[67] Recognition of the juridical personality of both the Apostolic See and the Vatican City-state is agreed upon, and canon law is made sovereign within its competence. "Canonical legislation [in Colombia] is independent of the civil, and forms no part of it" ({III}).[68] The standard provisions, furthermore, are observed, including clerical exemption from military service and taxation, legal equivalence of ecclesiastical with civil marriage, recognition of Catholic education, and shared rights and obligations regarding episcopacy, all justified by frequent references to canon law. To such familiar ecclesiological treaty norms, however, is added the somewhat ideational principle of the protection of Catholic Action, a lay ecclesiastical polity absent from the 1917 Code of Canon Law. "The State [of the Dominican Republic] guarantees the right of free organization and functioning of the Catholic associations of religious, social, and compassionate end, and in particular the associations of Catholic Action" ({XXV}).[69] "The Venezuelan State, in conformity with the Constitution, recognizes the right of organization of the Catholic citizens in order to promote the diffusion and achievement of the principles of Catholic faith and morals through the associations of Catholic Action" ({XV}).[70] The first concordat with Bolivia (*AAS* 50 [1958], 68–81) and the concordat with Peru (*AAS* 72 [1980], 807–12), meanwhile, largely follow the terms outlined above, though their subject matter is more restricted to missions.

Given that the army and the police, more specifically, are central to the enforcement of successful counter-revolution, a major ecclesiological innovation first appears within and largely defines the second concordat with Bolivia (*AAS* 53 [1961], 299–303): the military chaplain (*Vicariato Castrense*). In a manner to be duplicated in the subsequent concordats with Paraguay (*AAS* 54 [1962], 22–27), with El Salvador (*AAS* 60 [1968], 382–84), with Ecuador (*AAS* 75 [1983-I], 481–84), with Brazil (*AAS* 82 [1990], 126–29), and with Venezuela (*AAS* 87 [1995], 1092–96), terms and conditions are set forth for the institution of a largely autonomous office of chaplains to the army and the police, exempt from diocesan but endowed with personal jurisdiction over the spiritual welfare of the troops. With respect to canon law, DE VICARIIS CASTRENSIBUS (*AAS* 53 [1951], 562–65) is invoked, and the third concordat with Bolivia (*AAS* 81 [1989], 528 {I}) also introduces SPIRITUALI MILITUM CURAE (*AAS* 78 [1986], 481–86), in which military ordinates are established who report directly to the Apostolic See. The concordats with the Latin American states, therefore, confirmed and strengthened the spiritual resources of the armed personnel on the front lines of the waging of the Iberian Catholic counter-revolution.

The Theology of Liberation

The primary response to the counter-revolutionary posture of the Latin American Church as a whole was the development of an endogenous "liberation" theology to help give prophetic utterance to the sorrow and weeping of her abject millions of desperately poor and ruthlessly oppressed. The *Theology of Liberation* (*Teologia de Liberacion: Perspectivas*, [1972] 1975) of Peruvian Dominican Gustavo Gutiérrez is at once an extraordinarily compelling response to regional conditions, a bold and original synthesis of numerous narratives of modern philosophy, and a ravishing work of literature, the general intent being a spiritual regeneration of Roman Catholic ortho-*doxy* and ortho-*praxis* wherein the Biblical poor are transubstantiated into the Marxist proletariat. "To advance the social revolution," he explains, "means to abolish the present state of things and to attempt to replace them with something qualitatively different...it means to attempt to put an end to the domination of some countries by others, of some social classes by others, of some men by others."[71] He continues elsewhere, "Salvation comprehends all men and the whole of man...the fight for a just society is plainly inscribed in its own right in the history of salvation."[72] Liberation theology captured the imagination of Latin American Catholic faithful who lived amid abject poverty and beneath fascist regimes; yet its unprecedented utilization of Marxist imaginary sufficiently alarmed the Apostolic See that Joseph Cardinal Ratzinger, as Prefect of the Congregation for the Doctrine of the Faith, was approved to deliver two sustained rebuttals, in 1984 (*AAS* 76 [INSTRUCTIO DE QUIBUSDAM RATIONIBUS < < THEOLOGIAE LIBERATIONIS > > , 1984], 876–909) and in 1986 (*AAS* 79 [INSTRUCTIO DE LIBERTATE CHRISTIANA ET LIBERATIONE, 1987], 554–99), respectively. The dynamic tension between ecclesiology and idealism continues.

CASE CLUSTER IV: EUROPEAN SECULARISM, 1801–2020[73]

Positivist Theory

Within Western social thought since the 1848 revolutions, the term *secularization* has assumed wide varieties of meaning. Bryan R. Wilson in *Religion in a Secular Society* (1966) contends, "The whole significance of the secularization process is that society does not, in the modern world, derive its values from certain religious preconceptions which are then the basis for social organization and social action" (256). David Martin derives his *General Theory of Secularization* (1978) primarily by analyzing the intersections of critical historical junctures, comparative ecclesiologies, Reformed and Enlightened thought, and the relation between religion and nationalism. Charles Taylor in *A Secular Age* (2007) pursues the meta-transformation "from a society in which it was virtually impossible not to believe in God, to one in which faith, even for the staunchest believer, is one human possibility amongst others" (3). Without assuming the burden of the continuation of an extensive scholarly debate effectively summarized elsewhere,[74] this theoretical discussion shall concentrate on one influential form of European secular thought: the scientific or *positive* form.

Positivism is the conceptual derivation of Auguste Comte (1798–1857), whose highly influential epistemology consummates the *laïque* tendencies of the French Revolution. Intermittent and incompetent publication history has rendered his six-volume *Cours de philosophie positive* (1842) largely unavailable, but the *Introduction to Positive Philosophy* (Indianapolis: Hackett, 1988) consisting of its initial and theoretical chapters effectively furnishes the outline of what Comte confidently describes as the three-stage law of mental development. First, man in his primal state is *theological*, ascribing to gods and goddesses the observed phenomena of the universe. Theology is always false but was everywhere originally necessary. Next, he becomes *metaphysical*, understanding the world through ideal types and forms. This stage is transitional. Finally, beginning with Bacon, Descartes, and Galileo, man is clear for takeoff into the *positive* mental life consisting exclusively of the fruit of the scientific method. The resulting "main characteristic" of the positive philosophy Comte then proceeds to unfold "is precisely that of regarding as necessarily interdicted to human reason all those sublime mysteries which theological philosophy…explains with such admirable facility" (6). Astronomy, physics, chemistry, and physiology have already completed the transition to positivism, but the *social sciences*, argues Comte, regrettably remain encumbered with theology and metaphysics. Therefore, "nothing more remains to be done…than to complete the positive philosophy by including in it the study of social phenomena, and then to sum them up in a single body of homogenous doctrine" (30). Comte was a central theorist among the more educated, elite, and secular portions of French and European society at the time of the contentious abrogation of the Napoleonic concordat described below, with his positive epistemology inclining the appreciative reader toward the eradication of what remains of religious belief and morals within the study and government of human society.

This seminal conception of positive epistemology is pursued to the greatest imaginable extent in the towering scholarly achievements of Prof. Dr. Hans Kelsen (1881–1973), author of the Austrian Constitution of 1920, creator of the constitutional court as an instrument of government in a democracy, and distinguished research professor at Vienna, Cologne, Geneva and (fleeing fascism) the University of California, Berkeley.[75] In the monumental *General Theory of Law and State* (1945), Kelsen as a political scientist and jurist demonstrates his indebtedness to existing positive epistemology, stating, "Transformation of the science of social relationships from an ethical science into a causal sociology, explaining the reality of actual conduct and therefore indifferent to values, is largely accomplished today. It is, fundamentally, a withdrawal of social theory before an object which it has lost all hope of mastering" (391). In answer to the overall research question of WHY MUST I _____, Kelsen explains BECAUSE IT CONFORMS TO THE BASIC NORM. Jettisoning the unsustainable dualism of law and state derivative of Christian theology, Kelsen derives a "national legal order...defined as a relatively centralized coercive order whose territorial, personal, and temporal spheres of validity are determined by international law and whose material sphere of validity is limited by international law only" (351). His intersecting *Pure Theory of Law* ([*Reine Rechtslehre*, 1960] 2009), meanwhile, clarifies that the title refers to "a theory of positive law...The theory attempts to answer the question what and how the law *is*, not how it ought to be...Its aim is to free the science of law from alien elements" (1). For Kelsen, moral beliefs are always and everywhere in transition; therefore solution is to be found in a theory of legal positivism whereby a *norm* is something that ought to be or to take place, according to the *Grundnorm* establishing the validity of a coercive order called *law*. Theology and metaphysics therefore have no place within a positive science of law that "begins with the establishment of the constitution, continues via legislation or custom to the judicial decision, and leads to the execution of the sanction" (237).

The Concordats with Secular Europe

The positivist theory outlined above influenced the respective concordatorial diplomacy of France and Austria. Beginning with France, the decisive concordat with the French government of 15 July 1801 (*ASS* 37 [1904–1905], 76–78) served as the foundation for the relationship between Catholic Church and French State during the long nineteenth century. It furnishes, first, ecclesiological recognition, though uniquely bounded by state power. "The Catholic, Apostolic, Roman religion shall be freely exercised in France. Its worship shall be public, in conformity with policy ordinances which the Government in the interests of peace shall deem necessary" ({1}).[76] It also provides, second, the first appearance of an oath of episcopal loyalty. "I swear and promise to God upon the Holy Gospels, fidelity and obedience to the Government established by the Constitution of the French Republic. I promise to have no communications, to partake of no council, to enter upon no league, at home or abroad, which menaces the public peace; and if, within or without my diocese, I am informed of anything prejudicial to the State, I shall so disclose to the Government" ({VI}).[77] A special prayer for the regime, third, is agreed, which reads DOMINE, SALVAM FAC REMPUBLICAM; DOMINE, SALVOS FAC CÓNSULES (LORD, *save the Republic;* LORD, *save the Consuls* {VIII}). Finally, French episcopal nomination is entrusted to the First Consul (Napoleon), with the Holy See afterward providing the requisite canonical investiture.

In December 1905, however, a law separating church and state in France invalidated the treaty, resulting in the only historical example of a formal, unilateral abrogation of a concordat by a contracting party.[78] Triumphantly championed by French secularists, the immediate outcome of the law was a grave international incident, with the Church publishing its aggrieved version of events in *La Separation de L'Église et de L'État En France: Exposé et Documents* (*ASS* 38 [1905–1906], 433–702). The most important source document in concordatorial history, it is also the longest and most sustained intervention of the papacy *on any subject*, as well as uniquely aggressive in its accusation of specific civil officials. "The rupture of the Concordat and the separation," asserts the Holy See in a summary passage, "were searched and willed, formally, by the French Government, particularly by Mr. Combes" (15). Prime Ministers Pierre Waldeck-Rousseau and Émile Combes are accused of unlawful suppression of the Catholic faith, deliberate misrepresentation of the outcome of negotiations with the Church, and willful abuse of the bilateral system of episcopal investiture, in which the French state certainly has the concordatorial right to fill vacancies, but, in the indignant analysis of the Holy See, "must satisfy its obligation of naming worthy candidates, and of respecting the right of the Holy See to examine the titles of proposed candidates and to not admit those who lack qualities required for the episcopat."[79]

The papal representation—written exclusively in French, as if uniquely concerned with lay comprehension—advances three main points. First, the government of the day willfully misconstrued the provisions of the concordat with Napoleon's coterminous but unilateral organic articles of religion,[80] and led the public to believe that violations of the latter necessarily invalidated the former. The Holy See also argues that Roman Catholics have proven good republicans, with their patriotic record confounding any uncharitable assertions to the contrary. "The adversaries of the Church use a very evident sophism," the Holy See explains. "They arbitrarily identify the Republic with their anti-Christian laws and doctrines, and if the Church fails to accept them, they accuse it of systematic opposition to the Republic, finding pretext for further outrages."[81] In this respect, the Holy See had no choice but to protest the state visit (24 April 1904) of the French President to King Victor Emmanuel, but that incident had nothing to do with the existing terms of the concordat. Beginning in 1870, it is clarified, the papacy had adopted a policy of opposition to the visits of Catholic heads of state to the Italian king, with the selection of the Quirinal palace for that specific visit a clear attempt at provocation. Finally, the Holy See—in an exposition of enduring importance—explains that episcopal nomination means *désignation*, with concordatorial treaty law most frequently using the word NOBIS. In the papal interpretation of the treaty terms, the French head of state nominates a prospective bishop, the relevant ministry proposes him, and then the nuncio accepts the proposition. Putting to the reader a rhetorical question central to the history, theory, and practice of the entire subject matter, the Holy See, in an unusually Socratic mood, asks, "Dare we say that the Government is competent to decide the orthodoxy of the faith, theological and canonical doctrine, fervor, integrity of manners and of piety, such as are required in a bishop?"[82] In support of its unapologetic answer in the negative, 47 documents, mostly exchanges of letters between senior officials, are annexed to the report.[83]

The concordat between the Holy See and the Republic of Austria of 5 June 1933 (*AAS* 26 [1934], 249–84), meanwhile, was the first since the permanent departure from history of the Habsburg power. It was the product of the brief and unhappy fascistic regime of Chancellor Engelbert Dollfuß, who suspended Kelsen's federal constitution the same year only to be assassinated by local Nazis in 1934. Although the concordat contains no oath of episcopal loyalty or special prayers for the regime, it is otherwise very sustained and comprehensive, with all the usual assurances and guarantees. Austria was however then annexed to the greater German *Reich* in 1938, the Red Army took the city of Vienna by mid-April 1945, and an Allied and Associated State Treaty for the Re-establishment of an Independent and Democratic Austria was concluded on 15 May 1955.[84]

Five years later, a new concordatorial outcome appeared in the form of an Agreement (*Vertrag*) between the Holy See and the Republic of Austria for Regulating Property Relationships (*AAS* 52 [1960], 933–45). Beginning with this instance, the subsequent concordats with Austria less frequently invoke canon law, more narrowly define ecclesiology, and cite no encyclicals, with the main intent consisting of the restriction of the scope of Federal financial obligation to the Church through a complicated series of compensation arrangements, with specific amounts being agreed, and then subsequently adjusted. "The Catholic Church recognizes that the Republic of Austria is not obliged to undertake any further financial obligations beyond the services promised in this contract."[85] The Archdiocese of Salzburg receives certain quantities of fertile timberland ({V.2}), and the Diocese of Eisenstadt guaranteed a certain payout schedule ({VI}). The next agreement (*AAS* 62 [1970], 162–64) in what becomes a topical series increases the state payout, the one after that pledges more funds for the personnel of Catholic schools (*AAS* 64 [1972], 478–81), and the final three (*AAS* 68 [1976], 422–24; 82 [1990], 230–32; 90 [1998], 95–97) keep adjusting the existing figures for inflation, a seemingly crucial detail previously overlooked. During the same interval, meanwhile, another *Vertrag* on the School System (*AAS* 54 [1962], 641–52) enforced the right of the Church to educate in the Catholic manner ({I§1.1}), including the formation of any sort of ecclesiastical school consistent with the law ({II§1.1}). Catholic school is compulsory for Catholic pupils ({I§2.1}), who may install a cross on the classroom wall if comprising the numerical majority ({final protocol 2.b}). Although the transformation is by no means complete or absolute, the significant normative difference between the Dollfuß concordat of 1933 and those which have ensued with the democratic Austria[86] Kelsen (a Jew) wrote into existence is broadly consistent with his positivist extraction of law from philosophy, religion, ideology, and all other extraneous norms.

The Qualification of Positivist Theory

The legal relationships described above remain in effect. What has been compromised over the last several decades in some quarters, however, is general assurance of the sufficiency of positivist theory, given the consistency with which both the Cold War and the War on Terrorism demonstrated the profound importance of various forms of ideology to social organization. As the former was coming into focus during the late 1940s through the intrepid efforts of Prime Minister Churchill, Ambassador Kennan, General Marshall, and others, Kelsen brought forth *The Political Theory of Bolshevism: A Critical Analysis* (1949); and although he delivered a brilliant rebuttal to numerous problematic contentions within the Marxist-Leninist conceptual program, the bare necessity of intervention in an ideological conflict "on which, perhaps, the fate of mankind will depend" (2) would itself seem to demonstrate the inadequacy, and perhaps also the danger of theoretically relegating so much of human identity to the dustbin of history and to the margin of consciousness. The embedded character of law within larger social norm appears if anything more pronounced with respect to the Islamic world, throughout much of which positive doctrine appears largely unrecognizable. Partially in response to the horrific *Charlie Hebdo* massacre of 2015, French scholar Gilles Kepel published *Terreur dans l'Hexagone: Genèse du djihad français* (2017), wherein he explains, "the identitarian nationalism of the extreme right and the Islamic element...are unique bearers, as the French Communist Party formerly was, of a strong utopian tendency that reimagines a sinister social reality in projecting it in a myth where the left-for-dead of today become the victors of tomorrow."[87] Contemporary Europe continues to witness the deterioration of the plausibility of a strictly positive approach to the maintenance of public order.

CASE CLUSTER V: THE SECOND VATICAN REFORMATION, 1968–2016[88]

Christian Democratic Norms

Reflecting at once the theological norms of the postwar resurgence of Thomist thought, the comparative norms of the reconstruction of Western Europe by Christian Democratic political parties, and the international norms of the Charter of the United Nations and Statute of the International Court of Justice, the Second Vatican Ecumenical Council

(1962–1965) convoked by Pope John XXIII and adjourned by Pope Paul VI reconstituted the Roman Catholic Apostolic Church. At issue above all was the reactionary posture toward the outside world that the Church— but especially the papacy—had previously allowed itself, and in its place was agreed an acceptance of democratic self-determination rooted in Christian obedience. Among the sixteen documents of the council,[89] five are directly or indirectly referenced in the subsequent resulting case cluster.

First, a decree on the pastoral office of bishops [DECRETUM DE PASTORALI EPISCOPORUM MUNERE IN ECCLESIA {*Christus Dominus*} (*AAS* 58 [1966], 673–701)] clarifies the doctrine of Petrine primacy: whereas Christ specially instructed Peter to feed his sheep, and whereas the Roman pontiff is the legitimate successor to Peter, therefore the pope enjoys "ordinary power" (ORDINARIAE POTESTATIS {2}) over the Church. Consequently, the Church requests but does not require civil commonwealths to henceforth stand down from any further involvement in the nomination of bishops ({20}), a considerable advance toward further separation of church and state. Second, a dogmatic constitution of divine revelation [CONSTITUTIO DOGMATICA DE DIVINA REVELATIONE {*Lumen Gentium*} (*AAS* 58 [1966], 817–36)] reiterates the overall ecclesiology of the Church, explaining that the Cardinals succeed the Apostles as does the Holy Father St. Peter their Prince. Third, a declaration on religious liberty [DECLARATIO DE LIBERTATE RELIGOSA {*Dignitatis Humanae*} (*AAS* 58 [1966], 929–47)] opens with the proclamation that "the human person has the right to religious freedom."[90] Reflecting the overall tendency of such instruments as the American Bill of Rights, the French Declaration on the Rights of Man and Citizen, or the Universal Declaration of Human Rights, the document argues that this right derives from human dignity itself, and that it should always and everywhere receive constitutional protection. "Religious freedom in society is entirely consonant with the freedom of the act of Christian faith."[91] Fourth, a fresh pastoral constitution for the Church in today's world [CONSTITUTIO PASTORALIS DE ECCLESIA IN MUNDO HUIUS TEMPORIS {*Gaudium et Spes*} (*AAS* 58 [1966], 1025–1120)] articulates the following summation of Catholic social teaching:

> Whatever is opposed to life itself, such as any type of murder, genocide, abortion, euthanasia or willful self-destruction, whatever violates the integrity of the human person, such as mutilation, torments inflicted

on body or mind, attempts to coerce the will itself; whatever insults human dignity, such as subhuman living conditions, arbitrary imprisonment, deportation, slavery, prostitution, the selling of women and children; as well as disgraceful working conditions...are infamies indeed.[92]

When the concordats to be identified and discussed below consistently appeal in general terms to the norms of the Second Vatican Council, the import of the four documents above, central to the ecclesiological reconstitution of the Church, is primarily intended. But there are also three specific concordatorial references (*AAS* 92 [2000], 783 {preamble}; 93 [2001], 840 {preamble}; 97 [2005] 51 {preamble}) to the council's declaration on Christian education [DECLARATIO DE EDUCATIONE CHRISTIANA {*Gravissimum Educationis*} (*AAS* 58 [1966], 728–39)] which explains that the education of a Christian "has as its principal purpose this goal: that the baptized, while they are gradually introduced to the knowledge of the mystery of salvation, become ever more aware of the gift of Faith they have received, and that they learn in addition how to worship God the Father in spirit and truth."[93] The presence of satisfactory Catholic schools in a commonwealth, parental choice in the selection of schools, and moral instruction throughout the educational process are all of the utmost importance. "Consequently, this sacred synod proclaims anew what has already been taught in several documents of the magisterium, namely: the right of the Church freely to establish and to conduct schools of every type and level."[94]

The Concordats of the Council

Twenty-four subsequent concordats provide normative reference to the second Vatican ecumenical council, beginning with the Argentine Republic (*AAS* 59 [1967], 127–30), continuing with the Principality of Monaco (*AAS* 73 [1981], 651–53), and then greatly accelerating during the 1990s. The treaty *terms* among this cluster are representative of the subject matter, consisting primarily of the familiar guarantees of the apostolic mission of the Church, the inalienable right to Catholic education, the protections of sacramental marriage, the inviolability of the confessional seal, and the other characteristic outcomes of concordatorial diplomacy examined in the previous chapter, with the concordat with post-Communist Lithuania (*AAS* 92 [2000], 783–816) probably the strongest and most sweeping of the assortment. The treaty *norms*, however, appear much more idealistic than those of any previous case cluster, as the canon law tradition within the contracting commonwealth is seen in competition with newfound norms of both comparative and international law.

First, the concordats of the Vatican II generation demonstrate the considerable extent to which the institution of canon law within the contracting party is forced to acknowledge the democratizing norms of comparative law that complement and localize the conclusions of the ecumenical council. The textual evidence is contained mostly in the respective treaty preambles, and the first concordat of the cluster opens, "The Holy See reaffirming the principles of the Vatican II Ecumenical Council and the Argentine State inspired by the principle of liberty consecrated once again in the National Constitution,"[95] a statement that may be even more meaningful given the fascist *junta* that truly held power at the time. Proceeding to the second, Monégasque ecclesiology had been defined by the sovereign ordinance of 28 September 1887 enabling the prince to nominate the bishop[96]; but in accordance with *Christus Dominus*, the preamble to the new concordat is "convinced of the opportunity to introduce modifications to the norms established by said bull [QUMADMODUM SOLLICITUS, 15 March 1886] in order to conform to orientations given by the Vatican II Ecumenical Council" (*AAS* 73 [1981], 651 {preamble}).[97] In Asia, a democratized Philippines prefaces its English-language concordat by "Acting, on the part of the Holy See, in accordance with the declarations of the Second Vatican Council on religious liberty and the relations between the Church and the civil society, as well as the norms of Canon Law, and, on the part of the Philippines, with the principles of its Constitution and applicable laws" (*AAS* 101 [2009], 1062). The submission of such disparate instances—normally discouraged—here serves to illustrate the transnational trend of concordatorial law incorporating comparative applications of the ideals of Vatican II.

But the concordats of the Vatican II cluster also demonstrate international norms in competition with those of canon law, norms which articulate many of the Christian democratic or personalist ones of the council but on the basis of reason and secular humanism. In its post-Communist concordat, "The Republic of Lithuania," for example, is found "acting in accordance with its Constitution; holding the principles of freedom of conscience and religion as recognized and proclaimed by the international community" (*AAS* 92 [2000] 783 {preamble}). Founded by the crusading knighthood of St. John of Jerusalem (FRATERNITAS

HOSPITALARIA), Malta, meanwhile, could with strong justification claim to be the most pure and perfect Catholic state; yet even its concordat of the period explains, "Bearing in mind, on the part of the Republic of Malta, the principles enforced by its Constitution and by those International Bodies to which it adheres...it is opportune to reach a new and definitive Agreement on Church Schools" (*AAS* 85 [1993], 558 {preamble}). Although the source material for the international norms invoked in such references is seldom specified, the written work of the United Nations organization and its affiliated bodies appears intended.

The central *adjustment* with which both the comparative and international normative references described above are concerned, finally, is separation of church and state. The new concordat with the Italian Republic (*AAS* 77 [1985], 521–78) demolishes a central provision of the Lateran Pacts by disestablishing Roman Catholicism as the Italian state religion, instead describing the ecclesiastical and civil swords as henceforth "independent and sovereign" (*independenti e sovrani*, {1}) within their respective spheres. Another strong example is found in the preamble to the concordat with the Republic of Croatia (*AAS* 89 [1997], 277), which begins by "making reference, on the part of the Republic of Croatia to the norms of the Constitution, in particular articles 40 and 41 on religious liberty and liberty of conscience, and the Holy See to the documents of the Second Vatican Council and to the norms of canon law."[98] Bosnia and Herzegovina, meanwhile, headquartered the brief but appalling post-Yugoslav wars of ethno-religious nationalism during the early to mid-1990s; but being issued a highly internationalist constitution in 1995 through the Dayton Accords, proceeded to open its eventual concordat with the following:

> With reference on the part of Bosnia-Herzegovina to the constitutional principles by which it was created, and on the part of the Holy See to the documents of the Second Vatican Council and the norms of canon law...Respecting internationally recognized principles concerning the distinction between religion and the state and concerning freedom of religion; have established by mutual agreement what follows. (*AAS* 99 [2007], 939 {preamble})

The text then proceeds to rigorously partition church from state ({1}) and to guarantee papal control over episcopal nomination ({6.2}), but at the same time recognizes the juridical personality of the Church ({2}), guarantees Sabbath rest and ecclesiastical holidays ({9.1}), and furnishes sustained protections for Catholic Action and education.[99] In short, the Second Vatican Ecumenical Council inspired a whole new generation of concordats in which democratic comparative and international ideals both strongly and consistently appear.

Profession of International Order

As the following case cluster shall help demonstrate, the concordatorial diplomacy of Vatican II has contributed to a still more dramatic adjustment: the transformation of the Roman pontiff into global statesman, whereby the popes since the council have demonstrated their increasing willingness to publicly commit to certain salient international norms clearly not derived from canonical obligation. Perhaps the watershed historic moment for this ongoing alteration was the French-language address of 4 October 1965 of Pope Paul VI to the United Nations (*AAS* 57 [1965], 877–85). On the twentieth anniversary of the founding of that body, the Holy Father brought greetings in the name of the ongoing ecumenical council described above, and then prefaced his remarks toward those whom he regarded as his fellow heads of state by explaining, "Your brother…is invested…with but a miniscule and quasi-symbolic temporal sovereignty, the minimum necessary to be free to exercise his spiritual mission and to assure those who treat with him that he is independent of all sovereignty in this world."[100] Underscoring that the United Nations organization ought to be identified with the "all nations" of the Great Commission (Matt. 28-19-20), he continues "Whatever be your opinion of the Roman Pontiff…We are the bearer of a message for all humanity."[101] Central to that message is the equality of all nation-states before international law, the need to broadly instruct in the ways and means of global peace, and the urgency of disarmament at unilateral, bilateral, and multilateral levels. "You sanction the grand principle that relationships between peoples must be regulated by reason, by justice, by right, and by negotiation, and not by force, by violence, by war, and not by fear and trickery,"[102] the pontiff affirms, in seemingly unqualified endorsement of the organization.

Case Cluster VI: The Benediction of the Third World, 1993–2015[103]

Soul Force

The political theory of the Third World or Global South as a whole is defined by the comprehensive notion of RESISTANCE, to (neo)colonialist domination, to global capitalist expropriation, and—if with diminishing plausibility—to racialist hierarchicization. This resistance assumes two overall forms: the violent and the non-violent. The theory and practice of violent resistance on the part of the world's oppressed was developed primarily by Vladimir Ilyich Ulyanov (1870–1924), *nom de partie*, LENIN, the charismatic leader of the Communist revolution in Russia in 1917 and founder of the Soviet Union, who gainfully employed his years of imprisonment and exile in the preparation of four *Essential Works* (New York: Dover, 1987) marked by truly awesome analytical intelligence. *The Development of Capitalism in Russia* (1899) introduces the now familiar notion that large-scale mechanized agriculture rapidly heralds an unprecedented change to rural way of life, while *What is to be Done* (1902) urges an elite-driven, intentional, and self-conscious "revolutionary Social Democracy" to replace irredeemable bourgeois parliamentarism. Lenin's approach to international theory is mainly provided in *Imperialism, the Highest Stage of Capitalism* (1917), which holds that the increasing monopolization of finance capital in the West is and shall continue to result in attempts by its captive governments to dominate the less civilized world, an ingenious postulate which the appalling events of the intervening century have perhaps qualified but certainly not refuted. *The State and Revolution* (1917), finally, is perhaps the most important from the practical standpoint of serving as the primary template for subsequent violent and politicized resistance throughout the Third World. Lenin writes, "The proletariat needs state power, the centralized organization of force, the organization of violence, for the purpose of crushing the resistance of the exploiters and for the purpose of *leading* the great mass of the population...in the work of organizing socialist economy" (288, emphasis in original). Through the relentless efforts of his revolutionary successors in the People's Republic of China under Chairman Mao Tsetung, in Viet Nam under President Ho Chi Minh, in Africa under Dr. Kwame Nkrumah, and in Cuba under Commander in Chief Fidel Castro, to provide merely some of the most recognizable examples, one glimpses the almost immeasurable influence of Leninist thought throughout the non-Western world.

But many of the same post-colonial populations have also practiced an advanced doctrine of non-violent resistance constructed by Mahatma Gandhi (1869–1948), the spiritual leader of Indian independence in 1947. He describes his at-once political theory and moral theology as *Satyagraha* (New York: Dover, 2001 [1961]), a compelling "force of truth and love" designed to shame the oppressor into repentance and to inspire the oppressed toward deeper devotion to God. In complete contrast to Lenin, "Satyagraha," writes Gandhi, "can only be cultivated or wielded by those who will entirely eschew violence" (34). Celibacy, non-possession, civil disobedience, spinning, fasting, and prayer are all represented as manifestations of an all-inclusive practice initiated in British India in response to intensified domestic repression and to the continuation of imperial policies after World War I, a practice in which "the only weapon…is God, by whatsoever name one knows Him" (95). Central to Satyagraha is *Ahimsa* (love), which is Truth and which corresponds in numerous respects to the *agape* of John the Evangelist, whereby the other person is completely and unconditionally loved. Gandhi's intersecting *Autobiography* (1954) explores this and other similarities with Christian doctrine, which have produced the important consequence of selective concordatorial adoption of terms and concepts inspired by the extremely idealistic non-violent resistance theory derivative of the Indian *raj* but prevalent if not triumphant throughout the Third World.

Concordatorial Agape

An idealist posture of *Ahimsa* or *agape* has recently become manifest in select concordats with Third World states, especially those with weaker or non-existent canon law norms. "Acknowledging their adherence to the norms of international law…the Holy See and the Republic of Kazakhstan in accordance with the principles of respect and non-interference in internal affairs have agreed as follows" (*AAS* 92 [2000], 320 {preamble}). "The Organization of African Unity and the Holy See shall agree to…engage in regular consultations on matters of mutual interest such as education, health, human rights, and social affairs" (*AAS* 93 [2001], 15 {I}). The most decisive textual demonstrations of the ideals of soul force are however contained in the three remarkable concordats with the main parties to the Middle East conflict. The concordat with the

State of Israel (*AAS* 86 [1994], 716–29), alluding to but surmounting the catastrophic effect of concordatorial fascism upon the Jews, states, "The Holy See and the State of Israel are committed to appropriate cooperation in combatting all forms of anti-Semitism and all kinds of racism and religious intolerance, and in promoting mutual understanding among nations, tolerance among communities and respect for human life and dignity" ({2§1}). A nuncio is assigned to Israel ({14§2}), and the parties continue to "declare their respective commitment to the promotion of the peaceful resolution of conflicts among States and nations, excluding political violence and terror from international life" ({11§1}). Among the Arabs, meanwhile, the Apostolic See has concluded equally if not more idealistic concordats with both the Palestine Liberation Organization (*AAS* 92 [2000], 853–61) and with what is described as the State of Palestine (*AAS* 108 [2016], 168–85). Turning to that with the PLO, in its origin an Arab nationalist front with Marxian elements, the preamble calls for a "just and comprehensive peace" in the region that shall respect Palestinian national aspirations "on the basis of international law, relevant United Nations and its Security Council resolutions, justice and equity" (853–54). Joint desire is also expressed for the agreement of some kind of special instrument of government for Jerusalem that would place Jew, Christian, and Mohamedan equal before it, as well as protect holy sites and guarantee pilgrimage. With respect to the norms inspiring such terms, the PLO appears unambiguous in its "permanent commitment to uphold and observe the human right to freedom of religion and conscience, as stated in the Universal Declaration of Human Rights and in other international instruments" ({1.1}). Finally, the concordat with the State of Palestine confers Roman diplomatic recognition and approvingly notes ({1§2}) that the contracting parties are the only non-member observers of the United Nations. Most of the treaty terms consist of legal and technical clarifications of the competence of the Church and of its organs within Palestine, involving locations central of course to the life and ministry of Jesus; but such terms are grounded in the treaty's remarkable "Chapter II: Freedom of Religion and Conscience," which reads as a sustained program or manifesto of individual idealism incorporating Christian Democratic, non-violent universalist, and Kantian internationalist elements. The provisions of the Universal Declaration of Human Rights concerning freedom of and from religion are enthusiastically invoked ({4§1}), and Catholics in Palestine are guaranteed the rights to worship, to administer and to receive the sacraments, to maintain churches, and to educate and to marry according to religion ({4§3.5–9}). Further provisions include the right to refrain from oaths in violation of conscience, a guarantee of military chaplaincy in any prospective Palestinian army, and conscientious objection ({4§3.11–13}). Finally, a right of religious pilgrimage is introduced, whereby such devotional visitations, being "acts of religious worship, there shall be no interference by non-ecclesiastical authorities" ({17§3}). Unconditional love has therefore helped supply the deficiency of canon law with regard to the Holy Land, and in the concordats with Third World states more generally.

Pontifical Humanitarianism

These treaty outcomes belong to the ongoing transformation of the Roman pontiff into transnational activist and global humanitarian, whereby Christ's Vicar also fashions himself into People's Advocate. Perhaps the most pronounced single demonstration of this tendency is the *Laudato Si' De Communi domo colenda* (*AAS* 107 [2015], 847–945) of the current Pope Francis, a sustained treatise on the urgent necessity for global environmental action. Delivered on Pentecost—a day for which the most important pontifical pronouncements are often reserved—of the year 2015, Francis opens, "Faced as we are with global environmental deterioration, I wish to address every person living on this planet" ({3}).[104] What follows is a comprehensive examination of pressing ecological imperatives, ways of life, and philosophical mindsets held to be responsible, and moral solutions inspired by but not dependent upon Catholic theology and Franciscan practice. Amid moral indictments of cultures of waste and of pollution, ubiquitous failure to reduce carbon emission, and insensitivity to accelerating loss of biodiversity, Pope Francis consistently reveals himself as an aggrieved and passionate advocate of the poorest and most marginalized. "Access to safe drinking water is a basic and universal human right, since it is essential to human survival and, as such, is a condition for the exercise of other human rights" ({30}).[105] Climate change and other impending ecological disasters will most directly assail the already poor and wretched of the Third World, and consequently, the pontiff moves for the phasing out of fossil fuel consumption and the building of environmental governance at the global level, objectives obviously not rooted in the teaching *magisterium* of the Church, but in conformity with the call to love of her divine founder and head. Through public commitments such as those of *Laudato Si'*, the assumption of global idealism by the Bishop of Rome appears nearly complete.

* * *

The sections and subsections above furnish the only comprehensive analysis of all of the concordats of the Apostolic See. Between 1865 and 2020, inclusive, 167 treaties were concluded between the Apostolic See and a civil commonwealth, with their treaty norms ranging from ecclesiological to ideational based primarily on the respective dominance or inferiority of canon law within the contracting party. Six concordatorial case clusters have been presented as furnishing the full distribution of variation across the outcome or dependent variable of treaty norms: concordatorial fascism, 1906–1953 (15 observations), the German *Reich*, 1925–2019 (42 observations), Latin American counter-revolution, 1887–1994 (13 observations), European secularism, 1801–2020 (14 observations), the second Vatican reformation, 1968–2016 (30 observations), and the benediction of the Third World, 1993–2015 (9 observations). These case cluster results total 123 concordats within the grand total of 167 provided above.

What of the roughly one-quarter identified but not discussed? The most effective reply is that they do not necessarily deviate *from the theory*, but simply fail to clearly conform to a specific *case cluster*. Evenly distributed comparatively and longitudinally, the non-clustered concordats are a mix of defunct (Kingdom of Congo, 1906), tiny (Republic of San Marino, 1992), or simply isolated instances which usually result in a shorter treaty irrespective of larger canonical, comparative, or international trends. Bearing in mind that the consultation of so much official data is not easily replicable, it is appropriate at this juncture to insert authorial assurance and profession that nothing has been *withheld* which would bear directly upon the viability of the overall thesis.

An English Realist Synthesis

Having established the results of the research above, this final section shall provide useful theoretical reflection and contextualization. Do the norms of the numerous concordats of the Apostolic See appear to confirm any of the competing theories of international relations, and if so, in what ways and to what degree? Sufficient derivation of the outlines of international theory reveals concordatorial demonstration of the contentions of traditional English realism, wherein an anarchic but ordered international system of sovereign states perpetually destabilized by anxious self-help nevertheless contains, at its heart, a mustard seed of Christian redemptive love.

Realism in international affairs began to take shape in the political psychology of royal absolutism revealed through such works as the political testament of Cardinal Richelieu (1688), the *Nakaz* (1789) of Catherine the Great, or the *Politics Drawn from the Very Words of Holy Scripture* (*Politique tirée des propres paroles de l'Ecriture Sainte*, 1709) of Jacques-Benigne Bossuet for the consumption of the Dauphin; and it is today to be described as a mature and consolidated school, marked by "classical"[106] and "neoclassical"[107] varieties in addition to the *neorealism* or *structural realism* of the *Theory of International Politics* (1979) of Kenneth Waltz.[108] But from its origins in the advent, onset, and aftermath of the Second World War, realist international theory served primarily as a neo-Hobbesian *critique* of the perceived spiritual deficiencies of the liberal tradition that left the free world off guard against the totalitarian designs of the Axis, beginning with the interwar idealism that proved so tragically inaccurate. In an unsparing attack upon the *laissez-faire* optimism of his native United Kingdom, E.H. Carr concluded in 1939, "The breakdown of the 1930s was too overwhelming to be explained merely in terms of individual action or inaction. Its downfall involved the bankruptcy of the postulates on which it was based."[109] Following the war, George Kennan largely agreed with respect to his native United States, writing in 1951, "I see the most serious fault of our past policy formulation to lie in...the belief that it should be possible to suppress the chaotic and dangerous aspirations of governments in the international field by the acceptance of some system of legal rules and restraints."[110] Their ideas were systematically pursued in the magisterial *Politics Among Nations: The Struggle for Power and Peace* (1948) of Hans Morgenthau, and after the Cold War rarefied into the geographic determinism of John Mearsheimer's *Tragedy of Great Power Politics* (2001).

German and German-American realist authors dared to proceed even further, however, calling into question some of the most revered postulates of liberal thought. The extensive *oeuvre* of political theorist Carl Schmitt from the early years of the doomed Weimar Republic to the consolidation of the Federal Republic under American supervision may be understood as a lifelong confrontation with bourgeois, liberal parliamentarism, with one of his last writings concluding, "Our contemporary society…entails a value-free and scientific attitude, the commodification of all values and the augmentation of liberal human consumption."[111] Rev. Reinhold Niebuhr, at once anti-Communist but deeply alienated from the consumerist values he experienced in Detroit and observed throughout America as a whole, argued in *The Children of Light and the Children of Darkness* ([1944] 2015), "The conception of human nature which underlies the social and political attitudes of a liberal democratic culture is that of an essentially harmless individual," (366) although War and Holocaust were everywhere revealing the mortally dangerous inaccuracy of this conceit. There is finally the towering figure of Hannah Arendt, who in the soul-stirring conclusion to her *Origins of Totalitarianism* (1950) dwells upon the isolation, atomization, commodification, and above all depersonalization of the individual within the liberal society that plants the seed of its ultimate destruction, saying her peace in the following words: "What prepares men for totalitarian domination in the non-totalitarian world is the fact that loneliness…has become an everyday experience of the evergrowing masses of our century. The merciless process into which totalitarianism drives and organizes the masses looks like a suicidal escape from this reality" (478).

Such realist criticism and caution boldly contrast with the glowing hopes of the idealism responsible for much of international law and organization during the twentieth and twenty-first centuries. The collective security of William Penn's "Essay towards the Present and Future Peace of Europe" (1693)[112] and Immanuel Kant's more famous *Perpetual Peace* (*Zum ewigen Frieden*, 1795) became embodied—after the quieting of the Western Front—in the equally disastrous Weimar Constitution of 1919, the Covenant of the League of Nations of 1920, and the Kellogg-Briand Pact of 1928, and was perhaps also suggested by the ahistorical art and architecture of the period.[113] President Woodrow Wilson's six addresses to the United States Congress (22 January–15 April 1917) on the subject of war with Germany combined with his Fourteen Points after its defeat serve as the inaugural exposition for this liberal-idealist posture within international affairs. In his first speech (22 January), he asks the assembled legislature, "Is the present war a struggle for a just and secure peace or only for a new balance of power?"[114] After a further couple of months of U-boat attacks and other provocations, Wilson is prepared to answer (2 April) his own question. "Our object," he explains, "is to vindicate the principles of peace and justice in the life of the world as against selfish and autocratic power and to set up amongst the really free and self-governed peoples of the world such a concert of peace and of action as will henceforth insure the observance of those principles."[115] This must be done, he continues, because "the world must be made safe for democracy,"[116] and because "right is more precious than peace."[117]

Yet there has always been a humble conceptual territory between the realist contention as to the likelihood of war of all against all and the idealist assurances as to the prospects for perpetual peace, known today as English realism or the English School of international relations.[118] Professors Hedley Bull, Sir Herbert Butterfield, Martin Wight, and the other contributors to *Diplomatic Investigations* (1966) instinctively distrusted the excessive rationalism of Cold War American political science as well as the mutual irreligion of both the tendencies surveyed above. In accordance with their Christian beliefs or sympathies,[119] they sensed that Man, being corrupted by evil, had shown himself through history capable of all manner and degree of depravity, but also able to triumph over his egoistic proclivities through the power of redemptive love. This individual capacity for good or evil, in English realist philosophy, is replicated and enlarged in the life of nations, furnishing an organic and dynamic center between Hobbesian despair and death and Kantian sweetness and light. Its inaugural theorist was Hugo Grotius, and its modern rallying point is the work of Hedley Bull.

One of the greatest commentators on the forging of the religious peace of Europe, and the scion of its Reformed Church during the classical period of Dutch culture, Hugo De Groot (1583–1645) or Grotius is widely recognized as the founder of international law. His thesis and main ideas, however, were not at all secular by modern standards, but rather concerned with how Christian ethics and theology are to be correctly applied throughout the intensifying diplomatic, military, and economic interaction of the emerging system of sovereign states. The outline of this normative commitment is furnished in *The Truth of the Christian Religion* (1627), a shorter text intended for active seamen. "The Messiah was to be the Instructor of all Nations," Grotius explains, "that he should bring a vast Multitude of Strangers to the Worship of one God. Before the Coming of Jesus, almost the whole World was subject to false Worship, which began to vanish afterwards by Degrees, and…whole Nations and Kings were converted to the Worship of one God."[120] Grotius furthermore applies this designation of the Christian evangelical narrative as the transformative mighty working at the heart of international politics through two early works. His *Commentary on the Law of Prize and Booty* (1606?) was written at the request of the United Dutch East India Company to help justify the seizure of a Portuguese merchant ship near Singapore on account of the larger pattern of outlaw behavior by the Portuguese government,[121] while *The Free See* (1609) derives the positive absence of restrictions on navigation from the Judeo-Christian Golden Rule.[122]

Grotius furnishes a comprehensive exploration of this world-historical recreation of the relationship between Christian ethics and international realities in the monumental *Rights of War and Peace* (1625), the point of departure for all modern international theory and law. It rests on two main contentions. First, the moral system of the Sermon on the Mount, after the exhaustion of all other options, can and in some circumstances must accommodate political violence in defense of innocent life and certain justice. Were Jesus a *pacifist*, argues Grotius, then he would have said so explicitly; and in like manner Peter did not instruct the baptized Roman centurion Cornelius (Acts 10) to renounce the profession of arms, even in the service of imperialist power. "If CHRIST had intended to have abolished all capital Punishments, and the Right of (*making*) War," Grotius argues, "he would have done it in most plain and exact Terms, on Account of the great Importance and Novelty of the Thing."[123] Nevertheless, the regular coercion, occasional violence, and rare brutality necessary to preserve the vigor and well-being of a commonwealth must faithfully adhere to reasonable interpretations of the moral law, and in states of both peace and war. With regard to the former, all nations must respect the right of embassy (900), and ambassadors must be exempt from the laws of the receiving state (912). The right of burial of the dead (938), and the obligation to make restitution for injury sustained (1245) are also both inviolable. Concerning the latter, indecent assault (1301), the enslavement of prisoners (1372), the molestation of tombs and monuments to the dead (1470), the bombardment of undefended or defenseless places (1532), and perfidy (1626), among other potential war crimes, all contravene the moral duty of the individual Christian before God. The second main argument is submission to a lawfully constituted Christian state. "Civil Society being instituted for the Preservation of Peace," explains Grotius, "the State has a Power to prohibit the unlimited Use of that Right towards every other Person, to maintain publick Peace and good Order" (338). This Christian realist social contract like the materialist version of Hobbes and the theist version of Rousseau invalidates the private pursuit of justice (968), and derives from original consent (1108).[124]

Professor Hedley Bull revisits the outlines of this Grotian thought in *The Anarchical Society: A Study of Order in World Politics* ([1977] 2002), the modern thesis of the English School. Bull holds that between Hobbes and Kant meekly stands Grotius, and it is through the prism of Grotian *solidarism* that the international relations of the civilized world are most effectively understood. "Order," he opens, "is part of the historical record of international relations; and in particular…modern states have formed and continue to form, not only a system of states but also an international society" (22–23). *Interests*, *rules*, and *institutions* preserve this international order, of which two of the most important are the practice of diplomacy and the division of the Earth's surface into distinct sovereign states, both now almost universally accepted. Preservation of this global order—to which there are currently no plausible alternatives—must, when in conflict, take precedence over the pursuit of justice, given that justice requires order more than order requires justice. Order, summarizes Bull, "is the condition of the realisation of other values" (93).

The English realism surveyed above provides the most appropriate specifically international relations theoretical context for the concordatorial treaty norms identified and discussed throughout this chapter. The Apostolic See as an international actor fully institutionalizes and claims to oversee the Christian salvific narrative identified by Grotius as the heart of international relations, with its concordats serving as one of its primary evangelistic forces within particular nations. Although the treaty norms range from the comparatively ecclesiological to the comparatively ideational, few if any are found alongside either Hobbesian realism or Kantian idealism, but rather, through the prism of the Church militant, reflect what Bull characterizes as the solidarism of increasingly civilized global order nevertheless susceptible to violent reversal. The English School of International Relations, with its origins in the Christian tradition, therefore most closely aligns with how the Apostolic See through its concordats has consistently constructed world polity. Butterfield, though an immovable Methodist, concludes, "It would perhaps be regarded as legitimate to envisage the history of Europe as the story of a civilisation which developed under the presidency of the Church and which for many centuries bore an unmistakably Christian stamp. It would be necessary to be very cautious, however, in any attempt to make polemical use of this particular formulation of the narrative."[125]

Notes

1. Acknowledgement is once again in order of the considerable efforts of Anonymous, who out of secular humanist commitments have created "Concordat Watch," a website dedicated to identifying, understanding, and obstructing them. Although much of its data remains broken, incomplete, or erroneous, the presence of such a site indicates acute partisan interest in the subject matter.
2. And even if one remains suspicious of the truthfulness of the Apostolic See, further reflection upon the *grave and irreparable damage* to its international relations when or if the forgery of treaties were revealed can leave little to no serious doubt as to their authenticity.
3. *Cassell's Latin Dictionary*.
4. *Harper Collins German Concise Dictionary*.
5. This case cluster comprehends the following concordats, with those in bold primary: French Government (1801); Kingdom of Montenegro (1886); Government of Latvia (1922); Republic of Poland (1925); Government of Lithuania (1927); Kingdom of Romania (1927); Government of Czechoslovakia (1928?); **Lateran Pacts** (1929); **German Reich** (1933); Portuguese Republic (1940, 1950); Spanish State (1950, 1953); Swiss Federal Council (1978); Republic of Haiti (1984). The six case clusters are not necessarily completely discrete.
6. The term is adapted from the *clerical fascism* among especially Catholic religious implicated in the triumph of the dictators. See Matthew Feldman and Marius Turda, "'Clerical Fascism' in Interwar Europe: An Introduction," *Totalitarian Movements and Political Religions* 8, no. 2 (2007): 205–12.
7. Academic studies concerned primarily with conceptual delineation include Mabel Berezin, *Making the Fascist Self: The Political Culture of Interwar Italy* (Ithaca, NY: Cornell University Press, 1997); Michael Burleigh, *Sacred Causes: The Clash of Religion and Politics, from the Great War to the War on Terror* (New York: Harper Collins, 2007); Roger Eatwell, "Reflections on Fascism and Religion," *Totalitarian Movements and Political Religions* 4,

no. 3 (2003): 145–66; Emilio Gentile, *Contro Cesare: Religione e totalitarismo nell'epoca dei fascismo* (Milan: Feltrinelli, 2010), *Politics as Religion* (Princeton: Princeton University Press, 2006), "Political Religion: A Concept and its Critics, a Critical Survey," *Totalitarian Movements and Political Religions* 6, no. 1 (2005): 19–32, *The Sacralization of Politics in Fascist Italy* (Cambridge, MA: Harvard University Press, 1996), "Fascism as Political Religion," *Journal of Contemporary History* 25, no. 1 (1990): 229–51; A. James Gregor, *The Ideology of Fascism: The Rationale of Totalitarianism* (New York: Free Press, 1969); Roger Griffin, *Modernism and Fascism: The Sense of a Beginning under Mussolini and Hitler* (Cham, Switzerland: Palgrave Macmillan, 2007), *The Nature of Fascism* (New York and London: Routledge, 1993); G.L. Mosse, *The Fascist Revolution: Toward a General Theory of Fascism* (New York: H. Fertig, 1999); and David D. Roberts, "'Political Religion' and the Totalitarian Departures of Interwar Europe: On the Uses and Disadvantages of an Analytical Category," *Contemporary European History* 18, no. 4 (2009): 381–414.
8. Madeleine Albright, *Fascism: A Warning* (New York: Harper Collins, 2018); Mark Bray, *Antifa: The Anti-Fascism Handbook* (New York: Melville House, 2017); Federico Finchelstein, *From Fascism to Populism in History* (Oakland, CA: University of California Press, 2017); Jason Stanley, *How Fascism Works: The Politics of Us and Them* (New York: Random House, 2018).
9. "The Political Religions," in *The Collected Works of Eric Voegelin:* Vol. 5, *Modernity Without Restraint* (Columbia, MO: The University of Missouri Press, [*Die politischen Religionen*, 1938] 2000), 65.
10. In Benito Mussolini, *My Autobiography* (Mineola, NY: Dover, [1928] 2006), 236.
11. Although an acknowledged supporting actor in both the creation of the German concordat and the destruction of German democracy, relatively little appraisal exists in English. For an important recent contribution, see Martin Menke, "Ludwig Kaas and the End of the German Center Party," in Hermann Beck and Larry Eugene Jones (eds.), *From Weimar to Hitler: Studies in the Dissolution of the Weimar Republic and the Establishment of the Third*

> *Reich, 1932–1934* (New York and Oxford: Berghahn, 2019), 79–110.
12. "Der Konkordatstyp des faschistischen Italien," *Zeitschrift für ausländisches öffentliches Recht und Völkerrecht*, III. no. 1, (1933): 488–522.
13. Member of the Italian Royal Senate (1910–46) and author of *History as the Story of Liberty* (Indianapolis: Liberty Fund, [1941] 2000), he shall open the following chapter.
14. Ihre Beschränkung auf das rein religiöse Gebiet und das Verbot irgendwelcher in das Parteipolitische hineinragenden Betätigung liegt in gewissem Umfang zweifellos auch im wohlverstandenen kirchlichen Interesse.
15. Daß man hofft, die konkordatäre Begegnung zwischen dem Vatikan und dem > > totalitären Staat < < nicht als flüchtige Episode, sondern als lebensfähiges Dauerwerk in die Geschichte übergehen zu sehen.
16. The adjective is intended to exclude the Nazi puppet governments of occupied Europe, with which no concordat was contracted.
17. Also known as the CLAUSULA POLITICA. See Kaas (1933).
18. EGO IURO ET PROMITTO AD SANCTA DEI EVANGELIA, OBEDIENTIAM ET FIDELITATEM GUBERNIO PER CONSTITUTIONEM GALLICANAE REIPUBLICAE STATUTO. ITEM, PROMITTO ME NULLAM COMMUNICATIONEM HABITURUM, NULLI CONSILIO INTERFUTURUM, NULIAMQUE SUSPECTAM UNIONEM NEQUE INTRA, NEQUE EXTRA CONSERVATURUM, QUAE TRANQUILLITATI PUBLICAE NOCEAT; ET SI TAM IN DIOCESI MEA QUAM ALIBI, NOVERIM ALIQUID IN STATUS DAMNUM TRACTARI, GUBERNIO MANIFESTABO.
19. Davanti a Dio e sui Santi Vangeli, io giuro e proce metto, siccome si conviene ad un Vescovo, fedeltà allo Stato italiano. Io giuro e prometto di rispettare e di far rispettare dal mio clero il Re ed il Governo stabilito secondo le leggi costituzionali dello Stato. Io giuro e prometto inoltre che non parteciperò ad alci cun accord nè assisterò ad alcun consiglio che possa recar danno allo Stato italiano ed all'ordine pubblico e che non permetterò al mio clero simili partecipaci zioni. Preoccupandomi del bene e dell'interesse dello Stato italiano, cercherò di evitare ogni danno che possa minacciarlo.

20. These clauses open with the comprehensive assurance, L'insegnamento della religione cattolica nelle scuole elementary, professionali, medie) e superiori è material ordinaria d'insegnamento e sarà impartito in conformità con i principii della Chiesa Cattolica/ Der katholische Religionsunterricht in den Volksschulen, Berufschulen, Mittelschulen und höheren Lehranstalten ist ordentliches Lehrfach und wird in Übereinstimmung mit Grundsätzen der katholischen Kirche erteilt (AAS 25 [1933], 401 {21}).
21. Una preghiera per la prosperità del Reich e del popolo germanico/Ein Gebet für das Wohlergehen des Deutschen Reiches und Volkes eingelegt.
22. Davanti a Die e sui Santi Vangeli, giuro e prometto, come si conviene ad un Vescovo, fedeltà al Reich Germanico e allo Stato. Giuro e prometto di rispettare e di far rispettare dal mio clero il Governo stabilito secondo le leggi costituzionali dello Stato. Preoccupandomi, com'è mio dovere, del bene e dell'interesse dello Stato Germanico, cercherò, nell'esercizio del sacro ministero affidatomi, di impedire ogni danno che possa minacciarlo/Vor Gott und auf die heiligen Evangelien schwöre und verspreche ich, so wie es einem Bischof gezeimt, dem Deutschen Reich und dem Lande...Treue. Ich schwöre und verspreche, die verfassungsmässig gebildete Regierung zu achten und von meinem Klerus achten zu lassen. In der pflichtmässigen Sorge um das Wohl und das Interesse des deutschen Staatswesens werde ich in Ausübung des mir übertragenen geistlichen Amtes jeden Schaden zu verhüten trachten, der es bedrohen könnte.
23. Pius had also enthusiastically but secretly commissioned an American Jesuit, Father John La Farge, to draw up an explicitly anti-racist encyclical, but the pontiff passed away just as it was nearly ready for publication. See Frank J. Coppa, "Pope Pius XI's 'Encyclical" *Humani Generis Unitas* Against Racism and Anti-Semitism and the 'Silence' of Pope Pius XII," *Journal of Church and State* 40 (1998): 775–95.
24. A probing exploration of the acrimonious relations between the Italian fascist government and the Apostolic See equipped with its new Vatican City-state is contained in John F. Pollard, *The Vatican and Italian Fascism, 1929–1932* (Cambridge: Cambridge University Press, 1985).

25. See especially Richard Drake, "Julius Evola, Radical Fascism, and the Lateran Accords," *The Catholic Historical Review* 74, no. 3 (1988): 403–19.
26. Esprimendo tutti la penosa sorpresa di vedere perseguitata e colpita l'Azione Cattolica là, al Centro dell'Apostolato Gerarchico.
27. Una vera e propria statolatria pagana non meno in pieno contrasto coi diritti naturali della famiglia che coi diritti soprannaturali della Chiesa.
28. La concezione dello Stato che gli fa appartenere le giovani generazioni interamente e senza eccezione dalla prima età Ano alFetà adulta, non è conciliabile per un cattolico colla dottrina cattolica, e neanche è conciliabile col diritto naturale della famiglia.
29. Gleiches Blut gehört in ein gemeinsames Reich.
30. Gottfried Feder, *Das Programm der N.S.D.A.P. und seine weltanschaulichen Grundgedanken* (Munich: Central Publishing House of the Nazi Party, 1935).
31. Minister, Nazi Party Office of Foreign Affairs (*Außenpolitisches Amt der NSDAP*), 1933–1943; *Reich*-Minister for the Occupied Territories (*Reichsminister für die besetzten Ostgebiete*), 1941–1945. Sentenced to death by hanging by the International Military Tribunal for Germany (1 October 1946). Biographical accounts include Reinhard Bollmust, *Das Amt Rosenberg und seine Gegner: Studien zum Machtkampf im nationalsozialistischen Heurschaftssystem* (Stuttgart: Oldenbourg, 1970); Robert Cecil, *The Myth of the Master Race: Alfred Rosenberg and Nazi Ideology* (London: Batsford, 1972); Ernst Piper, *Alfred Rosenberg: Hitlers Chefideologie* (Munich: Karl Blessing, 2005); and Robert K. Wittman and David Kinney, *The Devil's Diary: Alfred Rosenberg and the Stolen Secrets of the Third Reich* (New York and London: HarperCollins, 2017).
32. Theoretical discussion should also at least identify however the *New Nobility of Blood and Soil* (Antelope Hill, [*Neuadel aus Blut und Boden*, 1930], 2021) of Nazi food and agriculture minister Richard Walter Darré. Although seconding Rosenberg's harsh criticism of the influence of Christian ecclesiastical polity in or rather over Germany, the eco-fascist *Obergruppenführer* is more interested in the reformulation of patrician than of pagan

values, calling for a House-of-Lords-style instrument of government to cultivate an agriculturally inclined, genetically refined neo-nobility.
33. Dall'atra parte si sia eretto a norma ordinaria lo svisare arbitrariamente i patti, l'eluderli, lo svuotarli e finalmente il violarli più o meno apertamente.
34. Se la razza o il popolo, se lo Stato o una sua determinate forma...-divinizzandoli con culto idolatrico, perverte e falsifica l'ordine, da Dio creato e imposto.
35. This case cluster comprehends the following concordats, with those in bold primary: **State of Bavaria** (1925), **Prussian Free States** (1929), **Baden Free State** (1932), **German *Reich*** (1933), Lands of North Rhine-Westphalia (1956, 1984), Lower Saxon Land (**1965**, 1973, 1989), Bavarian Free State (1966, 1968, 1970, 1974, 1978, 1988), Saarland (1968, 1969, 1975, 1985), Rhineland-Palatinate (1969, 1973), Lands of Saxony-Anhalt, Brandenburg, and the Saxon Free State (1994), Land of Brandenburg and the Saxon Free State (1994), Thuringian Free State (1994), Free and Hanseatic State of Hamburg, Land of Mecklenburg-West Pomerania, and Land of Schleswig–Holstein (1994), **Saxon Free State** (1996), **Thuringian Free State** (1997), Land of Mecklenburg-West Pomerania (1997), **Land of Saxony-Anhalt** (1998), Saarland (2001), Thuringian Free State (2002), Free Hanseatic State of Bremen (2003), Land of Brandenburg (2003), Free and Hanseatic State of Hamburg (2005, 2010), Bavarian Free State (2007), Land of Schleswig–Holstein (2009), Lower Saxon Land (1993, 2010, 2012), Land of Mecklenburg-West Pomerania (2015, 2019). Within this section, only the German shall be reproduced.
36. For a recent summation of the *Sonderweg* debate, see Jürgen Kocka, "Looking Back on the *Sonderweg*," *Central European History* 51, no. 1 (2018): 137–42.
37. Der Bayerische Staat gewährleistet die freie und öffentliche Ausübung der katholischen Religion (*AAS* 17 [1925], 42 {1.1}).
38. Der Freiheit des Bekenntnisses und der Ausübung der katholischen Religion wird der Preussische Staat den gesetzlichen Schutz gewähren (*AAS* 21 [1929], 42{1}).

39. Der gesetzliche Schutz der Sonntage, der staatlich anerkannten kirchlichen Feiertage und der kirchlichen Feiertage wird gewährleistet (*AAS* 96 [2004], 453 {2}).
40. Die kirchlichen Friedhöfe genießen den gleichen staatlichen Schutz wie die Kommunalfriedhöfe. Die Kirchengemeinden haben das Recht, neue Friedhöfe anzulegen (*AAS* 90 [1998], 483 {16}).
41. Die Kirche und das Land tragen gemeinsam Verantwortung für Schutz und Erhalt der kirchlichen Denkmale (*AAS* 90 [1998], 107 {17.1}).
42. Das Land wird bei den Rundfunkanstalten, an denen es beteiligt ist, darauf bedacht bleiben, daß die Satzungen Bestimmungen enthalten, nach denen das Programm das religiöse Empfinden der katholischen Bevölkerung nicht verletzt, der katholischen Kirche angemessene Sendezeiten eingeräumt werden und ihr eine angemessene Vertretung ihrer Interessen an den Fragen des Programms ermöglicht wird (*AAS* 57 [1965], 842 {10}).
43. Der Freistaat gewährleistet die Erteilung eines regelmäßigen katholischen Religionsunterrichts als ordentliches Lehrfach an der öffentlichen Schulen. Gegenstand des katholischen Religionsunterrichts ist die Vermittlung der katholischen Glaubens- und Sittenlehre (*AAS* 89 [1997], 615–16 {1–2}).
44. Das Recht der katholischen Kirche in Bayern auf einen angemessenen Einfluß bei der Erziehung der Schüler ihres Bekenntnisses wird unbeschadet des Erziehungsrechtes der Eltern gewährleistet (*AAS* 61 [1969], 166 {6.1}).
45. Der katholische Religionsunterricht ist in den öffentlichen Schulen ordentliches Lehrfach (*AAS* 89 [1997], 765 {12.1}).
46. Professoren und Hochschuldozenten (Hochschullehrer) für katholische Theologie und katholische Religionspädagogik werden erst berufen oder eingestellt, wenn sich das zuständige Staatsministerium bei dem zuständigen Diözesanbischof vergewissert hat, daß im Hinblick auf Lehre und Lebenswandel keine Bedenken bestehen (*AAS* 89 [1997], 617 {5.2}).
47. Lands of Saxony-Anhalt, Brandenburg, and the Saxon Free State (1994) (*AAS* 87 [1995], 129–37), Land of Brandenburg and the Saxon Free State (1994) (*AAS* 87 [1995], 138–45), and Free and Hanseatic State of Hamburg, Land of Mecklenburg-West

Pomerania, and Land of Schleswig- Holstein (1994) (*AAS* 87 [1995], 154–64).
48. Orden und religiöse Kongregationen können den kanonischen Bestimmungen gemäss frei gegründet werden (*AAS* 17 [1925], 42 {2}).
49. SOLIS UNIVERSITATIBUS ET FACULTATIBUS A SANCTA SEDE CANONICE ERECTIS VEL APPROBA TIS, A TQUE AD NORMAM HUIUS CONSTITUTIONIS ORDINA TIS, IUS EST CONFERENDI GRADUS ACADEMICOS, QUI VALOREM CANONICEM HABEANT. Article 34 of the supplementary norms of application (29 April 1979) furthermore explains that such canonical degrees shall henceforth be conferred in the name of the His Holiness.
50. Sɪɴɢᴜʟᴀᴇ UNIVERSITATES VEL FACULTATES PROPRIA STAUTA RECOGNITA SECUNDUM HANC CONSTITUTIONEM EXHIBERE DEBENT SACRAE CONGREGATIONI PRO INSTITUTIONE CATHOLICA ANTE DIEM I MENSIS IANUARII ANNO MCMLXXXI; SECUS IUS GRADUS ACADEMICOS CONFERENDI IPSO FACTO IIS SUSPENDITUR.
51. Its most important provisions include, "Treaties of the predecessor State cease to be in force in respect of the territory to which the succession of States relates" (15.a), and "A newly independent State is not bound to maintain in force, or to become a party to, any treaty by reason only of the fact that at the date of the succession of States the treaty was in force in respect of the territory to which the succession of States relates" (16).
52. Das Konkordat zwischen dem Heiligen Stuhl und dem Deutschen Reich vom 20. Juli 1933, der Vertrag des Freistaates Preußen mit dem Heiligen Stuhl vom 14 Juni 1929…bleiben unberührt (*AAS* 101 [2009], 555 {23}).
53. Unter Berücksichtigung des in Geltung stehenden Konkordats zwischen dem Heiligen Stuhl und dem Deutschen Reich vom 20. Juli 1933, soweit es das Land Brandenburg bindet, und in Würdigung des Vertrages des Freistaates Preußen mit dem Heiligen Stuhl vom 14. Juni 1929 schließen folgenden Vertrag (*AAS* 96 [2004], 626 {preamble}).
54. Excised from the *Reich* by the Versailles Treaty (100–08).

55. Allied Control Authority Germany, Enactments and Approved Papers, vol. VI (Office of Military Government for Germany (U.S.), 1 January 1947–31 March 1947), 28.
56. Bundesverfassungsgericht (1957), 'Urteil vom 26. März 1957. Reichskonkordat vom 20. Juli 1933. Niedersächsisches Gesetz über das öffentliche Schulwesen vom 14. September 1954', *Entscheidungen des Bundesverfassungsgerichts* (Tübingen, 1957).
57. In approved translation, "Subject to all rights and objections of interested parties, treaties concluded by the German *Reich* concerning matters within the legislative competence of the *Länder* under this Basic Law shall remain in force, provided they are and continue to be valid under general principles of law, until new treaties are concluded by the authorities competent under this Basic Law, or until they are in some other way terminated pursuant to their provisions.".
58. Das Reichskonkordat...hat durch den Zusammenbruch der nationalsozialistischen Gewaltherrschaft seine Geltung nicht verloren. Vertragspartner war das Deutsche Reich. Daher kann das Argument, das Konkordat gelte nur für die Dauer des nationalsozialistischen Systems, nicht überzeugen.
59. This case cluster comprehends the following concordats, with those in bold primary: Republic of Colombia (1887), **The Dominican Republic** (1954), Republic of Bolivia (1958, **1961**), Government of Paraguay (1961), **Republic of Venezuela** (1964), Government of El Salvador (1968), **Republic of Colombia** (1975), Republic of Ecuador (1978), Republic of Peru (1980), Republic of Bolivia (1986), Federal Republic of Brazil (1989), Republic of Venezuela (1994). Within this section, only the Spanish or Portuguese shall be reproduced.
60. The forty-third entry of which consists of the insistence that a contracting party to a concordat does not possess unilateral right of abrogation.
61. See especially John T. Graham, *Donoso Cortés: Utopian Romanticist and Political Realist* (Columbia: University of Missouri Press, 1974); R.A. Herrera, *Donoso Cortés: Cassandra of the Age* (Grand Rapids, MI: Eerdmans, 1995); John J. Kennedy, "Donoso Cortés as Servant of the State," *The Review of Politics* 14, no. 4 (1952): 520–55; Carl Schmitt, *Political Theology: Four Chapters on the Concept of Sovereignty* (Chicago: The University of Chicago Press,

[*Politische Theologie: Vier Kapitel zur Lehre von der Souveranität*, 1922] 2005); and Alberto Spektorowski, "Maistre, Donoso Cortés, and the Legacy of Catholic Authoritarianism," *Journal of the History of Ideas* 63, no. 2 (2002): 283–302.
62. Don Juan Manuel Orti y Lara, *Obras de Don Juan Donoso Cortés* (Madrid: Sociedad Editorial de San Francisco de Sales, 1893).
63. *Ibid.*, vol. I.
64. *La Iglesia representa la naturaleza humana sin pecado, tal como salió de las manos de Dios, llena de justicia original y de gracia santificante*, 40.
65. *La sumisión á la voluntad divina es el bien sumo*, 160.
66. *La Religión Católica, Apostólica, Romana sigue siendo la de la Nación Dominicana y gozará de los derechos y de las prerrogativas que le corresponden en conformidad con la Ley Divina y el Derecho Canónico.*
67. *El Estado Venezolano continuará asegurando y garantizando el libre y pleno ejercicio del Poder Espiritual de la Iglesia Católica.*
68. *La Legislación canònica es independiente de la civil y no forma parte de ésta.*
69. *El Estado garantiza el derecho de libre organización y funcionamiento de las asociaciones católicas con fin religioso, social y caritativo, y en particular de las asociaciones de Acción Católica.*
70. *El Estado Venezolano, de conformidad con la Constitución, reconoce el derecho de organización de los ciudadanos católicos para promover la difusión y actuación de los principios de la fe y moral católicas mediante las asociaciones de Acción Católica.*
71. *Propugnar la revolución social quiere decir abolir el presente estado de cosas e intentar reemplazarlo por otro cualitativamente distinto…intentar poner fin al sometimiento de unos países a otros, de unas clases sociales a otras, de unos hombres a otros*, 78.
72. *La salvación comprende a todos los hombres y a todo el hombre…la lucha por una sociedad justa se inscribe plenamente y por derecho propio en la historia salvífica*, 226.
73. This case cluster comprehends the following concordats, with those in bold primary: **French Government** (1801, 2008), Republic of Austria (1933, **1960**, **1962**, 1964, 1968, 1969, 1971, 1976, 1981, 1989, 1995, 2009, 2020).
74. See Philip S. Gorski, "Historicizing the Secularization Debate: Church, State, and Society in Late Medieval and Early Modern

Europe, ca. 1300 to 1700," *American Sociological Review* 65, no. 1 (2000): 138–67.

75. During Kelsen's lifetime, student Rudolf Aladár Métall published *Hans Kelsen, Leben und Werk* (Vienna: Verlag Franz Deuticke, 1969). See also Nicoletta Bersier Ladavac, "Hans Kelsen (1881–1973) Biographical Note and Bibliography," *European Journal of International Law* 9 (1998): 391–400.

76. Religio Catholica Apostolica Romana libere in Gallia Exercebitur. Cultus publicus erit, habita tamen ratione ordinationum quoad politiam, quas Gubernium pro publica tranquillitate necessarias existimabit.

77. Ego iuro et promitto ad Sancta Dei Evangelia, obedientiam et fidelitatem Gubernio per Constitutionem Gallicanae Reipublicae Statuto. Item, promitto me nullam communicationem habiturum, nulli consilio interfuturum, nuliamque suspectam unionem neque intra, neque extra conservaturum, quae tranquillitati publicae noceat; et si tam in diocesi mea quam alibi, noverim aliquid in Status damnum tractari, Gubernio manifestabo.

78. The events described unfolded under the French Third Republic (1870–1940), the constitution of which was comparable to the current Fifth (1958-) in its Chamber of Deputies and Senate, and Prime Minister and President. Prime Minister Émile Combes (1902–1905) of the Left-bloc was determined to defeat the Catholic Church in France, and his government was therefore central to the attacks upon it. The 1905 law in question, among other provisions, ended state financial support to religion, expropriated Church buildings and grounds—though still allowing the Church to use them—and prohibited religious symbols in public.

79. *Remplisse son devoir qui est de nommer des candidats dignes, et respecte le droit et le devoir du Saint Siège qui sont d'examiner les titres des candidats proposés et de ne point admetre ceux qui manqueraient des qualités requises pour l'épiscopat*, 12–13.

80. Their terms included state approval of all papal communications (1) and Catholic leadership assemblies (4), state suppression of all ecclesiastical establishments apart from cathedral chapters and seminaries (11), the absence of celebration other than the Sabbath without state authorization (41), and the confinement of

all Catholic services to their consecrated buildings and grounds (45).
81. *Les adversaires de l'Église usent d'un sophisme trop évident. Ils identifient arbitrairement la République avec leurs doctrines et leurs lois antichrétiennes, et si l'Église ne les accepte pas, ils l'accusent d'opposition systématique à la République, et en prennent prétexte pour de nouvelles violences*, 71.
82. *Oui oserait dire que le Gouvernement est compétent pour décider de l'orthodoxie de la foi, de la doctrine théologique et canonique, du zèle, d'intégrité des mœrs et de la piété, telles qu'elles sont requises dans un évêque?*, 87.
83. They range from 23 March 1900 to 30 July 1904.
84. The outcome of multilateral negotiations between the U.S.S.R., the United States, Great Britain, and France, the treaty mainly de-Nazifies and disarms Austria, as well as allows the Soviet Union to expropriate much of its oil.
85. Die Katholische Kirche anerkennt, dass die Republik Österreich über die in diesem Vertrag zugesagten Leistungen hinaus auf den darin behandelten Gebieten keine weiterenfinanziellen Verpflichtungen zu erfüllen hat (940 {VIII.1}).
86. There were also two agreements during the postwar interval establishing the diocese of Innsbrück-Feldkirch (*AAS* 56 [1963], 740–43) and then modifying it to the diocese of Feldkirch (*AAS* 60 [1968], 782–85), respectively.
87. *Le nationalisme identitaire d'extrême droite et le référent islamique…sont uniment porteurs, comme le PCF jadis, d'une forte charge utopique qui réenchante une réalité sociale sinistrée en la projetant dans un mythe où les laissés-pour-compte d'aujourd'hui seront les triomphateurs de demain*, 18.
88. This case cluster comprehends the following concordats, with those in bold primary: Argentine Republic (1968), Principality of Monaco (1981), Republic of Haiti (1984), **Republic of Italy** (1984), Republic of Malta (1991, 1993, 1995), State of Israel (1993), Republic of Croatia (**1996**, 1998), Republic of Poland (1993), **Republic of Lithuania** (2000), Slovak Republic (2000), Gabonese Republic (2001), Republic of Slovenia (2001), **Bosnia and Herzegovina** (2006), Republic of the Philippines (2007), Federative Republic of Brazil (2008), Republic of Mozambique (2011), **Republic of Equatorial Guinea** (2013), Republic of

Burundi (2013), Republic of Cape Verde (2013), Republic of Chad (2013), Central African Republic (2016), Democratic Republic of Congo (2016), Government of the Italian Republic (2016), Republic of Benin (2016), Republic of Congo (2017), Republic of San Marino (2018), Burkina Faso (2019).

89. They are, in combined order of proclamation or promulgation, as follows: [1] CONSTITUTIO DE SACRA LITURGIA {*Sacrosanctum Concilium*} 4 Dec. 1963; [2] DECRETRUM DE INSTRUMENTIS COMMUNICATIONIS SOCIALIS {*Inter Mirifica*} 4 Dec. 1963; [3] CONSTITUTIO DOGMATICA DE ECCLESIA {*Lumen Gentium*} 21 Nov. 1964; [4] DECRETUM DE OECUMENISMO {*Unitatis Redintegratio*} 21 Nov. 1964; [5] DECRETUM DE ECCLESIIS ORIENTALIBUS CATHOLICIS {*Orientalium Ecclesiarum*} 21 Nov. 1964; [6] DECRETUM DE PASTORALI EPISCOPORUM MUNERE IN ECCLESIA {*Christus Dominus*} 28 Oct. 1965; [7] DECRETUM DE ACCOMADATA RENOVATIONE VITAE RELIGIOSAE {*Perfectae Caritatis*} 28 Oct. 1965; [8] DECRETUM DE INSTITUTIONE SACERTOTALI {*Optatam Totius*} 28 Oct. 1965; [9] DECLARATIO DE EDUCATIONE CHRISTIANA {*Gravissimum Educationis*} 28 Oct. 1965; [10] DECLARATIO DE ECCLESIAE HABITUDINE AD RELIGIONES NON-CHRISTIANAS {*Nostra Aetate*} 28 Oct. 1965; [11] CONSTITUTIO DOGMATICA DE DIVINA REVELATIONE {*Dei Verbum*} 18 Nov. 1965; [12] DECRETUM DE APOSTOLATU LAICORUM {*Apostolicam Actuositatem*} 18 Nov. 1965; [13] DECLARATIO DE LIBERTATE RELIGOSA {*Dignitatis Humanae*} 7 Dec. 1965; [14] DECRETUM DE ACTIVITATE MISSIONALI ECCLESIA {*Ad Gentes*} 7 Dec. 1965; [15] DECRETUM DE PRESBYTERORUM MINISTERIO ET VITA {*Presbyterorum Ordinis*} 7 Dec. 1965; [16] CONSTITUTIO PASTORALIS DE ECCLESIA IN MUNDO HUIUS TEMPORIS {*Gaudium et Spes*} 7 Dec. 1965.

90. PERSONAM HUMANAM IUS HABERE AD LIBERTATEM RELIGIOSAM ({2}).

91. PRAESERTIM LIBERTAS RELIGIOSA IN SOCIETATE PLENE EST CUM LIBERTATE ACTUS FIDEI CHRISTIANAE CONGRUA ({9}).

92. QUAECUMQUE INSUPER IPSI VITAE ADVERSANTUR, UT CUIUSVIS GENERIS HOMICIDIA, GENOCIDIA, ABORTUS, EUTHANASIA ET IPSUM VOLUNTARIUM SUICIDUM; QUAECUMQUE HUMANAE PERSONAE INTEGRITATEM VIOLANT, UT MUTUATIONES, TORMENTA CORPORI MENTIVE INFLICTA, CONATUS IPSOS

ANIMOS COERCENDI; QUAECUMQUE HUMANAM DIGNITATEM OFFENDUNT, UT INFRAHUMANAE VIVENDI CONDICIONES, ARBITRARIAE INCARCERATIONES, DEPORTATIONES, SERVITUS, PROSTITUTIO, MERCATUS MULIERAM ET IUVENUM, CONDICIONES QUOQUE LABORIS IGNOMINIOSAE…PROBRA QUIDEM SUNT ({27}).

93. EO PRINCIPALITER SPECTAT UT BAPTIZATI DUM IN COGNITIONEM MYSTERII SALUTIS GRADATIM INTRODUCUNTUR, ACCEPTI FIDEI DONI IN DIES MAGIS CONSCII FIANT; DEUM PATREM IN SPIRITU ET VERITATE ADORARE ({2}).
94. QUARE HAEC S. SYNODUS IUS ECCLESIAE SCHOLAS CUIUS ORDINIS ET GRADUS LIBERE CONDENDI ATQUE REGENDI, IN PLURIMIS MAGISTERII DOCUMENTIS IAM DECLARATUM, DENUO PROLAMAT ({8}).
95. *La Santa Sede reafirmando los principios del Concilio Ecuménico Vaticano II y el Estado Argentino inspirado en el principio de la libertad reiteradamente consagrado por the la Constitución Nacional* ({preamble}).
96. See "*Création du diocèse de Monaco*," Comité National des Traditions Monégasques, September, 2017.
97. *Convaincus de l'opportunité d'apporter des modifications aux norms établies par ladite Bulle pour les conformer aux orientations données par le Concile Œcuménique Vatican II.*
98. Facendo riferimento, la Repubblica di Croazia alle norme della Costituzione, in particolare agli articoli 40 e 41 sulla libertà religiosa e la libertà di coscienza, e la Sante Sede ai documenti del Concilio Vaticano Secondo, e alle norme del Diritto Canonico / *Temeij eòi se Republika Hrvatska na odredbama Ustava, posebno na clancima 40. I 4L o vjerskoj slobodi i o slobodi savjesti, a Sveta Stolica na dokumentima Drugoga vatikanskog sabora i na odredbama kanonskoga prava.*
99. The subsequent concordat with Montenegro (*AAS* 104 [2012], 587–98) is similar in these and other respects.
100. *Votre frère…n'est investi…que d'une minuscule et quasi symolique souveraineté temporelle, le minimum nécessaire pour être libre d'exercer sa mission spirituelle et assurer ceux qui traitent avec lui qu'il est indépendant de toute souveraineté de ce monde,* 877.
101. *Quelle que soit votre opinion sur le Pontife de Rome…Nous sommes porteur d'un message pour toute l'humanité,* 878.

102. *Vous sanctionnez le grand principe que les rapports entre les peuples doivent être réglés par la raison, par la justice, le droit, et la négociation, et non par la force, ni par la violence, ni par la guerre, non plus que par le peur et par la tromperie,* 879.
103. This final case cluster comprehends the following concordats, with those in bold primary: **State of Israel** (1993), Republic of Kazakhstan (1998), **Palestine Liberation Organization** (2000), Organization of African Unity (2000), Ministry of Education of the Republic of China (2011), Republic of the Cameroon (2014), Ministry of Foreign Affairs of the State of Kuwait (2015), Government of the United Arab Emirates (2016), **State of Palestine** (2015).
104. Nunc Coram Universali Vastatione Orbis Terrarum, Singulis Personis Terram Incolentibus Dirigere Nos Volumus.
105. Potabilis Tutaeque Aquae Facultas Adhibendae Essentiale, Praecipuum Universaleque Est Hominum Ius, Quia Efficit Ut Personae Vivant, Atque Hanc Ob Rem Aliis Humanis Iuribus Fruantur.
106. See especially Michael C. Williams, "Why Ideas Matter in International Relations: Hans Morgenthau, Classical Realism, and the Moral Construction of Power Politics," *International Organization* 58, no. 4 (2004): 633–65; and Kenneth Thompson, *Political Realism and the Crisis of World Politics* (Princeton: Princeton University Press, 1960).
107. Gideon Rose, "Neoclassical Realism and Theories of Foreign Policy," *World Politics* 51, no. 1 (1998): 144–72.
108. An in parts strange exercise of Cartesian rationalism, Waltz asserts in a thesis passage, "We do not ask whether states are revolutionary or legitimate, authoritarian or democratic, ideological or pragmatic. We abstract from every attribute of states except their capabilities…What emerges is a positional picture, a general description of the ordered overall arrangement of a society written in terms of the placement of units rather than in terms of their qualities" (99). The contention appears tautological: great powers exude great power, and weak states demonstrate weakness. For further engagement, see David A. Baldwin, *Neorealism and Neoliberalism: The Contemporary Debate* (New York: Columbia University Press, 1993); Barry Buzan, *The Logic of Anarchy:*

Neorealism to Structural Realism (New York: Columbia University Press, 1993); Robert O. Keohane (ed.), *Neorealism and its Critics* (New York: Columbia University Press, 1986).
109. *The Twenty Years' Crisis, 1919–1939: An Introduction to the Study of International Relations* (New York: Harper & Row, [1939] 1964), 40.
110. *American Diplomacy* (Chicago: The University of Chicago Press, [1951] 2012), 102.
111. *Political Theology II* (Cambridge: Polity, [*Politische Theologie*, 1970] 2008), 54.
112. In Edwin B. Bronner (ed.), *The Peace of Europe, The Fruits of Solitude, and other Writings* (Rutland, VT: Everyman's Library, [1693] 1993): 5–22.
113. See for example the historically self-conscious discourses of Frank Lloyd Wright in *The Future of Architecture* (New York: Mentor Books, 1953).
114. *Why We are at War* (New York and London: Harper, 1917), 8.
115. *Ibid.*, 50.
116. *Ibid.*, 55.
117. *Ibid.*, 58.
118. For systematic introductions, see Tim Dunne, *Inventing International Society: A History of the English School* (Basingstoke, Hampshire: Palgrave Macmillan, 1998); and Andrew Linklater and Hidemi Suganami, *The English School of International Relations: A Contemporary Assessment* (Cambridge: Cambridge University Press, 2006).
119. See especially Herbert Butterfield, *Christianity and History* (New York: Scribner's, 1950), *Christianity in European History* (London: Collins, 1952), *Christianity, Diplomacy, and War* (London: Epworth, 1953), and *International Conflict in the Twentieth Century: A Christian View* (London: Routledge & Kegan Paul, 1960). For further engagement, see Ian Hall, "History, Christianity and Diplomacy: Sir Herbert Butterfield and International Relations," *Review of International Studies* 28, no. 4 (2002): 719–36; and Scott M. Thomas, "Faith, History, and Martin Wight: The Role of Religion in the Historical Sociology of the English School of International Relations," *International Affairs* 77, no. 4 (2001): 905–29.

120. (Indianapolis: Liberty Fund, [DE VERITATE RELIGIONIS CHRISTIANAE, 1627] 2012), 216.
121. (Indianapolis: Liberty Fund, [DE JURE PRAEDAE COMMENTARIUS, 1606?] 2006).
122. (Indianapolis: Liberty Fund, [MARE LIBERUM, 1609] 2004). His thesis passage is the following: "By law natural and divine it is commanded that thou do not that to another which thou would desire not have done to thee. Whereupon, seeing navigation can be hurtful to none but to him that saileth, it is meet that none either ought or can be barred" (45).
123. (Indianapolis: Liberty Fund, [DE IURE BELLI AC PACIS, 1625] 2005), 209.
124. The contributions of the three main eighteenth-century successors to Grotius occasionally surface in this context, and ought therefore to be acknowledged. Proceeding in order of increasing length and complexity, Jean-Jacques Burlamaqui's *Principles of Natural and Politic Law* (Indianapolis: Liberty Fund, [*Principes du droit naturel*, 1747] 2006) pursues the thesis that supreme law is begotten only of supreme being, while the *Law of Nations* (Indianapolis: Liberty Fund, [*Droit de gens*, 1758] 2008) of Emer de Vattel primarily endeavors to apply Christian natural law to the increasingly frequent, sustained, and complicated interactions among independent commonwealths. Christian Wolff's *Law of Nations Treated According to the Scientific Method* (Indianapolis: Liberty Fund, [JUS GENTIUM METHODO SCIENTIFICA PERTRACTATUM, 1749] 2017), meanwhile, comprehends much the same conceptual terrain; but the overall tendency indicative of Leibniz is more functional, with greater emphasis upon the instruments as opposed to merely the norms, and upon the obligations as opposed to merely the rights of international relations.
125. "The Christian and Historical Study," C.T. McIntire (ed.), *Writings on Christianity & History* (Oxford: Oxford University Press, 1979), 165.

CHAPTER 4

Concordatorial Fascism, 1906–53

In *History as the Story of Liberty* (*La storia come pensiero e come azione*, 1938), Italian Senator and philosopher Benedetto Croce boldly revisited the question, largely dormant since Westphalia, as to whether the Catholic Church ought to be regarded as an enemy of human freedom. "The Catholic religion," he charges, "has offered and offers the most grandiose and best assembled model for the mechanizations which other oppressive regimes attempt…from its art of weakening minds and making them docile towards itself and incapable of thought and of rebellion."[1] Although the fairness and impartiality of his accusation is open to question, the norms of the concordats with the reactionary rulers of Europe during the first half of the twentieth century, in the subsequent assessment of some learned commentators, appear to provide at least circumstantial evidence for its remote possibility.

(Im)pious Contracting Parties

Whereas the advanced study of international relations concentrates on the systemic pressures and constraints acting on sovereign states, the establishment of the intentions of the individual parties to a treaty characteristically belongs to the sub-discipline of diplomatic history; and separate inquiry might be made into the origination of any of the 167 concordats of the Apostolic See, or any of the 15 concordats of the current cluster. But in order to provide at least a partial comparative foundation, the following discussion shall survey the commitments, as available, of the respective pontiffs, pontifical legates, contracting plenipotentiaries, and heads of state or government as provided in Table 4.1 with regard to concordatorial, ecclesiastical, or religious policy more generally.

Beginning with the concerned pontiffs, the doctrine and practice of the Bishops of Rome is most consistently and vigorously expressed through encyclicals, public domain letters to bishops. Just as Peter, Paul, and some of the other apostles authored epistles of instruction, exhortation, consolation, and occasional reproof to the original Christian congregations, so the Holy Father composes encyclicals to bishops on vital questions confronting the Church militant here in earth. Intended for interested lay consumption also, encyclical communications thus locate what might be profanely described as Catholic policy formulation amid ever-evolving conditions and challenges.

Pope Leo XIII (1878–1903)[2] contracted the concordat with the Kingdom of Montenegro (*ASS* 19 [1886–1887], 219–23), and he authored a formidable 86 encyclicals. Eleven[3] faithfully, perhaps fanatically advance the rosary as the instrument through which the faithful obtain access to "the great Virgin Mary, the Mother of God, the guardian of our peace and the minister to us of heavenly grace, who is placed on the highest summit of power and glory in heaven;"[4] while three others assail Freemasonry as an international apostate conspiracy.[5] His encyclicals also consistently demonstrate suggestive *personification* of civil commonwealths as entities within the universal Church, with Italy providentially appointed to house the Chair of St. Peter ({*Etsi Nos*} *ASS* 14 [1881], 337–48), Hungary commissioned to wage a defensive war against the encroaching Mohamedans ({*Quod Multum*} *ASS* 19 [1886–1887], 97–106; {*Constanti Hungarorum*} *ASS* 26 [1893–1894], 129–36), and Scotland for some reason to be honored as "Special Daughter of the Holy See" (SANCTAE SEDIS SPECIALIS FILIA {*Caritatis Studium*} *ASS* 31 [1898–1899], 8).

The central tendency of Leo's many encyclicals however lies in the unfolding of a counter-revolutionary political theology intransigently opposed to a wide assortment of modern ideas, developments, and practices. *In Ipso* (1891) identifies a "combat ardently waged against the Church far and wide, although carried on in different ways for different places...to infiltrate every vein, as it were, of domestic and civil society

Table 4.1 Concordatorial fascism

Pontiff	CONTRACTING PARTY	Head of State or Government
(Pontifical Legate, Title)	(Contracting Location, Date, Language(s))	(Contracting Plenipotentiary, Title)
Pius VII	**FRENCH GOVERNMENT** (15 July 1801 [invoked 1906], Latin)	Napoleon Bonaparte
Leo XIII	**KINGDOM OF MONTENEGRO**	Nikola I
(Ludovico Iacobini, Cardinal Secretary of State)	(Rome, 18 Aug. 1886, Italian/Latin)	(Giovanni Sundécic, Secretary Particulaire)
Pius XI	**GOVERNMENT OF LATVIA**	Jānis Ćakiste
(Pietro Gasparri, Cardinal Secretary of State)	(The Vatican, 30 May 1922, French)	(Zigfiids A. Meierovics, Foreign Minister)
Pius XI	**REPUBLIC OF POLAND**	Stanisław Wojciechowski
(Pietro Gasparri, Cardinal Secretary of State)	(Warsaw, 2 June 1925, French)	(Amb. Ladislas Skrzynski and MP Stanislas Grabski)
Pius XI	**KINGDOM OF ROMANIA**	Ferdinand I
(Pietro Gasparri, Cardinal Secretary of State)	(The Vatican, 10 May 1927, French)	(V. Goldis, Minister for Religion and the Arts)
Pius XI	**GOVERNMENT OF LITHUANIA**	Antanas Smetona
(Pietro Gasparri, Cardinal Secretary of State)	(The Vatican, 27 Sep. 1927, French)	(Augustinas Voldemaras, Foreign Minister)
Pius XI	**GOVERNMENT OF CZECHOSLOVAKIA** (1928?, French)	Tomáš Garrigue Masaryk
Pius XI	**ITALY**	Victor Emanuel
(Pietro Gasparri, Cardinal Secretary of State)	(Rome, 11 Feb. 1929 [treaty portion], Italian)	(Benito Mussolini, Prime Minister)
Pius XI	**GERMAN *REICH***	Adolf Hitler
(Eugenio Pacelli, Cardinal Secretary of State)	(Vatican City-state, 20 July 1933, Italian/German)	(Franz von Papen, Vice Chancellor)
Pius XII	**PORTUGUESE REPUBLIC**	António Salazar

(continued)

Table 4.1 (continued)

Pontiff	CONTRACTING PARTY	Head of State or Government
(Luigi Maglione, Cardinal Secretary of State)	(Vatican City-state, 7 May 1940, Italian/Portuguese)	(Ministers Eduardo Augusto Marques andMario de Figueiredo, and Amb. Vasco Francisco Caetano de Quevedo)
Pius XII	**PORTUGUESE REPUBLIC**	António Salazar
(Domenico Tardini, Sec. of the S. Congregation for Extraordinary Ecclesiastical Affairs)	(Vatican City-state, 18 July 1950, Italian/Portuguese)	(Pedro Tovar de Lemos, Ambassador Extraordinaire)
Pius XII	**SPANISH STATE**	Francisco Franco
(Domenico Tardini, Sec. of the S. Congregation for Extraordinary Ecclesiastical Affairs)	(Vatican City-state, 5 Aug. 1950, Spanish)	(Joaquín Ruiz-Gimenez, Ambassador)
Pius XII	**SPAIN**	Francisco Franco
(Domenico Tardini, Sec. of the S. Congregation for Extraordinary Ecclesiastical Affairs)	(Vatican City-state, 27 Aug. 1953, Italian/Spanish)	(Minister Alberto Martin Artajo and Amb. Fernando Maria Castiella y Maiz)
Paul VI	**SWISS FEDERAL COUNCIL**	Swiss Federal Council
(Ambrogio Marchioni, Archbishop Nuncio)	(Berne, 2 May 1978, French)	(Amb. Emanuel Diez andCounsellor Alfred Wyser)
John Paul II	**REPUBLIC OF HAITI**	Jean-Claude Duvalier
(Achille Silvestrini, Archbishop)	(Port-au-Prince, 8 Aug. 1984, French)	(Jean-Robert Estimé, Minister of Foreign Affairs and Religion)

with the most dangerous poison of their errors,"[6] while *Tametsi Futura Prospicientibus* (1900) protests, "The world has heard enough of the so-called 'rights of Man.' Let it hear something of the rights of God."[7] His main application of this standpoint to social policy is however the famous *Rerum Novarum* (1891), an impressive reply to Marxist assertions of irremediable economic injustice mainly on the grounds that although the grievances of the international proletariat are indeed legitimate, the cure of communism-through-violence is worse than the disease of inequality-through-property.

A sacramental conservative political theory, meanwhile, opens with *Diuturnum* (1881), which declares, "The divine power of the Christian religion has given birth to excellent principles of stability and order for the State, while at the same time it has penetrated into the customs and institutions of States."[8] *Immortale Dei* (*ASS* 18 [1885], 161–80) continues with a reiteration of Augustinian natural law whereby the divinely appointed civil and ecclesiastical powers independently but in fraternal coordination carry out their respective functions, while *Libertas* (*ASS* 20 [1887], 593–613) insists that the freedom and autonomy of the individual proclaimed by Western secularism will careen out of control if not continually subjected to the Christian moral law and the pontifical teaching authority. *Sapientiae Christianae* (1890), finally, provides perhaps the most rigorous de-limitation of the competence of liberalization, stating, "If the laws of the State are manifestly at variance with the divine law, containing enactments hurtful to the Church, or conveying injunctions adverse to the duties imposed by religion, or if they violate in the person of the supreme Pontiff the authority of Jesus Christ, then, truly, to resist becomes a duty, to obey, a crime."[9] His encyclicals likewise identify numerous comparative applications.[10]

Pope Pius XI (1922–1939)[11] contracted the concordats with the Government of Latvia (*AAS* 14 [1922], 577–81), the Republic of Poland (*AAS* 17 [1925], 273–88), the Kingdom of Romania (*AAS* 21 [1929], 441–56), the Government of Lithuania (*AAS* 19 [1927], 425–34), the Government of Czechoslovakia (*AAS* 20 [1928], 65–66), Italy (*AAS* 21 [1929], 209–97), and the German *Reich* (*AAS* 25 [1933], 389–416); and he authored thirty-three encyclicals, the first of which provides a Christian response to the secular humanism of the Covenant of the League of Nations wherein, "The principal cause of the confusion, restlessness, and dangers which are so prominent a characteristic of false peace is the weakening of the binding force of law and lack of respect for authority, effects which logically follow upon denial of the truth that authority comes from God, the Creator and Universal Law-giver."[12] Amid a characteristic fusion of Thomist theology ({*Studiorum Ducem*} *AAS* 15 [1923], 309–26), Franciscan practice ({*Rite Expiatis*} *AAS* 18 [1926], 153–75), and Marian devotion by means of the rosary ({*Miserentissimus Redemptor*} *AAS* 20 [1928], 165–78; {*Ingravescentibus Malis*} *AAS* 29 [1937], 373–80) a general ecclesiological conservatism emerges across a wide front. The consecrated, celibate priesthood is reaffirmed on historical, theological, and spiritual grounds ({*Ad Catholici Sacerdotii*}

AAS 28 [1936], 6–23), while the blessings of marriage are clarified as the procreation of children, conjugal honor, and sacramental participation ({*Casti Connubi*} *AAS* 22 [1930], 539–92). Otherwise, encyclical intervention with regard to education, social welfare, and Communism appears especially robust.

Control of public education has always and everywhere been central to secularizing politics. Pius counters in *Divini Illius Magistri* (1929), "Education consists essentially in preparing man for what he must be and for what he must do here below, in order to attain the sublime end for which he was created."[13] So-called "co-education"—wherein boys and girls physically intermingle, above all in revealing outfits in the gymnasium—is morally dangerous, as are syllabi uninspected by ecclesiastical ordinaries and uninformed by the Christian moral law. *Quadragesimo Anno* (1931) meanwhile builds on *Rerum Novarum* to further articulate a distinctly Catholic approach to the social question relying on neither liberalism nor socialism. "There remain virtually only individuals and the State," the pontiff laments. "The so-called labor market…which is plunging all human society to destruction must be remedied as soon as possible."[14] Conceptual remedy includes recognition of how the wealth of the bourgeoisie and the privation of the proletariat are and have always been unacceptable on Christian grounds, while policy adjustment should concentrate on the demand for living wages and the enhancement of syndical vitality. Consequently, the grinding poverty and unemployment of the Great Depression are tragic but originated in a Biblically prohibited love of money ({*Nova Impendet*} *AAS* 23 [1931], 392–97; {*Caritate Christi Compulsi*} *AAS* 24 [1932], 177–94). Lastly, the astute response to Leninism of the perhaps insufficiently appreciated *Divini Redemptoris* (1937) argues that much of the transnational appeal of Marxist revolution derives from an alluring but perilous false messianic promise combined with the relentless exploitation, through effective propaganda, of the admitted abuse of workers. The contempt for divine word and commandment inherent in liberal order and the deeply misguided pursuit of justice through "socialism" are both pontifically acknowledged. Nevertheless, "Communism is intrinsically wrong, and no one who would save Christian civilization may collaborate with it in any undertaking whatsoever."[15] As an alternative, the faithful should direct their attention to the fortification and utilization of Catholic Action as a "social apostolate."[16]

His decisive contracting plenipotentiary, meanwhile, was Pietro Gasparri (1852–1934), whose crucial role in the compilation of the Code of Canon Law of 1917 was discussed in the second chapter. Also Archbishop Nuncio to Peru, Bolivia, and Ecuador, member of the Congregation for Extraordinary Ecclesiastical Affairs, and Cardinal Secretary of State, Gasparri adhered as jurist and advanced as diplomat a comprehensive conservatism, publishing several treatises on the sacraments[17] that prefigure the principles of the code and serving as contracting plenipotentiary for all of the concordats of Pius XI except that with the German *Reich*. With regard specifically to the indispensable concordat with Italy, Lupano remarks, "Every single deed and document in the laborious build-up to the Lateran Accords bore Gasparri's name."[18]

Pope Pius XII (1939–1958),[19] finally, contracted the concordats with the Portuguese Republic (*AAS* 32 [1940], 217–47; 42 [1950], 811–15) and with Spain (*AAS* 43 [1951], 80–86; 45 [1953], 625–56); and he authored forty-one encyclicals. A staunch advocate for the preservation of the cult of the saints[20] and of the immaculately conceived and cosmically glorified Virgin Mary,[21] two overarching ecclesiological notions otherwise emerge from his encyclical *oeuvre*. First, Pius stresses the *catholicity* of the Church. *Summi Pontificatus* (1939), his first encyclical, affirms upon the outbreak of war in Europe, "The human race is bound together by reciprocal ties, moral and juridical, into a great commonwealth directed to the good of all nations and ruled by special laws which protect its unity and promote its prosperity."[22] When those unspecified laws are violated by unspecified nations, Pius argues that the most wholesome remedy lies in the intercessory prayers of the Church throughout the world,[23] though he makes peculiar postwar mention of the rights of the Ruthenian Church in her communion with the Apostolic See,[24] the plight of Catholic Hungary amid the Soviet invasion of 1956,[25] and the peculiar challenges of missionaries to pre-industrial or pre-literate regions.[26] In response to the formation of the State of Israel in 1948, Pius XII also advanced the intersecting propositions of an international status for Jerusalem and immunity under international law for religious sites throughout the Holy Land.[27]

The *corporality* of the Church serves as the other unifying theme of that pontiff's encyclicals. "The Mystical Body of Christ is the Church," he clarified in *Mystici Corporis Christi* (1943),[28] one week before the Germans would open the largest tank battle in history near Kursk, Russia. Although the substance of the Eucharistic bread and wine is verily transubstantiated into Christ's literal Body and Blood, the divine head, hands, feet, side, mind, heart, arteries, tendons, ligaments, and muscles also incorporate the faithful into the risen, ascended, and glorified divine body. The physical heart of Christ, furthermore, being "hypostatically" (HYPOSTATICE) joined to the holy word, is rendered worthy of worship,[29] especially through a complete physical consecration wherein, "Holy virginity surpasses marriage in excellence."[30] The applications of this expansive Eucharistic theology appear primarily ecclesiological. *Mediator Dei* (1947) concerns the sacred liturgy pronounced completely subject to pontifical discretion in conformity with canon law. "We exhort you, Venerable Brethren, that each in his diocese or ecclesiastical jurisdiction supervise and regulate the manner and method in which the people take part in the liturgy, according to the rubrics of the missal and in keeping with the injunctions which the Sacred Congregation of Rites and the Code of canon law have published."[31] The formalistic approach to *Sacred Music* (*AAS* 48 [1956], 5–25) is similar, while the developing mediums of radio, film, and television are regarded as at once presenting evangelistic opportunities and moral dilemmas for the souls of Catholics ({*Miranda Prorsus*} *AAS* 49 [1957], 765–805).

The fascist rulers of Catholic Europe, for their part, reinforced through concordatorial diplomacy this relative confinement of the Church to ecclesiological norms. Among the civil contracting plenipotentiaries of the case cluster, two predominate. In his pre-war *Autobiography*,[32] Italian Prime Minister Benito Mussolini furnishes several mainstream remarks to the effect that church and state ought to preserve legal separation but cordial relations. German Vice-Chancellor Franz von Papen—an aristocratic conservative subsequently acquitted of all charges at Nuremberg—meanwhile states in his *Memoirs* that he sought through the *Reich* concordat "to establish a legal basis for the rights of the Christian Churches in Germany."[33] Initially pleased with the result and optimistic about the future of his Catholic religion in his rejuvenated Fatherland, Von Papen, no longer in Hitler's cabinet, continues, "During the years that followed, the gradual whittling away of the Concordat's provisions was to dash all my hopes."[34]

Among the authoritarian heads of state or government, General Franciso Franco ruled Spain with an iron first until 1975 on the basis of seven fundamental laws,[35] two of which concern ecclesiastical polity. *The Charter of the Spaniards* (*Fuero de los Españoles*, 1945) establishes Roman Catholicism as the state religion, and the *Law of Principles of the National Movement* (*Ley de Principios del Movimiento Nacional*, 1958) elaborates, "The holy Catholic, Apostolic, Roman Church, the one true faith inseparable from the national conscience, shall inspire its legislation."[36] Total internal repression in Spain and in adjacent Portugal under Dr. Salazar meanwhile liquidated the ideological opponents or enemies of the Catholic faith both despots publicly professed. The most sustained theological reflections are however reserved for an extremist head of state who next to absolute power, total domination, and world conquest, loved perhaps most the sound of his own voice.

The destruction of German democracy was as *rapid* as it was *complete*, a point perhaps insufficiently emphasized. *Reichspräsident* Hindenburg appointed Hitler *Reichskanzler* on 30 January 1933; and it is by no means out of the ordinary for a tottering parliamentary government to seek stability through the inclusion of marginal figures. But less than a month later (28 February), what came to be known as the "*Reichstag* Fire Decree"[37] virtually suspended civil liberties; and then on the twenty-third of March passage of a "Law to Rectify the Distress of the Folk and *Reich*" (*Gesetz zur Behebung der Not von Volk und Reich*), among other provisions, endowed the President and the Chancellor with the authority to make treaties in the absence of parliamentary consultation. The concordat of the following July was thus contracted under this legalized dictatorship. On 1 August 1934, Hitler abolished the office of *Reichspräsident*, the elderly and ailing Hindenburg passed away the next day, and from that time until the end of the war, Hitler's constitutional position was usually described as *Führer*, *Reich* Chancellor, and Supreme Commander of the *Wehrmacht*. Despite his omnipotence, Hitler never formally repealed the 1919 constitution, in which there was no German state church, but in which Catholic or Lutheran confessional establishments received recognition as public law corporations (137), Sabbath rest and religious holidays were guaranteed (139), and religious instruction was systematically provided in the schools (149).

The formative beliefs of the tyrant are contained in *Mein Kampf* (1936), which though turgid, weird, and altogether loathsome, satisfactorily demonstrates Hitler's conceptual binary as neither bourgeois versus proletariat, Catholic versus Protestant, nor even as Christian versus atheist, but rather as *Aryan versus Jew*, with his political theology absorbed in the imagined eternal racial conflict. Hitler asserts, "Human culture and civilization on this continent are inseparably bound up with the presence of the Aryan. If he dies out or declines, the dark veils of an age without culture will again descend on this globe."[38] The Nazis of course postured themselves as the sole resolute defenders of family, morals, and patriotism against the premature burial of godless Communism, but with regard to Roman Catholic ecclesiological reaction more specifically, the temporarily incarcerated future *Führer* states the following:

> In raising the Ultramontane question...the Jew reached his desired goal: Catholics and Protestants wage a merry war with one another, and the mortal enemy of Aryan humanity and all Christendom laughs up his sleeve...The significance of this [miscegenation] for the future of the earth does not lie in whether the Protestants defeat the Catholics or the Catholics the Protestants, but in whether the Aryan man is preserved for the earth or dies out.[39]

To coöpt the institutional Church, and to somewhat appropriate its *mythos* while of course preserving total National Socialist control would therefore to all appearances have been Hitler's primary objectives for a confessionally divided greater *Reich*.

Ecclesiological Treaty Norms

The resulting concordats of the period consistently demonstrate strict adherence to ecclesiological norms on the basis of dominant canon law traditions within historically Catholic countries. Beginning with a representative sample in chronological order, the concordat with the Government of Latvia (1922), the first with the Apostolic See, states, "The members of the Chapter, the Curates, and in general all the religious are nominated by the Archbishop of Riga according to the norms of canon law."[40] The same canon law is subsequently cited as the legal basis for the immunity of the buildings and grounds of churches, chapels, and cemeteries.[41] The concordat with the Republic of Poland three years later employs similar language, explaining, "The State guarantees to the Church the free exercise of its spiritual power and its ecclesiastical jurisdiction...in conformity to divine laws and canon law."[42] The Lithuanian concordat of 1927 likewise declares, "In all the public schools...religious teaching is obligatory...in conformity with canon law,"[43] while the far-reaching language of the second (1953) concordat with Spain under Phallangist rule translates as the following: "The Catholic, Apostolic, Roman religion shall continue being the only such of the Spanish nation and shall enjoy the rights and privileges pertaining thereto in conformity with Divine Law and canon law."[44] Within this overall framework of ecclesiological norms, two instruments predominate.

The first is an oath of episcopal loyalty, whereby Catholic bishops upon investiture in their dioceses must swear and promise allegiance to the contracting civil regime, notwithstanding its obvious or even professed authoritarianism. The canon law of the period defined an *oath* as "the invocation of the divine Name, in witness of the truth" (INVOCATIO NOMINIS DIVINI IN TESTEM VERITATIS, CIC/1917, c. 1316§1); and two previous permutations had materialized. King James I of England (1603–1625 [James VI of Scotland, 1567]), for his part, is generally remembered sympathetically for his relatively skillful management of the explosive theological politics whereby Catholicism threatened the realm from without and Puritanism from within. Nevertheless, David Hume as historian concludes regarding the King, "In his own person...he thought all legal power to be centered, by an hereditary and a divine right;"[45] and he imposed a verbose oath of allegiance on the bishops in 1606.[46] Two years later, James himself composed and published *Triplici Nodo, Triplex Cuneus. Or an Apologie for the Oath of Allegiance*, wherein he clarifies his royal intent. "The OATH was framed to be taken by my Subjects," he explains, "whereby they should make a cleare profession of their resolution, faithfully to persist in their obedience vnto mee...[and] many of my Subjects that were Popishly affected, aswell Priests, as Layicks, did freely take the same Oath."[47] The second as it were prototype appeared in the French Civil Constitution of the Clergy (1790), where the crucial language was "to be faithful to the nation, the law, and the king" (*d'être fidèle à la nation, à la loi, et au roi*, XXI). Its main unintended consequence, in the informed opinion of Madame de Staël, consisted in "putting political in the place of religious intolerance."[48]

The first oath of episcopal loyalty within the authoritarian concordatorial cluster appears in the 1801 treaty with Napoleon (*ASS* 37 [1904–1905], 77 {VI}), which introduces the words *swear* and *promise*, as well as the notion that bishops are bound to counsel their clergy to offer comparable obedience to the new regime, although no enforcement mechanism is specified.[49] The wording of the corresponding oath of the Archbishop of Antivari of Montenegro is nearly identical (*ASS* 19 [1886–1887], 220 {IV}), and that of the Czechoslovak religious similar (*AAS* 20 [1928], 66 {V}). The Latvian concordat slightly adjusts the verbiage, providing the oath as, "I swear before God and upon the Holy Gospels, as becomes a bishop, to respect and to make my clergy respect the Government established by the Constitution of the Republic of Latvia and to attempt nothing of such a nature as would compromise the public order" (*AAS* 14 [1922], 573 {V}),[50] terms repeated in the subsequent Polish (*AAS* 17 [1925], 277 {XII}) and Romanian (*ASS* 21 [1929], 444 {VI}) concordats.

The concordat with the Government of Lithuania builds on the preceding, but it noticeably expands the language and intensifies the commitments. Lithuanian bishops per the concordat of their commonwealth were compelled to pronounce the following:

> Before God and on the Holy Gospels, I swear and promise, as becomes a Bishop, fidelity to the Republic of Lithuania. I swear and promise to respect in all loyalty and to make my clergy respect the Government established by the Constitution. I furthermore swear and promise that I shall not participate in any combination, nor assist in any council that could portend danger to the Lithuanian state or to the public order. I shall not permit my clergy to participate in such actions. Solicitous of the wellbeing and interests of the State, I shall endeavor to avoid all danger to it of which I am familiar (*AAS* 19 [1927], 428 {XII}).[51]

These Lithuanian terms are not only inherently interesting but assume much greater historical importance upon the recognition that the subsequent oaths of episcopal loyalty provided in both the Lateran Pacts (*AAS* 21 [1929], 283 {20}) and the *Reich* concordat (*AAS* 25 [1933], 399 {16}) very closely correspond, a textual connection to be revisited at the conclusion of the chapter. The final examples of the imposition of an oath of episcopal loyalty via concordat appear in the Swiss (*AAS* 70 [1978], 468 {4}) and Haitian (*AAS* 78 [1984] 954 {5}) instances, both in the French language.

Second, the agreement to incorporate special public prayers for the contracting party appears in seven of the given concordats. Napoleon was content with, "*Domine, salvam fac Rempublicam / Domine, salvos fac Cónsules*" (*ASS* 37 [1904–1905], 77 {VIII}), and Nikola of Montenegro with, "*Domine salvam fac Principem*" (*ASS* 19 [1886–1887], 222 {XI}). The Republic of Poland meanwhile became first to agree to the inclusion of a common prayer for the prosperity of the republic and its president (*AAS* 17 [1925], 275 {VIII}), with Romania (*AAS* 21 [1929], 444 {VI}), Lithuania (*AAS* 19 [1927], 427 {VIII}), and Italy (*AAS* 21

[1929], 280 {12}) following suit. The precise wording of that of the *Reich* concordat—which furnishes the last historic example—is, "a prayer for the prosperity of the German Folk and *Reich*."[52]

Neither of these instruments is prolix, and amid the larger civil institutionalization of anti-Semitism, militarism, and totalitarianism might easily be overlooked by historians. But such extraordinary adjustments were always significant, and perhaps sometimes decisive in Catholic nations with dominant canon law traditions. By concerning themselves exclusively with the consolidation of ecclesiological norms, the concordats of this cluster offered little to no explicit resistance to the reactionary authoritarianism of their contracting parties, contributing to the divisive historiographical contention identified and discussed below.

Weeping and Gnashing of Teeth: The "Pius Wars"

"I was the accuser, God the accused," recalls Holocaust survivor Elie Wiesel in *Night* (1960). "My eyes were open and I was alone—terribly alone in a world without God and without man. Without love or mercy" (65). "It was as though in those last minutes he was summing up the lesson that this long course in human wickedness had taught us," continues Holocaust refugee Hannah Arendt in *Eichmann in Jerusalem* ([1963] 2006). "The lesson of the fearsome, word-and-thought-defying *banality of evil*" (252). "National Socialism was able to identify in a truly totalitarian fashion the aspirations of the individual German with the power objectives of the German nation," concludes Hans Morgenthau in *Politics Among Nations* ([1948] 1985). "Nowhere in modern history has that identification been more complete" (124).

The course of the Second World War in Europe from which these plaintive recollections are drawn is beyond the scope of this inquiry. Although primarily a gargantuan confrontation between the German and Russian armies, most of the western Eurasian landmass experienced—in the terminology subsequently employed at Nuremberg—conspiracy to wage wars of aggression, crimes against peace, war crimes, and crimes against humanity. The Catholic Church obviously having no guns and the pontiff no divisions, the question of the extent to which interwar concordatorial diplomacy may have inadvertently facilitated the consolidation of Axis power and influence has resulted in the most fraught and contentious scholarly debate of modern ecclesiastical history, which whatever its outcome has enveloped the concordat as an instrument of canon, comparative, and international law.

Beginning with the critical perspectives, some have questioned the conduct of the Catholic Church as a whole amid the rise and fall of European fascism. The most comprehensive indictment is Daniel Goldhagen's *A Moral Reckoning: The Role of the Catholic Church in the Holocaust and Its Unfulfilled Duty of Repair* (2003), which holds concerning the Church, "During the Nazi period, its pope and clergy did not just remain silent but, across a continent, had been actively and broadly complicit in the worst of crimes...Today the Church has enormous, unfulfilled moral duties of repair" (297). Ecclesiological collaboration with mass murder, in Goldhagen's aggrieved interpretation, is not however to come as a surprise, given that anti-Semitism provides the foundation for the Christian faith itself. "Christianity is a religion that consecrated at its core and, historically, spread throughout its domain a megatherian hatred of one group of people: the Jews" (3). Less fatalistic is the verdict of Michael Phayer in *The Catholic Church and the Holocaust, 1930–1965* (2000), which holds that although Pius XII could not have prevented the implementation of the Final Solution, he could and should have more clearly, consistently, and effectively communicated with religious across Europe about the mortal danger to Jewish lives and the obligations of Christians to assist them where and when possible.

The conduct of the Catholic Church in Germany has also repeatedly been subjected to critical analysis. In *German Catholics and Hitler's Wars* (1962), Gordon Zahn seeks to demonstrate the disquieting regularity with which Catholic priests exhorted departing soldiers to risk all for Folk and Fatherland. Guenter Lewy then expanded upon such a line of argument two years later in *The Catholic Church and Nazi Germany*, which argues, "In the failure to recognize the totalitarian goals of Hitler's state, which was regarded by the Church, as by many other Germans, as just another anti-Communist authoritarian regime that had its good as well as its bad sides, lay the basic error and tragedy of the leadership of German Catholicism in 1933" (54). Strongly conditioned against Marxist-Leninist norms in part by the encyclical *oeuvre* surveyed above, and shortly thereafter bound by the ecclesiological terms of the *Reich* concordat, the religious of the German Church as a whole were maneuvered into a place of reluctant subordination to the Nazis. But Kevin Spicer adds more recently in *Hitler's Priests: Catholic Clergy and National*

Socialism (2008) that 138 "brown priests"—after the primary color of the SA uniform—actively supported Hitler, especially during the earlier years focused on rearmament and economic recovery.

The peculiar rôle of the Apostolic See amid the authoritarian transformation of European order has likewise occasioned critical examination. Anthony Rhodes opens this particular conversation with *The Vatican in the Age of the Dictators, 1922–1945* (1973), which concludes, "There is no doubt…that mistakes were made by the Vatican in the 'Age of the Dictators'. Pius XI's belief that a series of concordats with the Dictators would promote the Church's apostolic activity more effectively than would Catholic political parties appears to have been, on the whole, mistaken" (355). Central to such apostolic activity is the sheer preservation of moral authority, which in the opinion of John F. Morley in *Vatican Diplomacy and the Jews during the Holocaust, 1939–1943* (1980) is compromised by the recognition that the nuncios and the Secretariat of State did not as he sees it remotely approach the limits of their potential effectiveness with regard to the relief of the persecuted Jews. This alleged passivity on the part of the Apostolic See retired to or trapped within the Vatican City-state appears all the more remarkable when applied not merely to a distant, turbulent front such as Ukraine or Poland, but also to happy Italy and to the Eternal City of Rome itself. Investigating specifically the conduct of the Apostolic See during the SS roundup of Roman Jews after the collapse of Mussolini's regime (October, 1943), Susan Zucotti in *Under His Very Windows: The Vatican and the Holocaust in Italy* (2002) attempts to locate the non-resistance of the curia primarily at the intersection of "the anti-Jewish bias of those concerned, their actual preference for the separation of Jews from Christians, their intense personal conservatism and lack of imagination, their narrow focus on their own Catholic constituency, and their fear of antagonizing the Fascists and Germans if discovered in acts of even the slightest opposition" (323).[53]

Still, other historians have singled out for criticism the conduct of individual popes. In *The Pope and Mussolini: The Secret History of Pius XI and the Rise of Fascism in Europe* (2014), David I. Kertzer concentrates on a tacit bargain whereby the organs of the Apostolic See would abstain from criticism of Italian anti-Semitic laws in exchange for continuity of operations among youth leagues and other organs of Catholic Action. Consequently, "the Vatican played a central role both in making the Fascist regime possible and in keeping it in power" (405).[54] Hubert Wolf more broadly explains in *Pope and Devil: The Vatican's Archives and the Third Reich* (2010) that the 2006 declassification of all secret archival material of the pontificate of Pius XI comprehends hundreds of thousands if not *millions* of individual documents, and therefore sweeping foregone conclusions ought to be discouraged on strictly evidentiary grounds. His own examination nevertheless induces him to conclude, "The 'representative of Christ on earth' and his colleagues believed themselves to be in a battle against the increasingly dangerous forces of modernity, anti-clerical liberalism, Communism, and National Socialism. They viewed the situation in Germany through Roman spectacles" (310).

The accusations greatly intensify, however, with respect to the conduct of Pius XII amid the World War and its included Holocaust. Otherwise undistinguished playwright Rolf Hochhuth may be credited with their ignition in his *Deputy* (*Der Stellvertreter*, 1963), in turn eventually brought to the screen in the *Amen* (2002) of Resistance filmmaker Costa-Gavras. In the drama, real-life SS 1LT Kurt Gerstein[55] is among the first to secretly witness the gas chambers in operation, his technical expertise having significantly contributed to their construction. Unable to get the attention of the neutral Swedish government and seemingly alone with this terrible forbidden knowledge, he befriends fictional liberationist priest Riccardo, and the pair contrive a completely unsuccessful plan to enlist the Apostolic See in their cause. Numerous investigators have subsequently regarded Hochhuth's depiction as no mere spiteful caricature, but rather as a considered opinion informed by historical fact. The initial assessment of Saul Friedländer in *Pius XII and the Third Reich* (1966) discovered Pacelli as a man to be deeply enamored of Germany—though not of Nazism—and as pontiff hopeful that a moderated version would provide the necessary shield for Western Christianity against the Bolshevism that loomed from the East. He was in particular, according to Carlo Falconi's *The Silence of Pius XII* (1970) fully informed as to the demonic behavior of the Ustaše, the Catholic Croat fascist front that drew a sovereign wealth of blood from their Serb, Eastern Orthodox neighbors.

Building on these researches, John Cornwell's *Hitler's Pope: The Secret History of Pius XII* (1999) both dramatically escalated the criticism of Pacelli's wartime conduct as well as disseminated the argument to the wider public. "Failure to utter a candid word about the Final Solution in progress proclaimed to the world that the Vicar of Christ was not moved to pity and anger," Cornwell charges. "From this point of view he was the ideal Pope for Hitler's unspeakable plan. He was Hitler's pawn. He was Hitler's Pope" (296–97). The consultation of all of Pacelli's encyclicals included above does indeed confirm that he never therein selected the words *Hitler, Nazi, Aryan, Holocaust, the Jews*, or anything else that would unambiguously identify the Third *Reich* perpetrating mass murder. The question for many has therefore subsequently become one of attempting to understand and account for such apparent silence. One of the primary and most biographically focused answers is that of Frank J. Coppa in *The Life & Pontificate of Pius XII: Between History and Controversy* (2013), which demonstrates that tactful silence rather than fruitless disputation had characterized Pacelli since adolescence, a disposition derivative of both an introverted and solitary personality as well as a strong predilection for diplomatic solutions. Coppa concludes, "Pius XII aimed to appease rather than arouse the dangerous dictatorial regimes as he sought peace for the Church and the world. He was thus both pope of peace and apostle of appeasement, hoping to attain the first through the latter" (150).[56]

In forceful and sustained reply, traditionalists continually confront what they perceive as a revision of the both interwar and wartime papal record on the basis of malice aforethought, ideological predilection, and lack of due diligence, together with some resulting good faith error. A useful and perhaps necessary *preface* to historical discussion of the Church and fascism is the testimony of Lt. Gen. Ion Mihai Pacepa (with Ronald Rychlak) in *Disinformation: Former Spy Chief Reveals Secret Strategies for Undermining Freedom, Attacking Religion, and Promoting Terrorism* (2013),[57] wherein the highest ranking defector from Warsaw Pact military intelligence seeks to demonstrate the KGB origin of some of the defamatory conclusions identified above. Falconi (1970), according to him, was viewing fabricated source documents, while Hochhuth—though real person and playwright—benefited immensely if obliviously from platform, publicity, and expertise provided by the organs of Soviet DEZINFORMATSIYA, the deliberate rewriting of history that serves as the true preoccupation of Russian counterintelligence. "Over the years, the pro-Nazi image of Pius XII, which had been seeded in the West by the Kremlin and watered by KGB agents and Western communists, generated a flurry of books, movies, and articles denigrating the heroic pontiff and helping the framing to succeed" (197).[58] Such acknowledgment helps induce more fruitful reading of the copious research notes principally concerned with Pius but addressing the Church as a whole of the prolific Sister Margherita Marchione, whose *Yours is a Precious Witness:*

Memoirs of Jews and Catholics in Wartime Italy (1997), *Pius XII: Architect of Peace* (2000), and *Consensus and Controversy: Defending Pope Pius XII* (2002) all appeared shortly before or after Cornwell. Relying heavily throughout on the testimony of surviving and eternally grateful Jews saved by secret operations directed from the precariously inviolate Vatican, Sister Margherita affirms in diametric contrast to Goldhagen, "Attacking Christianity because of the human weakness and personal failure of some to meet the difficult demands of the Catholic faith and charging the Church with such failure for having led to the Holocaust is seriously unjust" (2000: 100). She continues in her next submission, "Pope Pius XII was not 'silent', and his courageous acts during World War II are incontestable. Through public discourses, appeals to governments, and secret diplomacy, he was engaged more than any other individual or agency combined in the effort to curb the excesses of war and to rebuild the peace" (2002: 8), efforts which when properly examined demolish the invidious "black legend" caricature of a venal, anti-Semitic, and silent Nazi pontiff.

Many Jews *as Jews* have meanwhile long defended Pacelli, and the wartime conduct of the Apostolic See more generally. On behalf of the Anti-Defamation League, Joseph L. Lichten offered an initial response to *The Deputy* in "A Question of Judgment: Pius XII and the Jews" (1963), stating in his thesis passage, "No one who reads the record of Pius XII's actions on behalf of Jews can subscribe to Hochhuth's accusation. However, though the evidence moves against the hypothesis that a formal condemnation from Pius would have curtailed the mass murder of Jews, this is still a question of judgment" (31). Former Israeli consul Pinchas Lapide greatly enlarges upon this initial line in *Three Popes and the Jews* (1967), which holds that the pontificates of Pius XI, Pius XII, and John XXIII signaled a historical rediscovery and theological reinvestiture of the Judaic roots of Roman Catholicism despite the pagan Hitler's attempt at total severance, with the wartime Apostolic See responsible for saving more than 800,000 innocent lives. The reiteration of this record of achievement combined with a confrontation with agenda-driven historical revisionists induced Rabbi David G. Dalin to assert *The Myth of Hitler's Pope: How Pope Pius XII Rescued Jews from the Nazis* (2005), especially in contrast to the open and avowed anti-Semitism of the contemporaneous Grand Mufti of Jerusalem.

Unsurprisingly, many Catholics *as Catholics* have likewise rallied to the defense of their Apostolic See and Supreme Pontiff, though peculiar care should be taken in assessing the validity of the reasons why. Ecclesiological struggles *within* the Church, firstly, have according to some prolonged the black legends, with Michael O'Carroll's *Pius XII: Greatness Dishonoured* (1980) imputing the lasting impression of the elderly Pacelli as a bemused occultist to the machinations of John XXIII supporters, and with Ralph McInerny's *The Defamation of Pius XII* (2001) more generally seeing at work the hand of a "Culture of Death" (*xi*) derivative of larger moral relativism and surreptitiously militating against the steadfastness of the Petrine *magisterium*. Be that as it may, broad concurrence is observed between two of the most systematic traditionalist treatments of the subject: Pierre Blet's *Pius XII and the Second World War* (1997) and Ronald J. Rychlak's *Hitler, the War, and the Pope* (2000). The former is a one-volume distillation of the *Actes et Documents du Saint Siège relatifs à la Seconde Guerre Mondiale* (1965–1981), which "allows us to view the steps the pope took to ward off the calamity, to contain the conflict when it turned into a European and then a world war, and finally his efforts to alleviate suffering and to assist the victims" (2). With regard to, at minimum, Pius XII's encyclical omission of the final solution of the Jewish question being carried out in occupied Poland, Blet concludes, "Pius XII proceeded silently, with discretion, at the risk of appearing inactive or indifferent. And yet the work of assisting the war's victims was his favorite undertaking" (288). Finally, in December 1999, and on the other side of *Hitler's Pope*, Rychlak *replicated* Cornwell's research in the Vatican and painstakingly uncovered numerous distortions, exaggerations, and other perhaps comparatively minor but nonetheless sustained abuses of the source material, inducing a conviction as to his predecessor's polemical motives that do indeed appear confirmed by the mere titles of Cornwell's subsequent *The Pope in Winter: The Dark Face of John Paul II's Papacy* (2004) and *Church Interrupted, Havoc & Hope: The Tender Revolt of Pope Francis* (2021).[59] Viewing Pacelli's wartime conduct as a relatively straightforward application of *Summi Pontificatus*, and focusing on the simultaneous Nazi persecution of and Jewish reliance upon the Church, Rychlak concludes, "Perhaps the most valid criticism of Pius XII would be that he was too willing to compromise in order to achieve peace" (182), which if true and applicable is a more concrete way of saying that the utmost discretion necessary for successful diplomacy might appear to contravene the abundant moral clarity incumbent upon high priesthood.

Finally, the Catholic Church herself—rightfully allotted the last word—has most directly addressed some of these questions in *We Remember: A Reflection on the Shoah* (1998),[60] the eventual public report with pontifical endorsement of the Commission for Religious Relations with the Jews under the direction of Cardinal Eduard Idris Cassidy. Seemingly referring to the Western Middle Ages, it concedes, "Sentiments of anti-Judaism in some Christian quarters, and the gap which existed between the Church and the Jewish people, led to a generalized discrimination" (29). Continuing in an apparent reference to the Renaissance and Reformation periods, "In times of crisis such as famine, war, pestilence or social tensions, the Jewish minority was sometimes taken as a scapegoat and became the victim of violence" (30). Yet a crucial conceptual distinction is then drawn between the historic *anti-Judaism* of these earlier and the paganist *anti-Semitism* of the more recent period in Germany under Nazi rule and in Europe under Nazi occupation, with the latter both more psychotic and less Christian. "The Shoah was the work of a thoroughly modern neopagan regime. Its anti-Semitism had its roots outside of Christianity and, in pursuing its aims, it did not hesitate to oppose the Church and persecute her members also" (31). With regard to the most excruciating research question as to the conduct of the holy catholic church amid the roundups, deportations, gassings, and cremations of the Jews, the Commission concludes, "Did Christians give every possible assistance to those being persecuted, and in particular to the persecuted Jews? Many did, but...the spiritual resistance and concrete action of other Christians was not that which might have been expected from Christ's followers" (32).

As intended, the reader shall henceforth be left undisturbed to soberly reflect upon what is or is not stated or implied by such authoritative pronouncements. Scholarly if not necessarily spiritual insight shall likely grow as new documentation comes to light. The overall research question of this inquiry, however, as to the norms of concordats as a whole and their implications for international relations requires neither intervention in, nor prediction concerning the so-called "Pius Wars," canon law dominance resulting in ecclesiological treaty norms being the only major conceptual position herein assumed. What the preceding findings may however be able to contribute to this extensive body of existing literature is satisfactory answers to two recurring questions: *first*, which side first conceived or first proposed the idea of the *Reich* concordat?; and *second*, which side supplied its authoritarian ecclesiological norms?

Per the findings of the present research, the terms of the first question are somewhat transformed, given that a miniature interwar wave of concordats beginning with Latvia in 1922, continuing with Poland in 1925, with Romania and Lithuania in 1927, and finishing with Czechoslovakia in 1928 is observed and brought into focus. It can therefore be said with confidence that neither Hitler nor Mussolini simply conceived the idea of a concordatorial breakthrough out of thin air, given that the question of the establishment of extraordinary ecclesiastical relations with the Apostolic See was clearly open at the time throughout central and eastern Europe. In answer to the second, more solemn question of the origin of the oaths of episcopal loyalty, special prayers, and other authoritarian ecclesiological norms present in both the Lateran Pacts and the *Reich* concordat, the answer may with a high degree of confidence be pronounced in favor of the Apostolic See, especially as represented by Cardinal Secretaries of State Gasparri and Pacelli. Given the strong *continuity* in the terms of the concordats from Latvia in 1922 through the German *Reich* in 1933, inferential method recommends attribution to the common variable, in this case the Apostolic See, and more specifically its Secretariat of State. It is far more probable that the Apostolic See successfully negotiated with a series of contracting plenipotentiaries according to its own preferred terms and instruments than that independent nations should have reached similar treaty outcomes separately according to their own perceived self-interests. It is almost inconceivable that Mussolini or Hitler, and highly unlikely that Franz von Papen possessed the intention or capability to duplicate the access to and expertise in the canon law and concordatorial data available to the curial diplomatic staff. Rather the Apostolic See, it may safely be concluded, originated a policy of seeking concordatorial expression of ecclesiological norms by contracting Catholic nation-states beginning with Latvia in 1922 and climaxing with the German *Reich* in 1933.

Notes

1. (Carmel, IN: Liberty Fund, 2000), 282–83.
2. Born *Vincezo Gioacchino Raffaele Luigi Pecci*, 1810; ordained, 1837; Archbishop Nuncio to Belgium, 1843–46; Archbishop of Perugia, 1846–80; Cardinal, 1853; Camerlengo, 1877–78.
3. {*Supremi Apostolatus Officio*} ASS 16 [1883–84], 113–18; {*Superiore Anno*} ASS 17 [1884], 49–51; {*Vi È Ben Noto*} ASS 20

[1887], 209–15; {*Octobri Mense*} *ASS* 24 [1891–92], 193–203; {*Magnae dei Matris*} *ASS* 25 [1892–93], 139–48; {*Laetitiae Sanctae*} *ASS* 26 [1893–94], 193–99; {*Iucundu semper expectatione*} *ASS* 27 [1894–95], 118–22; {*Fidentem Piumque Animum*} *ASS* 29 [1896–97], 204–09; {*Augustissimae Viginis Mariae*} *ASS* 30 [1897–98], 129–35; {*Diuturni Temporis*} *ASS* 31 [1898–99], 146–49; {*Adiutricem*} *ASS* 28 [1895–96], 129–36.

4. MAGNAM DEI PARENTEM MARIAM VIRGINEM, QUAE PACIS NOSTRAE APUD DEUM SEQUESTRA ET CAELESTIUM ADMINISTRA GRATIARUM, IN CELSISSIMO POTESTATIS EST GLORIAEQUE FASTIGIO IN CAELIS COLLOCATA, *ASS* 16 [1883–84], 113.

5. {*Dall'Alto dell'Apostolico Seggio*} *ASS* 23 [1890–91], 193–206; {*Custodi di Quella Fede*} *ASS* 25 [1892–93], 214–18; {*Inimica Vis*} *ASS* 25 [1892–93], 274–77.

6. QUAE NIMIRUM LONGE LATEQUE IN ECCLESIAM CHRISTI ARDET DIMICATIO, ETSI VARIIS PRO VARIETATE LOCORUM ARTIBUS ARMISQUE EXERCETUR...PERNICIOSISSIMAM ERRORUM PESTEM IN OMNES VENAS DOMESTICAE CIVILISQUE COMMUNITATIS INFUNDERE, *ASS* 23 [1890–91], 518–22.

7. DE IIS, QUAE APPELLANTUR *IURA HOMINIS*, SATIS AUDIIT MULTITUDO: AUDIAT ALIQUANDO DE IURIBUS DEI, *ASS* 33 [1900–01], 285.

8. ATQUI TAMEN RELIGIONIS CHRISTIANAE DIVINA VIRTUS STABILITATIS ATQUE ORDINIS EGREGIA FIRMAMENTA REIPUBLICAE PEPERIT, SIMUL AC IN MORES ET INSTITUTA CIVITATUM PENETRAVIT, *ASS* 14 [1881], 4.

9. VERUM SI REIPUBLICAE LEGES APERTE DISCREPENT CUM IURE DIVINO, SI QUAM ECCLESIAE IMPONANT INIURIAM, AUT IIS, QUAE SUNT DE RELIGIONE, OFFICIIS CONTRADICANT, VEL AUCTORITATEM IESU CHRISTI IN PONTIFICE MAXIMO VIOLENT, TUM VERO RESISTERE OFFICIUM EST, PARERE SCELUS, *AAS* 22 [1890], 388.

10. {*Licet Multa*} *ASS* 14 [1881], 145–47; {*Cum Multa*} *ASS* 15 [1882], 241–46; {*Nobilissima Gallorum Gens*} *ASS* 16 [1883–84], 241–48; {*Iampridem*} *ASS* 18 [1885], 387–94; {*Pergrata*} *ASS* 19 [1886–87], 209–15; {*Officio Sanctissimo*} *ASS* 20 [1887], 257–71; {*Saepe Nos*} *ASS* 21 [1888], 3–5; {*Paterna Caritas*} *ASS* 21 [1888], 67–72; {*Quam Aerumnosa*} *ASS* 21 [1888], 248–60; {*Caritatis*} *ASS* 26 [1893–94], 523–32; {*Inter Graves*} *ASS* 26 [1893–94], 648–52; {*Litteras a Vobis*} *ASS* 27 [1894–95], 3–7;

{*Omnibus compertum*} *ASS* 33 [1900–01], 65–67; {*Reputantibus*} *ASS* 34 [1900–01], 321–25; {*In amplissimo*} *ASS* 34 [1901–02], 623–25.

11. Born *Ambrogio Damiano Achille Ratti*, 1857; ordained, 1879; Chief of the Ambrosian Library, 1907–14; Prefect of the Vatican Library, 1915–19; Archbishop Nuncio to Poland, 1919–21; Archbishop of Milan, 1921–22; Cardinal, 1922.

12. PRAECIPUAM QUANDAM CAUSUM TURBIDARUM RERUM, IN QUIBUS VIVIMUS, EAM ESSE QUOD, VALDE IMMINUTA SIT VEL IURIS AUCTORITAS VEL VERECUNDIA POTESTATIS, {*Ubi Arcano dei Consilio*} *AAS* 14 [1922], 687. He furthermore regards the secularizing regimes of France ({*Maximam Gravissimamque*} *AAS* 16 [1924], 5–11) and Spain ({*Dilectissima Nobis*} *AAS* 25 [1933], 261–75) as especially malignant.

13. QUONIAM OMNIS EDUCANDI RATIO AD EAM SPECTAT HOMINIS CONFORMATIONEM, QUAM IS IN HAC MORTALI VITA ADIPISCATUR OPORTET, UT DESTINATUM SIBI A CREATORE FINEM SUPREMAM CONTINGAT, LIQUIDO PATET, *AAS* 22 [1930], 51.

14. FERE SOLI REMANSERINT SINGULARES HOMINES ET RES PUBLICA…QUEM DICUNT LABORIS…HUIC PESSIMO MALO, QUO TOTA HUMANA SOCIETAS IN EXITIUM ABRIPITUR, QUAM CITISSIME ESSE MEDENDUM NEMO EST QUI NON INTELLEGAT, *AAS* 23 [1931], 203–04.

15. COMMUNISMUS CUM INTRINSECUS SIT PRAVUS, EIDEM NULLA IN RE EST ADIUTRIX OPERA AB EO COMMODANDA, CUI SIT PROPOSITUM AB EXCIDIO CHRISTIANUM CIVILEMQUE CULTUM VINDICARE, *AAS* 29 [1937], 96.

16. SOCIALI APOSTOLATU, *ibid.*, 99.

17. TRACTATUS CANONICUS DE MATRIMONIO (Paris and Lyon: Delhomme et Briguet, 1891–92); TRACTATUS CANONICUS DE SACRA ORDINATIONE (Paris and Lyon: Delhomme et Briguet, 1893–94); TRACTAUS CANONICUS DE SANCTISSIMA EUCHARISTIA (Paris and Lyon: Delhomme et Briguet, 1897).

18. "Pietro Gasparri (1852–1934)," in Orazio Condorelli and Rafael Domino (eds.), *Law and the Christian Tradition in Italy: The Legacy of the Great Jurists* (London: Routledge, 2020), 353.

19. Born *Eugenio Maria Giuseppe Giovanni Pacelli*, 1876; ordained, 1899; Secretary to the Congregation for Extraordinary Ecclesiastical Affairs, 1914–17; Archbishop Nuncio to Bavaria, 1917–25; Archbishop Nuncio to Germany, 1917–29; Cardinal, 1929; Cardinal Secretary of State, 1930–39; Camerlengo, 1935–39.
20. {*Orientalis Ecclesiae*} *AAS* 36 [1944], 129–44; {*Fulgens Radiatur*} *AAS* 39 [1947], 138–55; {*Doctor Mellifluus*} *AAS* 45 [1953], 369–84; {*Ecclesiae Fastos*} *AAS* 46 [1954], 337–56; {*Invicti Athletae*} *AAS* 49 [1957], 605–19.
21. {*Fulgens Corona*} *AAS* 45 [1953], 577–92; {*Ad Caeli Reginam*} *AAS* 46 [1954], 625–40.
22. IN UNIVERSAM MAGNAMQUE COALESCIT POPULORUM CONGREGATIONEM, QUAE AD ASSEQUENDUM OMNIUM GENTIUM BONUM DESTINATUR, AC PECULIARIBUS REGITUR NORMIS, QUAE ET UNITATEM TUTANTUR, ET AD RES COTIDIE MAGIS PROSPERAS DIRIGUNT, *AAS* 31 [1939], 437.
23. {*Communium Interpretes Dolorum*} *AAS* 37 [1945], 97–100; {*Quemadmodum*} *AAS* 38 [1946], 5–10; {*Optatissima Pax*} *AAS* 39 [1947], 601–04; {*Summi Maeroris*} *AAS* 42 [1950], 513–17; {*Mirabile Illud*} *AAS* 42 [1950], 797–800; {*Laetamur Admodum*} *AAS* 48 [1956], 745–48; {*Meminisse Iuvat*} *AAS* 50 [1958], 449–59.
24. {*Orientalis Omnes Ecclesias*} *AAS* 38 [1946], 33–63.
25. {*Luctuosissimi Eventus*} *AAS* 48 [1956], 741–44; {*Datis Nuperrime*} *ibid.*, 748–49.
26. {*Evangeli Praecones*} *AAS* 43 [1951], 497–528; {*Fidei Donum*} *AAS* 49 [1957], 225–48.
27. {*Auspicia Quadem*} *AAS* 40 [1948], 169–72; {*In Multiplicibus Curis*} *AAS* 40 [1948], 433–36; {*Redemptoris Nostri Cruciatus*} *AAS* 41 [1949], 161–64.
28. MYSTICI CORPORIS CHRISTI, QUOD EST ECCLESIA, *AAS* 35 [1943], 193.
29. {*Haurietis Aquas*} *AAS* 48 [1956], 316.
30. SANCTAM VIRGINITATEM EXCELLENTIA SUA MATRIMONIO PRAESTARE, {*Sacra Virginitas*} *AAS* 46 [1954], 170.
31. QUAMOBREM VOS ADHORTAMUR, VENERABILES FRATRES, UT III DIOECESI VEL ECCLESIASTICA DICIONE CUIUSQUE VESTRA MODUM RATIONEMQUE, QUIBUS POPULUS LITURGICAM ACTIONEM PARTICIPET, MODERARI ATQUE ORDINARE VELITIS

SECUNDUM NORMAS, QUAS < < M ISSALE > > STATUIT, ET SECUNDUM PRAECEPTA, QUAE SACRUM CONSILIUM RITIBUS PRAEPOSITUM ET CODEX IURIS CANONICI EDIDERE, *AAS* 39 [1947], 561.
32. Mineola, NY: Dover, [1928] 2006.
33. (New York: E.P. Dutton, 1953), 278.
34. *Ibid.*, 282.
35. *Fuero del Trabajo* (9 March 1938); *Ley Constitutiva de las Cortes* (17 July 1942); *Fuero de los Españoles* (17 July 1945); *Ley de Sucesion en la Jefatura del Estado* (26 July 1945); *Ley de Referendum* (22 Oct 1945); *Ley de Principios del Movimiento Nacional* (17 May 1958); *Ley Organica del Estado* (1 Jan 1967) [*Boletin Oficial del Estado* 9] (11 Jan 1967)].
36. *La Santa Iglesia Católica, Apostólica y Romana, única verdadera y fe inseparable de la conciencia nacional, que inspirará su legislación,* II.
37. Sovereign Ordinance of the *Reichspräsident* for the Protection of the Folk and State/ Verordnung des Reichspräsidenten zum Schutz von Volk und Staat.
38. Menschliche Kultur und Zivilisation sind auf diesem Erdteil unzertrennlich gebunden an das Vorhandensein des Ariers. Sein Aussterben oder Untergehen wird auf diesen Erdball wieder die dunklen Schleier einer kulturlosen Zeit senken, 421.
39. Am Aufwerfen ultramontanen Frage...Der Jude hat jedenfalls das gewollte Ziel erreicht: Katholiken und Protestanten führen miteinander einen fröhlichen Krieg, und der Todfeind der arischen Menschheit und des gesamten Christentums lacht sich ins Fäustchen, 629.
40. *Les membres du Chapitre, les Curés et en général tous les ecclésiastiques sont nommés par l'Archevêque selon les normes du Droit Canon, AAS* 14 [1922], 573 {VIII}.
41. *Ibid.*, 579 {XV}.
42. *L'Etat garantit à l'Eglise le libre exercice de Son pouvoir spirituel et de sa juridiction ecclésiastique...conformément aux Lois divines et au Droit Canon, AAS* 17 [1925], 274 {I}.
43. *Dans toutes les écoles publiques...l'enseignement religieux est obligitaire...conformément au Droit Canon, AAS* 19 [1927], 428 {XIII.1°}.

44. *La Religión Católica, Apostólica, Romana sigue siendo la única de la Nación española y gozará de los derechos y de las prerrogativas que le corresponden en conformidad con la Ley Divina y el Derecho Canónico, AAS* 45 [1953], 626 {1}.
45. *The History of England, from the Invasion of Julius Caesar to the Revolution of 1688* (Indianapolis: Liberty Fund, [1788] 1983), V, 19.
46. I A.B. doe trewly and sincerely acknowledge, professe, testifie and declare in my conscience before God and the world, That our Soueraigne Lord King IAMES, is lawfull King of this Realme, and of all other his Maiesties Dominions and Countreyes: And that the *Pope* himself, nor by any authority of the Church or Sea of *Rome*, or by any other meanes with any other, hath any power or authoritie to depose the King, or to dispose any of his Maiesties Kingdomes or Dominions, or to authorize any forreigne Prince to inuade or annoy him or his Countreys, or to discharge any of his Subjects of their Allegiance and obedience to his Maiestie, or to giue Licence or leaue to any of them to beare Armes, raise tumults, or to offer any violence or hurt to his Maiesties Royall Person, State or Gouernment, or to any of his Maiesties subiects within his Maiesties Dominions. Also I doe sweare from my heart, that, notwithstanding any declaration or sentence of Excommunication, or depriuation made or granted, or to be made or granted, by the *Pope* or his successors, or by any Authoritie deriued, or pretended to be deriued from him or his Sea, against the said King, his heires or successors, or any absolution of the said subiects from their obedience; I will beare faith and trew Allegiance to his Maiestie, his heires and successors, and him and them will defend to the vttermost of my power, against all conspiracies and attempts whatsoeuer, which shalbe made against his or their Persons, their Crowne or dignitie, by reason or colour of any such sentence, or declaration, or otherwise, and will doe my best endeuour to disclose and make knowne to vnto his Maiestie, his heires and successors, all Treasons and traitorous conspiracies, which I shall know or heare of, to be against him or any of them. And I doe further sweare, That I doe from my heart abhorre, detest and abiure as impious and Hereticall, this damnable doctrine and position, That Princes which be excommunicated or depriued by the *Pope*, may be deposed or murthered by their Subjects or any other

whatsoeuer. And I do beleeue, and in conscience am resolued, that neither the *Pope* nor any person whatsoeuer, hath power to absolue me of this Oath, or any part therof; which I vnto mee, and doe renounce all Pardons and Dispensations to the contrarie. All all these things I doe plainely and sincerely acknowledge and sweare, according to these expresse words by mee spoken, and according to the pleine and common sense and mentall euasion, or secret reseruation whatsoeuer. And I do make this Recognition and acknowledgement heartily, willingly, and trewly, vpon the trew faith of a Christian. So helpe me GOD.

47. King James VI and I, *Political Writings* (Cambridge: Cambridge University Press, 1994), 86.
48. *Considerations on the Principal Events of the French Revolution* (Indianapolis: Liberty Fund, 2008 [*Considérations sur les principaux événemens de la Révolucion française*, 1818]), 240.
49. EGO IURO ET PROMITTO AD SANCTA DEI EVANGELIA, OBEDIENTIAM ET FIDELITATEM GUBERNIO PER CONSTITUTIONEM GALLICANAE REIPUBLICAE STATUTO. ITEM, PROMITTO ME NULLAM COMMUNICATIONEM HABITURUM, NULLI CONSILIO INTERFUTURUM, NULLIAMQUE SUSPECTAM UNIONEM NEQUE INTRA, NEQUE EXTRA CONSERVATURUM, QUAE TRANQUILLITATI PUBLICAE NOCEAT; ET SI TAM IN DIOCESI MEA QUAM ALIBI, NOVERIM ALIQUID IN STATUS DAMNUM TRACTARI, GUBERNIO MANIFESTABO.
50. *Je jure devant Dieu et sur les Saints Evangiles, comme il convient à un Evêque, de respecter et faire respecter par le clergé le Gouvernement établi par la Constitution de la République de Lettonie et de ne rien entreprendre qui soit de nature à compromettre l'ordre public.*
51. *Devant Dieu et sur les Saints Evangiles, je jure et je promets, comme il convient à un Evèque, fidélité à la République de Lithuanie. Je jure et je promets de respecter en toute loyauté et de faire respecter par mon Clergé le Gouvernement établi par la Constitution. Je jure et je promets en outre que je ne participerai à aucun accord ni n'assisterai à aucun conseil pouvant porter atteinte à l'Etat lithuanien ou à l'ordre public. Je ne permettrai pas à mon Clergé de participer à de tells actions. Soucieux du bien et de l'intérêt de l'Etat, je tâcherai d'en écarter tout danger dont je le saurais menacé.*
52. Ein Gebet für das Wohlergehen des Deutschen Reiches und Volkes, *AAS* 25 [1933], 406 {30}.

53. See also Robert Katz, *Black Sabbath: A Journey Through a Crime Against Humanity* (New York: Macmillan, 1969). More generally, Giuliana Chamedes, *A Twentieth-Century Crusade: The Vatican's Battle to Remake Christian Europe* (Cambridge, MA: Harvard University Press, 2019) correctly identifies the organic connection between canon law dominance and ecclesiological treaty norms among the interwar concordats with the dictators, although her conceptual framing of the Apostolic See as a motivated transnational actor diverges from the present agnostic inquiry into the norms of a particular treaty form.
54. The same prolific historian, relying upon the newfound availability of documents regarding Pius XII from March, 2020, adds most recently that shortly after the papal coronation of 1939, Hitler directed the impeccably aristocratic Prince Philipp von Hessen to engage in direct talks with His Holiness, establishing previously unknown secret diplomacy. *The Pope at War: The Secret History of Pius XII, Mussolini, and Hitler* (New York: Random House, 2022).
55. See especially Valérie Hébert, "Disguised Resistance? The Story of Kurt Gerstein," *Holocaust and Genocide Studies* 20, no. 1 (2006): 1–33.
56. Jacques Kornberg, *The Pope's Dilemma: Pius XII Faces Atrocities and Genocide in the Second World War* (Toronto: University of Toronto Press, 2015) sees Pacelli prioritize the ecclesiological above the moral.
57. By the same author, *Red Horizons: The True Story of Nicolae & Elena Ceausescus' Crimes, Lifestyle, and Corruption* (Washington, D.C.: Regnery, 1990).
58. In an intersecting contention, the *strength* of General Pacepa's imputation of Sunni-Arab terrorism to Soviet instigation might potentially incur the risk of minimizing the endogenous imperatives of Islamic theology, the demonstration effects of Nazi anti-Semitism, and the perceived self-interests of Arab nationalism. It also remains unclear from his enhanced memoir why the KGB should have apparently refrained from targeting equally outspoken anti-Communist *Evangelical* clergy in like manner. See also John Koehler, *Spies in the Vatican: The Soviet Union's Cold War Against the Catholic Church* (New York: Pegasus Books, 2009).

59. Rychlak states specifically, "Cornwell decided that the easiest way to attack the Pope of today was to denigrate Pius XII. If he can prove that Pius was deeply flawed, especially in the current process of canonization, then he can argue that popes can be politically motivated. If that is the case, then he can argue that John Paul II is politically wrong about celibacy, women priests, artificial contraception, abortion, and other matters" (306).
60. Robert S. Rifkind, *Perspectives on* We Remember: A Reflection on the Shoah (New York: The American Jewish Committee, 1998).

CHAPTER 5

The German *Reich*, 1925–2019

"With every change in the political situation," writes German reactionary jurist and political theorist Carl Schmitt in the early essay *Roman Catholicism and Political Form* (1923), "all principles appear to change save one: the power of Catholicism."[1] Although concerned specifically with neither concordats nor Germany, Schmitt places on record his profound professional admiration for a Catholic Church of such undeniable comparative and longitudinal significance, consisting in part of a *complexio oppositorum* seemingly capable of absorbing within its formal structure the both variety and totality of human experience. "The political power of Catholicism," he continues, "rests neither on economic nor on military means but rather on the absolute realization of authority."[2] This case cluster chapter shall demonstrate how the dominance of Catholic canon law within the German *Reich* has resulted in the uniformly ecclesiological treaty norms of its 42 concordats with the Apostolic See.

Politik and Recht

Examination of Table 5.1 reveals the extensive assortment of religious and civil officials involved in the conclusion of these treaties; and therefore fruitful inquiry should concentrate on extracting informative patterns from the large set of data. Among the five pontificates identified, the most natural juncture for any intentional adjustment of policy would be that of Paul VI (1963–1978), being the first since the conclusion of the *Reich* concordat of 1933 and since the Viking funeral of the *Reich* in 1945. His seven encyclicals evince what might be described as a non-aggressive ecclesiological conservatism with respect to the Eucharist ({*Mysterium Fidei*} AAS 57 [1965], 753–74) and to the preservation of clerical celibacy ({*Sacerdotalis Caelibatus*} AAS 59 [1967], 657–97), but the global ideational norms introduced in *Ecclesiam Suam* (AAS 56 [1964], 609–59) and intensified in *Populorum Progressio* (AAS 59 [1967], 257–99) shall be reserved for Chap. 8 and with the contributions of John Paul II to also be considered in due course. Contextual introduction shall instead concentrate upon effective provision of the outlines of German comparative politics and law.

Two forces predominate within the political order of democratic Germany: Social Democracy, and Christian Democracy, representing historical materialist and Christian salvific conceptions of history, respectively.[3] Fully realized by 1890, and controlling for its temporary suspension under Nazism, the German Social Democratic Party[4] (*Sozialedemokratische Partei Deutschlands*) is the oldest in Continental Europe, the most influential testament of Karl Marx west of Leningrad, and the dauntless vessel of revolutionary hope for many extremely intelligent and highly idealistic people. There was Karl Kautsky, founder of *Die Neue Zeit* (1883–1923) and principal author of the heavily Marxist Erfurt Program of 1891. Karl Liebnecht was a distinguished member of the *Reichstag* and later Spartacist revolutionary martyr. Eduard Bernstein authored the decisive *Preconditions for Socialism* (1899).[5] But its exponent of the broadest popular appeal and most enduring conceptual significance remains Dr. Rosa Luxemburg (1871–1919).

A Jew from Romanov Poland, adolescence brought forth an inflammable desire for social justice, and advanced study in political economy in Zürich resulted in one of the first research doctorates awarded to a woman. In *The Accumulation of Capital* (1913), her most sustained scholarly and theoretical work, Luxemburg clarifies but also builds on Marx so as to explain, "A proper understanding of the fundamental categories of capitalist production, of value and surplus value...demands the understanding of this process in its historical development and of the categories themselves as historically conditioned forms of the general relations of labour. This means that only a socialist can really

Table 5.1 The German *Reich*

Pontiff	Contracting party	Head of State or Government
(Pontifical Legate, Title)	(Contracting Location, Date, Language(s))	(Contracting Plenipotentiary, Title)
Pius XI (Eugenio Pacelli, Nuncio)	**STATE OF BAVARIA** (Munich, 24 Jan. 1925, German/Italian)	Heinbich Held (Eugen von Knilling, Franz Matt, And Wilhelm Krausneck,
Pius XI (Eugenio Pacelli, Nuncio)	**PRUSSIAN FREE STATES** (Berlin, 14 June 1929, Italian/German)	Paul von Hindenburg (President Otto Braun, Ministers Carl Heinrich Becker, And Hermann Höpker-Aschoff)
Pius XI (Eugenio Pacelli, Cardinal Secretary of State)	**BADEN FREE STATE** (Konstanz, 12 Oct. 1932, Italian/German)	Paul von Hindenburg (President Josef Schmitt, Ministers Eugen Baumgartner, And Wilhelm Mattes)
Pius XI (Eugenio Pacelli, Cardinal Secretary of State)	**GERMAN *REICH*** (Vatican City-state, 20 July 1933, Italian/German)	Adolf Hitler (Franz von Papen, Vice Chancellor)
Pius XII (Luigi Muench, Nuncio)	**LAND OF NORTH RHINE-WESTPHALIA** (Bad Godesberg, 19 Dec. 1956, Italian/German)	Konrad Adenauer (Minister-President Fritz Steinhopf and Minister Paul Luchtenberg)
Paul VI (Corrado Bafile, Nuncio)	**LOWER SAXON LAND** (Hannover, 26 Feb. 1965, Italian/German)	Ludwig Erhard (Georg Diederichs, Minister-President)
Paul VI (Corrado Bafile, Nuncio)	**BAVARIAN FREE STATE** (Munich, 2 Sep. 1966, Italian/German)	Ludwig Erhard (Ludwig Huber, Minister for Teaching and Culture)
Paul VI (Corrado Bafile, Nuncio)	**SAARLAND** (Bad Godesberg, 9 April 1968, Italian/German)	Kurt Georg Kiesinger (Werner Scherer, Minister for Religion, Teaching, and Culture)
Paul VI (Corrado Bafile, Nuncio)	**BAVARIAN FREE STATE** (Munich, 7 Oct. 1968, Italian/German)	Kurt Georg Kiesinger (Minister-President Alfons Goppel, Ministers Ludwig Huber and Konrad Pöhner)
Paul VI	**RHINELAND-PALATINATE**	Kurt Georg Kiesinger

(continued)

Table 5.1 (continued)

Pontiff	Contracting party	Head of State or Government
(Corrado Baule, Nuncio)	(Mainz, 29 April 1969, Italian/German)	(Peter Altmeier, Minister-President)
Paul VI	SAARLAND	Willy Brandt
(Corrado Bafile, Nuncio)	(Bonn, 12 Nov. 1969, Italian/German)	(Alois Becker, Minister-President)
Paul VI	BAVARIAN FREE STATE	Willy Brandt
(Corrado Bafile, Nuncio)	(Bonn-Bad Godesberg, 17 Sep. 1970, Italian/German)	(Ludwig Huber, Minister for Teaching and Worship)
Paul VI	RHINELAND-PALATINATE	Willy Brandt
(Corrado Baule, Archbishop Nuncio)	(Mainz, 15 May 1973, Italian/German)	(Helmut Kohl, Minister-President)
Paul VI	LOWER SAXON LAND	Willy Brandt
(Corrado Bafile, Archbishop Nuncio)	(Hannover, 21 May 1973, Italian/German)	(Alfred Kubel, Minister-President)
Paul VI	BAVARIAN FREE STATE	Helmut Schmidt
(Corrado Bafile, Archbishop Nuncio)	(Munich, 4 Sep. 1974, Italian/German)	(Minister-President Alfons Goppel, Ministers Hans Maier and Ludwig Huber)
Paul VI	SAARLAND	Helmut Schmidt
(Corrado Bafile, Archbishop Nuncio)	(Bonn-Bad Godesberg, 21 Feb. 1975, Italian/German)	(Franz Josef Röder, Minister-President)
Paul VI	BAVARIAN FREE STATE	Helmut Schmidt
(Guido Del Mestri, Archbishop Nuncio)	(Munich, 7 July 1978, Italian/German)	(Alfons Goppel, Minister-President)
John Paul II	LAND OF NORTH RHINE-WESTPHALIA	Helmut Kohl
(Guido Del Mestri, Archbishop Nuncio)	(Düsseldorf, 26 March 1984, Italian/German)	(Johannes Rau, Minister-President)
John Paul II	SAARLAND	Helmut Kohl
(Joseph Uhaé)	(Saarbrücken, 12 Feb. 1985, Italian/German)	(Werner Zeyer)
John Paul II	BAVARIAN FREE STATE	Helmut Kohl
(Joseph Uhaé, Archbishop Nuncio)	(Munich, 8 June 1988, Italian/German)	(Franz Josef Strauß, Minister-President)
John Paul II	LOWER SAXON LAND	Helmut Kohl
(Joseph Uhaé, Archbishop Nuncio)	(Hannover, 8 May 1989, Italian/German)	(Herrn Ernst Albrecht, Minister-President)
John Paul II	LOWER SAXON LAND	Helmut Kohl
(Lajos Kada, Nuncio)	(Hannover, 29 Oct. 1993, German/Italian)	(Gerhard Schröder)

(continued)

Table 5.1 (continued)

Pontiff	Contracting party	Head of State or Government
John Paul II (Lajos Kada, Nuncio)	LANDS OF SAXONY-ANHALT, BRANDENBURG AND THE SAXON FREE STATE (Magdeburg, 13 April 1994, German/Italian)	Helmut Kohl (Minister-Presidents Christoph Bergner, Frank E. Portz, and Steffen Heittmann)
John Paul II (Lajos Kada, Nuncio)	THURINGIAN FREE STATE (Erfurt, 14 June 1994, German/Italian)	Helmut Kohl (Bernhard Vogel, Minister-President)
John Paul II (Lajos Kada, Nuncio)	FREE AND HANSEATIC STATE OF HAMBURG, LAND OF MECKLENBURG-WEST POMERANIA, AND LAND OF SCHLESWIG–HOLSTEIN (Hamburg, 22 Sep. 1994, German/Italian)	Helmut Kohl (Senate President Henning Voscherau, Minister-Presidents Steffie Schnoor and Marianne Tidick)
John Paul II (Giovanni Lajolo, Archbishop Nuncio)	SAXON FREE STATE (Dresden, 2 July 1996, German/Italian)	Helmut Kohl (Kurt Biedenkopf, Minister-President)
John Paul II (Giovanni Lajolo, Archbishop Nuncio)	THURINGIAN FREE STATE (Erfurt, 11 June 1997, German/Italian)	Helmut Kohl (Bernhard Vogel, Minister-President)
John Paul II (Giovanni Lajolo, Archbishop Nuncio)	LAND OF MECKLENBURG-WEST POMERANIA (Schwerin, 15 Sep. 1997, Italian/German)	Helmut Kohl (Berndt Seite, Minister-President)
John Paul II (Giovanni Lajolo, Archbishop Nuncio)	LAND OF SAXONY-ANHALT (Magdeburg, 15 Jan. 1998, German/Italian)	Helmut Kohl (Reinhard Höppner, Minister-President)
John Paul II (Giovanni Lajolo, Archbishop Nuncio)	SAARLAND (Saarbrücken, 19 Sep. 2001, German/Italian)	Gerhard Schröder (Peter Müller, Minister-President)
John Paul II (Giovanni Lajolo, Archbishop Nuncio)	THURGINIAN FREE STATE (Erfurt, 19 Nov. 2002, German/Italian)	Gerhard Schröder (Bernhard Vogel, Minister-President)

(continued)

Table 5.1 (continued)

Pontiff	Contracting party	Head of State or Government
John Paul II (Giovanni Lajolo, Archbishop Nuncio)	LAND OF BRANDENBURG (Potsdam, 12 Nov. 2003, German/Italian)	Gerhard Schröder (Matthias Platzeck, Minister-President)
John Paul II (Giovanni Lajolo, Archbishop Nucnio)	FREE AND HANSEATIC STATE OF BREMEN (Bremen, 21 Nov. 2003, German/Italian)	Gerhard Schröder (Henning Scherf, Senate President)
Benedict XVI (Erwin Josef Ender, Archbishop Nuncio)	FREE AND HANSEATIC STATE OF HAMBURG (Hamburg, 29 Nov. 2005, German/Italian)	Angela Merkel (Ole von Beust, President)
Benedict XVI (Erwin Josef Ender, Archbishop Nuncio)	BAVARIAN FREE STATE (München, 19 Jan. 2007, German/Italian)	Angela Merkel (Edmund Stoiber, Minister-President)
Benedict XVI (Jean-Claude Périsset, Archbishop Nuncio)	LAND OF SCHLESWIG–HOLSTEIN (Kiel, 12 Jan. 2009, German/Italian)	Angela Merkel (Peter Harry Carstensen, Minister-President)
Benedict XVI (Jean-Claude Périsset, Apostolic Nuncio)	LOWER SAXON LAND (Hannover, 6 April 2010, German/Italian)	Angela Merkel (Christian Wulff, Minister-President)
Benedict XVI (Jean-Claude Périsset, Archbishop Nuncio)	FREE AND HANSEATIC STATE OF HAMBURG (Hamburg, 18 May 2010, German/Italian)	Angela Merkel (Herlind Gundelach, Senator for Science and Research)
Benedict XVI (Jean-Claude Périsset, Archbishop Nuncio)	LOWER SAXON LAND (Hannover, 8 May 2012, German/Italian)	Angela Merkel (David McAllister, Minister-President)
Francis	LAND OF MECKLENBURG-WEST POMERANIA (Schwerin, 27 July 2015, German)	Angela Merkel
Francis (Nikola Eterović, Apostolic Nuncio)	LAND OF MECKLENBURG-WEST POMERANIA (Berlin, 4 June 2019, German)	Angela Merkel (Katy Hoffmeister, Justice Minister)

solve the problem of the reproduction of capital."[6] Luxemburg's resolute democratic conscience, however, appears rather more responsible than any theoretical refinements for her enduring normative appeal. A staunch opponent of Bolshevik tyranny, "Leninism or Marxism?" (1904) warned against excessive party centralization, concerns fully realized in her eventual "Russian Revolution" (1918) confronting Lenin's foreign aggression and domestic repression. "Reform or Revolution" (1908), finally, completes the deposition of the "revisionist" Bernstein to arrive at the decisive formulation whereby the petit-bourgeois pursue *reform* but the proletariat demand *revolution*. "Social Democracy," Luxemburg concludes, "sees Socialism come as a result of economic necessity—and the comprehension of that necessity—leading to the suppression of capitalism by the working masses."[7]

Following the eventual establishment of the Federal Republic, a revised party program agreed upon at Godesberg in 1959 postured a reciprocal relationship between the socialization of productive processes and democratization of political institutions, with SPD Chancellors Willy Brandt, Helmut Schmidt, Gerhard Schröder, and most recently Olaf Scholz taking and holding power. Meanwhile, the most recent Hamburg Program of 2007 constructs the above institutional history thus: "The German Social Democratic Party...fought for workers' rights, developed the social welfare state, and together with the trade unions it enabled disdained proletarians to become self-confident citizens with equal rights."[8] The party's current theoretical posture for its part might be characterized as *Marxism-without-Marx*, insofar as capitalist production remains the primary intended target, but without explicit reliance on dialectical reasoning, classless teleology, or resort to force. "Our history is shaped by the idea of democratic socialism, a society of free and equal people...guaranteeing civil, political, social and economic basic rights for all people living a life without exploitation, suppression and violence."[9]

In theoretical opposition proudly stands the Christian Democratic Union (*Christlich Demokratische Union*).[10] As mentioned in the preceding chapter, the *Rerum Novarum* (1891) of Leo XIII inspired a renewed pan-European effort to preëmpt Marxist revolutionary agitation in part through the intensification of Christian solidarity; but the party was founded immediately after World War II by the chairman of the constitutional convention and inaugural Chancellor Dr. Konrad Adenauer. An extremely devout lifelong Catholic who until Hitler served as the celebrated Mayor of Cologne, Adenauer sought adjustment at the deepest possible level, at that of *Weltanschauung* or worldview, explaining in his *Memoirs* (1965), "For many years I had believed that we needed a Christian party based on the foundations that both Catholics and Protestants had in common. Only this could, I thought, help us to counter the increasingly materialistic approach to political matters" (43). The new intended German majority party would therefore seek to *unite* both Catholic and Lutheran *Christians* in a new *democratic* regime, with the inaugural party program agreed at Neheim-Hüsten in 1946 grounding the political within a Christian as opposed to a materialist *Weltanschauung*, Nazi racism and Marxist Communism representing the two primary manifestations of the latter. As with the Social Democrats, the 2007 manifesto of the party of Chancellors Adenauer, Ludwig Erhard, Kurt Georg Kiesinger, Helmut Kohl, and Angela Merkel remains current, which declares, "The Basic Law is based on principles that are rooted in Christian beliefs. They have had a great/fundamental impact on our country and our society. It is not only the duty of the church but also the major responsibility of the state and the citizens to preserve it in our consciousness and to maintain and enforce it."[11]

With these ideological distinctions in mind, and turning once again to the contents of Table 5.1, it becomes obvious that the regularity with which German concordats have been concluded appears to preclude the possibility that either the Social or Christian Democrats as such are politically responsible. At least one such *Vertrag* has occurred on the watch of every former German Chancellor since 1949, and therefore an outcome or series of outcomes is identified that seems irrespective of parliamentary and partisan contention. All regions of Germany also appear represented, if not perhaps equally represented. The *sui generis* outcome whereby the individual states of the Federal Republic, called *Länder*, conclude their own concordats with the Apostolic See is therefore most clearly understood as a distinctive feature of German comparative constitutional law.

The Constitution of the German Reich (*Die Verfassung des Deutschen Reichs*) of 11 August 1919 contained the following key provision: "The maintenance of relations with foreign states is the sole responsibility of the *Reich*. In matters within the legal competence of the *Länder*, they may conclude treaties with foreign states, such treaties requiring the approval of the *Reich*" (78).[12] On this comparative basis concordats were agreed with the State of Bavaria (1925), the Prussian Free States (1929), and the Baden Free State (1932), with the Nazi seizure of power and the *Reich* concordat taking shape the following year. Regarding at least pre-war Nazism, the influential formulation of exilic jurist Ernst Fraenkel in *The Dual State: A Contribution to the Theory of Dictatorship* (1941) postures a comprehensive "Normative State" of extensive legal and administrative continuity from the Weimar period operative within the shadow of a circumscribed "Prerogative State" based on Nazi ideology irregularly institutionalized through violence and terror. Be that as it may, the 1949 constitution subsequently retained these same terms (32.1, 32.3), although the approving organ is now the "Federal Government" (*Bundesregierung*). Under German constitutional law, therefore, any of the sixteen *Länder* may agree to a concordat with the Apostolic See with the approval of the Federal Government in Berlin, a unique competence within comparative government consistently reflected in the large assortment of officials provided on the right-hand column of Table 5.1. Beginning with the concordat with North Rhine-Westphalia of 1956, the given head of state or government is the Federal Chancellor, and the contracting plenipotentiary members of the government of the given region. Although the exhaustive summary of German case law provided in Donald P. Kommers' *The Constitutional Jurisprudence of the Federal Republic of Germany* (1997) yields no directly applicable rulings, his analysis nonetheless explains that the Federal Constitutional Court in Karlsruhe per the Basic Law (100.2) has the authority to hear cases involving public international law actions and that the concordats of the *Länder* would therefore likely fall under the tradition of constitutional review (*Verfassungstreitigkeit*).

The Concordats of Worms

According to the first codification of the canon law, concordats are agreed with "various nations" (VARIIS NATIONIBUS, CIC/1917, c. 3), and according to the second with "other political societies" (ALIISVE SOCIETATIBUS POLITICIS, CIC/1983, c. 3) as well. Whether intentional or not, the latter reference is solely applicable to the German *Länder*, being the only national sub-divisions seen to conclude their own concordats. Under the 1919 constitution, concordats with Bavaria (*AAS* 17 [1925], 41–56), the Prussian Free State (*AAS* 21 [1929], 521–44), and Baden (*AAS* 25 [1933], 177–96) established a template closely adhered to by all subsequent German concordats based on the codification of three comprehensive ecclesiastical rights.

First, the numerous concordats with the German *Länder* recognize the right of the Catholic Church to carry out its apostolic mission according to the canon law. "The Bavarian State guarantees the free and public exercise of the Catholic religion," opens the first text of the above series. "It recognizes the right of the Church, within its jurisdiction, to make laws and regulations binding upon its members. It will neither prevent nor impede the exercise of these rights."[13] Where the ecclesiological formulation most clearly differs from the overall tendency of Anglo-American liberalism is in the legal agreement not so much to allow *individuals* to practice the Catholic faith—though this is nowhere denied—as to allow *the Church* to conduct itself according to its own laws within its own legal sphere. The same initial concordat with Bavaria continues, "Orders and religious congregations may be freely established according to the canonical provisions."[14] Somewhat further down, to pursue the matter, it reads, "The Bavarian State will provide appropriate subsidies to existing seminaries for boys and for priests in accordance with the provisions of the Code of Canon Law."[15] Such language characterizes the initial treaty articles of most observations within the series. Meanwhile, the concordat with Prussia—the same kingdom that had previously unleashed the *Kulturkampf*—grants religious freedom to the Catholic Church with an episcopal seat erected or if one counts Charlemagne restored to Aachen (*AAS* 21 [1929], 521 {1–2}), while the treaty with the Baden Free State (*AAS* 25 [1933], 177–96) confers legal freedom (*Freiheit*) upon the Catholic Church ({1}) and introduces its corporate right (*Recht*) to collect ecclesiastical taxes ({IV.4}).[16] Almost always accompanying such language acknowledging the apostolic mission and right of the Church to teach, preach, and administer the sacraments is the *precedent* set by the concordats with Bavaria in 1924, with Prussia in 1929, and with the German *Reich* in 1933, furnishing thereby the only series within the census in which subsequent concordats cite the example of earlier ones as part of their own normative justification.

Central to the operationalization of the apostolic mission of the Catholic Church through the German concordats is its acknowledged status as a public corporation, which allows that mission in various ways to be cognizable. Consecrated buildings and other ecclesiastical grounds are through the treaties typically removed from market competition and protected from demolition or expropriation. The initial concordat with Bavaria introduced such protections (*AAS* 17 [1925], 50 {10§4}) and that with Prussia followed (*AAS* 21 [1929], 526 {5.1}), establishing a consistent pattern. More specifically, canon law among other provisions insists upon the burial of the dead (CIC/1917, c. 1203; CIC/1983, c. 1176) in the hope of corporal resurrection and ecclesiastical possession of the necessary cemeteries dedicated to the purpose (CIC/1917, c. 1206; CIC/1983, c. 1240); and thus the first concordat with Lower Saxony initiates the characteristic concordatorial recognition of this right (*AAS* 57 [1965], 855 {§14.1}). The concordats with the German *Länder* also systematically recognize the utility and necessity of the *Kapital* required for the Church to carry out its legally acknowledged apostolic mission, although the treaty terms and resulting financial arrangements vary widely by case. In some versions, such as that of the Saxon Free State (*AAS* 89 [1997], 627 {21.1}), the Church simply conceded the liberty of imposing taxes in accordance with applicable laws, while in others, such as those of the Saarland (*AAS* 95 [2002], 429–32) or of Lower Saxony (*AAS* 87 [1995], 556–70), almost the entire document is dedicated to the precise definition of administrative and financial obligations within some particular policy space of the broader education field. The terms of most, however, lie between these two extremes, laying out guidelines for the financing of the Church's activities among other questions at the intersection of church and state. Such activities are furthermore seen to have generally *expanded* over time with regard to concordatorial acknowledgment of what is permissible for the Catholic Church in Germany to undertake. Beginning with the concordat with Lower Saxony (*AAS* 57 [1965], 842 {11.1}), the right of clerical visitation to hospitals, prisons, and other social institutions meeting the needs of the unfortunate and the downtrodden consistently appears.

Second, the concordats with the German *Länder* legally empower the teaching *magisterium* of the Roman faith, with the enumeration of Catholic educational rights and privileges comprising the bulk of the treaty texts. One central component is the establishment of Catholic primary and high schools on the same legal footing as state schools, comprehensive Catholic instruction in public schools, or some combination of both. The language of the comparatively recent concordat with Hamburg (*AAS* 98 [2006], 825–47) is representative: "Pursuant to article 7, paragraph 3 of the German Basic Law, the Free and Hanseatic City of Hamburg guarantees Catholic religious instruction as a regular subject in public schools according to the principles of the Catholic Church."[17] It continues, "Church educational institutions will continue to be guaranteed and funded within the framework of applicable law. This applies in particular to the Catholic school system."[18] In primary justification for these educational ecclesiological norms, the treaty texts routinely demand adherence to *missio canonica*, not a particular canon or canonical subject, but the principle whereby both religious and laity must receive explicit, written permission to carry out a Catholic teaching rôle. The concordat with Brandenburg (*AAS* 96 [2004], 625–52) states for example, "The granting of Catholic religious instruction requires an ecclesiastical authorization (*missio canonica*) by the responsible (arch)bishop...Authorization is only granted to persons with sufficient training."[19] The same bishops, local ordinaries, the Apostolic See, or some combination thereof may also continually verify the conformity of not only teachers, but also of textbooks, curricula, syllabi, and all other learning materials to Catholic doctrine and morals, and may intervene against any apparent deviation. "Without prejudice to overarching state law, the Catholic Church preserves the right of inspection of the religious instruction in public schools. The Land [of Schleswig–Holstein] appoints suitable teachers for this task by the suggestion of and in agreement with the Catholic Church."[20] "Subject matter and textbooks for Catholic religious instruction are to be determined in agreement with the diocesan bishops [of Saxony-Anhalt]."[21] Weimar Bavaria, once again, initiated such treaty terms (*AAS* 17 [1925], 46 {8§2}), which prevail throughout the series.

A spectrum of provisions also pertains to Catholic university instruction, the terms of which broadly align whether a Catholic university, a Catholic seminary, or a Catholic theological faculty at a non-Catholic university is in question. The concordat with the Baden Free State (*AAS* 25 [1933], 186 {IX}) states that theological instruction at the University of Freiburg will adhere to canon law, that with North Rhine-Westphalia (*AAS* 77 [1985], 295–96 {II.1}) that departments of Catholic theology will be reëstablished at the universities of Bochum, Bonn, and Münster, and that with the Bavarian Free State (*AAS* 62 [1970], 821 {1}) that the existing department of philosophical-theology (*Philosophisch-theologischen*) at the University of Augsburg will be replaced with a Catholic theological department. Whatever the specific institutional arrangements, the Apostolic See through its concordats insists upon the right of the Church to interpose against any profession inclining toward apostasy, heresy, or schism, or against any professors obstinately leading a sinful life. "If the diocesan bishop [in Bavaria] for valid reasons complains about one of the professors because of his teaching or moral conduct, the state will immediately arrange for a replacement through some other means."[22] "Professors and university lecturers [in Saxony] for Catholic theology and Catholic religious instruction are only appointed when the responsible state ministry has ascertained from the responsible diocesan bishop that there are no concerns with regard to life and doctrine."[23] University-level funding arrangements, meanwhile, consist of a portfolio of financial instruments including direct payments from state to church, favorable leases, legal recognition of both fixed and circulating capital, and reliance upon the ecclesiastical taxation system identified above. Concern for adult education is also consistently expressed, for beginning with the concordat with Lower Saxony (*AAS* 57 [1965], 842 {10})—television having become commonplace by that point—terms are agreed to guarantee adequate airtime for the Catholic position in any sort of public broadcast exploring questions of faith and morals.

The concordats with the German *Länder*, finally, emphasize the right of the Church to the government of its own ecclesiastical polity. As the Church is governed by bishops, this right is most importantly expressed through the creation and recognition of dioceses, beginning once again with the Prussian concordat establishing an episcopal seat at Aachen (*AAS* 21 [1929], 522 {2.2}) and the Baden concordat (*AAS* 25 [1933], 180 {4.1}) an arch-episcopal one at Freiburg, with geographic, institutional, and financial adjustments continuous throughout the series. The most interesting pattern, however, corresponds to the unification of the *Reich* following the implosion of the German Democratic Republic in 1989; for as Němec details in *Concordat Agreements between the Holy See and the Post-Communist Countries* (2012), a series of agreements appeared between the Apostolic See and the newly reconstituted *Länder* within German areas that had previously been Marxist-Leninist. Four are concerned purely with diocesan establishment: the concordat with Saxony-Anhalt, Brandenburg, and the Saxon Free State (*AAS* 87 [1995], 129–37) concerned with the creation of a new diocese in Magdeburg, the concordat with Brandenburg and the Saxon Free State (*AAS* 87 [1995], 138–45) regarding a new diocese in Görlitz, the concordat with Thuringia for a new diocese in Erfurt (*AAS* 87 [1995], 145–54), and the concordat with Hamburg, Mecklenburg-West Pomerania, and Schleswig–Holstein (*AAS* 87 [1995], 154–64) for a new archdiocese of Hamburg.

The textual appearance of such ecclesiological treaty norms is furthermore almost uniformly grounded in existing canon law. The idealist language in the preamble of the concordat with Hamburg (*AAS* 98 [2006], 826) concerned with human rights and the uniting of Europe[24] furnishes the sole deviation from a treaty series otherwise exclusively concerned with the construction of ecclesiastical polity on the basis of canon law. In addition to the characteristic invocations of the precedent established by the concordats with Prussia and with the German *Reich*, the apostolic constitutions DEUS SCIENTIARUM DOMINUS (AAS 23 [1931], 241–84) and its successor SAPIENTIA (*AAS* 71 [1979], 469–528) are referenced on eight separate occasions in support of the educational treaty terms discussed above.

The most solemn and binding instrument of ecclesiastical law, the apostolic constitution legally constructs some aspect of ecclesiastical polity; and DEUS SCIENTIARUM DOMINUS departs from the contention that as higher education through the founding of universities originated in the Church, it therefore ought rightfully to return unto her. More specifically, any Catholic institution of higher learning must be legally empowered by the Apostolic See, or else its degrees are rendered canonically invalid. The most crucial article is the first: "Universities and faculties of ecclesiastical studies are those authorized by the Holy See concerning sacred disciplines or those adjoining the sacred, with the right to confer academic degrees."[25] In fulfillment of this ecclesiastical constitutional law, ordinary power is invested in a Sacred Congregation of Seminaries and University Studies (SACRAE CONGREGATIONI DE SEMINARIIS ET STUDIORUM UNIVERSITATIBUS, 4), with valid degrees only conferred by adhering institutions (6), and applicability also explicitly extended to theological faculties at civil universities, with respect to any existing concordatorial provisions (11). DEUS SCIENTIARUM DOMINUS establishes the familiar Bachelor's, Master's, and Doctoral degrees, but clarifies that all shall be conferred in the name of the current pontiff, or in case of vacancy of the Apostolic See (7§1). Representing the same, a Grand Chancellor (MAGNUS CANCELLARUS) furthermore governs a Catholic university (14§1), in which the most prestigious subject is sacred theology, followed by canon law. Ensuing technical provisions pertain to the suitability of libraries, auditoriums, and laboratories.

In the wake of the Second Vatican Council the norms of which it explicitly references (38.1; 71),[26] the apostolic constitution SAPIENTIA CHRISTIANA followed and is mentioned repeatedly in the concordats with the German *Länder*. Emphasizing the necessity of professorial conformity to the doctrine and morals of the Catholic faith (25–26), but otherwise reiterating the terms of its predecessor, its crucial article is the following: "Only universities and faculties canonically erected or approved by the Holy See, and in conformity with the norms of this constitution, have the right to confer academic degrees possessing canonical value."[27] The apostolic constitutions DEUS SCIENTIARUM DOMINUS and SAPIENTIA CHRISTIANA thus provide the basis for the educational terms of the concordats with the German *Länder*, in turn, the most pronounced and prolix of the ecclesiological norms of its concordats derivative of the dominant position of Roman Catholic canon law within the German *Reich*.

THE QUESTION OF INTERNATIONAL VALIDITY

As demonstrated above, the German concordats conform to both the canon law of the Catholic Church and the comparative law of the Federal Republic. Their validity under *international* law, however, remains an unanswered question, as there is no other example within the census or universe of cases of concordatorial diplomacy operative at the sub-national level; and Germany is by no means the only federal state within the democratic or Catholic world. The author having despaired of encountering any existing opinion concerned in whole or in part with the question of the international legal validity of this otherwise obscure treaty series, the following initial treatment is offered as a foundation for prospective subsequent analysis.

To begin, the Charter of the United Nations (1945) speaks of the Organization it creates as, "based on the principle of the sovereign equality of all its Members" (2.1). Those Members consist of the original plus any other interested and approved "peace-loving states" (4.1), who together populate the General Assembly (9.1). On these terms, the German *Länder* are clearly not to be considered states within the international law and polity of the United Nations. Yet the Law of Nations preceded the appearance of the State, and the State preceded the appearance of the United Nations Organization, with lawful state existence therefore completely independent of UN membership. With regard to the concordats the German *Länder* regularly contract, the Vienna Convention on the Law of Treaties (1969) states the following: "'Treaty' means an international agreement concluded between States in written form and governed by international law, whether embodied in a single instrument or in two or more related instruments and whatever its particular designation" (2.1.a). But who or what are these *States* the convention speaks of?

The provisional answer intersects with the scholarly debate reviewed in Chap. 2 regarding the validity and competence of the Apostolic See as an international actor. At Montevideo in December 1933, the governments of the United States and those of Central and South America—there was no European participation—agreed a Convention on the Rights and Duties of States[28] which has subsequently served as the perhaps less than incontestable basis for the determination of international statehood. The convention begins, "The State [*El Estado/l'Etat/O Estado*] as a person of international law should possess the following qualifications: (*a*) a permanent population; (*b*) a defined territory; (*c*) government; and (*d*) capacity to enter into relations with the other states" (1). It continues, "The Federal State shall constitute a sole person in the eyes of international law" (2). As a category, the German *Länder* seemingly fail the test of one-delta, given the constitutional right of the federal government to veto, interpose, or nullify their concordats, or their treaties of any kind; and Article 2 precludes their personhood under international law. Preliminary textual investigation therefore returns a negative answer to the research question of whether the concordats with the subsidiary regions of Germany conform to international law.

The verdict of international legal commentary, if ever directly confronted with the question, would however likely prove somewhat more ambivalent. The current normative paradigm of international relations and law is held by many to have opened with Fedor Fedorovich Martens' magisterial *Contemporary International Law of Civilized Peoples* (1882),[29] the author having served as a prime conceptual mover of the Hague peace conferences that concluded nineteenth and inaugurated twentieth-century diplomacy. Martens submits Germany as the strongest example of a union of states as a complex but discrete subject of international law, "based on commonality of interests and respect for the internal and international autonomy of the members of the union." He immediately continues, crucially, "The last retain the right of international representation together with representation of the entire union; they all may conclude treaties and send embassies, with one limitation, that international transactions concluded by them or instructions given to diplomatic agents are not contrary to the interests of the entire union" (187–88). Slightly expanding upon the German international legal history he provides, the sixth article of the Treaty of Paris of 1814 stated, "The States of Germany shall be independent, and united by a federal tie,"[30] language revised and expanded in the first article of the subsequent Vienna Final Act of 1820, which states, "The German Confederation is a union under international law of the sovereign German princes and free cities, for the preservation of the independence and inviolability of the states included in its Confederation and for the maintenance of the domestic and external security of Germany."[31] Although nowhere explicitly stated, the subsequent federal governments created by the constitutions of the North German Confederation of 1867, of the German *Reich* of 1871, of the Weimar *Reich* of 1919, and finally of the Federal Republic of 1949 discreetly allowed to these states or *Länder* independent diplomatic competence as sending and receiving states; and therefore, according to this more case-specific method, the numerous concordats of the German *Länder* are to be provisionally considered valid under international law to the extent that this singularity of German constitutional practice has been tacitly approved through both long and continual observance. The legacy of Worms is therefore lasting and significant indeed.

Notes

1. (Westport, CT: Greenwood Press, [*Römischer Katholizismus und politische Form*, 1923] 1996), 4.
2. Ibid., 18.
3. The minority Free Democratic Party (*Freie Demokratische Partei*) is heavily *functionalist*, adhering to the position that the application of scientific method and advanced technology to public policy and administration can supply the deficiencies of dysfunctional parliaments and squabbling politicians. Formative texts of (West) German political science include Karl Dietrich Bracher, *The German Dilemma: The Relationship of State and Democracy* (London: Praeger, 1975); Ernst Fraenkel, *Deutschland und die westlichen Demokratien* (Baden-Baden: Nomos, [1964] 2011); and Franz Neumann, *The Democratic and the Authoritarian State: Essays in Political and Legal Theory* (Glencoe, IL: Free Press, 1957).

4. See especially Roger Morgan, *The German Social Democrats and the First International, 1864–1872* (Cambridge: Cambridge University Press, 1965); Carl E. Schorske, *German Social Democracy, 1905–1917: The Development of the Great Schism* (Cambridge, MA: Harvard University Press, 1983); and Leszek Kolakowski, *Main Currents of Marxism: Its Rise, Growth, and Dissolution* (Oxford: Clarendon Press, 1978), vol. II, chs. 2–4.
5. These were according to him a certain critical threshold of capitalist development followed by attainment of political power by the party of the workers, although at once guided and humbled by the painful acknowledgment that Marx and Engels were mistaken as to the impending catastrophic collapse of capitalist production. Eduard Bernstein, *The Preconditions for Socialism* (Cambridge: Cambridge University Press, [*Die Voraussetzungen des Sozialismus,* 1899] 1993).
6. (New Haven: Yale University Press, [*Die Akkumulation des Kapitels: Ein Beitrag zur ökonomischen Erklärung des Imperialismus,* 1913] 1951), 106.
7. *Reform or Revolution, and Other Writings* (Mineola, NY: Dover, 2006), 43.
8. Die deutsche Sozialdemokratie…Sie hat Arbeiterrechte erstritten, den Sozialstaat ausgebaut und zusammen mit den Gewerkschaften aus verachteten Proletarierinnen und Proletarien gleichberechtigte und selbstbewusste Staatsbürgerinnen und Staatsbürger gemacht, 12.
9. Unsere Geschichte ist geprägt von der Idee des demokratischen Sozialismus, einer Gesellschaft der Freien und Gleichen, in der unsere Grundwerte verwirklicht sind. Sie verlangt eine Ordnung von Wirtschaft, Staat und Gesellschaft, in der die bürgerlichen, politischen, sozialen und wirtschaftlichen Grundrechte für alle Menschen garantiert sind, alle Menschen ein Leben ohne Ausbeutung. Unterdrückung und Gewalt, also in sozialer und menschlicher Sicherheit führen können, 16.
10. See especially Noel D. Cary, *The Path to Christian Democracy: German Catholics and the Party System from Windthorst to Adenauer* (Cambridge, MA: Harvard University Press, 1996); Wolfram Kaiser, *Christian Democracy and the Origins of European Union* (Cambridge: Cambridge University Press, 2007); and

Stathis N. Kalyvas, *The Rise of Christian Democracy in Europe* (Ithaca, NY: Cornell University Press, 1996).
11. Das Grundgesetz beruht auf Werten, die christlichen Ursprungs sind. Sie haben unser Land und unsere Gesellschaft grundlegend geprägt. Sie im Bewusstsein zu halten, zu bewahren und ihnen Geltung zu verschaffen, verstehen wir nicht nur als Aufgabe der christlichen Kirchen, sondern auch als eine vorrangige Aufgabe von Staat und Bürgern, 279.
12. Die Plege der Beziehungen zu den auswärtigen Staaten ist ausschließlich Sache des Reichs. In Angelegenheiten, deren Regelung der Landesgesetzgebung zusteht, können die Länder mit auswärtigen Staaten Verträge schließen; die Verträge bedürfen der Zustimmung des Reichs.
13. § 1. Der Bayerische Staat gewahrleistet die freie und öffentliche Ausübung der katholischen Religion. § 2. Er anerkennt das Recht der Kirche, im Rahmen ihrer Zuständigkeit Gesetze zu erlassen und Anordnungen zu treffen, die ihre Mitglieder binden; er wird die Ausübung dieses Rechtes weder hindern noch erschweren. The subsequent treaty references will omit the corresponding Italian deemed non-essential to the case cluster analysis.
14. Orden und religiöse Kongregationen können den kanonischen Bestimmungen gemäss frei gegründet werden (2).
15. Der Bayerische Staat wird an die bestehenden, nach den Bestimmungen des Codex iuris canonici eingerichteten Knaben- und Priesterseminare angemessene Zuschüsse leisten (10§I.h).
16. German ecclesiastical taxation generally assumes the form of an 8–10% surcharge on income tax of baptized persons, withheld by the employer and remitted to a local revenue office. See Frederic Spotts, *The Churches and Politics in Germany* (Middletown, CT: Wesleyan University Press, 1973), pp. 193–99.
17. Die Freie und Hansestadt Hamburg gewährleistet gemäß Artikel 7 Absatz 3 des Grundgesetzes für die Bundesrepublik Deutschland die Erteilung des katholischen Religionsunterrichts als ordentliches Lehrfach an den öffentlichen Schulen in Übereinstimmung mit den Grundsätzen der Katholischen Kirche (5.1).
18. Kirchliche Bildungseinrichtungen werden weiterhin im Rahmen des geltenden Rechts gewährleistet und gefördert. Dies gilt in besonderem Maße für das katholische Schulwesen (6.1).

19. Die Erteilung des katholischen Religionsunterrichts setzt eine kirchliche Bevollmächtigung (missio canonica) durch den zuständigen (Erz-)bischof voraus...Die Bevollmächtigung wird nur Personen mit einer hinreichenden Ausbildung erteilt (628 {4.2}).
20. Unbeschadet des staatlichen Aufsichtsrechts behält die Katholische Kirche das Recht der Einsichtnahme in den Katholischen Religionsunterricht der öffentlichen Schulen. Das Land bestellt auf Vorschlag und im Einvernehmen mit der Katholischen Kirche geeignete Lehrkräfte für diese Aufgabe (5.5).
21. Lerninhalte und Lehrbücher für den katholischen Religionsunterricht sin dim Einvernehmen mit den Diözesanbischöfen festzulegen (*AAS* 90 [1998], 473 {4.2}).
22. Sollte einer der genannten Lehrer vom Diözesanbischof wegen seiner Lehre oder wegen seines sittlichen Verhaltens aus triftigen Gründen beanstandet werden, so wird der Staat unbeschadet der staatsdienerlichen Rechte alsbald auf andere Weise für einen entsprechenden Erstatz sorgen (*AAS* 66 [1974], 603 {3.3}).
23. Professoren und Hochschuldozenten (Hochschullehrer) für katholische Theologie und katholische Religionspädagogik werden erst berufen oder eingestellt, wenn sich das zuständige Staatsministerium be idem zuständigen Diözesanbischof vergewissert hat, daß im Hinblick auf Lehre und Lebenswandel keine Bedenken bestehen (*AAS* 89 [1997], 617 {5.2}).
24. –in der Achtung vor der Religionsfreiheit des Einzelnen sowie der Religionsgemeinschaften, -in dem Anliegen, die Menschenwürde und die Menschenrechte zu achten und zu schützen, -in der Einsicht, dass christlicher Glaube, christliches Leben und karitatives Wirken zugleich auch einen Beitrag zum Whole des Ganzen wie auch zur Stärkung des Gemeinsinns der Bürger in der pluralen Gesellschaft einer weltoffen, sich als Mittlerin zwischen den Völkern verstehenden Stadt leisten, -in dem Verlangen, damit auch zum friedlichen Aufbau eines immer enger zusammenwachsenden Europas beizutragen.
25. UNIVERSITATES ET FACULTATES STUDIORUM ECCLESIASTICORUM EAE SUNT, QUAE AUCTORITATE SANCTAE SEDIS AD DISCPLINAS SACRAS VEL CUM SACRIS CONEXAS TRADENAS ET EXCOLENDAS INSTITUUNTUR, CUM IURE CONFERENDI GRADUS ACADEMICOS.
26. To be taken up in Chapter 8, part 1.

27. SOLIS UNIVERSITATIBUS ET FACULTATIBUS A SANCTA SEDE CANONICE ERECTIS VEL APPROBATIS, ATQUE AD NORMAM HUIUS CONSTITUTIONIS ORDINA TIS, IUS EST CONFERENDI GRADUS ACADEMICOS, QUI VALOREM CANONICEM HABEANT, 6.
28. League of Nations Treaty Series, vol. CLXV, no. 3802, 1936.
29. F.F. Martens, *Contemporary International Law of Civilized Peoples* (Clark, NJ: Talbot, [1882] 2021).
30. *Les États de l'Allemagne seront indépendans, et unis par un lien fédératif.*
31. Der deutsche Bund ist ein völkerrechtlicher Verein der deutschen souverainen Fürsten und freien Städte, zur Bewahrung der Unabhängigkeit und Unverletzbarkeit ihrer im Bunde begriffenen Staaten und zur Erhaltung der innern und äußern Sicherheit Deutschlands. In Ernst Rudolf Huber (ed.), *Deutsche Verfassungsdokumente*, 1803–1850 (Stuttgart: W. Kohlhammer, 1978), p. 91. Clearly within the overall context of the preservation of the European and international balance of power, the intervening German Federal Act (*Deutsche Bundesakte*, 8 June 1815) belonging to the Congress of Vienna furthermore stated that individual members of the German Confederation (1815–66) could conduct their own foreign relations in conformity with the larger principle of collective security (11). Complications include the limitations of the aforesaid longitudinal interval, the highly imperfect correspondence between the arbitrary assortment of confederal members and the contracting parties of Table 5.1, and the dubious conformity of its concordats to the actual intentions of Castlereagh, Talleyrand, and Metternich.

CHAPTER 6

Latin American Counter-Revolution, 1887–1994

In *The Modern World-System I: Capitalist Agriculture and the Origins of the European World-Economy in the Sixteenth Century* (1974), Immanuel Wallerstein commendably reduces the violence of the Leninist and improves upon the inevitability of the Luxemburger logics of capital accumulation through the perspicacious introduction of a *geographic* division of labor in which core states surrounded by semiperipheral and then peripheral areas comprise the capitalist world-system, itself in turn partitioned from external areas. Although the constitutive norms of the Apostolic See are Christian salvific rather than historical materialist, even partial theoretical convergence with regard to Latin American comparative outcome encourages further exploration. Consequently, this case cluster chapter shall demonstrate how the dominant position of the canon law within the Central and South American concordatorial contracting states has again resulted in largely ecclesiological treaty norms.

Neocolonialism

Six out of the thirteen concordats provided in Table 6.1 were agreed between 1954 and 1968, inclusive, during the respective pontificates of Pius XII, John XXIII, and Paul VI. Apart however from unflagging support for global missionary endeavors—especially among indigenous peoples—none authored an encyclical in whole or in part directly concerned with the affairs of the Catholic Church in Latin America. The absence of ecclesiastical therefore results in an immediate procession to the available civil data.

Spanish and Portuguese colonization resulted in the importation and establishment of the authoritarian ecclesiological norms of the Iberian Counter-Reformation. In *Civil Power* (1528), Francisco de Vitoria justified royal prerogative through invocation of divine right,[1] while the illustrious Cardinal Bellarmine in *Controversies* (1586) defended within certain parameters the burning of obstinate heretics at the stake and in *The Temporal Power of the Pope* (1610) insisted that His Holiness may nullify oaths of allegiance to an excommunicated sovereign, a fiercely resisted notion within the bourgeoning Protestant commonwealths.[2] And in his monumental *Treatise on Laws and God the Lawgiver* (1612), Jesuit Francisco Suárez at once finalized the edifice of medieval scholasticism as well as provided the most elaborate *legal* confutation of the seemingly revolutionary evangelical thesis of justification by faith: "We shall pluck out the root of all the [Protestant] heresies, which is imputed justness, and we shall demonstrate...that the works of the just are weighed, estimated and imputed by God...Consequently, if they are good works, they are imputed for reward; if slightly evil, for temporal punishment...if they are grave sins, they are so imputed as actually to destroy the just character."[3]

Such norms were diffused and institutionalized through an indefinite but enduring canon, comparative, and international regime generally described as the royal patronage of the Indies (*real patronato de las Indias*), which began to take shape soon after Columbus' famous voyage and which resulted in the almost absolute control over the Church in South America by the Spanish crown. Three papal bulls were central to the creation, and two concordats to the clarification of the royal patronage, which manifested the most dominant comparative position of the canon law anywhere outside Europe. *Inter caetera* (4 May 1493) represented to the Spanish monarchy that "to lead the peoples dwelling in those islands and countries to embrace the Christian religion...you should

Table 6.1 Latin American counter-revolution

Pontiff	CONTRACTING PARTY	Head of State or Government
(Pontifical Legate, Title)	(Contracting Location, Date, Language(s))	(Contracting Plenipotentiary, Title)
Leo XIII	**REPUBLIC OF COLOMBIA**	Raphael Nuñes
(Rampolla del Tindaro, Cardinal Secretary of State)	(Rome, 31 Dec. 1887, Latin)	(Ioachim Ferdinandum Vélez, Legate Extraordinaire)
Pius XII	**THE DOMINICAN REPUBLIC**	Pedro Santana
(Domenico Tardini, Sec. of the S. Congregation for Extraordinary Ecclesiastical Affairs)	(Vatican City-state, 16 June 1954, Italian/Spanish)	(Rafael Leonidas Trujillo Molina, Generalissimo)
Pius XII	**REPUBLIC OF BOLIVIA**	Hernán Siles Zuazo
(Umberto Mozzoni, Nuncio)	(La Paz, 1 Feb. 1958, Italian/Spanish)	(Manuel Barrau Péláez, Minister of Foreign Relations and Religion)
John XXIII	**REPUBLIC OF BOLIVIA**	Hernán Siles Zuazo
(Domenico Tardini, Cardinal Secretary of State)	(Vatican City-state, 15 March 1961, Spanish)	(Fernando Diez de Medina, Ambassador Extraordinaire)
John XXIII	**GOVERNMENT OF PARAGUAY**	Alfredo Stroessner
(Carlo Martini, Nuncio)	(Asunción, 20 Dec. 1961, Spanish)	(Raúl Apena Pastor, Minister of Foreign Relations)
Paul VI	**REPUBLIC OF VENEZUELA**	Rómulo Betancourt
(Luigi Dadaglio, Nuncio)	(Caracas, 6 March 1964, Italian/Spanish)	(Marcos Falcón Briceño, Minister of Foreign Relations)
Paul VI	**GOVERNMENT OF EL SALVADOR**	Fidel Sánchez Hernández
(Bruno Torpigliani)	(San Salvador, 11 March 1968, Spanish)	(Alfredo Martínez Moreno)
Paul VI	**REPUBLIC OF COLOMBIA**	Misael Pastrana Borrero

(continued)

Table 6.1 (continued)

Pontiff	CONTRACTING PARTY	Head of State or Government
(Angelo Palmas, Archbishop Nuncio)	(Bogotá, 2 July 1975, Italian/Spanish)	(Alfredo Vásquez Carrizosa, Minister of Foreign Relations)
Paul VI	REPUBLIC OF ECUADOR	Alfredo Poveda Burbano
(Luigi Accogli, Nuncio)	(Quito, 3 Aug. 1978, Spanish)	(José Ayala Lasso, Minister of Foreign Relations)
John Paul II	REPUBLIC OF PERU	Francisco Morales Bermúdez Cerrutti
(Mario Tagliaferri, Nuncio)	(Lima, 19 July 1980, Spanish)	(Arturo García, Minister of Foreign Relations)
John Paul II	REPUBLIC OF BOLIVIA	Víctor Paz Estenssoro
(Santos Abril y Castellò, Nuncio)	(La Paz, 1 Dec. 1986, Spanish)	(Guillermo Bedregal Gutiérrez, Minister of Foreign Relations and Religion)
John Paul II	FEDERATIVE REPUBLIC OF BRAZIL	José Sarney
(Carlo Furno)	(Brasilia, 23 Oct. 1989, Portuguese)	(Paulo Tarso Flecha de Lima)
John Paul II	REPUBLIC OF VENEZUELA	Rafael Caldera
(Oriano Quilici, Nuncio)	(Caracas, 24 Nov. 1994, Spanish)	(Miguel Angel Burrelli Rivas, Minister of Foreign Relations)

appoint...worthy, godly, learned, skilled, and experienced men, in order to instruct the aforesaid inhabitants and residents in the Catholic faith and in sound morals."[4] *Eximae devotionis* (16 November 1501) conceded that tithes from the Spanish American church should go to the Spanish crown in exchange for retention of the resident clergy at its expense, while the scope of the terms of *Universalis ecclesiae* (28 July 1508) appears extremely comprehensive:

We [Julius II] concede with apostolic authority, other constitutions, ordinances, and laws to the contrary notwithstanding, to the said [King] Ferdinand and [Queen] Juana, and to the future kings of Castile and León, that nobody without their consent can construct or build in the above mentioned islands, now possessed or to be possessed, large churches; and we concede the right of patronage and of presenting qualified persons to cathedral churches, monasteries, *dignidades*, collegiates, and other ecclesiastical benefices and pious places.[5]

An appalled Bartolomé de Las Casas—the primary ethnologist and prosecutor of the conquest—would in short order gruesomely describe the genocide immediately perpetrated by the diabolical *conquistadors* upon the helpless indigenous peoples partially by appeal to such theocratic entitlement[6]; but the primary legal if not moral prerogatives of the royal patronage included authorization of the arrival and departure of clerics, approval of the construction of churches and missions, delineation of diocesan and parish boundaries, right of presentation of ecclesiastics for vacant bishoprics, archbishoprics, and canonicates, complete jurisdiction over the non-Catholic, veto, interposition, or nullification with regard to synods and church councils, and the operation of the Inquisition, the personnel of which were selected by, and reported solely to Madrid. The brief 1753 concordat, for its part, reiterated that such arrangements would continue to lie within, "the right of the king, by virtue of royal patronage," (*el derecho del rey, por* via *de patronato real*, I.II)[7]; and the 1851 concordat strongly reconfirmed the royal patronage as well, although exclusively with reference to Spain.[8] Mecham summarizes, "Never before or since did a sovereign with the consent of the pope so completely control the Catholic Church within his dominions...For this reason it can be contended with considerable truth that the king was more than a patron in America; he exercised quasi-pontifical authority."[9]

This authority would begin to be contested during the processes of Spanish American independence, won by all the states within the cluster except the Dominican Republic between 1809 and 1822. Fundamentally, these appear to have been liberal constitutionalist revolutions, which extended if not necessarily added to the republican norms of their recent American and French predecessors. In *Bases and Starting Points for the Political Organization of the Argentine Republic* (*Bases y puntos de partida para la organización política de la República Argentina*, [1835] 2017), the most influential work of political theory to emerge from the milieu of the new republics, Juan Bautista Alberdi explains in a summary section, "All the constitutions given in South America during the war of independence were the complete expression of the dominant necessity of…independence and exterior liberty…In their drafting our constitutions imitated the constitutions of the French Republic and the Republic of North America."[10] Although the sociological supremacy of the Catholic faith per se appeared excluded from the question, the nineteenth century consequently witnessed intermittent and inconclusive struggle between the papal claim to possess, the Spanish claim to retain, and the republican claim to succeed to the patronage of the Catholic Church in Spanish America.[11]

Proceeding to the postwar longitudinal interval in question, the deeply reactionary posture of much of South America proved an enticing postwar destination for Croatia's Ante Pavelić, SS criminals against humanity Adolf Eichmann, Josef Mengele, Klaus Barbie, Franz Stangl, and Walter Rauff, possibly *Reichsminister* Martin Bormann, and other former National Socialists who appear to have escaped Allied arrest mainly through South Tyrol to eventually disembark mainly in Argentina, thereafter to furtively reside under assumed names throughout the region.[12] The onset of the Cold War furthermore incidentally strengthened the hand of the pan-American Catholic Right, insofar as the recently created American Central Intelligence Agency (1947-) began to undertake continual operations of anti-Marxist repression throughout the region, in almost boastful defiance of international law and seemingly indifferent to the enormous human cost.[13] But identification and discussion of the politics of the respective contracting heads of state or government of this comparative regional tendency begins with Rafael Núñez, inaugural President of Colombia. He is author of *Essays of Social Criticism* (*Ensayos de Crítica Social*, 1874); but analysis may proceed at once to the decisive ecclesiological terms of the 1886 Colombian constitution for which he was largely responsible, and which remained in force until as recently as 1991. The document opens, "In the name of God, the supreme source of all authority," (*En nombre de Dios, fuente suprema de toda autoridad*), establishes Roman Catholicism as the national religion (III.38), declares public education to be provided in cooperation (*concordancia*) with the Church (41), and incorporates standard concordatorial language with regard to the freedom of the Church to manage its own affairs in accordance with the larger apostolic mission.[14] The first example of the comparative constitutional establishment of the instrument of the concordat per se is also provided in the following terms: "The Government shall be able to reach agreements with the Holy Apostolic See for the purpose of regulating the preceding questions, and of defining and establishing the relations between the civil and ecclesiastical power."[15] Núñez's eventual successor President Misrael Pastrana Borrero (1970–1994), meanwhile, belonged to a Colombian Conservative Party the 1849 thesis of which defends, "Christian morals and civilizing doctrines against the immorality and corrupt doctrines of materialism and atheism."[16]

A frightful proportion of the Catholic rulers of Central and South America, though not necessarily *as* Catholics completely succumbed however to the temptation to govern through terror as opposed to through law. Among the authoritarian strongmen within the findings, *Generalissimo* Rafael Trujillo of the Dominican Republic (1933–1961) and Alfredo Stroessner of Paraguay (1954–1989) were longest in power, although the latter was more competent, more representative of comparative trends, and at least ostensibly more devoted to a larger ideology, with the 1967 Declaration of Principles of his Colorado Party promising "consolidation of relations with the Holy See through the conclusion of concordats and other agreements that satisfy the spiritual interests of the country and the religious sentiments of the Paraguayan people."[17] Adding to this pair General Hernández of El Salvador, Admiral Burbano of Ecuador, and Marshall Bermúdez of Peru, the Apostolic See was concluding concordats with military regimes obsessed with internal repression.

Nevertheless, the question can however conclude upon a much more uplifting note: the life and doctrine of Prof. Dr. Rafael Caldera of Venezuela. By turns Solicitor General, President of the Chamber of Deputies, Senator for Life, founder of the *Partido Socialcristiano* ([COPEI] 1946-), and President (1969–1974, 1994–1999), he was a main contributor to the highly successful 1961 constitution and the individual most directly responsible for the importation and adaptation of the norms of European Christian Democracy to the Latin American political context. His writings at the intersections of political theology, political economy, sociology, and international and comparative politics are extensive[18]; yet he places his deepest political convictions on record in *Ideology: Christian Democracy in Latin America* (*Ideario: La democracia christiana en America Latina*, 1970). "The adjective *Christian* does not represent a religious position," he explains, "but the conviction that Christian values and the spirit of Christianity must be recognized in order to be able to confront with success the requirements of social justice and to defeat Marxism in the fight to conquer the soul of the people."[19]

Latin American political thought does include a secular-modernist center most clearly encapsulated in the 1948 Charter of the Organization of the American States, with its intriguing call for a model of "integrated development" (*desarrollo integral*, 30) comprehending science, technology, education, and culture. Politically, the Brazilian National Movement (*Movimento Democrático Brasileiro*) of President José Sarney (1985–1990) is by design centrist and catch-all. Yet the deeply unfortunate conditions described above have been most frequently comprehended and contested through the principles of Marxist criticism, with its overall imputation of social injustice to the historical unfolding of class conflict. "In opposition to the disintegration and anarchy of the capitalist world," proclaims the 1920 manifesto of the COMINTERN, "the Communist international sets up the united struggle of the international proletariat for the abolition of private property in the means of production, and for the reconstruction of national and world economy on a uniform economic plan instituted and maintained by a society of producers united by common interests and responsibilities."[20] Amid the interwar appearance of Marxist profession among the minimal but intrepid Latin American intelligentsia,[21] the 1930 arrival of the exilic People's Commissar of Military and Naval (1918–1925) and for Foreign Affairs (1917–1918) Leon Trotsky[22] at a villa outside Mexico City would result in a Latin American location for the development of the pioneering social theories of his Fourth International organized in defiance of Stalin.[23] In addition to his autobiography (1930) and informed perspective on *The Revolution Betrayed* (1937) by the Soviet bureaucracy, the most famous eventual victim of the Terror brought forth his *Russian Revolution* (1932) largely in vindication of what Trotsky calls the *law of combined development*, whereby the sudden appearance of modern productive forces within a traditional society creates revolutionary conditions. *The Permanent Revolution* (1930), meanwhile, powerfully argues that socialism cannot long endure in any comparative instance provided that capitalism still prevails internationally.

Both ideas remain central to developmental economics, but the most astute pupil and formidable practitioner of Latin American Marxism was a dauntless romantic whose violent exploits on behalf of the poor and the oppressed would render him the folk hero of almost the entire Third

World: Dr. Ernesto Guevara de la Serna, *nom de guerre*, CHE. Radicalized by the 1954 CIA coup against Jacobo Árbenz in Guatemala, he helped organize the Cuban Revolution five years later, with numerous diaries[24] chronicling the development of his doctrine and praxis. His address (11 December 1964) to the UN General Assembly, however, proved of profound ideological significance. "The final hour of colonialism has struck," Che prophesied, "and millions of inhabitants of Africa, Asia and Latin America rise to meet a new life and demand unrestricted right to self-determination and to the independent development of their nations."[25] He furthermore clarified, "As Marxists we have maintained that peaceful coexistence among nations does not encompass coexistence between the exploiters and the exploited, between oppressors and the oppressed."[26] Executed by the Bolivian military three years later, the enormous popular significance of the Che imaginary helped inspire sustained academic interest in a "dependency theory"[27] to attempt to account for the ubiquitous poverty, squalor, and immobility of the Latin American social situation. Most effectively formulated in *Dependency and Development in Latin America* (1979) by Fernando Henrique Cardoso—later President of Brazil—and Enzo Faletto, theirs is a qualified dialectical materialism comparatively sensitive to conflicts of interest and to demonstrations of agency within the affected peripheral society. "It is through contradictions that the historical process unfolds. Dependent development occurs through frictions, accords, and alliances between the state and business enterprises. But...both the state and business enterprises pursue policies that form markets based on the concentration of incomes and on the social exclusion of majorities" (199).[28]

Turning once again to the concerned heads of state or government, although the National Revolutionary Movement (*Movimiento Nacionalista Revolucionario*, 1942-) of repeat President Víctor Paz Estenssoro of Bolivia (1952–1956, 1960–1964, 1985–1989) incorporates some liberal, populist, and functionalist ideas, its formative doctrine primarily bewailed the "external dependency" (*dependencia externa*, VII) of the Bolivian economic and social order and promised, "an alliance of classes of workers, farmers, middle classes, and progressive bourgeoisie against imperialist despotism and internal allied forces."[29] His successor and rival Hernán Zuazo would at length move a left-splinter. Greatest however in personal charisma and in theoretical and historical significance was President of Venezuela (1945–1948, 1959–1964) and founder of the social democratic *Acción Democrática* Rómulo Betancourt. Author of

Venezuela: Oil and Politics (1978), and primary intellectual and political foil to Christian Democratic President Caldera, his inaugural address of 13 February 1959 marked a turning point in the unfinished struggle for Latin American social democracy. Although emphasizing an anti-Communist path to national economic independence and social justice with steadfast commitment to conformity to international law and isolation of abusive regimes,[30] he also signaled his interest in clarified extraordinary ecclesiastical relations with the Apostolic See thus: "Personally, I believe that the hour has come to initiate conversations with the Holy See in order to present to the Congress of the Republic, if considered convenient, the substitution of the inoperable instruments contained in the Law of Ecclesiastical Patrimony, legislation belonging almost to the prehistory of our public law, for the more flexible norms of a modern *modus vivendi*, carefully discussed between the contracting parties."[31] In the decisive Venezuelan case therefore, the presidential movement for a concordat was partially intended to modernize and to update the vestigial legal formulation, initiated with *Inter caetera* (1493), whereby the kings of Castile had been originally entrusted with the Catholic Church in Latin America.

Concordatorial Counter-Revolution

The inaugural concordat with the Republic of Colombia (*ASS* 21 [1888], 7–12) by reason of its establishment of Roman Catholicism as the state religion ({1}) reflects this dominant canon law position. But it is that with the Dominican Republic (*AAS* 46 [1954], 433–57) which more suggestively transitions out of the practice of concordatorial fascism and into the establishment of new treaty norms for those to come in the region. Roman Catholicism is denominated the national religion ({I}), recognition of "international juridical personality" (*la personalidad juridica internacional*) is conferred upon both its Apostolic See and Vatican City-state ({II.1}), and the Catholic Church as a whole, per the neo-Thomist formulation of Leo XIII in *Immortale Dei* (*ASS* 17 [1884], 161–80), is considered a "perfect society" (*sociedad perfecta*, {III.1}). A representative Sabbath prayer for the prosperity of the republic and its president is also agreed ({XXVI}).[32] Although these particular treaty terms were not to be repeated elsewhere, others would come to define standard regional procedure. The concordat constitutionally establishes all canonical holy days ({XVIII.1}), provides right of religious access to such humanitarian institutions as hospitals, orphanages, schools, and correctional facilities ({XIX}), and guarantees to the Church the right to establish schools "of any order and grade" (*cualquier orden y grado*, {21.1}). All such ecclesiological provisions reflect canon law dominance. But even amid the nightmarish despotism of Trujillo, an idealist candle is lit, wherein the concordat also recognizes the "free organization and function of Catholic associations with religious, social, and charitable ends, in particular the associations of Catholic Action."[33]

An intermittent series of four subsequent concordats displays similar treaty terms. Under canon law in force at the time, Apostolic Vicars or Prefects presided over Catholic territories not yet organized into dioceses (CIC/1917, c. 293); and a 1958 concordat with Bolivia (*AAS* 50 [1958], 68–81) recognized six such vicariates of Beni, Cuevo, Chiquitos, Pando, Reyes, and Châves, all endowed with juridical personality ({III.3}), the right to create schools ({V.2}), extensive immunity from taxation ({VIII}), and conferral of public financial support ({XIV.1}), together with other usual guarantees. Some of the unusually specific language employed in the comprehensive 1964 concordat with Venezuela under Betancourt (*AAS* 56 [1963], 925–32), meanwhile, appears to result from highly attentive diplomacy. "The Venezuelan state recognizes the free exercise of the right of the Catholic Church to promulgate Bulls, Briefs, Statutes, Decrees, Encyclical and Pastoral Letters within the remit of its competence."[34] "The Venezuelan state, in conformity with the constitution, recognizes the right of organization of the Catholic citizens to promote the diffusion and realization of the principles of the faith and Catholic morals through the associations of Catholic Action."[35] Both articles demonstrate the influence of Christian Democratic although not Social Democratic norms. The same treaty also recognizes the international legal personality of the Apostolic See and Vatican City-state ({III}), grants civil juridical personality to all Catholic institutions possessing it under the canon law ({IV}), and stipulates that bishops and archbishops must be Venezuelan ({VII}), a nationalist delimitation of the government of the Church to be repeated in the brief subsequent concordat with Peru (*AAS* 72 [1980], 808 {VII}). The terms of the next concordat with Colombia (*AAS* 67 [1975], 421–34) are similar, but its initial articles appear especially concerned with theory. "The state," it begins, "attentive to the traditional Catholic sentiment of the Colombian nation, considers the Catholic, Apostolic, and Roman religion as a fundamental element of the common good and of the integral development of the national community."³⁶ "Canonical legislation," the document continues, "is independent of the civil and forms no part of it, but shall be respected by the authorities of the Republic."³⁷ The Colombian concordat protects canonical marriage ({VII}), guarantees Catholic education at all levels ({X}), and accepts the consecration and pledges to respect the preservation of Catholic cemeteries ({XXVII}), as well as clarifies the pontifical right to name (*nombrar*, {XIV}) all bishops and archbishops. These and otherwise largely representative treaty terms are intended to advance the Christian personalist norms of a Church intended "to serve the human person" (*server a la persona humana*, {V}).

Yet more distinctive to the region is a subgroup of seven concordats concerned primarily with the ecclesiology of the armed forces of often highly repressive states. On 23 April 1951, the Apostolic instruction DE VICARIIS CASTRENSIBUS (*AAS* 43 [1951], 562–65) called for "new norms" (NOVAE NORMAE, preamble) regulating the relations between Church and Army, and created a new kind of official to implement them on the following terms: "He who carries out the ordinary office of the Military Vicar is endowed with a special jurisdiction to exercise the spiritual good of the committed faithful. The jurisdiction enjoyed by the Military Vicar is personal."³⁸ He may perform the divine office and offer benediction over new fortifications or ships; and subsequent concordats with Bolivia (*AAS* 53 [1961], 299–303), Paraguay (*AAS* 54 [1962], 22–27), El Salvador (*AAS* 60 [1968], 382–84), and Ecuador (*AAS* 75 [1983-I], 481–84) concern the incorporation of the Military Vicar into existing ecclesiastical polity. The language of that of Bolivia establishes the pattern. "The Holy See constitutes in Bolivia a Military Vicar in order to attend to the spiritual welfare of the members of the armed forces," according to the norms (*las normas*) of DE VICARIIS CASTRENSIBUS.³⁹ He may also discipline his military chaplains on the same canonical grounds ({VII}). As to the jurisdiction of the new Military Vicar and his chaplains, the language employed appears highly comprehensive, "extending to all the soldiers in active service, their wives, sons, relations, and domestic staff who billet with them in military establishments, to cadets in academies, and to all the civilians and religious who reside in military hospitals or in other institutions reserved for the military."⁴⁰ The Bolivian concordat also clarifies that Catholic religious are to be exempt from peacetime military service, though in the event of a general mobilization shall assist the armed forces ({X}).

The other three concordats, for their part, are very similar to that with Bolivia, save for the following modifications and clarifications. The treaty with Paraguay concluded the same year specifies that the Military Vicar shall be named (*nombrado*) by the Apostolic See in agreement with (*de acuerdo con*) the Paraguayan President (*AAS* 54 [1962], 22 {II}), and that his jurisdiction also extends to the police ({additional protocol}). The Paraguayan concordat also grounds clerical exemption from military service specifically in canons 121 and 614. The concordat with El Salvador (*AAS* 60 [1968], 382–84), meanwhile, furnishes an abridged version of that with Bolivia, while the concordat with Ecuador (*AAS* 75 [1983-I], 481–84) duplicates the Paraguayan extension of the jurisdiction of the Military Vicar to the national police, a treaty term in both instances suggestive perhaps of their true or full ideological intent.

The 1986 promulgation of the apostolic constitution SPIRITUALI MILITUM CURAE (*AAS* 78 [1986], 481–86) likewise resulted in a miniature assortment of three brief concordats the treaty norms of which were grounded in this particular development of the canon law. The document is based on the contention that the armed forces now require a "concrete and specific form of pastoral assistance,"[41] which is to be rendered no longer by *military vicars* (VICARIATUS CASTRENSES) but by military ordinaries (ORDINARIATIBUS MILITARIBUS) named by the Apostolic See (II§2), raised to episcopal dignity (II§1), and competent to charter seminaries (VI§3). The apostolic constitution furthermore explains that although the faithful are not exempt from diocesan jurisdiction, the military ordinary, if present, nevertheless enjoys *personal* (PERSONALIS, IV.1°), *ordinary* (ORDINARIA, IV.2°), and *proper* (PROPIA, IV.3°) jurisdiction. "Since all the faithful must cooperate to the edification of the Body of Christ," the Apostolic See enjoins, "let the Ordinary and his presbytery take care that the faithful, individually and collectively, play their strong apostolic and even missionary role among the soldiers with whom they live."[42] The concordat with Bolivia the same year (*AAS* 81 [1989], 528–31) incorporating the military ordinary into Bolivian ecclesiastical polity explicitly cites SPIRITUALI MILITUM CURAE in justification but adds that the norms of the canon law also continue to apply ({IX}), specifying in particular entries applicable to the solemnization of matrimony (CIC/1983, c. 1108, 1110, 1115, 1118, 1121). The Apostolic See also agrees to name the military ordinary in consultation with the Bolivian government ({III}). Subsequent concordats with Brazil (*AAS* 82 [1990], 126–29) and with Venezuela (*AAS* 87 [1995], 1092–96) duplicate these terms, although the former requires Brazilian citizenship for the military ordinary ({III.I}). Thus by what they have done, and by what they have left undone the Latin American concordats have perpetuated the authoritarian ecclesiological norms of the Iberian Counter-Reformation.

A Theology of Liberation

As a consequence of the counter-revolutionary ecclesiological treaty norms surveyed above, the task would fall neither to the Apostolic See nor to the contracting regimes, but rather to the excluded *bishops* of the region to independently demand ideational change, in the name of God but on behalf of their flock. At the conclusion of the most active longitudinal interval of the case cluster (1954–1968), a second general conference of Latin American bishops[43] convened at Medellín, Colombia, in August, 1968, and produced results that launched the comparative and to a lesser degree international tendency known as liberation theology, which seeks to reinvigorate the apostolic imagination through the qualified utilization of historical materialism.[44] Gutiérrez, its original and most decisive theorist, reflects upon the profound importance of the Medellín deliberations thus: "The name and reality of 'liberation theology' came into existence at Chimbote, Peru, in July 1968, only a few months before Medellín. Ever since Medellín, the development of liberation theology in Latin America has been accompanied by a continual awareness that we have entered into a new historical stage in the life of our peoples."[45]

The Medellín documents[46] are comprised of two sections. Chapters one through nine concern "Human Promotion" (*Promoción Humana*), and chapters ten through sixteen "The Visible Church and its Structures" (*La Iglesia visible y sus estructuras*). Justice (I), is followed by the demand for Peace (II), which surveys the rampant social marginalization, hopelessly alienated labor, interminable class conflict, extreme inequality of outcome, but above all systemic institutionalization of *violence* (*violencia*) purportedly encountered throughout Central and South America, and perpetrated by both state and non-state actors. "Here we denounce imperialism of whatever ideological variety,"[47] begin the aggrieved assembled priesthood. They continue with concern for the socio-economic renewal of the Family (III), and clarify that as to Education (IV), overwhelming emphasis is to be placed upon a "new type of society that we seek in the personalization of new generations, deepening mindfulness of their human dignity, favoring their free self-determination and promoting their communal sense."[48] Subsequent chapters pertaining to Youth (V), Ordinary Discipleship (VI), Catechism (VIII), and Liturgy (IX) demonstrate that whereas contemporary European Christian Democracy, broadly defined, sought to conserve Christian social order, Latin American liberation theology formulated a radical call to dynamically transform it. "The Latin American episcopate," states Medellín in the poverty of the Church chapter (XIV), "cannot remain indifferent to the tremendous social injustices on display in Latin America, which maintain the majority of our peoples in a terrible poverty."[49] Both laity (X) and religious (XI–XIII) must therefore comprehensively renew their minds and adjust their associations in preparation for the newfound salvific task of eliminating violence, oppression, terror, and poverty from the lives of the faithful of the Catholic Church in Latin America.

Several remarks concerning the relationship between Church and State within the seventh chapter entitled "Discipleship of the Elites," (*Pastoral de élites*) most directly confront however the treaty norms of the Latin American concordats identified and discussed above. Although the overwhelming emphasis of Medellín is social rather than political, the bishops furnish a critical position on the ecclesiastical patronage formulation derivative of Spanish colonialism and perpetuated with alterations through the concordats. "The Church must always maintain," they state, "its independence from the constituted powers...renouncing to be precise any and all legitimate instruments which, as a result of social context, arouse suspicion of an alliance with the constituted power, and likewise result in pastoral contradiction."[50] Direct and unqualified application of this norm would appear to preëmpt concordatorial diplomacy. The bishops in the same context also provide peculiar reference to the primary instruments of the gratuitous internal repression of their republics. "With regard to the armed forces, the Church must stress that, in addition to their specified normal functions, they uphold the mission of guaranteeing the political liberties of the citizens instead of obstructing them."[51] A pastoral call to furthermore promote positive immediately follows this injunction to preserve negative liberty. "Additionally, the armed forces preserve the possibility of educating, within their proper bounds, the new recruits in the future free and responsible participation in the political life of the country."[52] Such strong and distinctive normative results of the Medellín episcopal conference were subsequently made manifest in the call for a *Liberation of Theology* (1976) of Juan Luis Segundo, the fixation upon the transformational modality of "base communities" in the *Ecclesiogenesis*

(1977) of Leonardo Boff, and in the reconstruction of *Jesus the Liberator* (1991) of Jon Sobrino, catalyzing one of the most important idealist turns in modern ecclesiastical history.

NOTES

1. *Political Writings* (Cambridge: Cambridge University Press, 1991).
2. *On Temporal and Spiritual Authority* (Indianapolis: Liberty Fund, 2012).
3. *Selections from Three Works* (Indianapolis: Liberty Fund, 2015), 149. The same also authored *A Defence of the Catholic and Apostolic Faith* (1613) against King James and his oath of episcopal loyalty specifically, as well as *A Work on the Three Theological Virtues Faith, Hope, and Charity* (1621).
4. Populos in hujusmodi insulis et terris degentes ad Christianam religionem…ad terras firmas et insulas predictas viros probos et Deum timentes, doctos, peritos, et expertos, ad instruendum incolas et habitatoras prefatos in fide Catholica et bonis moribus. In Frances Gardiner Davenport (ed.), *European Treaties bearing on the History of the United States and its Dependencies to 1648* (Washington, D.C.: Carnegie Institution of Washington, 1917), 62.
5. In Mecham ([1934] 1966), 17.
6. *A Short Account of the Destruction of the Indies* (London: Penguin [*Brevísima relación de las destrucción de las Indias*, 1552] 1992).
7. In D. Pedro Rodriguez Campomanes, *Tratado de la regalia de España* (Paris: Libreria hispano-americana, 1830), 236.
8. Concordat concluded between His Holiness and Her Catholic Majesty, signed at Madrid on 16 March 1851 (adopted 16 March 1851, entered into force 11 May 1851) 1221 UNTS 301.
9. *Church and State in Latin America: A History of Politico-Ecclesiastical Relations* (Chapel Hill, NC: University of North Carolina Press, 1966), 36. See also Charles Boxer, *The Church Militant in Iberian Expansion* (Baltimore: Johns Hopkins University Press, 1978; and Eugene W. Shiels, *King and Church: The Rise and Fall of the* Patronato Real (Chicago: Loyola University Press, 1961). It furthermore seems extremely interesting to observe in passing that whereas the British monarch allotted the lands of

North America to select *individuals*, the papal monarch divided those of South America between the Spanish and Portuguese *states*.

10. Buenos Aires: Biblioteca del Congreso de la Nación, [1835] 2017. *Todas las constituciones dadas en Sud-América durante la Guerra de la Independencia fueron expression complete de la necesidad dominante de...la independencia y la Libertad exterior...En su redacción nuestras constituciones imitaban las constituciones de la República francesca y de la República de Norte-América*, 57–58. Señor Alberdi in the same decisive comparative regional study furnishes perhaps the inaugural formulation of complex interdependence via functional integration across national borders, emphasizing the mutual interest in the belated promotion of commercial treaties, open immigration, religious tolerance, interior settlement and development, public railways, private contracting, and river navigation among the fledgling South American republics.

11. As for a representative sample of each position, Matías Gómez Zamora in *Regio Patronato Español é Indiano* (Madrid: Compañía de Jesús, 1897) advances the canonist or papal position, Antonio Joaquin de Ribadeneyra in *Manual Compendio de el Regio Patronato Indiano* (Madrid: Antonio Marin, 1755) forcefully argues the regalist or Spanish view, and Dr. Juan Luis de Aquirre y Texada argues that because patronage is inherent in state sovereignty, a formerly royal domain may lay claim to it. In Faustino J. Legón, *Doctrina y Ejercicio del Patronato Nacional* (Buenos Aires: Libreria Nacional, 1920), 234–40.

12. See Ladislas Farago, *Aftermath: Martin Bormann and the Fourth Reich* (New York: Simon and Schuster, 1974); Uki Goñi, *The Real Odessa: Smuggling the Nazis to Peron's Argentina* (London: Granta, 2002); Daniel Stahl, *Hunt for Nazis: South America's Dictatorships and the Prosecution of Nazi Crimes* (Amsterdam: Amsterdam University Press, 2018); and Gerald Steinarcher, *Nazis on the Run: How Hitler's Henchmen Fled Justice* (Oxford: Oxford University Press, 2011).

13. From an immense literature involving facts and evidence still coming to light, see especially Peiro Gleijeses, *Shattered Hope: The Guatemalan Revolution and the United States, 1944–1954* (Princeton: Princeton University Press, 1991); Michael Grow, *U.S. Presidents and Latin American Interventions: Pursuing Regime Change in the Cold War* (Topeka: University of Kansas Press,

2008); J. Patrick McSherry, *Predatory States: Operation Condor and Covert War in Latin America* (Lanham, MD: Rowman & Littlefield, 2005); and Stephen G. Rabe, *The Killing Zone: The United States Wages Cold War in Latin America* (Oxford: Oxford University Press, 2016).

14. *La Iglesia Católica podrá libremente en Colombia administrar sus asuntos interiores y ejercer actos de autoridad espiritual y de jurisdicción eclesiástica, sin necesidad de autorización del Poder civil*, IV.53.

15. *El Gobierno podrá celebrar convenios con la Santa Sede Apostólica a fin de arreglar las cuestiones pendientes, y definir y establecer las relaciones entre la potestad civil y la eclesiástica*, IV.56. The 1997 Polish Constitution furnishes a similar provision (25.4).

16. *La moral del cristianismo y sus doctrinas civilizadoras contra la inmoralidad y las doctrinas corruptoras del materialism y del ateísmo*, 3. Mariano Ospina Rodríguez and José Eusebio Caro, "Programa Conservador de 1849," in *Manual del Conservador* (Bogotá: Directorio Nacional Conservador, 2020): 12–13.

17. *Afianzamiento de las relaciones con la Santa Sede, mediante la celebración de Concordatos y otros convenios que satisfagan los intereses espirituales del país y los sentimientos religiosos del pueblo paraguayo*, II.5.

18. *Especifidad de la democracia christiana* (Caracas: 2002); *Parlamento mundial: una voz latinoamericana* (Caracas: Ediciones del Congreso de la República, 1984); *La nacionalización del petróleo* (Caracas: Ediciones Nueva Politica, 1976); *La solidaridad pluralista de America Latina* (Caracas: Oficina Central de Informacion, 1973); *Temas de sociologia venezolana* (Caracas: Editorial Tiempo Nuevo, 1973); *El bloque latino-americano* (Caracas: Oficina Central de Informacion, 1970). The primary source for his presidential conversation, furthermore, is *Habla El Presidente: Dialogo seminal con el pueblo venezolano*, 5 vols. (Caracas: Ediciones de la Presidencia de la Républica, 1970–74).

19. *El adjetivo cristiano no representa una posición religiosa, sino la convicción de que los valores cristianos y el espíritu de la cristiandad son de reconocimiento fundamental para poder enfrentar con éxito los requerimientos de la justicia social y derrotar al marxismo en la lucha por conquistar el alma de los pueblos*, 55.

20. (Chicago: C.E.C. Communist Party of America, 1920), 33.

21. Especially memorable examples include José Carlos Mariategui, *Siete ensayos de interpretación de la realidad peruana* (Barcelona: Red ediciones, [1928] 2022); Diego Rivera, *Man at the Crossroads* ([Fresco] 1934); and María Alicia Rueda, *The Educational Philosophy of Luis Emilio Recabarren: Pioneering Working-Class Education in Latin America* (New York: Routledge, 2021).
22. Foremost perhaps among numerous personal interventions of imperishable historic significance was the negotiation of the Treaty of Brest-Litovsk (3 March 1918), which by reason of its cessation of hostilities between Russia and the Quadruple Alliance, *de jure* acknowledgment of Ukrainian and Baltic and de facto acknowledgment of Afghan and Persian independence, and institution of rules-based commercial interaction among the former belligerents ranks with that of Versailles as indispensable to future order in world politics.
23. Trotsky's "The Death Agony of Capitalism and the Tasks of the Fourth International: The Mobilization of the Masses around Transitional Demands to Prepare the Conquest of Power," *Bulletin of the Opposition* (May–June, 1938) accuses Stalin of serving, "merely as Goebbels' assistant" (36), insofar as Soviet bureaucracy and reaction have derailed the permanent revolution.
24. These include the initial *Motorcycle Diaries: Notes on a Latin American Journey* (New York: Seven Stories Press, 2003), *Latin American Diaries: The Sequel to* The Motorcycle Diaries (New York: Seven Stories Press), *Reminiscences of the Cuban Revolutionary War* (New York: Seven Stories Press), *Congo Diary: Episodes of the Revolutionary War in the Congo* (New York: Seven Stories Press, 2011), and the final, terminal *Bolivian Diary* (New York: Seven Stories Press, [1967] 2006). Che also famously compiled a manual on *Guerilla Warfare* (New York: BN Publishing, [1967] 2012).
25. In David Deutschmann and María del Carmen Ariet Garcia (eds.), *The Che Guevara Reader: Writings on Politics and Revolution* (New York: Seven Stories Press, 2013), 325.
26. *Ibid.*, 327.
27. Prominent variations include Andre Gunder Frank, *Capitalism and Underdevelopment in Latin America* (New York: Monthly Review Press, 1967); Raúl Prebisch, *The Economic Development of Latin America and Its Principal Problems* (New York: United Nations,

1950); and Walter Rodney, *How Europe Underdeveloped Africa* (London: Bogle-L'Ouverture, 1972).
28. Compare this theoretical synthesis to that of their martyred testator Trotsky: "The scientific task, as well as the political, is not to give a finished definition to an unfinished process, but to follow all its stages, separate its progressive from its reactionary tendencies, expose their mutual relations, foresee possible variants of development, and find in this foresight a basis for action." *The Revolution Betrayed* (Mineola, NY: Dover, [1937], 2004), 193.
29. *Alianza de clases de obreros, campesinos, clases medias y burguesia progresista contra el despotism imperialista y las fuerzas aliadas internas*, III. *Movimiento Nacionalista Revolucionario* (La Paz: National Electoral Court, 1987), 14.
30. What came to be known as the Betancourt Doctrine was of peculiar international significance. His exact words were, *Regímenes que no respeten los derechos humanos, que conculquen las libertades de sus ciudadanos y los tiranicen con respaldo de policías políticas totalitaristas, deben ser sometidos a riguroso cordon sanitario y erradicados mediante acción pacífica colectiva de la comunidad jurídica interamericana* /Regimes that fail to respect human rights, that violate the liberties of the citizens and that tyrannize them by means of totalitarian secret police, must be subjected to a rigorous sanitary cordon and eradicated through peaceful collective action of the pan-American legal community. In *Rómulo Betancourt: Selección de escritos politicos, 1929–1981* (Caracas: *Fundación Rómulo Betancourt*, 2006), 339. Trujillo the following year attempted to kill Betancourt in revenge. See especially Stephen G. Rabe, "The Caribbean Triangle: Betancourt, Castro, and Trujillo and U.S. Foreign Policy, 1958–1963," *Diplomatic History* 20, no. 1 (1996): 55–78.
31. (Betancourt, 2006), 341. *Personalmente, creo que ha llegado la hora de que se inicien conversaciones con la Santa Sede para presentarle al Congreso de la República formulas que permitan, si éste lo considera conveniente, la sustitución de los inoperantes cartabones contenidos en la Ley del Patronato Eclesiástico, legislación perteneciente casi a la prehistoria de nuestro derecho público, por las normas más flexibles de un modern* modus vivendi, *ciudadosamente discutido entre las partes contratantes.*

32. Dómine, salvam fac Rempublicam et Praesidem ejus. / < *Lord, save the Republic and its President.* >Et exaudi nos in die, qua invocavérimus te. / < *And hear us in the day we call to you.* >S alvum fac populum tuum, Dómine: et benedic hereditáti tuae. / < *Lord, save your people, and bless your heritage.* >Et rege eos et extólle illos usque in aeternum. / < *Govern them and lift them up forever.* >D ómine, exaudi orationem meam. / < *Lord, hear my prayer.* >Et clamor meus ad te veniat, / < *And may my cry come unto you.* > {Final Protocol, XXVI}.
33. *Libre organización y funcionamiento de las asociaciones católicas con fin religioso, social y caritativo, y en particular de las asociaciones de Acción Católica*, XXV.
34. *El Estado Venezolano reconoce el libre ejercicio del derecho de la Iglesia Católica de promulgar Bulas, Breves, Estatutos, Decretos, Cartas Encíclicas y Pastorales en el ámbito de su competencia*, II.
35. *El Estado Venezolano, de conformidad con la Constitución, reconoce el derecho de organización de los ciudadanos católicos para promover la diffusion y actuación de los principios de la fe y moral católicas mediante las asociaciones de Acción Católica*, XV.
36. *El Estado, en atención al tradicional sentimiento católico de la Nación Colombiana, considera la Religión Católica, Apostólica y Romana como element fundamental del bien común y del desarrollo integral de la comunidad nacional*, I.
37. *La Legislación canònica es independiente de la civil y no forma parte de ésta, pero será respetada por las autoridades de la República*, III.
38. Qui Vicarii Castrensis munus gerit ordinaria at speciali praeditus est iurisdictione in spirituale bonum commissorum fidelium exercenda. Iurisdictio qua fruitur Vicarius Castrensis est personalis, I-II.
39. *La Santa Sede constituye en Bolivia un Vicariato Castrense para attender al cuidado espiritual de los miembros de las Fuerzas Armadas*, I.
40. *Se extiende a todos los militares en servicio active, a sus esposas, hijos, familiars y personal doméstico, que convivan con ellos en los establecimientos militares, a los cadets de las Instituciones de formación, y a todos los religiosos y civiles que de manera estable vivan en los hospitals militares o en otras instituciones o lugares reservados a los militares*, VIII.

41. Concreta atque specifica curae pastoralis forma indigent, preamble.
42. Cum omnes fideles ad aedificationem Corporis Christi cooperari debeant, Ordinarius eiusque presbyterium curent ut fideles, laici Ordinariatus, sive uti singuli sive consocianti, suas partes gerant tamquam fermentum apostolicum, sed et missionale, inter ceteros milites cum quibus vitam agunt, IX.
43. *Segunda Conferencia General del Espiscopado Latinoamericano.* A Latin American Episcopal Council (*Consejo Episcopal Latinoamericano* [CELAM]) took shape from the first such conference in Río de Janeiro in 1955.
44. See especially William T. Cavanaugh, "The Ecclesiologies of Medellín and the Lessons of the Base Communities," *Cross Currents* 44, no. 1 (1994): 67–84; Patrick Cloffey and Joe Egan (eds.), *Movement or Moment? Assessing Liberation Theology Forty Years after Medellín* (Bern: Peter Lang, 2009); Rafael Luciani, "*Medellín 50 años después. Del Desarrollo a la liberación (I),*" *Revista Teologia* 55, no. 125 (2018): 120–38; and Juan-José Tamayo, "*Medellín, del cristianismo colonial al cristianismo liberador,*" *Rever* 18, no. 2 (2018): 13–34. Salient examples of liberation theology formulated and applied outside the original Latin American context include James H. Cone, *A Black Theology of Liberation* (Maryknoll, NY: Orbis, [1970] 2020); Letty M. Russell, *Human Liberation in Feminist Perspective: A Theology* (Philadelphia: Westminster, 1974); Richard Cleaver, *Know My Name: A Gay Liberation Theology* (Louisville, KY: Westminster John Knox, 1995); and George F. Tinker, *American Indian Liberation: A Theology of Sovereignty* (Maryknoll, NY: Orbis, 2008).
45. *A Theology of Liberation* (Maryknoll, NY: Orbis [*Teologia de la liberación: Perspectivas,* 1971] 1988), xviii.
46. *Iglesia y liberación humana. Los Documentos de Medellín* (Barcelona: Nova Terra, 1969).
47. *Denciamos aquí el imperialismo de cualquier signo ideológico,* II.10.
48. *Nuevo tipo de Sociedad que buscamos en la personalización de las nuevas generaciones, profundizando la conciencia de su dignidad humana, favoreciendo su libre autodeterminación y promoviendo su sentido comunitario,* IV.8.

49. *El Episcopado Latinoamericano no puede quedar indiferente ante las tremendas injusticias sociales existentes en América Latina, que mantienen a la mayoria de nuestros pueblos en una dolorosa pobreza*, XIV.I.1.
50. *La Iglesia deberá mantener siempre su independencia frente a los poderes constituidos...renunciado si fuera preciso aun a aquellas formas legítimas de presencia que, a causa del context social, la hacen sospechosa de alianza con el poder constituido*, VII.21.c.
51. *Con relación a las fuerzas armadas, la Iglesia deberá inculcarles que, además de sus funciones normales específicas, ellas tienen la mission de garantizar las libertades políticas de los ciudadanos en lugar de ponerles obstáculos*, VII.20.
52. *Por lo demás, las fuerzas armadas tienen la posibilidad de educar, dentro de sus propios cuadros, a los jóvenes reclutas en orden a la futura participación, libre y responsible, en la vida política del país*, ibid.

CHAPTER 7

European Secularism, 1801–2020

In 1789, the year of the outbreak of the great revolution in France, Emmanuel Joseph "Abbé" Sieyès affirmed in *What is the Third Estate?* (*Qu'est-ce que le Tiers état?*), the most sustained theoretical inquiry into the character of that revolution, "The nation forms itself solely by natural right. The government, on the contrary, pertains exclusively to positive right…The national will…has no need but for itself in order to be legal, since it is the origin of all legality."[1] Six years later, Immanuel Kant to some extent reformulated Sieyès' political into an international theory of *Perpetual Peace* (*ewigen Frieden*), constructing his both polity and ontology on the sequential propositions of comparative republicanism, international association through federal integration, and universal respect for the laws of hospitality, all to geographically and institutionally develop and deepen over time. "Differences of language and religion," Kant explains, "do indeed dispose men to mutual hatred and to pretexts for war. But the growth of culture and men's gradual progress toward greater agreement regarding their principles lead to mutual understanding and peace."[2] Framing the entire longitudinal interval of the modern use of the concordat, this case cluster chapter shall demonstrate the considerable influence of the legal revolution of European secularism upon the treaty norms of the French and Austrian nation-states where it triumphed through the enactment of positive law.

Pure Theory of Law

Beginning with the Napoleonic France of the consular (1799–1804), imperial (1804–1814), and final 100 days (20 March–18 July 1815) periods, the rapacious authoritarian rule of one man was established in a deeply traumatized Catholic nation, and hegemonic war unleased throughout most of a woefully unprepared sacramental Europe. Observing the passing Napoleon in person in Jena, Germany in 1806, the philosopher Hegel appeared enamored of, "The Emperor—this World-soul...seated upon a horse, surveying and mastering the world,"[3] an incarnation it is implied of his precious dialectic. Eight years thereafter and on the other side of the invasion of Russia, an exasperated Benjamin Constant in *The Spirit of Conquest and Usurpation* (*De L'Esprit de Conquête et de L'Usurpation*) possibly inaugurated democratic peace theory on the following terms: "A senseless war is therefore today the most frontal assault that a government can commit: it shakes, without compensation, all social guarantees. It places in peril all forms of liberty, injures all interests, menaces all assurances, weighs all fortunes, combines and authorizes all forms of domestic and international tyranny."[4] Madame De Staël—whom Bonaparte had exiled—interpreted the tyrant as a pathological embodiment of Machiavellian cynicism, introduced the term "counter-revolution" (483) to characterize his regime, and described his personality as consisting primarily in, "contempt of mankind, and consequently of all the laws, all the establishments, and all the elections of which the basis is respect for the human race."[5] Future French President Adolphe Thiers disagreed, viewing Bonaparte somewhat sympathetically as a liberal, modernizing force[6]; but Thomas Carlyle would counter once again with his early Victorian assessment of the Corsican upstart as a delusional and superficial sequel to Oliver Cromwell.[7] Relinquishing the both unbearable and unnecessary objective of the summary and analysis of every subsequent contention, construction, criticism, or curse concerning the Emperor of France and Soul of the World, this analysis shall concentrate upon the two primary and main secondary source for the normative commitments of French Emperor Napoleon Bonaparte.

The first is the *Civil Code of the French* (*Code Civil des Français*, 1804) of which the despot was very proud, and which furnished a tremendous advance in the enactment of a pure theory of law. Organized into three respective books concerning *persons*, *goods*, and *the means of acquiring property*, the first chapter of the Napoleonic code guarantees though does not enumerate "civil rights" (*droits civils*) for all Frenchmen that can only be lost through "civil death" (*mort civile*, I.I.II) in the form of capital punishment or certain forms of emigration and naturalization elsewhere. This foundation established, primary conceptual emphasis is placed on the articulation of the nature of *contract*, "a convention by which one or more persons engage themselves, to person or persons, to give, to do, or to not do something."[8] Contemporary French religious were much displeased by the application of this positivist logic to marriage, being de-sacralized through the code and relocated from the jurisdiction of ecclesiastical courts to that of a "Government Commissar" (*commissaire du Gouvernement*, I.VI.II.253) endowed with the authority to grant divorce on grounds of adultery, spousal abuse, conviction for a capital crime, or free consent of both parties. But with regard to the forthcoming development of the concordat at the intersection of canon, comparative, and international law, some of the language employed in the French code to articulate the decisive notion of the civil contract appears to have influenced the formation of some of the treaty terms described in the second chapter, with the most suggestive remark as follows: "Conventions legally formed take the place of law for those who make them. They cannot be revoked except by mutual consent, or for causes which the law authorizes."[9] This particular entry in the code likely served as a primary source and reference for the characteristic concordatorial term (page 12) of treaty modification solely by mutual consent of the contracting parties.

The other indirect entry into the mind of Napoleon amid fields of fire and seas of blood is the *Memorial of Saint Helen*, wherein the aristocratic political psychologist the Comte de Las Cases was able to observe and engage the exalted prisoner in a sustained series of interactions during his final, remote island exile.[10] The annotated diary opens with the abdication, exile, and arrival of Napoleon in June, 1815, and proceeds through the international travels of the author and correspondence with other contemporary historical figures, closing with a last will and testament (655–71) of 15 April 1821. Defiant to the unholy end, Bonaparte regards himself as having been "murdered by the English aristocracy" (*assassiné par l'oligarchie anglaise*, 5^0) despite his most determined efforts to accomplish "all for the French people" (*tout pour le peuple français*, 4^0). He nevertheless clarifies his adherence to the apostolic and Roman religion (*la religion apostolique et romaine*, 1^0) before disposing of his still extensive movable and immovable properties.

Sophisticated *conceptualization* of these materials, however, awaited the appearance in 1839 of the *Napoleonic Ideas* (*Des Idées Napoléoniennes*) of his nephew and future ruler (1852–1870) Napoleon-Louis Bonaparte, who distilled the materials described above together with systematic analysis of the emperor's domestic and foreign policies into something resembling a coherent political theory. However implausible must appear the author's repeated assurances that the imperialist rule of his illustrious uncle was thoroughly benign, much less that he served as an instrument of Providence (146) for the reconstitution of Europe (149), the characterization of Bonaparte as the *executor* (17) of the revolution is interesting, as is the theory built thereon. "The Emperor Napoleon never committed the fault of many men of state, that of wishing to subject the nation to any abstract theory," his heir explains. "He studied, on the contrary, with care the character of the French people, their needs, their present state; and, from these criteria, he formulated a system that he subsequently modified according to circumstances."[11] The strongly approved creation of republican instruments of government including the Council of State, the Grand Elector, and the Court of Cassation (113–18) bear witness to the enduring commitment to this *systeme*; and likewise regarding financial and administrative modernization, agricultural improvements, educational advances, public monuments and memorials, and in particular the introduction of universal CONSCRIPTION, "one of the grand institutions of the century" (*une des plus grandes institutions du siècle*, 98) which at once recruited active troops from the whole nation, and placed the whole nation on reserve status. As for foreign relations, the emperor is approvingly held to have extended the "benefits of a clear administration" (*bienfaits d'une administration éclairée*, 156) to the Italian, Swiss, German, Polish, Dutch, and Spanish subject nations, and by this policy to have prepared the way for a European confederation that would somehow facilitate comparative self-determination. "The politics of the Emperor...consisted in founding a solid European association, and in making this system repose on complete nationalities and the satisfaction of general interests."[12] Wherefore the political norms of Napoleon Bonaparte, based upon the most reliable available evidence, appear to coalesce into a *highly aggressive liberal republicanism*, though obviously sparing the rational utility of a modernizing emperor.[13]

Turning now to the Austria of the second republic (1945-), further inquiry reveals that every head of state or government and every contracting plenipotentiary identified in Table 7.1 belonged to no parliamentary party apart from the Social Democratic Party of Austria (*Sozialdemokratische Partei Österreichs*, [SPÖ] 1889-) or the Folk Party of Austria (*Österreichischen Volkspartei*, [ÖVP] 1945-).[14] What norms prevail within these two Austrian parties that appear to regularly alternate in power but with comparable frequency to conclude concordats? Amid satisfactory existing coverage of their "grand coalitions" principally intended to preserve the democratic peace,[15] of their derivative *Proporz* system of equity in patronage and largesse,[16] and of the intersecting "corporatist" (*berufsständisch*) regimes of Austrian political economy,[17] the question is both necessary with respect to the case cluster findings as well as useful on its own terms.

The contemporary Austrian folks and social democrats represent democratized versions of the two primary authoritarian tendencies whose violent quarrel sealed the fate of the first Austrian republic (1920–1934); and therefore analysis should concentrate upon the comparatively unfamiliar circumstances surrounding its strange death and eventual reconstitution. The peace treaty between the victorious Allied and Associated powers and prostrate Austria signed at Saint-Germain-en-Laye in September, 1919, robbed the fledgling democracy of its freedom and honor much as that of Versailles recently had Germany, with the limitation of total Austrian force strength to 30,000 (120), prohibition of all submariner (140) and aerial capability (144), and subjection to the nearly omnipotent reparations commission (VIII) foremost among its many vindictive terms. The following year, its reluctant signatory Dr. Karl Renner appointed Professor Kelsen to chair a secretariat tasked with the composition of a new constitution[18]; and the decisive result was the Federal Constitutional Law (*Bundes-Verfassungsgesetz* [B-VG]). The balloon-shaped Austrian borders fixed by the international treaty, Kelsen drew up a federal state consisting of nine *Länder* and various municipalities, with many subject matter divisions and checks and balances between these legal units,[19] all beneath a directly elected Federal President as head of state and a Federal Chancellor as head of government. His instrument of government for Austria furthermore abolishes the death penalty (85), establishes the office of ombudsman (148.a), and incorporates "self-administering bodies" (*Selbstverwaltungskörper*) into public law, provided their internal statutes are democratic and in conformity with all applicable laws (120.a–c). But two features appear especially significant. First, Kelsen originates the Constitutional Court (*Verfassungsgerichtshof*) as an instrument of political justice in democracy, endowing it

Table 7.1 European secularism

Pontiff (Pontifical Legate, Title)	Contracting party (Contracting location, Date, Language(s))	Head of State or Government (Contracting plenipotentiary, Title)
Pius VII	**FRENCH GOVERNMENT** (15 July 1801 [invoked 1906], Latin)	Napoleon Bonaparte
John XXIII (Giovanni Dellepiane, Nuncio)	**REPUBLIC OF AUSTRIA** (Vienna, 23 June 1960, Italian/German)	Julius Raab (Ministers Bruno Kreisky and Heinrich Drimmel)
John XXIII (Opilio Rossi, Nuncio)	**REPUBLIC OF AUSTRIA** (Vienna, 9 July 1962, Italian/German)	Alfons Gorbach (Ministers Bruno Kreisky and Heinrich Drimmel)
Paul VI (Opilio Rossi, Nuncio)	**REPUBLIC OF AUSTRIA** (Vienna, 7 July 1964, Italian/German)	Josef Klaus (Ministers Bruno Kreisky and Theodor Piffl-Percevic)
Paul VI (Opilio Rossi, Nuncio)	**REPUBLIC OF AUSTRIA** (Vienna, 7 Oct. 1968, Italian/German)	Josef Klaus (Ministers Kurt Waldheim and Theodor Piffl-Percevic)
Paul VI (Opilio Rossi, Nuncio)	**REPUBLIC OF AUSTRIA** (Vienna, 29 Sep. 1969, Italan/German)	Josef Klaus (Ministers Wilfried Platzer and Alois Mock)
Paul VI (Opilio Rossi, Archbishop Nuncio)	**REPUBLIC OF AUSTRIA** (Vienna, 8 March 1971, Italian/German)	Bruno Kreisky (Ministers Rudolf Kirchschläger and Leopold Gratz)
Paul VI (Opilio Rossi,	**REPUBLIC OF AUSTRIA** (Vienna, 9 Jan. 1976, Italian/German)	Bruno Kreisky (Ministers Erich Bielka

(continued)

Table 7.1 (continued)

Pontiff (Pontifical Legate, Title)	Contracting party (Contracting location, Date, Language(s))	Head of State or Government (Contracting plenipotentiary, Title)
Archbishop Nuncio) John Paul II	REPUBLIC OF AUSTRIA	and Fred Sinowatz) Bruno Kreisky
(Mario Cagna, Archbishop Nuncio) John Paul II	(Vienna, 24 July 1981, Italian/German) REPUBLIC OF AUSTRIA	(Willibald Pahr and Fred Sinowatz, Federal Ministers) Franz Vranitzky
(Donato Squiccairini, Archbishop Nuncio) John Paul II	(Vienna, 10 Oct. 1989, Italian/German) REPUBLIC OF AUSTRIA	(Alois Mock and Hilde Hawlicek, Federal Ministers) Franz Vranitzky
(Donato Squiccairini)	(Vienna, 21 Dec. 1995, Italian/German)	(Wolfgang Schüssel and Elisabeth Gehrer)
Benedict XVI (Dominique Mamberti, Cardinal Secretary of State)	FRENCH REPUBLIC (Paris, 18 Dec. 2008, French)	Nicolas Sarkozy (Bernhard Kouchner, Minister for Foreign and European Affairs)
Benedict XVI (Edmund Farhat, Apostolic Nuncio)	REPUBLIC OF AUSTRIA (Vienna, 5 March 2009, Italian/German)	Werner Faymann (Michael Spindelegger)
Francis (Pedro López Quintana, Apostolic Nuncio)	REPUBLIC OF AUSTRIA (Vienna, 12 Oct. 2020, German)	Sebastian Kurz (Susanne Raab)

with competence to arbitrate disputes between all other courts (138.1.1–2) and between the Federation and the *Länder* (138.2), as well as to rescind ordinances contrary to the law (139.3–6). It also pronounces upon the legality of treaties (140a.1), and upon any contravention of international law (145). Second, Kelsen's otherwise unflappable positivist equanimity—whereby the political is completely excluded from the legal—is broken exclusively with respect to the primary educational policy provision, where the redoubtable Doctor of Law and Philosophy appears to have disdained concealment of his abiding normative commitments: "Democracy, humanity, solidarity, peace, and justice as well as openness and tolerance toward people are the foundational values of the school...In cooperative partnership between students, parents, and teachers, children and adolescents are to be permitted the optimal intellectual, mental, and physical development to enable them to become healthy, self-confident, contented, high-achieving, obedient, skillful, and creative persons...open to the political, religious, and ideological thinking of others and capable of participating in the cultural and economic life of Austria, Europe, and the world."[20]

The good intentions of this positive legal order notwithstanding, it began almost immediately to succumb to the rising tide of politicized, paramilitary violence throughout post-imperial central Europe,[21] which in Austria came to assume the primary form of a *Heimwehr* in the service of the clerical or corporate fascist regime.[22] Sensing the growing threats to his creation, Kelsen during the 1920s authored numerous essays in defense of the constitution,[23] culminating in "The Essence and Value of Democracy" (*Vom Wesen und Wert der Demokratie*, 1929) wherein the former is defined as participatory formation of the will of the state, and the latter as a positive worldview affording lasting protection from transcendental normative tyranny.[24] Yet in this tragic instance the philosopher's stone was dashed to pieces by the *kommando's* truncheon, with the brief (12–16 February 1934) civil war between the Christian social and social democratic forces furnishing sufficient pretext for the institution of the "Austro-fascist" dictatorship of Chancellor Dr. Engelbert Dollfuβ.

A conceptually challenging regime that hoisted its arresting *Kruckenkreuz* somewhere between Mussolini, Hitler, and the Apostolic See, but that awkwardly combined ecclesiological and ideational elements of each,[25] the Dollfuβ dictatorship briefly but decisively embodied the norms of the Austrian Folk or People's Party, however infrequently this debt may be acknowledged.[26] Just like Hitler, Dollfuβ opened his international policy with a concordat in June, 1933 (*AAS* 26 [1934], 249–84) that recognized the Catholic Church as a comparative public law corporation governed according to canon law ({II}), established university instruction in Catholic theology according to DEUS SCIENTIARUM DOMINUS ({V§1}), rendered religious instruction in the schools compulsory ({VI§1}), and very comprehensively pledged the Austrian state to the financial support of the Church in Austria,[27] a commitment to be shortly revisited. The following September 11th marking the one hundred and fiftieth anniversary of the failed Ottoman siege of Vienna,[28] the Chancellor in a major address to his Fatherland Front asserted, "We want the social, Christian, German state of Austria on a corporatist basis, under strong authoritarian leadership!"[29]; and he evidently believed he had secured it through the subsequent May, 1934 constitution. "In the name of Almighty God, from whom all justice flows," the document opens, "the Austrian people receive this their Christian, German, federal constitution on a corporatist basis;"[30] which pursuant to its preamble recognized the Church under public law (29), endowed it with the right to levy ecclesiastical taxes (29.3), and explicitly established the preceding concordat (30.4). Dollfuß was assassinated three months later, Austria annexed four years later, and the Austrian concordat and constitution dissolved into the greater German *Reich*.

Following the war, Herr Dr. Karl Renner reëmerged from excusable self-isolation and with the agreement of the occupying Allied powers became inaugural President of Austria (1945–1950). The eighteenth child of indigent Moravian vintners, Renner in his previous position as Chancellor (1918–1920) had reluctantly signed the debilitating Treaty of Saint-German-en-Laye and commissioned Kelsen to draft the democratic constitution; and in his pre-Dollfuß years in Vienna, he had figured prominently among the "Austro-Marxist" assortment of social scientists[31] including Max Adler, Otto Bauer, and Rudolf Hilferding together building the ideas of Austrian social democracy through their periodicals *Marx-Studien* (1904-) and *Der Kampf* (1907-), conceptual work largely ineffective from 1914 and illegal from 1934. His *Institutions of Private Law and their Social Functions* ([*Die Rechtsinstitute des Privatrechts und ihre soziale Funktion*, 1929] 1949) being the most sustained theoretical exposition of Austro-Marxism prior to its suppression, as well as the only such work translated into English and widely read outside Austria, furnishes the implied overall thesis of Austrian social democracy.

The most intransigent form of European secularism is of course that of Karl Marx, who in the Communist Manifesto (1848), *Capital* (1867), and throughout his otherwise continual and coruscating *oeuvre*[32] never retreats from the position that conflict between social classes is solely responsible for the movement of history, and that accelerating conflict between bourgeois and proletarian classes is certain to portend the revolutionary end of history. Subsequent theoretical applications by his disciples such as Trotsky's *The* [Great] *War and the International* (1914) or Lenin's *The* [Soviet] *State and Revolution* (1917) tend however to tacitly acknowledge the obvious importance of other variables, with Renner's task the successful incorporation of positive law into socialist theory. The main idea is that the prevailing notion of private property generally satisfactory with reference to land and to personal possessions fails to accurately reflect post-industrial social reality, insofar as there are no real *contracts* with workers in service industries such as cooking or cleaning, no meaningful *privacy* in capitalist property such as hotels and railroads, and no possible *adjustment* of the predicament whereby, "the worker, though he can exchange one individual capitalist for another, cannot escape the Capitalist. There is no doubt that in the sphere of production the bourgeoisie as a class has absolute control of the non-propertied classes as far as the law is concerned" (116). Legal norms must therefore, by implication, be realigned to once again accurately reflect the newfound distributions of power in a society transformed by capitalist production.

The constitutive norms of the respective Austrian folk and social democratic parties derived above, finally, persist in less militant forms in their current party platforms.[33] In 2015 the Folks, after identifying themselves as *Christian democratic* (*christdemokratische*, 5), declaring their commitment to a prospective "eco-social market economy" (*Ökosozialen Markwirtschaft*, 6), and stressing the location of solidarity within Christian charity, explain, "We acknowledge the significance of churches and religious communities for understanding and for the yearning for transcendence as well as for education and charitable engagement."[34] They also register opposition to abortion (32). The primary ethic of the Austrian Social Democrats, in contrast, is expressed through *solidarity* (*solidarität*), in which marginalized economic and social groups combine their efforts in pursuit of political justice. "We advocate for a different economic order," their 2018 party platform states, "designed in a democratic, solidarist, and environmental way."[35] This different economic order will somehow achieve multilateral disarmament (19) and resolution of the "climate catastrophe" (*Klimakatastrophe*, 44) abroad, while securing full employment (32), universal housing (41), and LGBTQIA + rights at home. Such are the norms of Austrian politics within the scope of Kelsen's pure theory of law, in turn the most sophisticated rendition of the tradition of positive law.

Positivist Concordats

Germaine De Staël in her epic account of the French revolutionary period characterizes the celebration of the Napoleonic concordat of 15 July 1801(*ASS* 37 [1904–1905], 76–78) in Nôtre-Dame as a "full-dressed rehearsal" for his subsequent coronation, festooned with the livery and regalia of monarchy.[36] The preamble to the first modern concordat consists of a "mutual recognition" (UTRINQUE RECOGNITA) between the French Government and the Holy See, whereby the former explicitly concedes the majoritarian position of the Catholic religion among the French citizenry, and the latter the advantages of both the constitutional establishment of the same and its personal profession by the Consuls. The subsequent terms of the concordat then give substance to these ideas, with article one reading in full, "The Catholic, Apostolic, and Roman religion shall be freely exercised in France; its worship shall be public, conforming itself with police regulations which the government shall judge necessary for the public tranquility."[37] The bishops of France are to accept these terms ({III}), and a regime is agreed whereby the First Consul shall *nominate* (NOMINABIT, {IV}) priests for vacant bishoprics and archbishoprics, to be followed by their investiture of "canonical institution" (INSTITUTIONEM CANONICAM, {IV}) by the Holy See.

The two decisive instruments of an oath of episcopal loyalty and special prayers for the regime ensue, with the first as follows:

> I swear and promise to God, on the Holy Gospels, to be obedient and faithful to the Government established by the constitution of the French Republic. I promise also to have no dealings, to be present at no council, to belong to no league, whether at home or abroad, which may be contrary to the public peace; and if, in my diocese or elsewhere, I learn that anything is being plotted to the prejudice of the state, I will make it known to the Government.[38]

Priests will also be administered the same oath at some unspecified future time by unspecified civil officials ({VII}), making for the only comprehensive application of the device. Second, the refrain, DOMINE, SALVAM FAC REMPUBLICAM; DOMINE, SALVOS FAC CÓNSULES will henceforth conclude the celebration of every Mass in France ({VIII}).

A final assortment of mutual concessions concludes the terms of the concordat. The French government is given a veto on the installation of parish priests ({X}), and though it need not subsidize must allow cathedral chapters and seminaries ({XI}). The Holy See renounces all claims to ecclesiastical property stolen, expropriated, nationalized, or otherwise irretrievably lost through the recent revolutionary convulsions ({XIII}), but the consular government likewise pledges to guarantee acceptable salaries for priests and bishops ({XIV}). The Holy See, finally, extends to the First Consul the same "rights and privileges" (IURA AC PRIVILEGIA, {XVI}) attached to the previous regime, but extracts the guarantee that any prospective assumption of power by a non-Catholic First Consul shall automatically dissolve the concordat, enabling the contracting parties to begin anew ({XVII}).

The canon law of the Catholic Church and the international law of the civilized nations both remained in rudimentary forms in July, 1801; and therefore the remaining *comparative law* of France most likely serves as the primary means by which to help elucidate the treaty norms of the decisive concordat described above. Consultation of the respective French constitutions of 1791, Year One (1793), Year Three (1795), and Year Eight (1799) appear to support the overall contention of the case cluster that the disestablishment though not destruction of the canon law in France and Austria has resulted in the positioning of the treaty norms of their concordats midway between the ecclesiological and ideational.

The Declaration of the Rights of Man and Citizen (*Déclaration des Droits de l'Homme et du Citoyen*) of 1789 is the principle normative statement of the French Revolution; and being prefixed to the first French Constitution of 3–4 September 1791, its tenth article reads, "None should be disquieted on account of their even religious opinions, provided that their manifestation does not disturb the public order by law established."[39] This initial framing of religious belief and practice within the parameters of the preservation of the positive legal order reappears ten years later if with slightly altered wording in the first article of the concordat. Although the 1791 constitution itself proved unable to salvage the political situation through its establishment of a constitutional monarchy heavily reliant on British precedent, its imposition of *oaths of office* for the citizenry (II.5), for the Members of the National Assembly (I.V.6), and for the King (II.I.4) would have familiarized the contracting parties with such procedure, and the respective wording does appear comparable to the oath of episcopal loyalty recorded above. The French oath of citizenship for example reads, "I swear to be faithful to the Nation, to the law, and to the king and to maintain with all my power the Constitution of the Kingdom, as decreed by the national constituent assembly in 1789, 1790, and 1791."[40] The subsequent 1793 constitution, meanwhile, abolishes the monarchy, revises and expands the Declaration of the Rights of Man and Citizen, and otherwise contains no theological content, avoiding entirely the question of the Catholic Church in France.

The Constitution of Year Three, for its part, appropriates a major swathe of territory from the canon law through its comprehensive nationalization of the educational system, making allowance only for French public schools,[41] and originating conflicts in France between *laïque* and Catholic education partially resolved through the recent 2008 concordat (*AAS* 101 [2009], 59–64) reserving to the Apostolic See prerogative over all degrees conferred by Catholic universities, but otherwise attempting to establish protocols for mutual recognition.[42] The same instrument of government furthermore creates though does not specify, "national celebrations, in order to maintain fraternity between citizens and to attach them to the constitution, the country, and the laws,"[43] helping build up a civil religion which then as now competes with the norms of sacramental observance. The Constitution of Year Eight that provided the legal pretense for Napoleonic rule, finally, contained no articles of religion, but explicitly granted to the Consuls[44] comprehensive treaty-making power (49), which thus systematically preconditioned a solution to the overarching question of church and state in France on the basis of the establishment of extraordinary ecclesiastical relations, via concordat.

The positivist legal revolution within the similarly Catholic country of Austria has also resulted in the norms of its concordats appearing somewhere between the strongly ecclesiological and strongly ideational, beginning with the July, 1960 concordat (*ASS* 52 [1960], 933–45) establishing apparently the only existing contract whereby the national government of a Western democratic state is actively paying money directly to the Catholic Church. Agreed five years after the Austrian state treaty, it concerns "property relationships" (*vermögensrechtlichen beziehungen*), and commits the new republic to pay the Church fifty million schillings per annum ({II.a}) together with the rough equivalent salary of 1,250 Catholic religious employees ({II.b}), to restore all immovable property seized in the *Anschluss* ({III.1}), and to transfer about 14,000 acres of timberland to the Archdiocese of Vienna ({III.2}) and 1,400 to the Archdiocese of Salzburg ({III.3}). These terms agreed, "All claims from existing and future compensation regulations of the

Republic of Austria for property damage caused by persecution are finally settled. The Catholic Church recognizes that the Republic of Austria has no further financial obligations in the areas dealt with in this contract beyond the benefits promised."[45] The concordat included however the representative clarification of adjustment by mutual consent ({IX}); and this procedure has been utilized no less than seven times, with the direct payment enumerated above subsequently increased to 67 million schillings in 1969 (*AAS* 62 [1970], 164 {I}), to 97 million in 1976 (*AAS* 68 [1976], 423 {I}), to 128 million in 1981 (*AAS* 74 [1982], 273 {I}), to 158 million in 1989 (*AAS* 82 [1990], 231 {I}), to 192 million in 1995 (*AAS* 90 [1998], 96 {I}), to 17.2 million euros in 2009 (*AAS* 101 [2009], 938 {I}) following the establishment of European monetary union, and finally to 20.7 million euros in October, 2020 (*AAS* 113 [15SEP2021], 96 {I}), the most recent concordat recorded within the *Acts of the Apostolic See*.

During the same interval, Austria also agreed two concordats (*AAS* 56 [1963], 740–43; *AAS* 60 [1968], 782–85) respectively creating a Diocese of Innsbrück-Feldkirch and then partitioning the same into two, each receiving state financial support for their organization and reorganization. But the other early and decisive concordat with democratic Austria (*AAS* 54 [1962], 641–52) concerned the perennial question of Catholic education, with the Church securing the right to provide compulsory instruction to all Catholic pupils in public schools ({I§1.(1)}), though an exception is carved out for trade schools overseen by unspecified guilds ({I§2.(1–2)}). Per the educational canons, furthermore, teachers must align with the *missio canonica* and hold Austrian citizenship ({I§3.(2–3)}), administrators must provide full cooperation to religious inspectors appointed by the Church (I§4.(2)}), and learning materials must not discredit Catholic faith and morals ({I§5.(2)}). Any type of Catholic school may be founded in Austria ({II§1.(1)}), together with supplementary institutions including "kindergartens, after-school care, daycare, dormitories, and such like" (*Kindergärten, Schülerhorte, Schülertagesheime, Schülerheime, und ähnliche Einrichtungen*, {II§1.(3)}). Financially, a one-time payment to the Diocese of Eisenstadt is included to help defray the costs of establishing a Catholic school system in Burgenland ({III}), but more broadly the Austrian republic commits to supporting the Catholic schools through financial grants (*Zuschüsse*, {II§2.(1)}) necessary to maintain their personnel, although a subsequent concordat (*AAS* 64 [1972], 478–81) clarifies that grant money may be customized according to the curricular requirements peculiar to the individual school. As if in defiance of the pure theory of law, the final protocol concludes the concordat by upholding the right of a majority of Christian pupils in a public school classroom to *install a cross*. Therefore in both France and Austria, positivist legal revolution intentionally irrespective of social reality resulted in the permanent disestablishment though not destruction of Roman Catholic canon law, comparative adjustments in turn primarily responsible for the neither fully ecclesiological nor fully ideational norms of the French and Austrian concordats.

"Identitarian" Reaction

In the European context alone, the clear and present dangers, emerging threats, or at the very least overdue qualifications to full confidence in the positive or pure theory of law have become almost too extensive to enumerate, with "Identitarian"[46] political actors increasingly populating parliaments, staging mass rallies, organizing on the internet, confounding the authorities, and challenging the familiar taxonomies of urban/rural, left-leaning/right-leaning, agricultural/industrial, or religious/secular, among others, constitutive of European political science since Lijphart.[47] Attempting in this place neither a critical analysis of the varieties of political theory encountered among so-called Identitarian elements in Europe nor the provision of any advice to established civil or ecclesiastical powers, the author shall instead enthusiastically resubmit for further consideration the first, most comprehensive, and most resolute critique of the deficiencies of the pure theory of law, and consequently a work of the utmost moment: *The Authoritarian State* of Eric Voegelin.

In a neglected monument of comparative law, empirical political science, and realist political theory suppressed after the *Anschluss* and undiscovered until after the war, German-American Prof. Dr. Eric Voegelin in *The Authoritarian State: An Essay on the Problem of the Austrian State* (*Der autoritäre Staat: Ein Versuch über das österreichische Staatsproblem*, 1936) furnishes the most important contrarian treatment of the 1920 Kelsen constitution for Austria together with its supporting doctrine of the positive law.[48] Initially a postgraduate student at the University of Vienna under the supervision of Kelsen, Voegelin fled the Nazis with his wife in 1938, attained American citizenship in 1944, and served with distinction at the universities of Louisiana State, postwar Munich, and Stanford, where he would repeatedly return to the theme of the direct responsibility borne by Kantian philosophy and positive law for the eventual triumph of National Socialism among the German *Volk* and within the German *Reich*. With regard to Austrian constitutional law, Voegelin's longitudinal interval runs from the 1848 revolutions with their fatiguing procession of the Supreme Patent, Bohemian Charter, and Pillersdorff instruments of government—all full of contrasts, and indicative of the deepest turmoil—to the 1934 constitution under Dollfuß, described as authoritarian, "by its authorial endeavors in establishing, preserving, and developing the state" (338). Amid the resplendent illiberalism of late Hapsburg political thought, Voegelin insists that the successive constitutional laws of Austria cannot be comprehended in isolation, however rigorous the selective reading, but only as the historical and social totality of a modern state in desperate search for a self-conscious people. "The lack of a politically united people imbued with the will to existence—that is, of a demos—is precisely *the* problem of the Austrian constitution" (243).

This main problem according to Voegelin is however rendered even more insoluble by the introduction of a pure theory of law both unable to withstand analytical scrutiny and in Austria or in any other case liable to ultimately exacerbate existing disorder. The first deficiency of the positive law doctrine is its complete incomprehension of the *creation* of a particular legal order, with Kelsen arbitrarily distinguishing the law from the state—when of course, other forms of political authority have always existed—and more importantly constructing the former as the orderly agora of reason, method, and cleanliness but the latter as a sinister wilderness of ignorance and violence. "The political power that institutes as *auctoritas*, as the author of a legal order," Voegelin explains, "is not viewed with equanimity, as it would befit a scholar, but with horror as the eruption of something incomprehensible, abnormal, a-rational" (216). The positive law of a state, furthermore, actually consists of *many* discrete legal orders rather than just one (172), with the present inquiry concentrating upon the concordatorial intersection of the canon, comparative, and international. Yet the most grievous error of the pure theory of law in the assessment of early Voegelin is its central contention that the interpretation, elaboration, and application of legal norms can and must occur without reference to the intersecting political science that can alone elucidate the terms employed within the norms. "Norms relating to actions of the type 'voting', 'election', 'nomination', and 'legislation', or to correspondingly acting subjects, such as 'people', 'king', 'parliament', and 'minister'," he forcefully argues, "cannot be understood unless we know what they 'mean'. What they 'mean', however, is not inherent in the norm itself; rather, it must be drawn upon as a content-related premise based on the judgments of a political science oriented toward reality when interpreting the norm" (207). Consequently, the very questions of sociology, ideology, and ethics that the pure theory of law would relegate to the political domain ostensibly for the sake of its own internal cohesion emerge upon closer inspection as indispensable to the articulation and effectiveness of the law.

His physical safety secured from totalitarian rule, Voegelin continued his articulation of a realist political theology at variance with established positivism, idealism, formalism, and rationalism. "The Political Religions" (1938) accounts for the mesmeric appeal of the Nuremberg rallies or October Day parades by reason of their modified utilization of the psychological structure of traditional religious belief, while the postwar "New Science of Politics" (1952) and "Science, Politics, and Gnosticism" (1959) reformulates the gamut of totalitarian intellectual tendencies as modern varieties of Christian Gnosticism.[49] Thus with Identitarian political forces in France, Austria, and elsewhere increasingly evading the comprehension much less the sanction of the pure legal order, wider utilization of its most forceful criticism in the thought of Eric Voegelin is strongly recommended.

Notes

1. Emmanuel Joseph Sieyès, *Qu'est-ce que le Tiers état?* (Paris: Éditions du Boucher, [1789] 2002), 54.
2. Immanuel Kant, *To Perpetual Peace: A Philosophical Sketch* (Indianapolis, IN: Hackett, [*Zum ewigen Frieden: Ein philosophischer Entwurf*, 1795] 2003), 25.
3. Den Kaiser-diese Weltseele...auf einem Pferde sitzend, über die Welt übergreift und sie beherrscht. In Wolfgang Welsch and Klaus Vieweg (eds.), *Das Interesse des Denkens Hegel aus heutiger Sicht* (Münich: Wilhelm Fink Verlag, 2004), 233.
4. *Une guerre inutile est donc aujourd'hui le plus grand attentat qu'un gouvernement puisse commettre: elle ébranle, sans compensation, toutes les garanties sociales. Elle met en peril tous les genres de liberté, blesse tous les intérêts, trouble toutes les sécurités, pèse sur toutes les fortunes, combine et autorise tous les modes de tyrannie*

intérieure et exterieure, 63. His explicit confrontation, furthermore, with "numerous authors…in the service of the dominant system," (*nombre d'écrivains…au service du système dominant*, 64) demonstrates one of the earliest examples of self-conscious intentionality within international theory.

5. *Considerations on the Principal Events of the French Revolution* (Indianapolis: Liberty Fund, [*Considérations sur les principaux événemens de la Révolution Françoise*, 1818] 2008), 517.
6. *The History of the French Revolution* (Cambridge: Cambridge University Press [*Histoire de la Révolution française*, 1823] 2011–12).
7. *On Heroes, Hero-Worship, and the Heroic in History* (New Haven: Yale University Press, [1841] 2013): 162–95.
8. *Une convention par laquelle une ou plusieurs personnes s'obligent, envers une ou plusieurs autres, à donner, à faire ou à ne pas faire quelque chose*, III.III.I.1101.
9. *Les conventions légalement formées tiennent lieu de loi à ceux qui les ont faites. Elles ne peuvent être révoquees que de leur consentement mutuel, ou pour les causes que la loi autorise*, III.III.III.1143.
10. *Le Mémorial de Sainte-Hélène* (Paris: Bibliothèque de la Pleiade, [1835] 1956).
11. *L'Empereur Napoléon ne commit pas la faute de beaucoup d'hommes d'état, de vouloir assujettir la nation à une théorie abstraite…il étudia, au contraire, avec soin le caractère du people français, ses besoins, son état present; et, d'après ces données il formula un systeme, qu'il modifia encore suivant les circonstances*, 104.
12. *La politique de l'Empereur…consistait à fonder une association européene solide, en faisant reposer son système sur des nationalités completes et sur des intérêts généraux satisfaits*, 177.
13. The contracting partner to his 1801 concordat Pope Pius VII (1800–23) might have agreed with this conclusion, as *Diu Satis* (15 May 1800), the first of his four encyclicals, furnishes a rather incoherent reply and ineffectual attempt at pastoral consolation amid the upheavals of the French Revolution. Otherwise, *Ex quo Ecclesiam* (24 May 1800) clarifies that any practicing Roman Catholic may on his or her own initiative select any priestly confessor, as if to expedite the process.
14. Their respective affiliations are the following: Heinrich Drimmel (ÖVP); Elisabeth Gehrer (ÖVP); Alfons Gorbach (ÖVP); Leopold

Gratz (SPÖ); Hilda Hawlicek (SPÖ); Rudolf Kirchschläger (SPÖ); Josef Klaus (ÖVP); Bruno Kreisky (SPÖ); Sebastian Kurz (ÖVP); Alois Mock (ÖVP); Theodor Piffl-Percevic (ÖVP); Julius Raab (ÖVP); Susanne Raab (ÖVP); Wolfgang Schüssel (ÖVP); Fred Sinowatz (SPÖ); Franz Vranitzky (SPÖ); Kurt Waldheim (ÖVP). Erich Bielka, Willibald Pahr, and Wilfried Platzer were independents.

15. See especially Julian Aicholzer and Johanna Willmann, "Forecasting Austrian National Elections: The Grand Coalition Model," *International Journal of Forecasting* 30, (2014): 55–64; Wade Jacoby, "Grand Coalitions and Democratic Dysfunction: Two Warnings from Central Europe," *Government and Opposition* 52, no. 2 (2017): 329–55; and Wolfgang C. Müller, "Austria: Tight Coalitions and Stable Government," in Müller and Kaare Strøm (eds.), *Coalition Governments in Western Europe* (Oxford: Oxford University Press, 2000): 86–125.

16. Concerned exclusively with the question is Reinhard Heinisch, *Populism, Proporz and Pariah—Austria Turns Right: Austrian Political Change, its Causes and Consequences* (New York: Nova Science Publishing, 2002).

17. Conversation begins with Peter J. Katzenstein, *Corporatism and Change: Austria, Switzerland, and the Politics of Industry* (Ithaca, NY: Cornell University Press, 1984). His coverage of the Swiss watch, Austrian steel, and mutual textile industries within larger institutional contexts is comprehensive, but there is no sustained engagement with the revolutions in legal norm to be emphasized here. See also Jill Lewis, "Austria in Historical Perspective: From Civil War to Social Partnership," in Stefan Berger and Hugh Compston (eds.), *Policy Concertation and Social Partnership in Western Europe* (New York: Berghahn, 2002): 19–34.

18. For further historical context, see Sara Lagi, "Hans Kelsen and the Austrian Constitutional Court (1918–1929)," *Revista Co-herencia* 9, no. 16 (2012): 273–95.

19. Specifically, the Federation is endowed with legislative and executive power over foreign and defense policy, the financial system, the administration of justice, transportation, internal improvements, public health, and public buildings and grounds (10). On most more specific questions of public order and quality of life, execution is delegated to the *Länder* (11–12). The *Länder* may also

with the approval of the Federal Government make treaties with commonwealths bordering on Austria (16.1).
20. Demokratie, Humanität, Solidarität, Friede und Gerectigkeit sowie Offenheit und Toleranz gegenüber den Menschen sind Grundwerte der Schule, auf deren Grundlage sie der gesamten Bevölkerung, unabhängig von Herkunft, sozialer Lage und finanziellem Hintergrund, unter steter Sicherung und Weiterentwicklung bestmöglicher Qualität ein höchstmögliches Bildungsniveau sichert. Im partnerschaftlichen Zusammenwirken von Schülern, Eltern und Lehrern ist Kindern und Jugendlichen die bestmögliche geistige, seelische und körperliche Entwicklung zu ermöglichen, damit sie zu gesunden, selbstbewussten, glücklichen, leistungsorientierten, pflichttreuen, musischen und kreativen Menschen warden, die antwortung für sich selbst, Mitmenschen, Umwelt und nachfolgende Generationen zu übernehmen. Jeder Jugendliche soll seiner Entwicklung und seinem Bildungsweg entsprechend zu selbständigem Urteil und sozialem Verständnis geführt warden, dem politischen, religiösen und weltanschaulichen Denken anderer aufgeschlossen sein sowie befähigt warden, am Kultur- und Wirtschaftsleben Österreichs, Europas, under der Welt (14.5a).
21. See especially Robert Gerwarth and John Horne (eds.), *War in Peace: Paramilitary Violence in Europe after the Great War* (Oxford: Oxford University Press, 2012).
22. See C. Earl Edmondson, *The Heimwehr and Austrian Politics, 1918–1936* (Athens, GA: University of Georgia Press, 1978).
23. "*Der Vorentwurf der österreichischen Verfassung,*" *Neue Freie Presse* (11–14 Feb. 1920), "*Der Drang zu Verfassungsreform,*" *Neue Freie Press* (6 Oct 1929), "*Die Grundzuege der Verfassungsreform,*" *Neue Freie Presse* (20 Oct 1929); "*La garantie juridictionelle de la Constitution (La Justice constitutionelle),*" *Revue du Droit Public et de La Science Politique en France et a l'Étranger* 35 (1928): 197–257.
24. In Arthur J. Jacobson and Bernhard Schlink (eds.), *Weimar: A Jurisprudence of Crisis* (Berkeley: University of California Press, [*Vom Wesen und Wert der Demokratie*, 1929] 2000): 84–109.
25. For further exploration, see especially Dieter A. Binder, "The Christian Corporatist State: Austria from 1934 to 1938," in Rolf Steininger, Günter Bischof, and Michael Gehler (eds.), *Austria*

in the Twentieth Century (New York: Routledge, 2002): 72–84; R. John Rath, "The First Austrian Republic—Totalitarian, Fascist, Authoritarian, or What?", in Rudolf Neck and Adam Wandruszka (eds.), *Beiträge zur Zeitgeschichte. Festschrift Ludwig Jedlicka zum 60. Geburtstag* (St. Pölten: Verlag Niederösterreichisches Pressehaus, 1976): 163–81; and Emmerich Tálos, *Das Austrofaschistische Herrschaftssystem. Österreich 1933–1938* (Vienna: LIT Verlag, 2013).

26. Academic integrity requires acknowledgment of the central conceit of modern Austrian politics: that the nation was a helpless victim rather than an eager accomplice of the Third *Reich*. Begin with Günter Bischof, Alexander Lassner, and Anton Pelinka (eds.), *The Dollfuß/Schuschnigg Era: A Re-assessment* (Brunswick: Transaction, 2003).

27. Die Republik Oesterreich wird der katholischen Kirche in Oesterreich gegenüber stets ihre finanziellen Pflichten erfüllen, welche auf Gesetz, Vertrag oder besonderen Rechtstiten beruhen ({XV§1}). "The Austrian Republic will always fulfill its financial obligations to the Catholic Church in Austria, whether based in law, treaty, or peculiar legal rights.".

28. The absence of any direct evidence notwithstanding, the author has always suspected that the exact correspondence to the date of the eventual Al Qaeda attacks upon the United States may have been intentional.

29. Wir wollen den sozialen, christlichen, deutschen Staat Österreich auf ständischer Grundlage, unter starker, autoritärer Führung! In Edmund Weber (ed.), *Dollfuß an Österreich. Eines Mannes Wort und Ziel* (Vienna: Reinhold, 1935), 25. This *Trabrennplatzrede* or "track speech," as it came to be known, weaponizes much of the Catholic social teaching of in particular *Quadragesimo Anno* (*AAS* 23 [1931], 177–228).

30. Im Namen Gottes, des Allmächtigen, von dem alles Recht ausgeht, erhält das österreichische Volk für seien christlichen, deutschen Bundesstaat auf ständischer Grundlage diese Verfassung. B.G.Bl. 1934 I. Nr. 239.

31. This neglected school or tendency is explored in Mark E. Blum, *The Austro-Marxists, 1890–1918: A Psychobiographical Study* (Lexington, KY: The University of Kentucky Press, 1985); and

Tom Bottomore and Patrick Goode (eds.), *Austro-Marxism* (Oxford: Clarendon Press, 1978).

32. The *Economic and Philosophic Manuscripts of 1844* (Amherst, New York: Prometheus Books, 1988) introduces such concepts as the theory of alienated labor, the futility of wage increases, and the correspondence between atheism and communism. *The German Ideology* (Amherst, NY: Prometheus, [1845] 1998) and *The Poverty of Philosophy* (Amherst, NY: Prometheus Books, [*Misère de la philosophie*, 1847] 1995) survey the fraught relationship between historical materialism and the ideas of Hegel and of Proudhon, respectively, while Marx's high hopes for proletarian revolution in neighboring France are on display in such works as *The Civil War in France* (Chicago: Charles H. Kerr, 1934), *The Class Struggles in France* (New York: International Publishers, [1848] 1964), and *The Eighteenth Brumaire of Louis Bonaparte* (New York: International Publishers, [*Der 18te Brumaire des Louis Napoleon*, 1852] 1963), with comparative interest extended to the less persuasive *Civil War in the United States* (New York: International Publishers, [1937] 2016). *The Revolutions of 1848, Surveys from Exile,* and *The First International & After* (New York: Vintage, 1974) collectively furnish Marx's speeches, editorials, party memoranda, and other political documents, while *Grundrisse* (New York: Penguin, [1939] 1993), finally, comprises a formidable series of research notes that reiterate many of the ideas of *Capital*.

33. *Grundsatzprogramm 2015 der Österreichischen Volkspartei*, 12 May 2015; and *SPÖ Grundsatzprogramm*, 2018.

34. Wir anerkennen die Bedeutung von Kirchen und Religionsgemeinschaften für Sinnstiftung und die Sehnsucht nach Transzendenz sowie für Bildung und karitatives Engagement, 20.

35. Darum treten wir für eine andere Wirtschaftsordnung ein. Eine Ordnung, in der Wirtschaftsprozesse demokratisch, solidarisch und umweltverträglich gestaltet sind, 26.

36. *Considerations*, 454. The latter event is depicted in the famous *Sacre de Napoléon* (1808) of court painter Jacques-Louis David.

37. RELIGIO CATHOLICA APOSTOLICA ROMANA LIBERE IN GALLIA EXERCEBITUR. CULTUS PUBLICUS ERIT, HABITA TAMEN RATIONE ORDINATIONUM QUOAD POLITIAM, QUAS GUBERNIUM PRO PUBLICA TRANQUILLITATE NECESSARIAS EXISTIMABIT, I.

38. Ego iuro et promitto ad Sancta Dei Evangelia, obedientiam et fidelitatem Gubernio per Constitutionem Gallicanae Reipublicae statuto. Item, promitto me nullam communicationem habiturum, nulli consilio interfuturum, nul-Iamque suspectam unionem neque intra, neque extra conservaturum, quae tranquillitati publicae noceat; et si tam in dioecesi mea quam alibi, noverim aliquid in Status damnum tractari, Gubernio manifestabo, VI.
39. *Nul ne doit être inquiété pour ses opinions, même religieuses, pourvu que leur manifestation ne trouble pas l'ordre public établi par la loi.*
40. *Je jure d'être fidèle à la Nation à la loi et au roi et de maintenir de tout mon pouvoir la Constitution du Royame, décrétée par l'Assemblée nationale constituante aux années 1789, 1790, et 1791*, I.5. The religious law of 12 July 1790 had likewise imposed an oath of exclusively episcopal loyalty (II.XXI), but without provisioning any wording.
41. *Il y a dans la République des écoles primaires où les élèves apprennent à lire, à écrire, les éléments du calcul et ceux de la morale. La République pourvoit aux frais de logement des instituteurs préposés a ces écoles*, 296.
42. With central importance attached to the designation of the respective French and Apostolic *Centre national de reconnaissance académique et de reconnaissance professionnelle* and *Bureau du Saint-Siège pour les reconnaissances académiques* as competent to make the necessary administrative decisions ({3}).
43. *Fêtes nationales, pour entretenir la fraternité entre les citoyens et les attacher à la Constitution, à la patrie et aux lois*, 301.
44. First Consul Napoleon, Second Consul Cambacérès, and Third Consul Lebrun.
45. Alle Ansprüche aus schon Bestehenden und künftigen Entschädigungsregelungen der Republik Österreich für Verfolgungssachschäden endgültig abgegolten. Die Katholische Kirche anerkennt, dass die Republik Österreich über die in diesem Vertrag zugesagten Leistungen hinaus auf den darin behandelten Gebieten keine weiteren finanziellen Verpflichtungen zu erfüllen hat, VIII.1.
46. See especially Ralf Haverts, *Radical Right Populism in Germany: AfD, Pegida, and the Identitarian Movement* (New York: Routledge, 2021); Mark Sedgwick (ed.), *Key Thinking of the Radical*

Right: Behind the New Threat to Liberal Democracy (Oxford: Oxford University Press, 2019); and José Pedro Zúquete, *The Identitarians: The Movement against Globalism and Islam in Europe* (Notre Dame: University of Notre Dame Press, 2018). Deeply implicated throughout is the critical commentary of French aristocrat Alain de Benoist (b. 1943), lead organizer of the *Groupement de Recherche et d'Etudes pour la Civilisation Européene* (GRECE) and editor of *Nouvelle École* (1968-). The author would describe his decisive *Manifesto for a European Renaissance* (London: Arktos, [*Manifeste pour une renaissance européene*, 1999] 2012) with Charles Champetier as generally insightful and occasionally moving in its plaintive descriptions of French, European, and international normative deficiencies and dislocations, but highly amateurish in its vast and vague suggestions of prospective legal and institutional remedies.

47. Perhaps the greatest West European comparative political scientist renowned for his exacting research methods, the Dutch-American Arend Lijphart derives and commends "consociational" or "consensus" democracy, especially amid social cleavages. *The Politics of Accommodation: Pluralism and Democracy in the Netherlands* (Berkeley: University of California Press, [1968] 2022); *Democracy in Plural Societies: A Comparative Exploration* (New Haven: Yale University Press, 1977); *Democracies: Patterns of Majoritarian and Consensus Government in Twenty-One Countries* (New Haven: Yale University Press, 1984); *Patterns of Democracy: Government Forms and Performance in Thirty-Six Countries* (New Haven: Yale University Press, 1999). With the benefit of hindsight, the professional inability to make proper methodological allowance for the authoritarian, totalitarian, revolutionary, and now *identitarian* might have been foreseen, as in Lijphart's case in particular the overwhelming emphasis upon comparative institutional design in the attainment of political justice appears to distract him from the both prior and larger question of the provision of national defense, insofar as none of his preferred consensus democracies of the European continent successfully resisted the Hitlerite predation, and would have likely proven equally defenseless against the Stalinist in the absence of cover from his suspect "majoritarian" Anglo-Saxon democracies.

48. Eric Voegelin, *The Authoritarian State: An Essay on the Problem of the Austrian State* (Columbia, MO: University of Missouri Press, [*Der autoritäre Staat: Ein Versuch über das österreichische Staatsproblem*, 1936] 1999).
49. "The Political Religions [*Die politischen Religionen*, 1938]," in Manfred Henningsen (ed.), *Modernity without Restraint* (Columbia, MO: University of Missouri Press, 2000), 19–73; "The New Science of Politics [1952]," in Manfred Henningsen (ed.), *Modernity without Restraint* (Columbia, MO: University of Missouri Press, 2000), 75–241; "Science, Politics, and Gnosticism [*Wissenshcaft, Politik, und Gnosis*, 1959]," in Manfred Henningsen (ed.), *Modernity without Restraint* (Columbia, MO: University of Missouri Press, 2000), 244–313.

CHAPTER 8

The Second Vatican Reformation, 1968–2019

"If the democracies are to win the peace after having won the war, it will be on condition that the Christian inspiration and the democratic inspiration recognize each other and become reconciled," wrote Thomist philosopher Jacques Maritain in *Christianity and Democracy* ([*Christianisme et démocratie*, 1943] 2011). He continued, "It [lasting victory] is…a question of passing from bourgeois democracy, drawn dry by its hypocrisies and by a lack of evangelical sap, to an integrally human democracy" (16–17). The postwar ideational rejuvenation of Roman Catholic political theology attains the summit of its expression in the world-historical Second Vatican Ecumenical Council (1962–1965),[1] a de facto constitutional convention for the Catholic Church that reconciled her to democratic politics, and that in subsequent decades produced a large cluster of concordats wherein its idealistic norms supplied the deficiency of inferior canon law position among the respective contracting parties.

Pontifical Idealism

Pope John XXIII (1958–1963)[2] convoked the council; and he is the first of three pontiffs whose encyclicals directly reference and wholeheartedly endorse the conciliar intentions and results. Author of eight encyclicals, *Ad Petri Cathedram* (*AAS* 51 [1959], 497–531) on Truth, Unity and

Peace, in a Spirit of Charity, his first, announces his bold intentions to convene an ecumenical council, to revise the Code of Canon Law, and to likewise draw up an intersecting code to govern the oriental churches.[3] His encyclical coverage continues with regard to hagiography ({*Sacerdotii Nostri Promordia*} *AAS* 51 [1959], 673–79; {*Aeterna Dei Sapientia*} *AAS* 53 [1961], 785–803), the rosary ({*Grata Recordatio*} *AAS* 51 [1959], 673–78), missions ({*Princeps Pastorum*} *AAS* 51 [1959], 833–64), penance ({*Paenitentiam Agere*} *AAS* 54 [1962], 481–91), and other perennial themes, all of which indicate a political theology respectful of tradition but open to innovation most clearly manifest in *Mater et Magistra* (1961) and *Pacem in Terris* (1963).

Mater et Magistra (*AAS* 53 [1961], 401–64), on Christianity and Social Progress furnishes a significant advance in Catholic social teaching. Proudly building theory directly on *Rerum Novarum* and *Quadragesimo Anno*, His Holiness argues that economic is embedded within social growth, of which the most important and enduring adjustments are always moral. A living wage sufficient for a male worker to support wife and child should be forthcoming in a timely manner, the historic antagonism between bourgeois and proletariat should be pacified through commitment to brotherly love, working men should be comprehensively empowered, and the mission of the International Labor Organization[4] actively supported. Although natural law sanctions private ownership, it also prescribes right personal and communal use, which may be expected to reduce extreme inequality and the violent instability occasioned thereby. This remedy, per the correct elements of Marxist analysis, applies within a society, but it also holds internationally in ways that appear to have escaped Marx's attention. "Probably the most difficult problem today concerns the relationship between political communities that are economically advanced and those in the process of development," the Holy Father hypothesizes. "The nations of the world are becoming more and more dependent on one another and it will not be possible to preserve a lasting peace so long as glaring economic and social imbalances exist."[5]

Equally significant is *Pacem in Terris* (*AAS* 55 [1963], 257–304), on Establishing Universal Peace in Truth, Justice, Charity, and Liberty. Per the long-standing edifice of Roman Catholic natural law, the pontiff opens, "Laws clearly indicate how a man must behave toward his fellows in society...what principles must govern the relations between States; and finally, what should be the relations between individuals or States on the one hand, and the world-wide community of nations on the other."[6] Thermo-nuclear disarmament is specified as the most empirically unqualified of such principles, but others more susceptible to continual negotiation and reformulation include recognition of global economic interdependence, self-determination for all historically oppressed peoples, and commitment to the norms of the Universal Declaration of Human Rights.

His successor Paul VI (1963–1978)[7] adjourned the ecumenical council, and he authored seven encyclicals. Ecclesiological emphasis is placed upon the practice of common prayer for peace ({*Mense Maio*} *AAS* 57 [1965], 353–58; {*Christi Matri*} *AAS* 58 [1966], 745–49), fidelity to the doctrine of transubstantiation of the Eucharist ({*Mysterium Fidei* (*AAS* 57 [1965], 753–74), the total commitment to the apostolic mission of the Church necessitating clerical celibacy ({*Sacerdotalis Caelibatus*} *AAS* 59 [1967], 657–97), and the profound respect for the mystery of the divine order that must not be cheapened and degraded through the use, and even more so through the mindset of contraception ({*Humanae Vitae*} *AAS* 60 [1968], 481–503). Two encyclicals however systematically reformulate catholic or universal ideals and apply them directly to the maturing international order.

"How is the Church to adapt its mission to the particular age, environment, educational, and social conditions of men's lives?",[8] the Bishop of Rome inquires in *Ecclesiam Suam* (*AAS* 56 [1964], 609–59), on the Church. Proceeding from *Satis cognitum* (1896) and *Mystici corporis* (1943), the answer lies mainly in the form of sustained dialogue between the Church and the world, with each interlocutor practicing self-examination, empathy, and active listening. Drawing the conceptual line at the atheism deemed unworthy of engagement, the international theory of Paul VI enunciated in 1964 and never subsequently revoked by his pontifical successors resembles the concentric diagram below (Fig. 8.1).

Humanity, even in apostasy, is to be *loved*, as God loved the world. The comparative religions are likewise to be appreciated for the elements of the true God within them, although among these the Jewish is obviously the closest to the Roman Catholic. *Christians*, meanwhile, include the apostolic worshippers of the Holy Land predating the See of Rome, the Eastern or Byzantine churches the legitimacy of which is discreetly acknowledged, and the Protestants held to be in schism, although not assigned all blame for the Wars of Religion. At the center of these concentric circles lie believing and practicing Roman Catholics, with whom

Fig. 8.1 The International theory of Paul VI

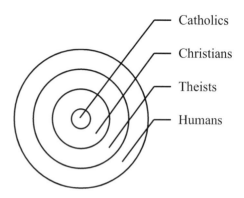

the Holy Father, like the other categories of persons, does enter into charitable dialogue, but also from whom he uniquely expects faithful obedience.

The overriding concern of *Ecclesiam Suam* for world order is further developed in *Populorum Progressio* (*AAS* 59 [1967], 257–99) tasking itself with the formulation of justice in world society. Although communist dictatorship is condemned and socialist utopianism opposed, the dire consequences of capitalist expropriation especially throughout the newly independent Third World remain to be conceded and rectified. "No one may appropriate surplus goods solely for his own private use when others lack the bare necessities of life,"[9] the Holy Father asserts. "Economics is supposed to be in the service of man."[10] Consequently, a moral and therefore sustainable developmental model must begin with education emphasizing cooperation in addition to competition, and must continue with professional development utilizing human in addition to technical expertise. The Catholic Church throughout the world opposes all forms of nationalism and racism, and holds that the surplus goods of more affluent states ought to be donated to those whose peoples lie in need. Such a global social policy shall above all serve the three major purposes of, " (1) mutual solidarity—the aid that the richer nations must give to developing nations; (2) social justice—the rectification of trade relations between strong and weak nations; [and] (3) universal charity—the effort to build a more humane world community, where all can give and receive, and where the progress of some is not bought at the expense of others."[11]

The 14 encyclicals of Pope John Paul II (1978–2005),[12] finally, furnish sustained exploration and commendation of the documents of the Second Vatican Council,[13] as well as take the genre to new heights of theoretical and literary sophistication. A probing both moral ({*Veritatis Splendor*} *AAS* 85 [1993], 1133–1228) and analytical philosopher ({*Fides et Ratio*} *AAS* 91 [1999], 5–88) devoted to the Virgin Mary ({*Redemptoris Mater*} *AAS* 79 [1987], 261–433), attuned to the Holy Spirit ({*Dominum et vivificantem*} *AAS* 78 [1986], 809–900), and committed to the Eucharistic Mystery ({*Ecclesia de Eucharistia*} *AAS* 95 [2003], 433–75), His Holiness emphasizes missions ({*Redemptoris Missio*} *AAS* 83 [1991], 249–340), especially among the Slavs ({*Slavorum Apostoli*} *AAS* 77 [1985], 779–813). Otherwise, upon the near completion of the attainment of independence by the Third World nations he opens with *Redemptor Hominis* (*AAS* 71 [1979], 257–324), concerned with the overall position of the Church in the world,[14] stressing deep introspection within the Church, active dialogue with other religions, and earnest entreaty to heads of state or government, "to respect the rights of religion and of the Church's activity. No privilege is asked for, but only respect for an elementary right" (III.17). Some of these notions initially delivered in the abstract become much more concrete in *Ut Unum Sint* (*AAS* 87 [1995], 921–92), on commitment to ecumenism, wherein the Supreme Pontiff dwells upon the need for outreach to the Orthodox and visitation to the Protestant ecclesiastical communities, outlining an ecumenical movement seeking the ultimate communion of all the baptized, and proclaiming a Great Jubilee of the Holy Year 2000 as a prospective milestone. "The Church must breathe with her two lungs!...Byzantium and Rome" (II.54), declares the Holy Father in the name of the Great Physician.

Four major encyclicals meanwhile formulate the Johanine Pauline social theology. *Laborem Exercens* (*AAS* 73 [1981], 577–647), on human work problematizes the matter thus: "While in the past the '*class question*' was especially highlighted as the centre of this issue, in more recent times it is the '*world question*' that is emphasized" (1.2). Although liberalism is correct that science and technology can emancipate and empower, realism is also correct that the same can marginalize and oppress; and consequently the needs of man ought to remain paramount throughout the productive process, with such adjustments as the preservation of Sabbath rest, the standardization of a family wage, civilized bargaining between workers and management, and if that fails orderly and commensurate use of the strike or walkout strongly recommended. "It is respect for the objective rights of the worker," the Holy Father explains, "that must constitute *the adequate and fundamental criterion* for shaping the whole economy, both on the level of the individual society and State and within the whole of the world economic policy and of the systems of international relationships that derive from it" (IV.17).

Sollicitudo Rei Socialis (*AAS* 80 [1988], 513–86), for the twentieth anniversary of *Populorum Progressio*, second, intensifies the focus upon enduring deficiencies of social and economic justice among the emerging nations. Although all states within the international system must at all times adhere to the natural law, the leaders of the rich and powerful states have a peculiar obligation to feed the hungry, heal the sick, lift up the poor, and otherwise not merely dispense justice, but show mercy to the populations of the small, weak, and precarious states. Invoking the norms of the United Nations charter, introducing the notion of a "development of peoples," and stressing the acute housing shortages, chronic unemployment, and sovereign debt of "Fourth world" nations within the overbearing bipolar imperialism of the Cold War, the pontiff explains that "interdependence must be transformed into solidarity" (V.39). What His Holiness acknowledges as *structures of sin* resulting from the compounded sins of many individuals also include the "superdevelopment" of the capitalist world, which has long willfully ignored the social and ecological harms of industrialization while posturing strictly technical solutions to problems in large measure moral. "The Church's social doctrine is not a 'third way' between liberal capitalism and Marxist collectivism," the pontiff clarifies in a summary passage, "but rather the accurate formulation of the results of a careful reflection on the complex realities of human existence, in society and in the international order, in the light of faith and of the Church's tradition" (VI.41).

Centesimus Annus (*AAS* 83 [1991], 793–867), on the hundredth anniversary of *Rerum Novarum*, third, furnishes the most explicit pontifical reflection upon the revolutionary events of 1989, which contemporary rereading, incidentally, almost completely vindicates. Extolling the past foresight of Pope Leo in predicting the eventual disconfirmation of the nostrum of socialist transformation, but also confronting the contemporary dangers of the prevailing norms of democratization, national security, and consumerism, the pontiff contends, "The United Nations…has not yet succeeded in establishing, as alternatives to war, effective means for the resolution of international conflicts. This seems to be the most urgent problem which the international community has yet to resolve" (II.21). The first pope to hail from the crucified Polish nation,

John Paul II imputes the ultimate Soviet collapse to the demoralizing character of state atheism and condemns the totalitarian destruction of freedom of thought, conscience, and association. But he also, ominously, cautions the Western democracies against equating the temporal destruction of socialism with the spiritual vindication of capitalism, against the proclivity to confuse the relative defeat of the enemy with the absolute victory of the self. "The Marxist solution has failed," he concludes, "but the realities of marginalization and exploitation remain in the world, especially the Third World, as does the reality of human alienation, especially in the more advanced countries. Against these phenomena the Church strongly raises her voice" (IV.42).

Evangelium Vitae (*AAS* 87 [1995], 401–522), on the value and inviolability of human life, finally, provides the most direct pontifical confrontation yet seen with legalized acts of killing such as abortion, euthanasia, embryonic research, and suicide. "The absolute inviolability of innocent human life is a moral truth clearly taught by Sacred Scripture, constantly upheld in the Church's Tradition and consistently proposed by her Magisterium" (III.57), he insists. All are equal, but what is described as *procured* abortion is especially heinous because the victim is INNOCENT, being completely incapable of having done any wrong to the mother. The Holy Father both releases practicing Catholics from any obligation to obey any laws condoning such wanton destruction, as well as exhorts the faithful to conscientiously object. "To be actively pro-life," he clarifies, "is to contribute to the renewal of society through the promotion of the common good" (III.101).

With regard to the contracting parties of the case cluster, examination of Table 8.1 reveals the large number and international distribution of the concordats pursuant to the norms of the Second Vatican Council. How might such diverse data be succinctly communicated? In this instance, satisfactory reply may be offered in the form of *an advocate*, worthily selecting to speak on behalf of these numerous Vatican II states Samuel P. Huntington, the Professor Emeritus of Political Science and International Affairs at Harvard University whose ideas long informed the policies of Allied and Associated governments. Although Huntington was not expert in the ecclesiastical polity of the Catholic religion, a dynamic intersection is observed between the treaty norms of the concordats of the cluster and those he considers internationally decisive in *The Third Wave: Democratization in the Late Twentieth Century* (1991), here submitted as a sufficient synthesis report on the prevailing political disposition of the contracting parties.

Occupying perhaps the conceptual turning point of his extensive *oeuvre*,[15] Huntington asks, "What changes in plausible independent variables in, most probably, the 1960s and 1970s produced the dependent variable, democratizing regimes in the 1970s and 1980s?" (45). His inductive answers or independent variables are five-fold: (1) the crisis of legitimacy of authoritarian regimes; (2) the postwar economic boom; (3) the transnational movement for Christian democracy directly associated with Vatican Council II; (4) external policy adjustments in Brussels, Washington, and Moscow in addition to in the Vatican; and (5) the eventual force of emulation. The Huntington *of 1991* remains a classical liberal political scientist. "The essence of democracy is the choosing of rulers in regular, fair, open, competitive elections in which the bulk of the population can vote" (257). "Poverty is...probably the principal obstacle to democratic development. The future of democracy depends on the future of economic development" (311). Yet in walking himself and the reader through the various factors provided above and the resulting *transformations* in Spain, Brazil, or Hungary, *replacements* in the Philippines or Romania, and *transplacements* in Poland, Czechoslovakia, Uruguay, or Hungary, however, the author's peculiar, and seemingly unexpected fascination with the rôle of the Apostolic See in conjunction with local bishops in the non-violent dismantling of autocratic power in these and other countries is clearly evident. "The third wave of the 1970s and 1980s was overwhelmingly a Catholic wave," he writes. "Overall, roughly three-quarters of the countries that transited to democracy between 1974 and 1989 were Catholic countries" (76).[16] Four of these—the Republic of the Philippines, the Federative Republic of Brazil, the Argentine Republic, and the Republic of Poland—likewise appear in Table 8.1. More importantly, the ideational adjustments of Vatican Council II and to a lesser degree liberation theology are held to have provided Catholic oppositional elements in Europe, Latin America, and Asia much of the normative commitment required to stand by local ordinaries in the praying, fasting, and chanting away of reviled strongmen. "In country after country the choice between democracy and authoritarianism became personified in the conflict between the cardinal and the dictator. Catholicism was second only to economic development as a pervasive force making for democratization in the 1970s and 1980s. The logo of the third wave could well be a crucifix superimposed on a dollar sign" (85). The postgraduate

Table 8.1 The second vatican reformation

Pontiff (Pontifical Legate, Title)	Contracting party (Contracting location, Date, Language(s))	Head of State or Government (Contracting plenipotentiary, Title)
Paul VI (Umberto Mozzoni, Nuncio)	**ARGENTINE REPUBLIC** (Buenos Aires, 28 Jan. 1968, Italian/Spanish)	Juan Carlos Onganía (Nicanor Costa Méndez, Minister of Foreign Relations and Religion)
John Paul II (Achille Silvestrini, Archbishop)	**PRINCIPALITY OF MONACO** (Vatican City-state, 25 July 1981, French)	Rainier III (César Charles Solamito, Ambassador Extraordinaire)
John Paul II (Agostino Casaroli, Cardinal)	**ITALIAN REPUBLIC** (Vatican City-state, 18 Feb. 1984, Italian)	Bettino Craxi
John Paul II (Achille Silvestrini, Archbishop)	**REPUBLIC OF HAITI** (Port-au-Prince, 8 Aug. 1984, French)	Jean-Claude Duvalier (Jean-Robert Estimé, Minister of Foreign Affairs and Religion)
John Paul II (Pier Luigi Celata)	**REPUBLIC OF MALTA (2)** (Valletta, 28 Nov. 1991, Italian/English)	Edward Fenech Adami (Ugo Mifsud Bonnici)
John Paul II (Pier Luigi Celata, Archbishop Nuncio)	**REPUBLIC OF MALTA** (Valleta, 3 Feb. 1993, Italian/English)	Eddie Fenech Adami
John Paul II (Józef Kowalczyk, Archbishop Nuncio)	**REPUBLIC OF POLAND** (Warsaw, 28 July 1993, Italian/Polish)	Hanna Suchocka (Krzysztof Skubiszewski, Minister of Foreign Relations)
John Paul II (Claudio M. Celli)	**STATE OF ISRAEL** (Jerusalem, 13 Dec. 1993, English/Hebrew)	Yitzhak Rabin (Yossi Beilin)
John Paul II	**REPUBLIC OF MALTA**	Eddie Fenech Adami

(continued)

Table 8.1 (continued)

Pontiff (Pontifical Legate, Title)	Contracting party (Contracting location, Date, Language(s))	Head of State or Government (Contracting plenipotentiary, Title)
(Pier Luigi Celata) John Paul II	(Valletta, 6 Jan. 1995, Italian/English) **REPUBLIC OF CROATIA** (3)	(Guido de Marco) Zlatko Mateša
(Giulio Einaudi) John Paul II	(Zagreb, 19 Dec. 1996, Italian/Croatian) **REPUBLIC OF CROATIA**	(Jure Radie) Zlatko Mateša
(Giulio Einaudi) John Paul II (Erwin Josef Ender)	(Zagreb, 9 Oct. 1998, Italian/Croatian) **REPUBLIC OF LITHUANIA** (3) (Vilnius, 5 May 2000, English/Lithuanian)	(Jure Radió) Andrius Kubilius (Algirdas Saudargas)
John Paul II (Erwin Josef Ender)	**REPUBLIC OF LATVIA** (8 Nov. 2000, English/Latvian)	Einars Repše (Ingrīda Labucka)
John Paul II (Angelo Sodano, Cardinal Secretary of State)	**SLOVAK REPUBLIC** (Vatican City-state, 24 Nov. 2000, Italian/Slovak)	Mikuláš Dzurinda (Prime Minister)
John Paul II (Jean-Louis Tauran, Cardinal Secretary of State)	**GABONESE REPUBLIC** (Vatican City-state, 26 July 2001, French)	Jean-François Ntoutoume Emane (André Mba Obame, Minister for National Education)
Benedict XVI (Alessandro D'Errico)	**BOSNIA AND HERZEGOVINA** (Sarajevo, 19 April 2006, English)	Ahmet Hadžipašić (Ivo Miro Jović)
Benedict XVI (Fernando Filoni)	**REPUBLIC OF THE PHILIPPINES** (Manila, 17 April 2007, English/Italian)	Gloria Macapagal Arroyo (Alberto G. Romulo)

(continued)

Table 8.1 (continued)

Pontiff (Pontifical Legate, Title)	Contracting party (Contracting location, Date, Language(s))	Head of State or Government (Contracting plenipotentiary, Title)
Benedict XVI (Dominique Mamberti, Cardinal Secretary of State)	FEDERATIVE REPUBLIC OF BRAZIL (Vatican City-state, 13 Nov. 2008, Portuguese/Italian)	Luiz Inácio Lula da Silva (Celso Amorim, Minister for Foreign Affairs)
Benedict XVI (Tarciso Bertone, Cardinal Secretary of State)	MONTENEGRO (Vatican City-state, 24 June 2011, Italian/Montenegrin)	Filip Vujanović (Igor Lukšić)
Benedict XVI (Antonio Arcari, Nuncio)	REPUBLIC OF MOZAMBIQUE (Maputo, 7 Dec. 2011, Italian/Portuguese)	Armando Guebuza (Oldemiro Júlio Marques Baloi, Minister of Foreign Affairs)
Francis (Dominique Mamberti, Cardinal Secretary of State)	REPUBLIC OF CAPE VERDE (2) (Praia, 10 June 2013, Italian/Portuguese)	José Maria Neves (Jorge Alberto da Silva Borges, Minister of Foreign Affairs)
Francis (Franco Coppola, Archbishop Nuncio)	REPUBLIC OF BURUNDI (Bujumbura, 5 July 2013, French)	Pierre Nkurunziza (Laurent Kavakure, Minister of Exterior Relations and International Cooperation)
Francis (Piero Pioppo, Apostolic Nuncio)	REPUBLIC OF EQUATORIAL GUINEA (Mongomo, 25 Oct. 2013, Italian/Spanish)	Teodoro Obiang Nguema Mbasogo (Agapito Mba Mokuy)

(continued)

Table 8.1 (continued)

Pontiff (Pontifical Legate, Title)	Contracting party (Contracting location, Date, Language(s))	Head of State or Government (Contracting plenipotentiary, Title)
Francis (Jude Thaddeus Okolo)	**REPUBLIC OF CHAD** (N'Djaména, 6 Nov. 2013, French)	Idriss Déby (Moussa Faki Mahamat)
Francis (Paul R. Gallagher, Archbishop Secretary for Relations With the State)	**DEMOCRATIC REPUBLIC OF CONGO** (Vatican City-state, 20 May 2016, French)	Joseph Kabila (Raymond Tshibanda, Minister for Foreign Affairs and Interational Cooperation)
Francis (Franco Coppola,ara> Archbishop Nuncio)	**CENTRAL AFRICAN REPUBLIC** (Bangui, 6 Sep. 2016, French)	Faustin-Archange Touadéra (Charles Armel Doubane, Minister of Foreign Affairs and African Integration)
Francis (Paul R. Gallagher, Secretary for Relations with States)	**GOVERNMENT OF THE ITALIAN REPUBLIC** (Vatican City-state, 15 Oct. 2016, Italian)	Giuseppe Conte (Pier Carlo Padoan, Minister of Economics and Finance)
Francis (Brian Udaigwe, Apostolic Nuncio)	**REPUBLIC OF BENIN** (Cotonou, 21 Oct. 2016, French)	Patrice Talon (Aurélien A. Agbénonci, Minister for Foreign Affairs and Cooperation)
Francis (Pietro Parolin, Cardinal Secretary of State)	**REPUBLIC OF CONGO** (Brazzaville, 3 Feb. 2017, Italian/French)	Denis Sassou Nguesso (Clément Mouamba, Prime Minister)
Francis	**REPUBLIC OF SAN MARINO**	Stefano Palmieri and Matteo Ciacci

(continued)

Table 8.1 (continued)

Pontiff (Pontifical Legate, Title)	Contracting party (Contracting location, Date, Language(s))	Head of State or Government (Contracting plenipotentiary, Title)
(Emil Paul Tscherrig, Apostolic Nuncio)	(San Marino, 28 June 2018, Italian)	(Nicola Renzi, Secretary of State for Foreign Affairs)
Francis (Paul R. Gallagher, Secretary for Relations with States)	**BURKINA FASO** (Vatican City-state, 12 July 2019, French)	Roch Marc Christian Kaboré (M. Alpha Barry, Minister of Foreign Affairs and Cooperation)

student or the democratic activist may or may not regard this analysis as sound or sufficient, and it is of course for Huntington to substantiate his own reasonings. But per the findings of a celebrated study within international political science that overlap and complement the idealistic turn unfolded below in the norms of the concordats of the Second Vatican Council, the various treaty negotiations were unfolding within an international systemic context of the Catholic Church as a whole very publicly facilitating lasting gains in political freedom and constitutional transformation.

THE CONCILIAR CONCORDATS

The preambles to all of the concordats of the cluster explicitly invoke the *norms*, the *principles*, or sometimes the *documents* of the Second Vatican Ecumenical Council; and they were agreed with contracting parties in which Roman Catholic canon law had been either internally repressed, externally overthrown, recently introduced, ineffectively enforced, or otherwise rendered *INFERIOR* in comparative national position, a deficiency either verbally acknowledged or reasonably surmised from the treaty texts and contexts. "The Republic of Latvia guarantees to the Catholic Church the restoration of unlawfully alienated property" (*AAS* 95 [2003], 105 {10}). "The Central African Republic pays particular attention to the documented demands for the return of patrimonial goods pertaining to the Catholic Church expropriated beginning in 1962."[17] Malta had been a British colony, and Poland, Croatia, Bosnia and Herzegovina, Lithuania, and Latvia had been Communist.[18] The applicable concordats also seem to implicate an admixture of French *laïcité* and Black Marxism in obliquely referenced injuries to the Church in the newly independent southern African cases. Regardless of the comparative developments responsible, the norms of the concordats of the highly international cluster likewise became more ideational, stressing the adherence of the Church to values.

Within the extensive assortment, the two purest and most representative examples are the Agreement between the Holy See and the Republic of Lithuania Concerning Juridical Aspects of the Relations between the Catholic Church and the State (*AAS* 92 [2000], 795–808) and the Accord between the Holy See and the State of Burkina Faso on the Juridical Status of the Catholic Church in Burkina Faso (*Accord entre le Saint-Siège et l'État du Burkina Faso sur le Statut Juridique de l'Église Catholique au Burkina Faso, AAS* 113 [15SEP2021], 73–87), which respectively initiate and complete a treaty template to which most of the intervening concordats almost identically adhere, though differences in language naturally affect the precise wording. Most of the important normative content of the Vatican II concordats may therefore be imparted through sustained examination of the Lithuanian concordat identified above, with the corresponding texts from that with Burkina Faso footnoted in support.

Guadium et Spes (7 December 1965), the Pastoral Constitution on the Church in the Modern World formulates the overarching conciliar political theology as follows: "The Church and the political community in their own fields are autonomous and independent. Yet both, under different titles, are devoted to the personal and social vocation of the same men."[19] The Lithuanian concordat likewise codifies such neo-Augustinian thought. "The Holy See and the Republic of Lithuania agree that the Catholic Church and the State shall be independent and autonomous each within their own field and, adhering to the said principle shall cooperate closely for the spiritual and material welfare of every individual and of society" (796 {1.1}).[20] The treaty continues in the next article, "All institutions of the Catholic Church in the Republic of Lithuania, which enjoy the status of public or private juridical persons in accordance with Canon Law, shall have the rights of a juridical person in civil law according to the legal acts of the Republic of Lithuania" (796 {2.2}).[21] Although it is the *intersection* of the Church and the commonwealth subsequently pursued throughout, analysis may begin with the ecclesiastical power, clarified in *Lumen Gentium* (21 November 1964), the Dogmatic Constitution on the Church. "The pope's power of primacy over all, both pastors and faithful, remains whole and intact. In virtue of his office, that is as Vicar of Christ and pastor of the whole Church, the Roman pontiff has full, supreme and universal power over the Church. And he is always free to exercise this power."[22] Central to the exercise of such primacy is the transmission of orders and information, provisioned according to canon and comparative law throughout the conciliar concordats. "The Republic of Lithuania shall guarantee the Catholic Church, its juridical and natural persons freedom to maintain contacts and to communicate without restrictions with the Holy See and other ecclesiastical institutions recognized by Canon Law both within Lithuania and abroad" (796 {3}).[23] Yet beneath the Supreme Pontiff, the Church is governed by bishops, who according to *Christus Dominus* (28 October 1965) or the Decree Concerning the Pastoral Office of Bishops, "enjoy full and perfect freedom and independence from any civil authority. Hence, the exercise of their ecclesiastical office may not be hindered, directly or indirectly."[24] Likewise, the concordat with Lithuania declares, "The competent authority of the Catholic Church shall have the exclusive right to regulate freely ecclesiastical life, to establish and suppress ecclesiastical provinces, archdioceses, apostolic administrations…parishes, religious houses, and other ecclesiastical persons" (797 {5.1}).[25] As stated in the case cluster summary in Chapter 3, the Vatican II treaty terms largely perpetuate those of the concordats preceding the council, but like their conciliar source material their accompanying ideational norms are newly articulated. *Inter Mirifica* (4 December 1963), or the Decree on the Media of Social Communications for example clarifies, "The Church *welcomes* and *promotes* with special interest…the press, movies, radio, television and the like…It is, therefore, an inherent right of the Church to have at its disposal and to employ any of these media insofar as they are necessary and useful for the instruction of Christians and all its efforts for the welfare of souls" (emphases added).[26] The Lithuanian concordat likewise reads, "The Catholic Church shall be guaranteed the right to print, publish and distribute books, newspapers and magazines, as well as to engage in other publishing activities related to its mission" (800 {12.1}).[27]

The Lithuanian concordat derivative of the conciliar documents also demonstrates increasingly ideational norms pertaining to the civil power. *Dignitatis Humanae* (7 December 1965), or the Declaration on Religious Freedom demonstrates almost full accommodation to the terms of such instruments as the British (1688) or American Bills of Rights (1789), the Declaration on the Rights of Man and of Citizen (1789), or the Universal Declaration of Human Rights (1948) pertaining to freedom both of and from religion, stating, "It is necessary that religious freedom be everywhere provided with an effective constitutional guarantee and that respect be shown for the high duty and right of man freely to lead his religious life in society."[28] The treaty writes this norm into law as follows: "The Republic of Lithuania shall guarantee the right of the faithful to establish organizations to achieve the aims proper to the Catholic Church and to conduct their activities" (801 {14.1}).[29] Long and perhaps painful experience seems to have also convinced the Church of the necessity of commitment to concrete, specific, and tangible aspects of such religious liberty. *Dignitatis Humanae* continues, "Religious communities also have the right not to be hindered, either by legal measures or by administrative action on the part of the government, in the selection, training, appointment, and by transferal of their own ministers, in communicating with religious authorities and communities abroad, in erecting buildings for religious purposes, and in the acquisition and use of suitable funds or properties."[30] The Lithuanian concordat therefore concedes all these rights to "ecclesiastical juridical persons" (799 {10.1}),[31] identified throughout as bishops and all applicable ordinaries. The text continues, "The Catholic Church shall have the right to build churches and other buildings for ecclesiastical purposes, as well as to extend and restore those already in existence" (799 {11.1}).[32]

Such adjustments are elaborated in various ways. As discussed in Chapter 2, the inaugural Concordat of Worms of 1122 concerned the question as to whether the initiative for the investiture or appointment of bishops resided with Catholic Church or German *Reich*. After the passage of more than eight centuries, *Christus Dominus* appears to return a final answer. "This holy council desires that in future no more rights or privileges of election, nomination, presentation, or designation for the office of bishop be granted to civil authorities. The civil authorities...are most kindly requested to voluntarily renounce the above-mentioned rights and privileges."[33] Such voluntary renunciation has subsequently occurred primarily *in writing*, via *concordat*, with that of Lithuania indicatively declaring, "The appointment, transfer and removal from office of bishops and those canonically equivalent to them shall be within the exclusive competence of the Holy See" (797 {6.2}).[34] Notwithstanding this historic change, the Supreme Pontiff and the Catholic Church on one side and the contracting parties to concordats on the other are still expected to coordinate their efforts within the scope of the natural law. *Guadium et Spes* explains elsewhere, "Whoever promotes the human community at the family level, culturally, in its economic, social and political dimensions, both nationally and internationally, such a one, according to God's design, is contributing greatly to the Church as well."[35] Lithuania and the Apostolic See write this norm into contractual international law as follows: "The competent authorities of the Republic of Lithuania and the competent authorities of the Catholic Church shall cooperate in ways acceptable to both Parties on educational, cultural, family and social issues and, in particular, in the field of protecting public morals and human dignity" (796 {1 2}).[36] *Apostolicam Actuositatem* (18 November 1965), or the Decree on the Apostolate of the Laity, finally, enlarges upon this strong Christian Democratic interest in securing the widest possible involvement of all Catholics in the work of the Church. "With a constantly increasing population, continual progress in science and technology, and closer interpersonal relationships, the areas for the lay apostolate have been immensely widened particularly in fields that have been for the most part open to the laity alone."[37] Indicative of this normative commitment, the Republic of Lithuania shall through its concordat, "recognize the freedom of the Catholic Church to carry out its pastoral, apostolic and charitable mission. The Catholic Church shall pursue its social, educational and cultural activities in accordance with Canon Law and the procedure prescribed by the laws of the Republic of Lithuania" (796–97 {4}).[38]

As stated above, this concordat with Lithuania of 5 May 2000 and the footnoted concordat with Burkina Faso of 12 July 2019 respectively begin and end, and together exemplify the prevailing pattern. Peculiar features of the remaining cases in the cluster nevertheless suggest several supplementary remarks. The Argentine concordat initiates the cluster with its normative reference to the "principles" (*principios*, AAS 59 [1967], 127) of the ecumenical council, while the first concessions of the civil prerogative of the appointment of bishops were made by the Monégasque Prince (*AAS* 73 [1981], 652 {II}) and by the Haitian President (*AAS* 76 [1984], 953). Textually, the Lithuanian concordat was based on that with newly independent Croatia agreed at Zagrebu in December, 1996 (*AAS* 89 [1997], 277–302), with its tripartite division into separate treaties respectively concerned with juridical questions, educational and cultural cooperation, and military chaplaincy, the last reflecting the counter-revolutionary norms described in the case chapter on Latin America. Subsequent Vatican II concordats agreed with former Communist Slovakia (*AAS* 93 [2001], 136–55), Latvia (*AAS* 95 [2003], 102–20), Bosnia and Herzegovina (*AAS* 99 [2007], 939–46), and Montenegro (*AAS* 104 [2012], 587–98), meanwhile, strongly suggest demonstration effects, with the most recent comparative regional extension to Africa beginning with the concordat with Mozambique (*AAS* 104 [2012], 567–86) also intriguing. Although the explicit invocation within the miniseries of the norms, principles, or documents of Vatican Council II remains unchanged, and the treaty terms are representative of both the case cluster and of concordats as a whole, recognition of the rights and duties of the local Episcopal Conferences is also incorporated into the concordats with the Republic of Burundi (*AAS* 106 [2014], 196 {5§1}), the Democratic Republic of Congo (*AAS* 112 [2020], 192 {3§2}), the Central African Republic (*AAS* 111 [2019], 733 {3§2}), the Republic of Benin (*AAS* 110 [2018], 1290 {3§3}), the Republic of Congo (*AAS* 111 [2019], 1178 {12}), and with Burkina Faso, although the latter also mentions the bishops of adjacent Niger (*AAS* 113 [15SEP2021], 74 {2§2}). This most recent variation may or may not materialize elsewhere; but in any event, the 37 concordats that depart from the Second Vatican Ecumenical Council consistently demonstrate more ideational norms than previously apparent within Roman Catholic extraordinary ecclesiastical relations.

The Standardization of Catholic Norms

The culmination of the normative transformation initiated by Vatican Council II and subsequently codified in a large international cluster of concordats is the insufficiently appreciated *Compendium of the Social Doctrine of the Church* (2004), the major conceptual undertaking of the Pontifical Council for Justice and Peace.[39] Consisting of 583 entries divided into the 12 chapters of (1) God's plan of love for humanity, (2) the Church's mission and social doctrine, (3) the human person and human rights, (4) principles of the Church's social doctrine, (5) the family, (6) human work, (7) economic life, (8) the political community, (9) the international community, (10) safeguarding the environment, (11) the promotion of peace, and (12) social and ecclesial action in overall pursuit of an "integral and solidary humanism," the compilation is intended to accomplish ideationally what the 1984 revision of the canon law achieved ecclesiologically, with Cardinal Secretary of State Angelo Sodano explaining in the forward, "Those who share the same Baptism with us, as well as the followers of other Religions and all people of good will, can find herein fruitful occasions for reflection and a common motivation" (XXIII). Although the following analysis shall concentrate upon the eighth and ninth chapters respectively concerned with the finalization of Catholic political and international theory, it bears emphasizing that normative *unity* and *coherence* is reinforced throughout, delivering per the Angelic Doctor not merely interdependence of parts, but indivisibility of substance.

The eighth chapter concerned with the political community synthesizes the long development of Roman Catholic natural law, with terms including thoughtful submission to established authority ({380}), recognition of the divine origin of political power ({383}), and clarification of the HUMAN PERSON as the essential political referent ({384}). "The rights and duties of the person," the council states, "constitute an *objective norm* on which *positive law* is based and which cannot be ignored by the political community" ({388}, emphases added). Holy Communion being a public rite and blessed sacrament to always be openly celebrated within human community, the Church is keen to clarify a social theology embodying the right relationships between, in particular, the church and the state and the individual and the state, while retaining her overall indifference to form of government. Reiterating the council's insistence upon the inalienable right to religious freedom ({421}), the compendium clarifies, "Although the Church and the political community both manifest themselves in visible organizational structures, they are by nature different because of their configuration and because of the ends they pursue" ({424}). The political community may go about pursuing its appointed ends provided it preserves legal recognition for the Church ({426}), and refrains from torture ({404}) and execution ({405}). The same is said to threaten the individual, meanwhile, primarily through corruption ({411}), bureaucracy ({412}), and directives "contrary to the demands of the moral order, to the fundamental rights of persons or the teachings of the Gospel" ({399}), which concerned Catholics need not obey, while the individual endangers himself principally through an insidious *ethical relativism* dismissive of the moral law ({407}). "An authentic democracy is…the fruit of a convinced acceptance of the values that inspire democratic procedures: the dignity of every human person, the respect of human rights, commitment to the common good as the purpose and guiding criterion for political life" ({407}).

The ninth chapter then furnishes the outlines of a Roman Catholic international political theory. Departing from the immutable exigencies of the natural law, the more recent advances in international law through the Hague, Geneva, and Vienna conventions are said to sustain international order ({434}), with the rejection of both the use and the threat of force central to the UN Charter the subject of peculiar commendation ({438}). "The Church is a companion on the journey towards an authentic international community, which has taken a specific direction with the founding of the United Nations Organization in 1945" ({440}). The Catholic Church views the United Nations, however, less as a vessel for the partial civilization of great power conflict than as the beginning of the inclusion of all humanity into an international legal order within which the Church will retain its preferential love for the poor ({449}), and the Apostolic See retain or enlarge its inherent rights to send and receive diplomatic agents, to fully participate in international organizations, to mediate international conflicts, and to enter into "mutual agreements" with civil commonwealths ({444–53}). "The Holy See, or Apostolic See," the compendium submits, "enjoys full international subjectivity as a sovereign authority that performs acts which are juridically its own. It exercises an external sovereignty recognized within the context of the international community…and is marked by organizational unity and independence" ({444}). Thus with the publication of the *Compendium of the Social Doctrine of the Church* shortly after the opening of the new century and millennium, the normative ideals of the Church militant here in earth became fully incorporated into the international law and world polity of the United Nations.

Notes

1. Primary source collections apart from the formidable *Acts of the Apostolic See* include Robert Barron and Matthew Levering, *The Word on Fire Vatican II Collection*, 2 vols. (Washington, D.C.: Word on Fire, 2021–23); Austin Flannery (ed.), *Vatican Council*

II: The Conciliar and Postconciliar Documents (Collegeville, MN: Liturgical Press, [1975] 2014); and Edward P. Hahnenberg, *A Concise Guide to the Documents of Vatican II* (Cincinnati, OH: St. Anthony Messenger Press, 2007). Ecclesiastics have long struggled to get the material widely seen and actively read by the laity.

2. Born *Angelo Giuseppe Roncalli*, 1881; ordained, 1904; Archbishop of Areopolis, 1925–34; Archbishop Nuncio to France, 1944–53; Cardinal, 1953; Patriarch of Venice, 1953–58.

3. Eventually appearing as a CODEX CANONUM ECCLESIARUM ORIENTALIUM (*AAS* 82 [1990], 1061–1364) consisting of 1,546 canons, the codification of the canon law of the oriental assemblies does not necessitate adjustment of the thesis or reconsideration of the subject matter, its primary purpose being the clarification of the laws of ecclesiastical polity for the churches of the Alexandrian, Antiochene, Armenian, Chaldean, and Constantinopolitan rites, wherein the four Patriarchs of Constantinople, Alexandria, Antioch, and Jerusalem preside over hierarchs of archbishops, metropolitans, eparchial bishops, exarchs, and apostolic administrators, all of whom are assigned both rights and duties in their formalized communion with the Apostolic See. More specifically, the Latin wording of its fourth canon concerned with concordats is almost identical to that of the 1983 revision discussed in Chap. 2.

4. The oldest intact element of the United Nations system, the Versailles Treaty (1919: XIII) authorized an International Labour Organization in affiliation with the League of Nations in Geneva, which following the latter's obsolescence was incorporated into the newfound United Nations.

5. VERUM NOSTRIS HISCE DIEBUS QUAESTIO UNA FORTASSE OMNIUM MAXIMA HAEC AFFERTUR, QUAE NIMIRUM NECESSITUDINES CIVITATIBUS IN RE OECONOMICA PROGRESSIS CUM CIVITATIBUS, QUARUM OECONOMICAE PROGRESSIONES SINT IN CURSU, INTERCEDERE DEBEANT…EO VEL MAGIS QUOD, CUM CIVITATES VIDEANTUR COTIDIE MAGIS ALIAE EX ALIIS QUODAMMODO PENDERE, FIERI NON POTEST UT DIU UTILEM PACEM EAEDEM SERVENT, SI EARUM OECONOMICAE ET SOCIALES CONDICIONES NIMIOPERE AB ALIARUM DISCREPENT, 440.

6. HIS ENIM LEGIBUS PRAECLARE ERUDIUNTUR HOMINES, QUIBUS PRIMUM MODIS MUTUA SUA COMMERCIA IN HUMANO CONVICTU MODERENTUR; QUIBUS DEINDE MODIS RATIONES COMPONENDAE

SINT, QUAE CIVIBUS CUM PUBLICIS SUAE CUIUSQUE CIVITATIS MAGISTRATIBUS INTERCEDUNT; QUIBUS TUM MODIS MUTUO EOIITINGANTUR RESPUBLICAE; QUIBUS POSTREMO MODIS INTER SE CONTINEANTUR HINC SINGULI HOMINES ET CIVITATES, ILLINC UNIVERSARUM GENTIUM SOCIETAS; QUAE SOCIETAS, UT TANDEM CONDATUR, COMMUNIS OMNIUM UTILITAS VEHEMENTER REQUIRIT, 259.

7. Born *Giovanni Battista Enrico Antonio Maria Montini*, 1897; ordained, 1920; Referendary Prelate of the Apostolic Signatura, 1926–38; Substitute for General Affairs, 1937–53; Archbishop of Milan, 1954–63; Cardinal, 1958.

8. QUOUSQUE OPORTET ECCLESIA SE AD RERUM TEMPORUMQUE RATIONES CONFORME, IN QUIBUS SUA MUNERA GERAT?, 646.

9. NEMINI LICET BONA, QUAE SIBI SUPERENT, UNIRE AD PRIVATA COMMODA SEPONERE, CUM ALII REBUS CAREANT VITAE NECESSARIIS, 269.

10. CUM RES OECONOMICAS, QUOD RURSUS GRAVITER ADMONERE IUVAT, HOMINI DUMTAXAT INSERVIRE OPORTEAT, 270.

11. PRIUS EST OFFICIUM MUTUAE NECESSITUDINIS, AUXILIUM NEMPE A DIVITIORIBUS NATIONIBUS AFFERENDI IIS, QUAE AD PROGRESSIONEM ADHUC NITUNTUR; DEINDE OCCURRIT OFFICIUM IUSTITIAE SOCIALIS, QUAE IN EO EST POSITA, UT RATIONES MERCATORIAE, POPULIS FORTUNATIORIBUS CUM INFIRMIORIBUS INTERCEDENTES, IN MELIUS RESTITUANTUR; DENIQUE OFFICIUM CARITATIS UNIVERSALIS, QUA PRO OMNIBUS CONSORTIO HUMANIOR PROMOVETUR, IN QUA CUNCTI DARE DEBEANT ET ACCIPERE, NEQUE ALIORUM PROCESSUS PROGRESSIONEM PRAEPEDIAT ALIORUM, 279.

12. Born *Karol Józef Wojtyla*, 1920; ordained, 1946; Archbishop of Krakow, 1964–1978; Cardinal, 1967.

13. They are *Sacrosanctum Concilium* (*AAS* 56 [1964], 97–138); *Inter Mirifica* (*AAS* 56 [1964], 145–57); *Lumen Gentium* (*AAS* 57 [1965], 5–71); *Unitatis Redintegratio* (*AAS* 57 [1965], 90–112); *Orientalium Ecclesiarum* (*AAS* 57 [1965], 76–89); *Christus Dominus* (*AAS* 58 [1966], 673–701); *Perfectae Caritatis* (*AAS* 58 [1966], 702–12); *Optatum Totius* (*AAS* 58 [1966], 713–27); *Gravissimum Educationis* (*AAS* 58 [1966], 728–39); *Nostra Aetate* (*AAS* 58 [1966], 740–44); *Dei Verbum* (*AAS* 58 [1966], 817–35); *Apostolicam Actuositatem* (*AAS* 58 [1966], 837–64);

Dignitatis Humanae (*AAS* 58 [1966], 929–46); *Ad Gentes* (*AAS* 58 [1966], 947–90); *Presbyterorum Ordinis* (*AAS* 58 [1966], 991–1024); and *Gaudium et Spes* (*AAS* 58 [1966], 1025–1120), all in Latin.

14. Beginning with the pontificate of John Paul II and in accordance with the internationalist turn herein explored, encyclicals are comprehensively made available in numerous world languages on the Vatican website; and the author therefore feels content to henceforth rely exclusively upon the approved English, per the clearly intended manner of the consultation of the material.

15. Otherwise, the prior service Huntington opened his distinguished academic career with *The Soldier and the State: The Theory and Politics of Civil-Military Relations* (Cambridge, MA: Harvard University Press, 1957), which argues that the benign disorder of American liberalism is no longer suitable for the national security exigencies of the Cold War, and that instead a neo-conservatism respectful of the discipline, hierarchy, uniformity, and camaraderie of military life ought to be encouraged, with the armed forces subject to a regime of "objective civilian control." With Zbigniew Brzezinski he subsequently co-authored *Political Power: USA/USSR* (New York: Penguin, 1964), a sustained comparative analysis of the respective political systems headquartered in Washington and Moscow which suggests continual evolution but not necessarily systemic convergence. *Political Order in Changing Societies* (New Haven: Yale University Press, 1968), meanwhile, imputes the unexpected instability of the Third World primarily to the collision between accelerating social change and widening political mobilization with insufficiently responsive political institutions, calling into question the meliorative logic of much developmental policy. *The Clash of Civilizations and the Remaking of World Order* (New York: Simon & Schuster, 1996) in the aftermath of the Soviet collapse famously prophesied the international replacement of capitalist versus Marxist ideology with transnational cultural affinity, emphasizing the vindictiveness with which the benighted Islamic might seek to do an injury to the victorious Western Christian civilization. *Who Are We? The Challenges to America's National Identity* (New York: Simon & Schuster, 2004), finally, submits that the American constitution and political culture derivative of the English Reformation may prove unable to assimilate the massive

Hispanic immigrant population derivative of the Iberian Counter-Reformation, threatening the unity of the nation. Although an ultimate normative commitment to the Christian liberal-conservatism and acute interest in institutional design of Tocqueville is perceptible throughout, the critical reflection of half a century appears to display a gradual followed by an accelerating shift in the attribution of justice from political to cultural form, not excluding the concomitant reduction in the scope for positive action that such an adjustment would seem to impose.

16. The slow first wave is specified as 1828 to 1926, and the faster second wave as 1943 to 1962.
17. *La République Centrafricaine accordera une attention pariculière aux demandes documentées de retrocession des biens patrimoniaux appurtenant à l'Église catholique, expropriés à partir de 1962 (AAS 111 [2019], 739 {17§1}).*
18. In its final institutional forms, European Communism consisted of a Union of Soviet Socialist Republics (СОЮЗА СОВЕТСКИХ СОЦИАЛИСТИЧЕСКИХ РЕСПУЬЛИК, 7 Oct. 1977) in turn comprised of Russian, Ukrainian, Byelorussian, Uzbek, Kazakh, Georgian, Azerbaijan, Lithuanian, Moldavian, Latvian, Kirghiz, Tajik, Armenian, Turkmen, and Estonian Soviet Socialist Republics, and of a Socialist Federal Republic of Yugoslavia (*Socijalističke Federativne Republike Jugoslavije*, 21 Feb. 1974) in turn comprised of the Socialist Republics of Bosnia-Herzegovina, Croatia, Macedonia, Montenegro, Serbia, Slovenia, and the Socialist Autonomous Provinces of Vojvodina and Kosovo. The People's Republics of Albania, Bulgaria, Hungary, Poland, and Rumania, the German Democratic Republic, and the Czechoslovak Republic were furthermore joined to the Soviet Union through a Treaty of Friendship, Cooperation, and Mutual Assistance concluded at Warsaw in 1955.
19. Communitas politica et Ecclesia in proprio campo ab invicem sunt independentes et autonomae. Ambae autem, licet diverso titulo, eorumdem hominum vocationi personali et sociali inserviunt (*AAS* 58 [1966], 1099).
20. *Les Hautes Parties contractantes réaffirment que l'Église Catholique et l'État du Burkina Faso sont, chacun dans son ordre, souverains, indépendants et autonomes et déclarent s'engager, dans leur relations, à respecter un tel principe et à œuvrer ensemble pour le bien-être*

spirituel et matériel de la personne humaine, comme en faveur de la promotion du bien commun (73–74 {1}).
21. *Le Burkina Faso reconnaît également la personnalité juridique de toutes les entités de l'Église Catholique que possèdent cette prerogative en vertu du droit canonique et qui restent régies par leurs règles propres* (74 {2§2}).
22. ROMANUS ENIM PONTIFEX HABET IN ECCLESIAM, VI MUNERIS SUI, VICARII SCILICET CHRISTI ET TOTIUS ECCLESIAE PASTORIS, PLENAM, SUPREMAM ET UNIVERSALEM POTESTATEM, QUAM SEMPER LIBERE EXERCERE VALET (*AAS* 57 [1965], 26).
23. *Le Burkina Faso garantit à l'Église Catholique, tant à ses fidèles en general qu'aux responsables et aux members de ses institutions, la liberté de communiquer et de se maintenir en relation avec le Saint-Siège et les Conférences Épiscopales d'autres Pays* (75 {4}).
24. IN SUO APOSTOLICO MUNERE OBEUNDO, QUOD ANIMARUM SALUTEM INTENDIT, EPISCOPI PER SE PLENA AC PERFECTA GAUDENT LIBERTATE ATQUE INDEPENDENTIA A QUACUMQUE CIVILI POTESTATE. QUARE NON LICET EORUM MUNERIS ECCLESIASTICI EXERCITIUM DIRECTE VEL INDIRECTE IMPEDIRE (*AAS* 58 [1966], 682).
25. *Il appartient exclusivement à l'Autorité ecclésiastique de fixer librement les lois et règlements et tous les actes juridiques dans le domaine de sa competence, ainsi que d'ériger, modifier ou supprimer des institutions ecclésiastiques en general, qu'il s'agisse de circonscriptions ecclésiastiques ou de toutes autres entités de l'Église Catholique* (74 {2§3}).
26. MATER ECCLESIA EA EXCIPIT AC PROSEQUITUR...CINEMATOGRAPHEUM, RADIOPHONIA, TELEVISIO ET ALIA HUIUSMODI...ECCLESIAE ERGO NATIVUM IUS COMPETIT QUODVIS HORUM INSTRUMENTORUM GENUS, QUATENUS AD CHRISTIANAM EDUCATIONEM OMNEMQUE SUAM DE ANIMARUM SALUTE OPERAM SUNT NECESSARIA VEL UTILIA, ADHIBENDI ATQUE POSSIDENDI (*AAS* 56 [1964], 146).
27. *Dans l'exercise de sa mission spirituelle, il est reconnu à l'Église Catholique la liberté d'éditer, de publier, de divulger et de vendre des livres, journaux, revues en support dur ou en format électronique, ainsi du respect de l'ordre public* (78 {11§1}).
28. PROINDE UT PACIFICAE RELATIONES ET CONCORDIA IN GENERE HUMANO INSTAURENTUR ET FIRMENTUR, REQUIRITUR UT

UBIQUE TERRARUM LIBERTAS RELIGIOSA EFFICACI TUTELA IURIDICA MUNIATUR ATQUE OBSERVENTUR SUPREMA HOMINUM OFFICIA ET IURA AD VITAM RELIGIOSAM LIBERE IN SOCIETATE DUCENDAM (*AAS* 58 [1966], 941).

29. Le Burkina Faso reconnaît et protège le droit des fidèles catholiques de s'associer selon les norms du droit canonique ou simplement celles de l'État pour des activités (79 {14§1}).

30. COMMUNITATIBUS RELIGIOSIS PARITER COMPETIT IUS, NE MEDIIS LEGALIBUS VEL ACTIONE ADMINISTRATIVA POTESTATIS CIVILIS IMPEDIANTUR IN SUIS PROPRIIS MINISTRIS SELIGENDIS, EDUCANDIS, NOMINANDIS ATQUE TRANSFERENDIS, IN COMMUNICANDO CUM AUCTORITATIBUS ET COMMUNITATIBUS RELIGIOSIS, QUAE IN ALIIS ORBIS TERRARUM PARTIBUS DEGUNT, IN AEDIFICIIS RELIGIOSIS ERIGENDIS, NECNON IN BONIS CONGRUIS ACQUIRENDIS ET FRUENDIS (*AAS* 58 [1966], 932–33).

31. Identical French wording by concordat Burkina Faso: *personnes juridiques ecclésiastiques* (77 {9§1}).

32. Dans le cadre de la legislation civile, l'Église Catholique a le droit de construire des églises et des édifices ecclésiastiques, d'en agrandir et d'en modifier la configuration (78 {10§1}).

33. QUAPROPTER AD ECCLESIAE LIBERTATEM RITE TUENDAM ET AD CHRISTIFIDELIUM BONUM APTIUS ET EXPEDITIUS PROMOVENDUM IN VOTIS EST SACROSANCTI CONCILII UT IN POSTERUM NULLA AMPLIUS CIVILIBUS AUCTORITATIBUS CONCEDANTUR IURA AUT PRIVILEGIA ELECTIONIS, NOMINATIONIS, PRAESENTATIONIS VEL DESIGNATIONIS AD EPISCOPATUS OFFICIUM; CIVILES VERO AUCTORITATES, QUARUM OBSEQUENTEM ERGA ECCLESIAM VOLUNTATEM SACROSANCTA SYNODUS GRATO ANIMO AGNOSCIT PLURIMIQUE FACIT, HUMANISSIME ROGANTUR UT PRAEDICTIS IURIBUS VEL PRIVILEGIIS, QUIBUS IN PRAESENS PACTO AUT CONSUETUDINE FRUANTUR, CONSILIIS CUM APOSTOLICA SEDE INITIS, SUA SPONTE RENUNTIARE VELINT (*AAS* 58 [1966], 683).

34. La nomination, le transfert, la révocation et l'acceptation de la renunciation des Évêques relèvent de la compétence exclusive du Saint-Siège (76 {7§2}).

35. QUICUMQUE ENIM COMMUNITATEM HUMANAM IN ORDINE FAMILIAE, CULTURAE, VITAE OECONOMICAE ET SOCIALIS,

NECNON POLITICAE TAM NATIONALIS QUAM INTERNATIONALIS, PROMOVENT, SECUNDUM CONSILIUM DEI COMMUNITATI QUOQUE ECCLESIALI (*AAS* 58 [1966], 1065).
36. *Pour les domaines d'éducation, de formation et d'assistance sociale réglés aussi par conventions ou protocoles internationaux, l'État burkinabè reconnaît aux institutions de l'Église Catholique la liberté d'appliquer des mesures interprétatives qui respectent plus étroitement la doctrine catholique* (79 {13§2}).
37. AUGESCENS ENIM IN DIES NUMERUS HOMINUM, SCIENTIARUM ATQUE TECHNICARUM ARTIUM PROGRESSUS, ARCTIORES INTER HOMINES NECESSITUDINES NON SOLUM IN IMMENSUM DILATARUNT APOSTOLATUS LAICORUM SPATIA (*AAS* 58 [1966], 837).
38. *Le Burkina Faso reconnaît à l'Église Catholique, en ses différents rites, le libre exercice de sa mission apostolique, en particulier pour ce qui concerne le pouvoir d'auto-organisation, la liberté de culte, le gouvernement de ses fidèles* (75 {5}).
39. Little is textually revealed concerning this particular formation except that Cardinal François-Xavier Nguyên Van Thuân began, and upon his death Cardinal Renato Raffaele Martino completed the manuscript, which subsequently appeared in English from the Vatican press. See also A. Alexander Stummvoll, *A Living Tradition: Catholic Social Doctrine and Holy See Diplomacy* (Eugene, OR: Cascade Books, 2018).

CHAPTER 9

The Benediction of the Third World, 1993–2016

"The history of the subaltern classes is necessarily fragmented and episodic," contends Antonio Gramsci in the most famous passage from his carceral period in Turi di Bari on Mussolini's orders. "Subaltern classes are subject to the initiatives of the dominant class, even when they rebel; they are in a state of anxious defense. Every trace of autonomous initiative is therefore of inestimable value."[1] By reason of his at once coherent but flexible notion of the SUBALTERN class resulting from the division of society through capitalist production but also entering upon a political domain characterized by the *hegemony* or *dominance* of entrenched countervailing norms, Gramsci helped bridge the newfound liminal space between the economic determinism of textualist Marxist thought and the profound institutional challenges confronting a Third World in its transitions to independence, a theoretical contribution subsequently reflected in the militant demand for political consciousness of Frantz Fanon,[2] the strong reliance on philosophical *consciencism* of Ghana's Kwame Nkrumah,[3] and the account of existing *Orientalism* (1978) of Edward W. Said.[4] This final empirical chapter shall therefore demonstrate how, in meaningful dialogue with rapidly evolving international norms, the deeply inferior position of the Roman Catholic canon law within a cluster of Third World states has consequently resulted in the profoundly idealist normative posture of their respective concordats with the Apostolic See.

© The Author(s), under exclusive license to Springer Nature Switzerland AG 2024
M. R. Royce, *Ecclesiology, Idealism, and World Polity*, Palgrave Studies in Religion, Politics, and Policy, https://doi.org/10.1007/978-3-031-57033-9_9

Pontifical Constructivism

This final transformation of concordatorial treaty norms is theoretically delineated in the two main encyclicals of Francis (2013-),[5] the reigning Supreme Pontiff and only one to hail from the Global South. The unprecedented resignation of his predecessor Benedict XVI (2005–2013)[6] left the current pope with unfinished research notes for *Lumen Fidei* (*AAS* 105 [2013], 555–96), which proclaimed a Year of Faith to coincide with the fiftieth anniversary of the convocation of the Second Vatican Council. Pope Francis writes in a very personal and distinctive manner however in *Laudato Si'* (*AAS* 107 [2015], 847–945), on Care for our Common Home, and in *Fratelli Tutti* (*AAS* 112 [2020], 969–1074) on Fraternity and Social Friendship, together the most significant faith-based theoretical attempts at the social construction of idealist world polity.

Both explicitly reliant upon the life and doctrine of Saint Francis of Assisi,[7] *Laudato Si'* is the first papal encyclical equally addressed to all human beings. Bewailing global expropriation, universal commodification, and enduring or increasing stratification, its ambitious overall intent is to save an endangered planet by provoking the normative reconsideration of complex interdependence. "The basic problem," His Holiness contends, "is the way that humanity has taken up technology and its development *according to an undifferentiated and one-dimensional paradigm*" (106, emphasis in original). This unnamed paradigm is furthermore held to benefit unspecified elite interests. "The twenty-first century, while maintaining systems of governance inherited from the past, is witnessing a weakening of the power of nation states, chiefly because the economic and financial sectors, being transnational, tends to prevail over the political" (175).[8] As a result, excessive garbage and carbon dioxide have been allowed to accumulate, even as the poorest segments of the global population still have no reliable access to safe drinking water and indigenous communities still have no direct representation in developmental decisions directly affecting their lived experience, with UN scientists correct as to the scale but UN representatives powerless to achieve the rectification of such calamities. Both the Earth and the Poor therefore, in unison, cry unto God; and our shared response must lie in the reiteration of the distinction between technical and moral progress, the recognition of the unity of ecological and of social healing, and the reconstruction of an "ethics of international relations" (51) which, whatever its prospective institutionalization, must adhere to the following contention: "Interdependence obliges us to think of *one world with a common plan*...A global consensus is essential for confronting deeper problems, which cannot be resolved by unilateral actions on the part of individual countries" (164, emphasis in original).

Brexit, Trump, Lockdown, and other intervening comparative and international convulsions appear obliquely referenced in *Fratelli Tutti* (*AAS* 112 [2020], 969–1074), the most recent papal encyclical on fraternity and social friendship. Co-sponsored by Grand Imam Ahmad El-Tayeb,[9] and inspired by the Rev. Dr. Martin Luther King, Jr., Archbishop Desmond Tutu, and Mohandas Gandhi, it pursues much the same theme of a world groaning in travail, but widens the previous concentration on ecological renewal in order to identify and discuss numerous other prevailing social injustices, as well as strikes a much darker tone both in its identification of an "invisible dictatorship of hidden interests" (75) skillfully exercising world domination but also in the self-induced "frenzy of texting" (49), "feverish exchange of opinions on social networks" (200), and "neither the time nor the energy...to say 'excuse me', 'pardon me', 'thank you'" (224) symptomatic of the spiritual aridity, specious reasoning, and selfish behavior of the international netizens that *Laudato Si'* had five years earlier boldly attempted to call to action. Categorically rejecting the death penalty in remembrance of the carnage of Auschwitz and Hiroshima, *Fratelli Tutti* first constructs political theory on universal openness to other persons and cultures, preëmptively declaring nationalism of any kind completely out of order. "Other cultures are not 'enemies' from which we need to protect ourselves," Francis declares, "but differing reflections of the inexhaustible richness of human life" (147). Consequently, in particular, receiving states must fully assimilate migrants, regardless it would seem of the expense or the amount. Unspecified "narrow forms of nationalism," the pope holds, "err in thinking that they can develop on their own heedless of the ruin of others, that by closing their doors to others they will be better protected" (141). This fraternal foundational norm then enables the sketching of a POLYHEDRAL (190) international theory to display both the *art* and *architecture* of world peace (231), including but not limited to the United Nations Charter. Although specific suggestions are either delegated to diverse actors according to the principle of subsidiarity, or else simply tabled for future decision by more responsible heads of state or government, the pontifical instruction as a whole reverberates with, among other constructivist formulations, the empowering *Theory of Communicative Action* (1981) of Jürgen Habermas, the overriding emphasis on *Human Security* (2007) amid post-Westphalian devolutionary wars of Mary Kaldor, and the lifelong autobiographical description of the public intellectual *Citizen Pilgrim* (2021) of Richard Falk. "An appropriate and authentic openness to the world presupposes the capacity to be open to one's neighbour within a family of nations," Pope Francis concludes. "Cultural, economic and political integration with neighbouring peoples," he continues, "should therefore be accompanied by a process of education that promotes the value of love for one's neighbour, the first indispensable step towards attaining a healthy universal integration" (151).

Turning from the ecclesiastical to the civil side, the deeply inferior position of the canon law within the Third World contracting parties of Table 9.1 ought to incline the analyst to expect what is indeed the result: little to no previous conceptualization of the proper relationship between the Catholic Church and the civil commonwealth. The concordats within this final cluster of cases, as shall be demonstrated, *initiate* rather than alter or finalize that relationship. Yet the following preliminary remarks, tailored to the specific question at hand, will likely still prove useful.

The three contracting parties to the primary Middle East conflict appearing within the cluster ought to be introduced first and together. The political theory of Zionism directly responsible for the formation of the State of Israel derives from Theodor Herzl's *The Jewish State* (*Der Judenstaat*, 1896), which seeks to politically awaken, transnationally organize, and then mass migrate the mainly European diaspora back to the Biblical Holy Land, there to organize a secular republic that would not be constrained by the Mosaic law and a liberal economy that would not be overthrown by the Communist manifesto; but otherwise the Jews are expected to form themselves into political factions and ideological tendencies in the usual manner. For Herzl, a Jew is principally a national community member rather than a specimen of a particular race or an adherent of a particular religion. "A State is formed," he explains, "not by pieces of land, but rather by a number of men united under sovereign rule. The people is the subjective, land the objective foundation of a State, and the subjective basis is the more important of the two."[10]

The Jewish state Herzl did not live to see is governed according to thirteen Basic Laws, eleven of which had been passed by the agreement

Table 9.1 The benediction of the Third World

Pontiff	Contracting party	Head of State or Government
(Pontifical Legate, Title)	(Contracting Location, Date, Language(s))	(Contracting Plenipotentiary, Title)
John Paul II (Claudio M. Celli)	**STATE OF ISRAEL** (Jerusalem, 13 Dec. 1993, English/Hebrew)	Yitzhak Rabin (Yossi Beilin)
John Paul II (Angelo Sodano, Cardinal)	**REPUBLIC OF KAZAKHSTAN** (Vatican City-state, 24 Sep. 1998, English/Kazakh/Russian)	Nursultan Nazarbayev (Kasymzhomart K. Tokaev)
John Paul II (Celestino Migliore)	**PALESTINE LIBERATION ORGANIZATION** (Vatican City-state, 15 Feb. 2000, English)	Yasir Arafat (Emile Jarjoui)
John Paul II (Silvano Tomasi, Archbishop Nuncio)	**ORGANIZATION OF AFRICAN UNITY** (Adis Ababa, 19 Oct. 2000, French/English)	Salim Ahmed Salim (Secretary General)
Benedict XVI (Zenon Grocholewski, Cardinal)	**MINISTRY OF EDUCATION OF THE REPUBLIC OF CHINA** (Taipaei, 2 Dec. 2011, English)	Ma Ying-jeou (Ching-Ji Wu)
Francis (Piero Pioppo, Archbishop Nuncio)	**REPUBLIC OF THE CAMEROON** (Yaounde, 13 Jan 2014, French/English/Italian)	Paul Biya (Pierre Moukoko Mbonjo, Minister of External Relations)
Francis (Paul R. Gallagher, Secretary for Relations with States)	**STATE OF PALESTINE** (Vatican City-state, 26 June 2015, English)	Mahmoud Abbas (Riad Al-Malki, Minister of Foreign Affairs)
Francis	**MINISTRY OF FOREIGN AFFAIRS**	Sabah IV

(continued)

Table 9.1 (continued)

Pontiff	Contracting party	Head of State or Government
(Paul R. Gallagher, Secretary for Relations with States)	**OF THE STATE OF KUWAIT** (Vatican City-state, 10 Sep. 2015, English/Arabic)	(Sabah Khaled Al-Hamad Al-Sabah, First Dep. Prime Minister and Minister of Foreign Affairs)
Francis (Paul R. Gallagher, Secretary for Relations with States)	**GOVERNMENT OF THE UNITED ARAB EMIRATES** (Vatican City-state, 15 Sep. 2016, English/Arabic)	Khalifa bin Zayed Al Nahyan (Abdullah bin Zayed Al-Nahyan)

of its 1993 concordat. The Knesset Basic Law (1958) establishes a parliament in Jerusalem based on proportional representation, with prospective candidates whose life or doctrine contravenes Israeli independence or gives succor to its enemies preëmptively rendered ineligible (7a.(a)(1–3)). The Israeli Lands law (1960) prohibits any territorial alienation, the President of the State law (1964) provides for a characteristic head of state elected by the Knesset for seven years, and the Military law (1976) charters the Israel Defense Forces. The Government (2001), Judiciary (1984), and State Comptroller (1988) Basic Laws outline law and policymaking, while the State Economy (1975) and Freedom of Occupation (1994 [1992]) Basic Laws provide structure to the political economy. Per Herzl, no substantive role is assigned to the rabbinical authorities in any of the Israeli Basic Laws, with the *declarations* rather than oaths of its lawmakers and officers likewise containing no religious asseveration. The Basic Law: Human Dignity and Liberty (1992) furnishes however the following normative statements, the strongest theretofore passed by the Knesset[11]:

> The basic human rights in Israel are based on the recognition of the value of the human being, the sanctity of his life, and his being a free person, and they shall be upheld in the spirit of the principles included in the Declaration of the Establishment of the State of Israel (1). The purpose of this Basic Law is to protect human dignity and liberty, in order to embed

the values of the State of Israel as a Jewish and democratic State, in a basic law (1a).

The said Israel establishment declaration chaotically finalized in Tel Aviv on the historic night of 14 May 1948, as one might expect, recounts the exilic wanderings, Nazi attack, and Zionist reformation of the Jewish people, but also insists upon their right under international law pursuant to the Balfour Declaration, the League of Nations, and the United Nations to self-determination in ERETZ-ISRAEL.

Such Zionist immediately and irrevocably contravened Arab self-determination, however, with a resulting Palestine National Liberation Movement (*Harakat al-Tahrir al-Watani al Filistini* [AL-FATEH]) taking shape during the early 1960s under politically conscious engineering student Yasser'Arafat. Although the work of no political theorist is as clearly decisive among the Arabs of Palestine as that of Herzl was among the Jews of the diaspora, hijacker Leila Khaled's memoir *My People Shall Live: The Autobiography of a Revolutionary* (2008 [1973]) occupies perhaps the most prominent position within the popular romance and mythos of Al-Fateh. "We did not leave [Haifa] voluntarily, and if we did, what law or morality gave the Zionists the right to occupy our homes and take our possessions? That is the question which the realistic historian must answer" (11–12). A United Nations select committee in 2022—on the opposite shore of an ocean of debate and argument—deemed them to have done so by the force of arms rather than by the law of nations[12]; but meanwhile a young Khaled in hiding from the authorities clarifies, "The supreme objective of the Palestine liberation movement is the total liberation of Palestine, the dismantlement of the Zionist state apparatus, and the construction of a socialist society in which both Arabs and Jews can live in peace and harmony" (91). The largely complementary Palestinian National Charter approved by the PLO in Cairo in 1968 reflects this Marxian framing of subaltern Arab Palestinians waging just war against international Zionist imperialism,[13] with its first article declaring, "Palestine is the homeland of the Arab Palestinian people; it is an indivisible part of the Arab homeland, and the Palestinian people are an integral part of the Arab nation." The Islamic religion is not mentioned in a national charter that nonetheless insists that "armed struggle" (9) consisting of "commando action" (10) provides the only possible recourse for a stateless nation whose territory was partitioned in contravention of the UN Charter (19), and whose enemies represent international "Zionist and imperialist aggression" (153). The final utopian result shall however "provide the Holy Land with an atmosphere of safety and tranquility, which in turn will safeguard the country's religious sanctuaries and guarantee freedom of worship and of visit to all, without discrimination" (16). The PLO subsequently submitted an interfaith declaration of Arab Palestinian independence to the UN General Assembly (A/43/827) in November, 1988, which eventually responded in November, 2012 with a resolution (A/RES/67/19) "to accord to Palestine non-member observer State status in the United Nations, without prejudice to the acquired rights, privileges and role of the Palestine Liberation Organization in the United Nations as representative of the Palestinian people" (3{2}), a conceptual ambiguity shared exclusively with the Apostolic See.

The contracting party to the concordat with the Republic of Kazakhstan, meanwhile, was Nursultan Nazarbayev, its omnipotent post-Soviet ruler. Although the Kazakh constitution assigns all power to the President (44), Nazarbayev's highest law otherwise suggests intentional ideological ambiguity, with the oaths of its officers containing no religious assertation (42.1) and the text as a whole failing to display any apparent constitutive norms. Consequently, stalwart comparative jurist William E. Butler concludes in his recent translation of the *Civil Code of the Republic Kazakhstan* (2021) that his subject furnishes, "a legal system in transition from the socialist legal tradition to a destination as yet undetermined" (back cover). The following article, corresponding to similar wording in the concordat, does however in context conclusively demonstrate the deeply inferior position of the canon law in the Republic Kazakhstan: "Activities of *foreign* religious associations on the territory of the Republic, as well as the appointment of heads of religious associations in the Republic by *foreign* religious centers shall be carried out in coordination with the respective state institutions of the Republic" (5.5, emphases added).

Continuing down Table 9.1, the at once political, comparative, and international theory responsible for the Organization of African Unity chartered at Addis Ababa in May, 1963 derives from *Africa Must Unite* (1963), by Doctor of Philosophy, founder of the Convention People's Party, inaugural President of the Republic of Ghana, and Pan-African philosopher[14] Kwame Nkrumah. The author of a *Consciencism* (1964) political outlook primarily concerned with the construction of an African socialist humanism, *Africa Must Unite* urges the institutional, economic, and developmental confederation of the newly independent African nations for both the absolute gain of leapfrogging human and the relative gain of safeguarding national security, primarily against the *neocolonialism* of a European Common Market that could insidiously reconstruct much the same former exploitation, abuse, and dependency. "In fledgling states," Nkrumah explains, "imperialist interests flourish where there is an atmosphere of dissension. They are endangered in an atmosphere of national unity and stability" (76). Reflecting upon American, German, European, Soviet, Chinese, and Indian precedents, Nkrumah holds that although the attainment of the first overarching objective—independence—has been achieved, the African nations must immediately set about bringing to completion the next major goal of unity, sketched as a centralized developmental plan safeguarded by common foreign and security policies. Although non-Communist, Nkrumah demonstrates and acknowledges primary conceptual reliance upon the materialist conception of history in the formulation of the constitutive norms of his Convention People's Party, "people's parliamentary democracy" (70), and pioneering efforts to create a miniature UN for Africa: "If the true interest of all peoples is pursued, there must come an end to all forms of exploitation and oppression of man by man, of nation by nation; there must come an end to war. There must result peaceful co-existence and the prosperity and happiness of all mankind" (203).[15]

The constitutive norms of the Republic of China as a whole, next, are encapsulated in *The Three Principles of the People* (*San Min Chu I*, 1938) of Father of the Republic and Eternal Premier of the Kuomintang, MEDICINAE DOCTOR Sun Yat-sen (1886–1925), who the year before his death delivered sixteen long lectures in Canton setting forth the political philosophy of the Chinese Revolution. Critically reflecting upon the vast extent but chronic division, the large population but limited ability, and the geopolitical precariousness but political immaturity of post-imperial China, Dr. Sun contends, "The life of mankind has flowed from theocracy on to autocracy and from autocracy now on to democracy, and there is no way to stem the current" (116). Consequently, he continues, "The watchword of our revolution is '*Min-ts'u, Min-ch'uan, Min-sheng*' (People's Nationalism, People's Sovereignty, People's Livelihood)" (123). Throughout extensive discourses on the contributions but misconceptions of Rousseau and Marx, the ambivalence of the recent results under Lenin, and the profound importance of building upon but also deviating from the liberal revolutions in America, France, and elsewhere, these three principles are richly connoted but never precisely denoted, although a distinction is eventually drawn between political power residing with the people and public administration of the state machine (*Chi-kuan*) entrusted to trained professionals. "The political power will be given into the hands of the people, who will have a full degree of sovereignty and will be able to control directly the affairs of state," Dr. Sun explains. "The other power is government, and we will put that entirely in the government organs, which will be powerful and will manage all the nation's business" (225).[16]

Lastly, the political theology of the Emirate of Kuwait and of the United Arab Emirates both constituted in 1962 demonstrate the agonistic intersection of the Islamic theology of the *Noble Qur'ân*, the Arab nationalism of T.E. Lawrence's *Seven Pillars of Wisdom* (1933), and the commercial liberalism of Adam Smith's *Wealth of Nations* (1776). The Constitution (Law Number I) of the hereditary Emirate of Kuwait (11 November 1962 / 14 Jumada al-Thani 1382) opens, "Kuwait is an Arab state, independent and fully sovereign...The religion of the State is Islam, and the Islamic Shari'a shall be a main source of legislation" (1–2). The UAE constitution, in apparent coordination, likewise states, "The Union is part of the Great Arab Nation...Islam is the official religion of the Union. The Islamic Shari'ah shall be a main source of legislation in the Union" (6–7). The Islamic and the Arab dimensions are reiterated throughout both constitutions, but the remaining third body of norms reflects the development of both commonwealths within the commercial world-system of the British Commonwealth. "Property, capital, and work are fundamental constituents of the social structure of the State and of the national wealth" (16), continues the Kuwaiti constitution. Consequently, the government shall encourage saving and investing (23), promote scientific research (36), and guarantee public education (40). The United Arab Emirates are meanwhile constituted principally as a free trade area and customs union (11), with commitments to public education (17), the protection of private property (21), and equality before the law (25), wherein, "the basis of the national economy...shall be the achievement of economic productivity, raising the standards of living and the achievement of prosperity for citizens" (24). More generally, "the foreign policy of the Union shall be directed towards support for Arab and Islamic causes and interests and towards consolidation of the bonds of friendship and cooperation with all the principles of the Charter of the United Nations and ideal international standards" (12), although the latter are left unspecified.

Constructivist Concordats

The demonstration of purely idealist treaty norms in inverse relation to the completely inferior position of the canon law within the contracting parties of this final cluster of Third World concordats consists of three sequential points. First, the treaty texts themselves often explicitly make clear that the Catholic Church enjoyed no previous legal incorporation, political position, or social prominence prior to agreement. "Concerning Catholic legal personality at canon law the Holy See and the State of Israel will negotiate on giving it full effect in Israeli law" (*AAS* 86 [1994], 720 {3§3}). Although no textual outcome of such intended deliberations appears in the *Acts of the Apostolic See*, the remark illustrates the point. Similarly, "the authorities of the Republic of Kazakhstan shall grant residence permits to members of the Catholic Church *from abroad*" (*AAS* 92 [2000], 320 {2}, emphasis added). The Memorandum of Understanding with Kuwait, meanwhile, is based on the conviction "that consultations and exchange of information…will contribute to the deepening of mutual understanding" (*AAS* 108 [2016], 1164 {preamble}).

Second, the idealist norms of the United Nations are in consequence directly referenced in the constructivist concordats. Passed by the General Assembly (A/RES/217(III)) in December, 1948, the Universal Declaration of Human Rights/*Déclaration universelle des droits de l'homme* is the most important such statement since the French version of 1789, and the only fully incorporated into international law. Beginning with, "recognition of the inherent dignity and of the equal and inalienable rights of all members of the human family," the document proceeds to enumerate "a common standard of achievement for all peoples and all nations," a standard which must include freedom of association, expression, asylum, conscience, and religion, freedom from slavery, torture, discrimination, persecution, and arbitrary arrest and/or imprisonment, and the right to life, liberty, marriage, due process of law, and "a social and international order in which the rights and freedoms set forth in this Declaration can be fully realized" (28). By reason of the explicit textual references to the Declaration in the concordats with the State of Israel (*AAS* 86 [1994], 716 {1§1}), the Palestine Liberation Organization (*AAS* 92 [2000], 854 {1.1}), the African Union (*AAS* 93 [2001], 15 {preamble}), and the State of Palestine (*AAS* 108 [2016], 171 {II.4§1}), the respective contracting parties legally and normatively commit themselves to the social construction of such a world order. The same principle applies with respect to the six Vienna Conventions (1961–1986) that govern the exchange of ambassadors, consular relations, the delineation of treaty forms, and other international laws of peace, with this indispensable treaty series cited approvingly in the concordats with the Kuwaiti Foreign Ministry (*AAS* 108 [2016], 1164 {preamble}), the UAE government (*AAS* 108 [2016], 1169 {preamble}), and the Cameroon (*AAS* 106 [2014], 292 {9.1}).

Third, the various texts of the cluster also invoke, where applicable, corresponding comparative ideals. The concordat with the Organization of African Unity (*AAS* 93 [2001], 15–18), for example, invokes in its preamble the 1963 charter based upon "a common determination to promote understanding among our peoples and co-operation among our states in response to the aspirations of our peoples for brotherhood and solidarity." The OAU likewise invokes the UN Charter together with the Universal Declaration of Human Rights, and it establishes a regional system consisting of Member States, an Assembly of Heads of State and Government, a Council of Ministers, and Administrative Secretary-General along the UN pattern, all wherein "Member States pledge to settle all disputes among themselves by peaceful means" (XIX). The concordat with the Taiwanese Ministry of Education (*AAS* 105 [2013], 96 {II.2.ii}), likewise, incorporates the thirteenth article of the national constitution which holds, "The people shall have freedom of religious belief," while the preamble to the concordat with Cameroon (*AAS* 106 [2014], 289) grounds the treaty in the recognition "that the Constitution of the Republic of Cameroon establishes a secular [*laïcité/laicità*] state."

With these general principles established, more sustained critical attention may be directed toward the strongest and most highly idealistic attempts to (re)construct international relations via concordat. The extraordinary ecclesiastical relations established in sequence with the State of Israel (*AAS* 86 [1994], 716–29), with the Palestine Liberation Organization (*AAS* 92 [2000], 853–61), and with the State of Palestine (*AAS* 108 [2016], 168–85) collectively furnish the most robust demonstrations of the ideational treaty norms of the cluster and the census, wherein the Apostolic See comes full circle on its legacy of medieval crusading so as to renew the quest for peace in the Holy Land on the basis of international law and norm, and wherein three non-Catholic contracting parties together seal a new covenant with the Bishop of Rome solemnly appointed their mediator and advocate.

The Declaration of Principles on Interim Self-Government Arrangements between Israel and the PLO signed in Washington on 13

September 1993 (A/48/486, 'OSLO I') attempted to restart a peace process whereby Israeli forces would withdraw from Gaza and Jericho, Palestinian politics would be democratized, and security forces from both communities would carefully coordinate control in a West Bank socially resurrected through a "Marshall Plan" of forthcoming economic and developmental assistance. *Three months later*, the Apostolic See signed in Jerusalem a "Fundamental Agreement" with the same State of Israel (*AAS* 86 [1994], 716–29), wherein both parties state up front their mindfulness, "of the singular character and significance of the Holy Land." Clarifying Israeli commitment to the norms of the Universal Declaration of Human Rights ({1§1}) and Apostolic commitment to those of *Dignitatis Humanae* and *Nostra Aetate* ({1§2}), what follows in article 2 is one of the boldest normative statements within contractual international law, so intense that it must be recorded in full:

§1. The Holy See and the State of Israel are committed to appropriate cooperation in combatting all forms of antisemitism and all kinds of racism and of religious intolerance, and in promoting mutual understanding among nations, tolerance among communities and respect for human life and dignity.

§2. The Holy See takes this occasion to reiterate its condemnation of hatred, persecution and all other manifestations of antisemitism directed against the Jewish people and individual Jews anywhere, at any time and by any one. In particular, the Holy See deplores attacks on Jews and desecration of Jewish synagogues and cemeteries, acts which offend the memory of the victims of the Holocaust.

Such sweeping commitments provided, the concordat continues by expressing shared interest in the promotion of Christian pilgrimage ({5§1}), characteristic recognition of the right of the Church to own property on Israeli soil ({10§1}),[17] and "respective commitment to the promotion of the peaceful resolution of conflicts among States and nations, excluding violence and terror from international life" ({11§1}). An exchange of Apostolic Nuncio and Israeli Ambassador follows ({14§1}).

Likewise, after the establishment of official relations in 1994 and several years of research and development, a Basic Agreement between the Holy See and the Palestine Liberation Organization (*AAS* 92 [2000],

853–61) was signed in the Vatican on 15 February 2000, the preamble of which calls for, "a peaceful solution of the Palestinian-Israeli conflict...on the basis of international law, relevant United Nations and its Security Council resolutions, justice and equity," in which, more specifically, there ought to be a "special Statute for Jerusalem, internationally guaranteed" rendering its three Abrahamic faiths legally equal, and assuring their adherents access to holy buildings and grounds. Standard ecclesiological concessions include acknowledgment of the right of the Church to carry out its apostolic mission ({5}), legal autonomy within its own sphere ({6}), and the promise of public incorporation whereby, "Full effect will be given in Palestinian Law to the legal personality of the Catholic Church and of the canonical legal persons" ({7}). Otherwise, two highly idealist normative statements stand out. First, "the PLO affirms its permanent commitment to uphold and observe the human right to freedom of religion and conscience, as stated in the Universal Declaration of Human Rights" ({1.1}). Second, "the Parties are committed to appropriate cooperation in promoting respect for human rights, individual and collective, in combatting all forms of discrimination and threats to human life and dignity, as well as to the promotion of understanding and harmony between nations and communities" ({2.1}). Thus although subsequent eruptions of communal violence including, but not limited to the Second Intifada tragically derailed the peace process, two extremely ideational concordats of the Apostolic See provided a less widely acknowledged[18] contribution during an auspicious historic interval.

Nevertheless, on the other side of intervening Palestinian uprising, Zionist reaction, and global War on Terror, the Church renewed its concordatorial efforts in the region with the Comprehensive Agreement between the Holy See and the State of Palestine (*AAS* 108 [2016], 168–85), signed in the Vatican on 26 June 2015 by Archbishop Paul R. Gallagher and Palestinian Foreign Minister Dr. Riad Al-Maliki. In conceptual vitality, instrumental clarity, and originality of vision, intention, and outcome, the concordat with Palestine is in a class of its own, rivaled only by the purely ecclesiological Lateran Pacts with which this entire account of the normative transformation of concordats began. Its contents therefore bring the overall thesis to decisive conclusion.

The preamble opens with a resounding affirmation of, "the inalienable rights of the Palestinian people to self-determination, freedom, security and dignity in an independent state of their own...in accordance with international law and all relevant United Nations resolutions, as well as for an independent, sovereign, democratic and viable State of Palestine on the basis of the pre-1967 borders." What follows is the social construction of a dynamic relationship between the Catholic Church and the Palestinian State according to seven issue area chapters—a unique textual feature—the contents of which are as a whole much more ideational than ecclesiological. "Fundamental Principles and Norms" (I) opens by explaining that on the basis of the previous agreement with the PLO, "the Holy See recognizes the State of Palestine and welcomes its admission to the United Nations as a Non-Member Observer State" ({1§2}). In exchange, the newly acknowledged State of Palestine pursuant to the 1988 independence declaration, "shall, in accordance with Palestinian law and internationally accepted human rights standards, permit without undue restrictions the exercise of the above freedoms of religion, belief, worship and the performance of the religious functions to the Catholic Church, to any canonical legal person and to any Catholic person" ({2§3}). An annotated list of sixteen concrete realizations contained within this sweeping assurance follows in "Freedom of Religion and Conscience" (II), wherein the Palestinian state, after again committing itself to the terms of the Universal Declaration of Human Rights ({4§1}), specifies ({4§3.1–16}) freedom to adhere to any religion without discrimination, freedom to publicly or privately worship, the right to peaceably assemble, the freedom to maintain religious organizations, the corporate right of the Church to transnational correspondence and entry and exit of religious personnel, the freedom of the Church to publish, the personal right of Catholics to marriage and burial according to canon law, recognition of Catholic holy days, the right of pilgrimage upon or across Palestinian territory, the right to refuse civil oaths deemed irreligious, the guarantee of religious freedom and observance within any armed forces, the right to conscientiously object, religious freedom for the imprisoned and the hospitalized, and parental right of access to Christian education.

Chapter 3 entitled "Ecclesiastical Rights, Rights to Self Organization, Jurisdiction and Personnel" furnishes strong ideational justification for ecclesiological terms. It begins with characteristic provisions as to the right of the Church to carry out its spiritual mission ({5§1}) and to govern and administer within its own legal sphere ({5§2}), although a peculiar Papal Representative ({6§1}) is appointed to serve as overall although not sole ordinary of the place. The chapter continues, "The State of Palestine recognizes the legal personality of the Catholic Church and of all canonical legal persons deemed by the Canon Law of the

Church to be legal persons, and recognizes that they are governed in their internal matters by the relevant provisions of Canon Law" ({7§1}). Various provisions operationalize this recognition ({7§2–5}), culminating in the conferral of diplomatic immunity to Palestinian agents according to the Vienna Convention of 1961 ({7§7}). Supported by the subsequent "Personal Status" (IV) chapter, diplomatic immunity is likewise conferred upon both the Latin Patriarch of Jerusalem and Custos of the Holy Land ({8§1}),[19] together with the "necessary multi-entry and residence permits" for their staff ({10§1}). All Catholic religious are meanwhile completely exempt from involuntary Palestinian military service ({11§1}) or any kind of official search ({12§4}), and the confessional seal once again declared inviolable ({12§5}).

"Freedom of Religion and Sacred Places" (V), next, comprehensively assures the comparative preservation of world religion throughout Palestinian territory. "The sacred character of the Holy Places shall be respected and protected" ({16§1}). "All forms of worship shall be constantly guaranteed" ({17§1}). "The freedom of pilgrimage to the Holy Land for Catholics is recognized as pertaining to the freedom of worship" ({17§2}). With regard to the preceding assurance specifically, the text furthermore clarifies that the passage of Christian pilgrims must never be interdicted nor their choice of spiritual guides overruled ({17§3}), although the Apostolic See commits to prioritize the engagement of locals for this purpose ({17§4}). The Church as a whole is once again entitled to all manner of ecclesiastical premises ({18§1}).

"Charitable, Social and Cultural Institutions; Means of Communication" (VI), develops the comprehensive right of the Church to maintain Catholic schools, although "subject to" ({19§1}), "in accordance with" ({19§2}), and under the potential "supervision" ({20§2}) of the Palestinian government. "Palestinian authorities will guarantee the right of Christian pupils to Christian religious education in public schools in coordination with the relevant ecclesiastical authority" ({20§4}). Catholic teaching is also promised ongoing presence within Palestinian state broadcasting ({23§1}), and the Church guaranteed the right to the use of private media as well ({23§2}). Finally, "Ecclesiastical Property Rights and Taxation" (VII) develops the main idea, "the Church has the right to acquire, retain and administer property whether movable or immovable" ({25§1}). Such property of the Roman Catholic Church within the territory of the State of Palestine is furthermore categorically declared immune from expropriation ({26§1}) and exempt from taxation ({27§1}), along with the salaries of all Catholic religious from any state income tax ({28§1}). Thus the only concordat of the Apostolic See with a contracting party not fully incorporated into international law conclusively demonstrates the papal intention and capability to directly engage in the ideational construction of international community.

Interfaith Idealism

The consummation of this idealist turn under Pope Francis is a normative declaration inconceivable in any earlier era: "Of Human Brotherhood and Communal Living" (*AAS* 111 [De Humana Fraternitate pro Pace Mundiali et communi convictu] 349–56), completed 4 February 2019 at Abu Dhabi by the Supreme Pontiff and his unlikely co-author Prof. Dr. Ahmed Mohamed Ahmed El-Tayeb, by turns Grand Mufti of Egypt and President and Grand Sheikh of al-Azhar University, and consequently the putative senior cleric of Sunni Islam.[20] Meeting in the U.A.E. two and a half years after the conclusion of its concordat, their interfaith declaration stresses the prevention of further damage to the institution of the family, the importance of the provision of educational and employment opportunities for women, and the clarity of international law regarding the protection of synagogues, churches, mosques, and all houses of worship. The respective representatives of the Catholic Church and al-Azhar likewise agree that materialist systems of norms mortally endanger the mindset of religious obedience, as well as that the profusion of extreme political theologies has begun to precipitate "a third world war being fought piecemeal" (*terza Guerra mondiale a pezzi*, 351). But some of the most progressive remarks of their joint resolution evince an interfaith idealism that appears to approach religious syncretism. "The pluralism and the diversity of religions," they both argue, in apparent contradiction to the fundamentals of both their creeds, "are willed by God in His wisdom" (*Il pluralism e le diversità di religione…sono una sapiente volontà divina*, 353). By extension, reason the pontiff and the imam, seeming manifestations of religion as a source of violent conflict instead result from political oppression, economic exploitation, social maladjustment, or other external factors which unscrupulous religious actors might take advantage of, but which have no theological basis in any religious doctrine. "Terrorism," they pronounce, "is not due to religion…It is due, rather, to an accumulation of incorrect interpretations of religious texts and to policies linked to hunger, poverty, injustice, oppression and pride."[21] Thus by reason of its unprecedented attempt to achieve normative unison between the Roman Catholic and the Sunni Muslim religions, "Of Human Brotherhood," demonstrates the strongest papal idealism yet seen, or easily imagined.

Notes

1. *Prison Notebooks* (New York: Columbia University Press, [*Quaderni del carcere*, 1937] 1996), vol. II, 21 {§ < 14 > }. Gramsci is necessary though not sufficient to explain the ironic convergence of the Left, Al-Fateh, and Islam characteristic of the international demonstrations that erupted following the Hamas incursion and rampage of 7 October 2023.
2. *The Wretched of the Earth* (New York: Grove Press, [*Les damnés de la terre*, 1961] 2004): "We believe the conscious, organized struggle undertaken by a colonized people in order to restore national sovereignty constitutes the greatest cultural manifestation that exists...that national consciousness is the highest form of culture" (178–79).
3. *Consciencism: Philosophy and Ideology for De-colonization* (New York: Monthly Review Press, 1964): "African society has one segment which comprises our traditional way of life; it has a second segment which is filled by the presence of Islamic tradition in Africa; it has a final segment which represents the infiltration of Western Europe into Africa, using colonialism and neocolonialism as its primary vehicles" (68).
4. "In any society not totalitarian...certain cultural forms predominate over others, just as certain ideas are more influential than others; the form of this cultural leadership is what Gramsci has identified as *hegemony*, an indispensable concept for any understanding of cultural life in the industrial West. It is hegemony, or rather the result of cultural hegemony at work, that gives Orientalism the durability and the strength I have been speaking about" (7, emphasis in original).
5. Born *Jorge Mario Bergoglio*, 1936; ordained, 1969; Provincial Superior of the Society of Jesus in Argentina, 1973–79; Archbishop of Buenos Aires, 1998–2013; Cardinal, 2001.
6. Because the ecclesiological to ideational concordatorial norms are principally ascribed to the dominance or inferiority of canon law

within the contracting party, every encyclical or indeed every pontiff need not be identified and discussed. But lest the omission appear awkward, the three encyclicals of Benedict XVI—*Deus Caritas Est* (*AAS* 98 [2006], 217–52), on Christian Love, *Spe Salvi* (*AAS* 99 [2007], 985–1027), on Christian Hope, and *Caritas in Veritate* (*AAS* 101 [2009], 641–709), on Integral Human Development in Charity and Truth—are representative though not especially pioneering expressions of Catholic devotional and social teaching. The last is the boldest through its existential call for, "a person-based and community-oriented cultural process of world-wide integration that is open to transcendence," (42), a proposition actively pursued by his successor.

7. Large accretion of legend surrounds the central figure of Roman Catholic popular piety. For certain, he was author together with other devotional fragments of the famous "Canticle of the Sun," along with an epistle addressed to all the faithful (1215?) that probably informed the framing of the two distinctive Franciscan encyclicals. His ecclesiological RULE OF THE FRIARS MINOR (1209, 1223), meanwhile, establishes above all an obedient, chaste, and propertyless brethren, who are furthermore obliged to continually pray and to seasonally fast, and to completely avoid both money and women, with fornicators expelled. Paschal Robinson, *The Writings of Saint Francis of Assisi* (Philadelphia: The Dolphin Press, 1906).

8. The general contention that international economic, financial, and/or technological prevails upon comparative political power appears in too many disparate variations to succinctly enumerate, but the application of Francis perhaps most naturally suggests the arc of critical analysis opened by Noam Chomsky in *American Power and the New Mandarins* (New York: The New Press, [1969] 2002), which despite significant differences of context and emphasis comparably assails, "the dominance of liberal technocracy…supported by an apathetic, obedient majority, its mind and conscience dulled by a surfeit of commodities" (5).

9. To be properly introduced in section three.

10. Theodor Herzl, *The Jewish State: An Attempt at a Modern Solution of the Jewish Question* (New York: Jewish Publication Society of America, [*Der Judenstaat*, 1896] 2011), 67.

11. Basic Law: Israel—the Nation State of the Jewish People (2018) would furnish major escalation through its imposition of an *exclusive* right of the Jewish people to self-determination in Israel, along with clarification of the official state symbols, language, and compelling interest in a perpetual "ingathering of the exiles" (5).
12. Report of the Independent International Commission of Inquiry on the Occupied Palestinian Territory, including East Jerusalem, and Israel. United Nations General Assembly, A/77/328. "The Commission finds that there are reasonable grounds to conclude that the Israeli occupation of Palestinian territory is now unlawful under international law owing to its permanence and to actions undertaken by Israel to annex parts of the land de facto and de jure...The settlement enterprise is the principal means by which those results are achieved" (75).
13. In Leila S. Kadi, *Basic Political Documents of the Armed Palestinian Resistance Movement* (Beirut: PLO Research Center, 1969): 137–42.
14. By the same author, all from Panaf of London: *Towards Colonial Freedom* (1945); *Ghana: Autobiography of Kwame Nkrumah* (1957); *I Speak of Freedom* (1958); *Neo-colonialism: The Last Stage of Imperialism* (1965); *Axioms of Kwame Nkrumah* (1967) *Challenge of the Congo: A Case Study of Foreign Pressures in an Independent State* (1967); *Voice from Conakry* (1967); *Dark Days in Ghana* (1968); *The Struggle Continues* (1968); *Class Struggle in Africa* (1970); *Revolutionary Path* (1973); *Rhodesia File* (1974).
15. Specifically, Nkrumah convened the initial Conference of Independent African States in April, 1958, with union between Ghana and Guinea in particular achieved the following November.
16. By the same author, *Memoirs of a Chinese Revolutionary: A Programme for National Reconstruction in China* (Taipei: China Cultural Service, 1953) furnishes an assortment of deductive and inductive proofs, together with supporting documents in furtherance of the overarching epistemology as to "the easiness of action and the difficulty of knowledge" (75), whereby theoretical veracity is essential to social transformation. "If the men of my day will sincerely combat...the [wrong] formula 'knowledge is easy but action is difficult', and at the same time bend their energies to agitation for the fundamental watchwords of our Revolution

(nationalism, democracy, the foundations of the Chinese Constitution), China will rapidly become a strong and mighty Republic" (84).
17. Although, as has been consistently demonstrated, a standard feature of canon law, this treaty term would appear to entail at least a partial exception to Basic Law: Israel Lands (1960) identified above prohibiting any transfer, partition, or other alienation.
18. No scholarly book has yet been written on the specific subject of the three concordats with the parties to the Arab/Israeli conflict. Until then, see Leonard Hammer, "The 2015 Comprehensive Agreement Between the Holy See and the Palestinian Authority: Discerning the Holy See's Approach to International Relations in the Holy Land," *Oxford Journal of Law and Religion* 6, no. 1 (2017): 162–79.
19. The former cleric is last in precedence, though equal in dignity to his brothers in Christ from Constantinople, Alexandria, and Antioch (CCEO/1990, c. 59§2), and the latter is Minister Provincial of the CUSTODIA TERRÆ SANCTÆ, the Franciscans serving the Holy Land.
20. Further clarity shall not be forthcoming in this place given that the author has otherwise been unable to locate any book or significant apologetic communication intended for a Western democratic audience personally composed by him.
21. *Il terrorismo…non è dovuto alla religione…me è dovuto alle accumulate interpretazioni errate dei testi religiosi, alle politiche di fame, di povertà, di ingiustizia, di oppression, di arroganza*, 354.

CHAPTER 10

A Distinguished Treaty Form

In her capstone submission of a long and distinguished career in political infused with ethical theory, Jean Bethke Elshtain in *Sovereignty: God, State, and Self* (2008) approaches the conceptual context for nearly a millennium of concordatorial engagement thus: "The dominant theory of rule for a thousand years of Western Christian history…[was] the so-called two swords doctrine. The two swords are *regnum* and *sacerdotium*, respectively, earthly and spiritual dominion" (11). She further clarifies, "The saga of sorting this out gave the history of the Western half of Christendom a distinctive dynamic that channeled cultural energy, conflict, and contestation" (12).

Per the above epic saga, this inquiry opened with the following research question: *What are the norms of concordats as a whole, and what are the implications for international relations?* It is now prepared to yield its final answers. Over the course of the last nine centuries (ANNO DOMINI 1122–2022), the Holy or Apostolic See has agreed 196 international treaties with civil commonwealths, 167 since continual records were initiated in 1865, of which one has been unilaterally abrogated and one subjected to judicial review. Taking shape at the intersection of Catholic canon, comparative constitutional, and public international law, the terms of concordats are primarily intended to advantage the Church with regard to its juridical personality, ordinary power, teaching

© The Author(s), under exclusive license to Springer Nature 271
Switzerland AG 2024
M. R. Royce, *Ecclesiology, Idealism, and World Polity*,
Palgrave Studies in Religion, Politics, and Policy,
https://doi.org/10.1007/978-3-031-57033-9_10

magisterium, sacramental marriage, and other points of contact with the authority of the State, while their norms range from the ecclesiological to the ideational. Ecclesiological treaty norms pertain to the Church as an institution, and prevail where canon law has occupied a long-standing, continual, exclusivist, or otherwise dominant position. Ideational treaty norms pertain to the Church as an adherent to values, and prevail where canon law has occupied a new, inconstant, negligible, or otherwise inferior position. Treaties being law, and law being self-referential, the variables are problematized according to the texts of the concordats themselves, with most of the results grouped into six case clusters that represent the full spectrum of variation across the dependent variable of treaty norms: Concordatorial Fascism (1906–53); the German *Reich* (1925–2019); Latin American Counter-Revolution (1887–1994); European Secularism (1801–2020); Vatican II States (1968–2019); and Third World States (1993–2016). The primary conceptual implication for international relations is general vindication of its "English" school of Christian realist theory which pursuant to Hugo Grotius envisions self-help under anarchy as neither doomed to Hobbesian enmity nor destined for Kantian friendship; and the primary empirical implication is the demonstrated legality, vitality, ingenuity, and therefore attained distinction of the concordat as an instrument of papal diplomacy amid changing world polity.

Appendix: The Secret Concordat with China

In January, 1933, author of *The Good Earth* (1931) and future Nobel laureate Pearl S. Buck publicly submitted a devastating critique of the condition of the prototypical American missionary in the post-imperial China whose people she had adored and whose language she had mastered, declaring, "The vast people, the age-old history, the fathomless differences of race, even the enormous opportunity combined with his own apparent lack of success, dwarfed him…He is lost."[1] Because the face of Christ must ultimately be reflected in those of persons and groups, she testifies, missionary efforts must go on; but the missionary must in transubstantial normative shift begin to completely spiritually identify with the both moral and material needs of the receiving community. To such existing evangelistic difficulties Buck initially identified would in the intervening years be added the specter of Communism, the truncheon of dictatorship, and the political religion of the worship of the supreme leader.

Per the sobering intelligence of Miss Buck, the author has consulted every official statement[2] pertaining to a development unique within

---

[1] "Is There a Case for Foreign Missions?", *Harper's Monthly Magazine* (Jan, 1933): 147.

[2] Holy See Press Office: "*Communiqué* on the extension of the Provisional Agreement between the Holy See and the People's Republic of China regarding the appointment of

canon, comparative, and international history: the public announcement but textual concealment of a concordat with the People's Republic of China. The following facts are confirmed. On 22 September 2018, a "provisional agreement" concerned with episcopal *appointment* or *nomination*—both words are used—was signed in Beijing by Undersecretary for Relations with States Antoine Camilleri and Chinese Deputy Foreign Minister Wang Chao. Its importance subsequently "was highlighted" at a seemingly unscripted encounter at the Munich Security Conference in 2020 between Archbishop Paul Gallagher and Chinese Foreign Minister Wang Yi, with what is described as the "experimental implementation phase" renewed for two years on 22 October 2020 and 2022, rendering the agreement, based on the most recent recorded assurance, binding through 22 October 2024. Withheld from both the *Acts of the Apostolic See* and the United Nations Treaty Series, the text remains classified; but this brief appendix chapter, according to the same methodology as those of the preceding six treaty clusters, shall nevertheless seek to satisfactorily examine, to the degree possible, this grotesquely deviant case.

The Clandestine Church

Beginning as usual with the prevailing conditions on the papal side, Francis inherited the initiative to seek overtures to the Chinese government from his predecessor Benedict XVI, who on Pentecost (27 May) 2007 released a conceptually sophisticated Letter of the Holy Father to the Bishops, Priests, Consecrated Persons and Lay Faithful of the Catholic Church in the People's Republic of China (*AAS* 99 [2007], 553–81). Normatively, the document belongs to the extraordinary ecclesiastical relations pursuant to Vatican Council II, citing repeatedly *Gaudium et Spes*, *Lumen Gentium*, *Dignitatis Humanae*, and *Christus Dominus* in

---

Bishops" (22 Oct 2022); "*Communiqué* on the extension of the Provisional Agreement between the Holy See and the People's Republic of China regarding the appointment of Bishops" (22 Oct 2020); "Press Release from the Secretariat of State: Bilateral Meeting between the Holy See—People's Republic of China" (14 Feb 2020); "Pastoral Guidelines of the Holy See Concerning the Civil Registration of Clergy in China" (28 Jun 2019); "Informative Note on the Diplomatic Relations of the Holy See" (7 Jan 2019); "*Communiqué* concerning the signing of a Provisional Agreement between the Holy See and the People's Republic of China on the appointment of Bishops" (22 Sep 2018). The author found no corresponding announcements from the *People's Daily*.

an attempt to belatedly introduce some order into the anarchic relations between the Catholic Church and the Chinese state. "The solution to existing problems," explains Pope Benedict, "cannot be pursued via an ongoing conflict with the legitimate civil authorities; at the same time, though, compliance with those authorities is not acceptable when they interfere unduly in matters regarding the faith and discipline of the Church."[3] The main ecclesiological problems he unfolds are as follows, although all identifying information is withheld. First, some bishops in China in communion with the Apostolic See have been secretly consecrated. Second, some bishops have been publicly consecrated with the approval of the regime, and then given the extremity of the Chinese situation received into communion with Rome. Other such bishops, third, have been officially consecrated but not it would seem have sought Catholic communion. The Chinese faithful,[4] fourth, are for their part chronically confused as to the proper lines of communication and divisions of authority; and consequently the Chinese Bishops Conference cannot be recognized. The regime has also been interfering with papal communication with even those bishops known to it. At one ecclesiological extreme, Pope Benedict insists, "The proposal for a Church that is 'independent' of the Holy See, in the religious sphere, is incompatible with Catholic doctrine."[5] Yet at the same time, the holy catholic church may be compelled to adopt a clandestine (*clandestinità*, 569) posture amid suffering (*sofferto*). In addition to concluding exhortations to intensify clerical formation and celibacy, and to henceforth lift up in prayer the church in China on 24 May, but without any peculiar reference to or recommendation of the established principles of concordatorial diplomacy, the Supreme Pontiff assures, "I trust that an accord [*accordo*] can be reached with the Government so as to resolve certain questions regarding the choice of candidates for the episcopate, the publication of the appointment [*nomina*] of Bishops, and the recognition—concerning

---

[3] La soluzione dei problemi esistenti non puo' essere perseguito attraverso un permanente conflitto con le legittime Autorita' civili; nello stesso tempo, pero', non e' accettabile un'arrendevolezza alle medesime quando esse interferiscano indebitamente in materie che riguardano la fede e la disciplina della Chiesa, 558.

[4] The Association of Religion Data Archives puts the 2020 number of Chinese Catholics at ten million, or 0.69 percent of the national population.

[5] Il progetto di una Chiesa « indipendente», in ambito religioso, dalla Santa Sede e' incompatibile con la dottrina cattolica, 566–67.

civil effects where necessary—of the new Bishops on the part of the civil authorities."[6]

Pontiff	Contracting party	Head of State or Government
(Pontifical Legate, Title)	(Contracting Location, Date, Language (s))	(Contracting Plenipotentiary, Title)
Francis (Antoine Camilleri, Undersecretary for Relations with States)	**People's Republic of China** (Beijing, 22 Sep. 2018, ?)	Xi Jinping (Wang Chao, Deputy Foreign Minister)

Meanwhile, the prevailing norms of the contracting People's Republic of China are diffused throughout the punishing *Governance of China* (2014–2022), the four-volume chronicle of all the public communications of General Secretary of the Central Committee of the Communist Party and President Xi Jinping.[7] Throughout his recorded ceremonial appearances at all manner of party gatherings, diplomatic receptions, social engagements, or other official functions,[8] President Xi at once pays continual tribute to while avoiding any acknowledgment of deviation from the previous theoretical contributions of Mao Zedong Thought, Deng Xiaoping Theory, the "Three Represents" of Jiang Zemin, and

---

[6] Auspico che si trovi un accordo con il Governo per risolvere alcune questioni riguardanti sia la scelta dei candidati all'episcopato sia la pubblicazione della nomina dei Vescovi sia il riconoscimento — agli effetti civili in quanto necessari — del nuovo Vescovo da parte delle Autorita' civili, 571–72.

[7] By the same author, *Up and Out of Poverty* (Beijing: Foreign Languages Press, 2016) covers his previous (1988–90) position as Party secretary of Ningde Prefecture in Fujian Province.

[8] Volume I covers the period 12 Nov 2012 to 13 Jun 2014, and consists of 72 speeches, three interviews, two meeting minutes, one memorandum, and one public letter. Volume II covers the period 18 Aug 2014 to 29 Sep 2017, and consists of 97 speeches, two meeting minutes, and two directives. Volume III covers the period 18 Oct 2017 to 13 Jan 2020, and consists of 87 speeches, one report, one meeting minute, two public letters, and one directive. Volume IV covers the period 3 Feb 2020 to 10 May 2022, and consists of 106 speeches, two letters, and one memorandum.

the "Scientific Outlook on Development" of Hu Jintao,[9] with his own submission mainly provided in, "Secure a Decisive Victory in Building a Moderately Prosperous Society in All Respects and Strive for the Great Success of Socialism with Chinese Characteristics for a New Era," the supremely important report to the 19th National Congress of the Communist Party of China (vol. iii: 1–79, 18 October 2017) synthesizing the overall goals and outlook of his regime.

Sifting through layers of collective groupthink including, but not limited to the *Five-sphere Integrated Plan*, *Four-pronged Comprehensive Strategy*, *Three Guidelines for Ethical Behavior*, *Three Basic Rules of Conduct*, *Eight Rules*, and *Four Cardinal Principles*, one arrives at the overall self-definition, "China is a socialist country of people's democratic dictatorship under the leadership of the working class based on an alliance of workers and farmers" (37–38), as well as the overall self-assessment, "the principal challenge facing Chinese society in the new era is the gap between the unbalanced and inadequate development and the ever-growing expectation of the people for a better life" (20). Several annotated lists of necessary initiatives across mostly domestic political, economic, and social policy are then provided, of which the most important are the initial fourteen points of ensuring party leadership, committing to a people-centered approach, deepening reform, adopting a new developmental vision, ensuring popular sovereignty, ensuring law-based governance, upholding core socialist values, improving living standards, ensuring harmony between man and nature, pursuing holistic national security, upholding total party leadership over the armed forces, upholding the "one country, two systems" principle, building global community, and exercising full and rigorous party governance. Although largely institutionalist, functionalist, and reformist in substance, President

---

[9] Mao Zedong Thought seeks to base the revolution on the super-majority Chinese peasantry rather than on the then almost non-existent Chinese proletariat, and is concentrated in the little red *Quotations from Chairman Mao Tsetung* (Peking: Foreign Languages Press, 1972). The central edict of Deng Xiaoping Theory is to *Build Socialism with Chinese Characteristics* (Beijing: Foreign Languages Press, 1985). The *Three Represents* (Beijing: Foreign Languages Press, 2002) of Jiang Zemin incumbent upon the Communist Party are the productive forces, cultural development, and majority interests of China. "The Scientific Outlook on Development" of Hu Jintao, finally, refers to the sustained characterization by Marx and Engels of their shared conceptual efforts as a provable and falsifiable science, rather than as a (Christian) religious hope, (Hegelian) philosophical exercise, or (anarchist) utopian dream.

Xi's most sustained and indicative submission to date assigns absolutely no rôle to constructive criticism within a social or loyal opposition within a political order wherein, "the whole Party obeys the Central Committee" (66).[10] Such normative constraints to all appearances applied to contracting plenipotentiary Wang Chao.

Wormsian Shadow Boxing

Although the normative commitments and subject matter of the secret, clandestine, or classified concordat with China are addressed above, any remarks concerning its specific terms must remain almost completely speculative. Given the absolute linguistic incomprehension between the pontifical Secretariat of State and the Chinese Central Committee, it is by no means improbable that the document signed in Beijing on 22 September 2018 is in English. Legally, the term *provisional* (*provvisorio*) is meaningless, given that treaties are law, and laws are not provisional or experimental, but rather coercive and binding. Otherwise, the agreement likely opens with an assertion of the unalienable right of the Catholic Church to carry out its spiritual mission, and almost certainly continues with guarantees of episcopal communication with priests and laity, with each other, and with the Apostolic See, a universal attribute of canon law, regular concordatorial treaty term, and as represented by Pope Benedict above a deeply endangered religious liberty in China. Yet how, specifically, the document attempts to resolve the overlapping jurisdiction claimed by the Apostolic See and the Chinese government concerning the *nomina* of bishops in China is at present impossible to conjecture.

A Return to Secrecy?

The recent submissions of Deeks (2017) and of Donaldson (2017)[11] have helped rekindle academic interest in a question long thought dormant,

---

[10] According to article 36 of the 2018 constitution, Chinese citizens have religious freedom, and the Chinese government cannot discriminate among the adherents of different religions. But the text also reads, "Religious bodies and religious affairs are not subject to any foreign domination," which the Chinese government could obviously invoke against the Apostolic See. See Zhibin Xie, "Religion and State in China: A Theological Appraisal," *Journal of Church and State* 63, no. 1 (Winter, 2021): 1–22.

[11] Ashley S. Deeks, "A (Qualified) Defense of Secret Agreements," *Arizona State Law Journal* 49, special issue (2017): 713–94; Megan Donaldson, "The Survival of the Secret

immaterial, or obsolete: the secret treaty. The main finding of the former is that the entry into secret agreements by the American and by other governments continues unabated, and the main argument that they should not necessarily be normatively condemned; while the latter holds that empirically, legally, and normatively, the distinction between secret and public treaties is not so straightforward. Although the subject demands its own proper inquiry, satisfactory treatment with peculiar reference to the concordats may be offered in this place.

Whether any peculiar significance ought to be assigned to a treaty, concordat, or other binding instrument between sovereign states that is for whatever reason *kept secret* was not a conceptual question of much interest to the foundational theorists of international law prior to the outbreak of the Great War. Grotius does not take note of this variation, while Textor is content to stipulate that the terms of a prospective secret must not contradict those of an existing public treaty.[12] Neither Van Bynkershoek, Wolff, nor Vattel distinctly remark upon the subject, while De Callieres merely explains that the secret is as he sees it but one of three treaty classifications, the other two being public and what he calls *eventual*, "because their execution depends on certain events which it is held must occur and without which the treaty is void."[13] Synthesizing these and other authors, Martens decisively frames the question as one of treaty publication if not necessarily *publicity* procedurally included within the essential process of ratification, without which no international law instrument can enter into force.[14]

Treaty: Publicity, Secrecy, and Legality in the International Order," *American Journal of International Law* 111, no. 3 (2017): 575–627.

[12] Johann Wolfgang Textor, *Synopsis of the Law of Nations* (Washington, D.C.: Carnegie, [SYNOPSIS JURIS GENTIUM, 1680] 1916), 257. "Briefly, the answer is that, if the contracting parties are not hindered by any prior treaty or other like bond, a secret alliance is permitted.".

[13] *Parce que leur execution depend de certain évenemens que l'on juge devoir arriver & sans lesquels ces Traitez sont de nul effet. De La Maniere de Negocier avec Les Souverains* (Amsterdam: 1716), 186.

[14] *Contemporary International Law of Civilized Peoples* (Clark, NJ: The Lawbook Exchange, [1882] 2021), 311–12. He also pertinently states, "Attempts have repeatedly been made in the science of international law to divide (or classify) international treaties into certain types. But the experiments made so far of this kind have not been very successful" (325).

His being the prevailing interpretation of international law in 1914, the lasting disgrace of secret diplomacy instead originated in Trotsky's vivid conception of the historic responsibility of socialist internationalism. Still from exile, he had written in *The War and the International* ([1915] 1971), "The exposure of diplomatic trickery, cheating, and knavery is one of the most important functions of Socialist political agitation" (34), and in concluding the same volume called for, "The United States of Europe—without monarchies, without standing armies, without ruling feudal castes, without secret diplomacy" (74). According to the most well-attested sources, President Wilson at least familiarized himself with Trotsky and drew direct conceptual inspiration from the Bolshevik peace decree of 26 October/8 November 1917, the first official Soviet act in foreign relations abolishing secret diplomacy and promising a "just, democratic" peace,[15] terms reformulated into the "open covenants of peace, openly arrived at" constituting the first of Wilson's Fourteen Points (8 January 1918), with article 18 of the subsequent Covenant of the League of Nations on which he staked his reputation requiring the registration of all treaties with the Secretariat in Geneva.[16]

The resulting interwar has been more heavily scrutinized than any other period of international history; and although it included secret agreements, and secret clauses within otherwise public agreements,[17] the basis of critical reflection, with regard to the deepening world crisis, is Hitler's *broken* rather than secret promises, combined with the tragic synthesis of Allied idealism, appeasement, disinterest, and denialism that made it possible for the Führer to repeatedly renege on his insincere assurances. Likewise, the total hegemonic war soon unleased by the Axis

---

[15] E.H. Carr, *The Bolshevik Revolution, 1917–1923*, vol. III (Baltimore: Penguin, 1953), 21–23. The minimal contemporary recognition of the organic connection between Trotskyite socialist and Wilsonian liberal internationalism is a powerful testament to the enduring significance of Stalinist falsification.

[16] "Every treaty or international engagement entered into hereafter by any Member of the League shall be forthwith registered with the Secretariat and shall as soon as possible be published by it. No such treaty or international engagement shall be binding until so registered."

[17] Belonging very much to the mindset of appeasement, the secret (Sir Samuel) Hoare-(Pierre) Laval pact of 1935 would if not leaked have granted much of Abyssinia to Mussolini, while the (Vyacheslav) Molotov-(Joachim von) Ribbentrop pact of 1939 included secret spheres of influence in addition to its public domain non-aggression clauses.

Powers exchanged misdemeanors for felonies, and swallowed up felonies within atrocities; and consequently the comparatively minor question of treaty secrecy factually and normatively receded from view.

Nevertheless, the question was revisited in the Charter of the United Nations and Statute of the International Court of Justice of 26 June 1945, the primary instrument of international law. Article 102, paragraph 1 of the Charter reads, "Every treaty and every international agreement entered into by any Member of the United Nations after the present Charter comes into force shall as soon as possible be registered with the Secretariat and published by it."[18] Almost all the contracting parties to the concordats are such Members of the United Nations. Paragraph 2 continues, "No party to any such treaty or international agreement which has not been registered in accordance with the provisions of paragraph 1 of this Article may invoke the treaty or agreement before any organ of the United Nations." As it happens, of the 145 concordats agreed since the entry into force of the UN Charter, only *eleven* appear to have been properly registered,[19] indicating both the devastating methodological inadequacy of the United Nations Treaty Series as a primary source as well as the normatively disturbing impunity with which UN Members may be habitually disregarding this particular obligation of the Charter. Kelsen's *Law of the United Nations* (1950) remains the most exhaustive analysis of the document's legal problems, and he foresaw such complications arising from even the seemingly straightforward procedure of treaty registration (696–705, 721–24).

---

[18] The wording and therefore perhaps the import of the subsequent Vienna Convention on the Law of Treaties (1969) varies ever so slightly: "Treaties shall, *after their entry into force*, be transmitted to the Secretariat of the United Nations for registration or filing and recording, as the case may be, for publication" (80.1, emphasis added).

[19] Brazil (2008), France (2008), Latvia (2000), Lithuania (2000, 2012), Poland (1993), Spain (1950, 1953, 1976, 1979, 1994).

From the depths of the Cold War Thomas Schelling initiated,[20] amid its slow thaw Robert Jervis continued,[21] and throughout the asymmetries and ambiguities of qualified unipolarity their more recent successors remain engaged[22] upon the informational, institutional, psychological, and reputational components of secrecy within international bargaining and negotiation, particularly the merits of Fearon's deductive supplements to neorealist international theory.[23] But the abstract question of secrecy within international *bargaining* is distinct from if adjacent to the concrete question of secrecy within international *law*, where what follows is a punctuated equilibrium of oddities that may defy any attempt at generalization. Nestled between the fall of Berlin and the Berlin airlift was a top secret British-U.S. Communication Intelligence Agreement (5 March 1946) providing comprehensive and ongoing sharing of classified information, initiating the formation of the publicly acknowledged "Five Eyes" network.[24] The Swiss Confederation and Communist Poland appear to have secretly agreed following the war to redirect the misplaced money of each other's citizens to the opposite government, adding another layer

---

[20] *The Strategy of Conflict* (Cambridge, MA: Harvard University Press, 1960) concerned not, "with the efficient *application* of force but the *exploitation of potential force*" (5, emphasis in original) fuses rationalism and empiricism to locate strategic interaction between harmonious interests and incurable divisions, and between zero-sum games like CHESS and purely collaborationist games like CHARADES, with emphasis on qualitatively intuitive tacit bargaining. *Arms and Influence* (New Haven: Yale University Press, [1966] 2020) furnishes sustained inductive reasoning through plausible scenarios and contingency plans for international security crises, provocatively introducing in the process the term COMPELLENCE to capture the coercive logic of strategic deterrence, but when present on the *offense* or the initiative, like America in Vietnam.

[21] Much inspired by the work of Schelling and of Glenn Snyder, *Perception and Misperception in International Politics* (Princeton: Princeton University Press, [1976] 2017) probes how decision-makers across sovereign states perceive each other, and the causes, forms, and treatments of characteristic misperceptions.

[22] Muhamet Bas and Robert Schub, "Mutual Optimism as a Cause of Conflict: Secret Alliances and Conflict Onset," *International Studies Quarterly* 60, no. 3 (2016): 552–64; Shuhei Kurizaki, "Efficient Secrecy: Public versus Private Threats in Crisis Diplomacy," *American Political Science Review* 101, no. 3 (2007): 543–58; Keren Yarhi-Milo, "Tying Hands Behind Closed Doors: The Logic and Practice of Secret Reassurance," *Security Studies* 22, no. 3 (2013): 405–35.

[23] "Bargaining, Enforcement, and International Cooperation," *International Organization* 52, no. 2 (Spring, 1998): 269–305; "Rationalist Explanations for War," *International Organization* 49, no. 3 (Summer, 1995): 379–414.

[24] Approved for Release by NSA on 08 Nov 2014, MDR Case #78,775.

of complexity to postwar Jewish efforts to recover deposits from Swiss private banks.[25] Physical survival of the notorious Protocol of Sèvres proclaimed from the rooftops the guilt of the Israeli, French, and British governments in their combined attack upon Egypt in 1956,[26] while an "escaped criminals" extradition treaty between Pyongyang and Beijing has been known to exist for many years.[27] In the intelligence sector, the dreaded Operation Condor designed to cleanse the southern cone of Marxism appears to have originated in a secret bilateral agreement between Paraguayan intelligence and the Argentine army,[28] while Pakistan until perhaps 2013 adhered to something similar permitting American drone strikes against Islamists.[29] The submission of further examples would continue to intrigue but not inform. The point is that the scarcity, irregularity, and perhaps relative unimportance of the secret treaty has heretofore discouraged attempts to endow it with any special meaning within international relations theory.

Thus returning to the shallow secret Chinese concordat, and proceeding on the supposition that the Chinese government adheres to the Chinese Constitution (2018 [1982]), ratification of treaties belongs to the Standing Committee of the National People's Congress (67.15), although the text is unclear on whether it may act in secret. Assuming that it may, the outcome would indeed be a binding instrument of international law, although not cognizable before the International Court of Justice. But there are equally profound ecclesiological implications, for until this exceptional instance there had *never* been a secret concordat. Cornweil (2008 [1999])[30] provides sustained coverage of a minor Pacelli

[25] Anita Ramasastry, "Secrets and Lies? Swiss Banks and International Human Rights," *Vanderbilt Journal of Transnational Law* 31, no. 2 (March, 1998): 325–456.

[26] Avi Shlaim, "The Protocol of Sèvres, 1956: Anatomy of a War Plot," *International Affairs* 73, no. 3 (July, 1997): 509–30.

[27] Stephy Kwan, "More than an Ignorant Bystander: Chinese Accountability and the Repatriation of North Korean Defectors," *International Journal of Korean Unification Studies* vol. 26, no. 2 (2017): 95–138.

[28] *Asunto: Acuerdo Bilateral de Inteligencia FF.AA.* PARAGUAY/*Ejército* ARGENTINO, September 12, 1972. National Security Archive [Archive of Terror, Asuncion, Paraguay], 6 May 2015.

[29] Rosa Brooks, "Drones and the International Rule of Law," *Ethics & International Affairs* vol. 28, no. 1 (2014): 83–103.

[30] John Cornwell, *Hitler's Pope: The Secret History of Pius XII* (New York: Penguin, [1999] 2008), 48–58.

ecclesiological installment: a concordat with Serbia (24 June 1914) that does not appear within the *Acts of the Apostolic See*, and therefore the findings of the present study. The author is inclined however to impute this sole omission purely to editorial oversight, rather than to the unlikely intention to suppress a document openly discussed in contemporary newspapers. Likewise, Rhodes (1973)[31] contends that accompanying secret language to the *Reich* concordat addressed mutual opposition to the Soviet Union, clerical military service, and the fate of baptized Jews; but his account is not strongly sourced, not repeated anywhere else, and not within the power of the author to verify.

The Provisional Agreement between the Holy See and the People's Republic of China on the appointment of bishops of 22 September 2018 is therefore the first concordat in Church history the text of which has been withheld, a highly ominous development for the integrity of the subject matter. Might the agreement of this pact portend a return to treaty secrecy, or the beginning of concordatorial secrecy? The very nature of the instrument inclines toward negative answers, given that for a concordat *to be effective*, it is necessary for bishops, and useful for priests and laity to *know what it says*. Roman Catholics within the contracting party to a concordat can neither assert unknown rights nor discharge unknown duties; wherefore a secret would be an almost null concordat. Nonetheless, having thus probed available canon, comparative, and international law regarding this deviant observation, only time will tell whether it has thrown the practice of extraordinary ecclesiastical relations into lasting confusion.

---

[31] Anthony Rhodes, *The Vatican in the Age of the Dictators, 1922–1945* (New York: Holt, Rinehart, and Winston, 1973), 179–80. More generally, one might variously encounter *clauses within, appendices to,* or *language accompanying* a concordat or other treaty, with such potential case-specific differences potentially requiring meticulous framing and exposition.

Index

A
Acts of the Apostolic See (AAS), 38
Acts of the Holy See, 38
Adenauer, Konrad, 155
Agape, 93
Ahimsa, 93
Alberdi, Juan Bautista, 176
Apostasy, 69

B
Bellarmine, Robert, 172
Benedict XVI, 23, 274
Betancourt, Rómulo, 180–182
Bishops. *See* Episcopacy
Bolshevism, 86
Buck, Pearl S., 273
Bull, Hedley, 101
Butterfield, Herbert, 37

C
Caldera, Rafael, 177–178
Centesimus Annus, 226

Charlie Hebdo, 86
Che Guevara, 189
Christian Democratic Union, 155
Christus Dominus, 87, 236–237
CIA, 179
Civil Code of the French, 196–197
Civil Constitution of the Clergy, 129
Compendium of the Social Doctrine of the Church, 238–239
Comte, Auguste, 81
Congregation for extraordinary ecclesiastical affairs, 9
Constant, Benjamin, 196
Cortés, Juan, 76–78
Croce, Benedetto, 64, 119

D
Declaration of the Rights of Man and Citizen, 206
Deng Xiaoping Theory, 277
Dependency theory, 179
De Staël, Germaine, 196, 205

Deus Scientiarum Dominus, 162, 202
De Vicariis Castrensibus, 182
Dignitatis Humanae, 87, 236
Divini Redemptoris, 124
Dollfuß, Engelbert, 84, 202

E
Ecclesiological, 61, 62
Education, 19, 73, 158–161. *See also Sapientia Christiana*
El-Tayeb, Ahmed Mohamed, 265
Enabling Act, 63
English realism, 97
Episcopacy, 17, 19, 79
Episcopal oath of loyalty, 65, 129–131, 205
Evangelium Vitae, 227
Evola, Julius, 2, 68–69
Ex-Nazis, 209–210

F
Fanon, Frantz, 249
Farinacci, Roberto, 68
Fearon, James, 282
Folk Party of Austria, 199
Francis, 22–23, 93–96, 250
Franco, Francisco, 126
Fratelli Tutti, 250–252

G
Gandhi, Mahatma, 93–95
Gasparri, Pietro, 8, 124, 125
Gaudium et Spes, 87, 274
Geneva Conventions, 19
Gentile, Giovanni, 63
German Constitutional Court, 76
Gramsci, Antonio, 249
Gravissimum Educationist, 88
Grotius, Hugo, 99–101
Gutiérrez, Gustavo, 80

H
Helsinki Final Act, 19
Herzl, Theodor, 252, 254
Hindenburg, Paul von, 1
Hitler, 1, 126, 127
Huntington, Samuel, 227–233

I
Idealist international theory, 98
Ideational, 61
Inter Mirifica, 235
International Military Tribunal for Germany, 19
Israeli Basic Laws, 254

J
Jervis, Robert, 282
John Paul II, 22, 74, 224
John XXIII, 221

K
Kaas, Ludwig, 1, 64, 65
Kant, Immanuel, 98, 195
Kazakhstan, 259–260
Kelsen, Hans, 62, 82, 85, 86, 199–202, 281
Khaled, Leila, 255
King James, 129
Kuwait, 258

L
Laborem Exercens, 225
Länder, 71, 72
Las Casas, Bartolomé, 175
Lateran Pacts, 15, 21, 65–68
Laudato Si', 95–96, 250
Law of separation, 10
Lenin, Vladimir, 92
Leo XIII, 120
Lijphart, Arend, 218

Lumen Gentium, 87, 235
Luxemburg, Rosa, 150–155

M
Mao Zedong Thought, 277
Maritain, Jacques, 221
Marriage, 18
Marx, Karl, 216
Mater et Magistra, 222
Medellín, 184–185
Mein Kampf, 127–128
Military chaplain, 79, 182–183
Mit Brennender Sorge, 69
Montevideo Convention, 21, 31
Mussolini, Benito, 126

N
Napoleon, 10, 83, 130, 196
Napoleon-Louis Bonaparte, 198
Neoliberalism, 20
Nkrumah, Kwame, 92, 256, 257
Non abbiamo bisogno, 68–69
Nuncio, 21
Núñez, Rafael, 176, 177

O
OAS, 178
OAU, 260
Ordinary power, 16

P
Pacelli, Eugenio, 1–3, 63, 134–137, 139, 283
Pacem in Terris, 222
Pacta sunt servanda, 13
Paganism, 69, 70
Palestine, 255, 256, 260–262
Papen, Franz von, 126
Paul VI, 91, 221–224

Perfect society, 77
Pius XI, 134, 136
Pius XII, 123–126, 132–136, 172–175. *See also* Pacelli, Eugenio
PLO, 255
Populorum Progressio, 224
Prayers for the regime, 17–19, 85, 205
Prussia, concordat with, 74–75

R
Ratzinger, Joseph, 80
Realist international theory, 97–99
Reich Concordat, 2, 63–67, 75
Renner, Karl, 199, 203
Rerum Novarum, 122, 155
Resistance, 92, 93
Rosenberg, Alfred, 2, 69–70
Royal patronage, 172, 175

S
Said, Edward, 249
Saint-Germain-en-Laye, 199
Sapientia Christiana, 73–74, 162
Satyagraha, 93. *See also* Gandhi, Mahatma
Schelling, Thomas, 282
Schmitt, Carl, 149
Scientific Outlook on Development, 277
Secret treaties, 279
Secret Vatican Archives, 38
Separation of church and state, 87
Shoah, 138–139
Sieyès, Joseph, 195
Social Democratic Party, 150
Sollicitudo Rei Socialis, 226
Sonderweg, 71
Spirituali Militum Curae, 183
Stroessner, Alfredo, 177

Suárez, Francisco, 172
Succession of states, 74, 75
Sun Yat-sen, 257
Syllabus of Errors, 77

T
Three Represents, 277
Treaty for the Re-estalishment of an Independent and Democratic Austria, 85
Treaty registration, 281
Trotsky, Leon, 178, 280
Trujillo, Rafael, 177

U
United Arab Emirates, 258
United Nations, 90
   Charter of, 19, 86, 281
Universal Declaration of Human Rights (UDHR), 19, 94, 259

V
Vatican City-state, 39
Vienna Conventions, 14, 75
Vitoria, Francisco, 172
Voegelin, Eric, 63, 209–211

W
Wallerstein, Immanuel, 171
Weimar Constitution, 98
Wilson, Woodrow, 98, 280
Worms, Concordat of, 4, 7, 71, 236

X
Xi Jinping, 276